THE POLITICAL IDEAS OF MARX AND ENGELS

[I]

Marxism and Totalitarian Democracy, 1818–1850

University of Pittsburgh Press

The Political Ideas of
MARX
and
ENGELS

Marxism and Totalitarian Democracy,
1818–1850

RICHARD N. HUNT

Library of Congress Cataloging in Publication Data

Hunt, Richard N.
Marxism and totalitarian democracy, 1818–1850.

(His The political ideas of Marx and Engels, 1)
Bibliography: p. 345
1. Marx, Karl, 1818–1883—Political science.
2. Engels, Friedrich, 1820–1895—Political science.
3. Totalitarianism. I. Title.
JC233.M299H85 vol. 1   335.4s   [335.43'8'3219]
ISBN 0-8229-3285-7   74-13536

Extracts from *Birth of the Communist Manifesto,* edited by Dirk J. Struik, *The Revolution of 1848-49: Articles from the "Neue Rheinische Zeitung,"* translated by S. Ryazanskaya, and *Anarchism and Anarcho-Syndicalism* are reprinted by permission of International Publishers.

Passages from Werner Blumenberg, "Die Aussagen des Peter Gerhardt Röser" and Boris Nicolaievsky, "Last Meeting of the Central-Behörde" first appeared in German in the *International Review of Social History* and are translated here with the permission of that journal.

Excerpts from *The Political Philosophy of Bakunin,* ed. G. P. Maximoff, are © 1953 by The Free Press, a division of the Macmillan Publishing Co. Inc., and are reprinted by permission of the publisher.

Passages excerpted from *Writings of the Young Marx on Philosophy,* edited by Loyd Easton and Kurt H. Guddat, copyright © 1967 by Loyd D. Easton and Kurt H. Guddat, are reprinted by permission of Doubleday & Company, Inc.

Marx's *Critique of Hegel's 'Philosophy of Right'* was first published by the Cambridge University Press.

To my mother,
Verda Engst Hunt,
who has always imagined the equality of man
was supposed to be taken seriously,
a rusticity that may also betray itself
in the pages that follow.

The more Socialist theories claim to be "scientific," the more transitory they are; but Socialist values are permanent. The distinction between theories and values is not sufficiently recognized, but it is fundamental. On a group of theories one can found a school; but on a group of values one can found a culture, a civilization, a new way of living together among men.

IGNAZIO SILONE

Contents

Preface

THE IMPOSING GROWTH of non-Communist scholarship on Marx during the last several years has swept away many Cold War vulgarities and, by focusing interest on his early philosophical writings, exposed the profound humanist roots of Marx's value system. But there has been no equivalent volume of new interest in the specifically political ideas and values of Marx and Engels. The conventions of the Cold War assign the two men unambiguously to the totalitarian camp, identifying them completely with the repressive one-party dictatorships that have been created in their names. Communists themselves, while rejecting the label "totalitarian," have been equally insistent that Marx and Engels opposed Western-style "bourgeois" democracy and favored "proletarian dictatorship" under the guidance of a single vanguard party, at least until the mythic day when the state itself would disappear.

Of course, not everyone accepts such a view of Marx and Engels' political ideas. Most Social Democratic writers have been unwilling to sign over the entire Marxist heritage to the Communists: following the path blazed by Kautsky in his classic debate with Lenin, they have argued that Marx and Engels were essentially Western-style parliamentary democrats who would have been appalled at the behemoth dictatorships erected in the twentieth century. That both Social Democrats and Communists can lay claim to the Marxist political inheritance has led a number of specialists (notably ex-Communists like Sidney Hook and Bertram Wolfe) to conclude that the masters left an "ambiguous legacy," a mass of political writings so vague and contradictory that both democrats and totalitarians can find ample sustenance in them. It is possible to refine this interpretation, as have, for example, Isaiah Berlin and George Lichtheim, to suggest that Marx and Engels went through two distinct phases of political development, that their youthful revolutionism made them—in twentieth-century parlance—"Communists" up to 1850, but that they matured into "Social Democrats" thereafter. Still another possibility, and a particularly striking one, has been suggested by J. L. Talmon, who argues that Marx must be placed in a separate tradition of totalitarian democracy (in contrast to liberal democracy) that runs from Rousseau and Robespierre, through Babeuf and Blanqui, down to Marx and his followers.

What has hindered an accurate reconstruction of Marx and Engels' political values, apart from polemicizing among ideologists with vested interests to defend, is the aggravating care both men took to conceal those values behind a mask of scientism. Their "scientific" socialism was supposed to be distinguished from its utopian forerunners precisely by the absence of vain and idle moralizing, and the consequent refusal to offer detailed blueprints of a "good society." No doubt Marx and Engels wanted to be judged on their theories, not on their values. Thus in their better-known writings they left only a handful of statements about their political goals, and even these are often masquerading as scientific observations or predictions. This material is indeed frustratingly cryptic and ambiguous, especially when examined by itself and apart from any biographical or historical context. Yet the customary procedure for writers on Classical Marxist political philosophy has been to trot out this tired stable of well-known passages and perform familiar tricks with endless variations in the perfect vacuum of abstract ideas. Such a limited body of evidence cannot really settle the key issues, as has been recognized by a few recent scholars like Shlomo Avineri, Iring Fetscher, and Hal Draper, who have pursued less-known evidence in a more systematic way. Breaking genuinely new ground, these specialized monographs offer hope that at least some of the debates about Marx and Engels' political ideas can be resolved instead of merely being perpetuated.

This same perhaps extravagant hope has motivated the present study, and is the only possible justification for putting into the world yet another book on Marxism. In part, I have tried to synthesize a fresh, post–Cold War, and comprehensive account of Marx and Engels' political ideas from the new monographic literature available. But most of the interpretations set forth below are not those of other scholars; for better or worse they represent my own attempts to pursue less-known evidence in a more systematic way. My approach has been to combine a number of separate procedures in a phalanx, powerful enough—I hope—to gain new ground in the area. First, I have treated Marx and Engels together, not as a single mind of course, but as a collaborative team, and I believe this has illuminated a crucial paradox in the Marxist theory of the state. Second, I have examined *everything* Marx and Engels wrote (through 1850 for the present volume), convinced that such Germanic thoroughness must find its due reward. And indeed, many famous but notoriously ambiguous texts, for example, in the *Communist Manifesto*, can be elucidated with the help of contemporaneous essays and letters that are almost unknown. Comprehensiveness has also permitted the frequent use of negative evidence: it can be asserted, for instance, that Marx and Engels nowhere called for a "dictatorship of the proletariat" or a "permanent revolution" prior to 1850. Third, I have tried to combine the topical treatment of ideas with a biographical-historical approach to Marx and Engels' lives, so that their ideas would not appear in some timeless, spaceless vacuum of pure thought, but would be firmly rooted in the appropriate nineteenth-century historical matrix. And finally, I have attempted to transcend the abstractions of pure thought in another way, by measuring what Marx and Engels wrote against what they did, against their actual behavior in radical organizations and as participants in the revolution of 1848.

My findings have convinced me that all the general interpretations noted at the outset are either wrong or inadequate, that Marx and Engels were neither totalitarians nor garden-variety parliamentary democrats, neither "Communists" nor "Social Democrats." I have not found their writings so full of vagaries and contradictions that any interpretation can be drawn from them with equal plausibility, nor can I perceive any sharp change of political outlook or values around the year 1850. What they envisaged for the future society, from its very beginning, was a kind of participatory democracy organized without any professional leaders or administrators at all, which has nowhere been established in a national government, and which requires some effort of imagination and historical understanding for the present-day reader to grasp. To make such an effort to comprehend Marx and Engels' half-concealed prophetic vision, to appreciate its real moral grandeur, to ask hard questions about its applicability in our own time—to grapple with all these things may repay the effort if one believes, like Silone, that socialist values are somehow more fundamental and enduring than socialist theories.

The broad scope of this study has necessitated a division into two volumes according to a principle that is partly chronological and partly topical. Chronologically, the present volume deals with Marx and Engels' early intellectual development and with their lives down through

1850; volume 2 will take up their "mature" years after that date. Topically, the volume at hand seeks to test the most intriguing if ultimately unconvincing of the aforementioned interpretations—the view advanced by Talmon and others that Marx and Engels belong to a tradition of totalitarian democracy. Our concern for the early period of the masters' lives leads naturally enough to a stress on those issues—revolutionary strategy, the role of the party, political terror, and postrevolutionary government—that will allow a final assessment of the totalitarian democracy thesis. Viewed from a different angle, volume 1 emphasizes what separates Marx and Engels from the later doctrines of Leninism; volume 2 will stress what separated them from the later attitudes of social democracy.

I would like to express my particular appreciation to all those friends, colleagues, and students—too numerous to name individually—who read the manuscript or listened to the exposition of my findings, and who served as a sounding board for the interpretations developed in the following pages. The research materials were gathered at the Internationaal Instituut voor Sociale Geschiedenis in Amsterdam, the Library of Congress in Washington, and the Hillman Library at the University of Pittsburgh, and I am grateful to the staffs of those institutions for many kindnesses. To the University of Pittsburgh, and especially its International Dimensions Program, I am indebted for grants that made two research trips possible. Beth Luey has been a superb copy editor and has improved the manuscript far more than duty required. Most of all, I would like to thank my wife, Françoise, who continued at her own job much longer than planned so as to give me sufficient free time to finish my work.

Marxism and Totalitarian Democracy, 1818–1850

Introduction:
The Concept of Totalitarian Democracy

THE WORD "TOTALITARIAN" did not exist before the twentieth-century regimes it is supposed to describe. It gained currency in the 1930s as a means of singling out those common traits which were curiously shared by Nazi Germany and Stalinist Russia (and perhaps similar regimes), and which distinguished them from other forms of government, including earlier forms of absolutism and dictatorship.[1] As classically defined by Carl J. Friedrich, these common and distinctive characteristics include: (1) an official chiliastic ideology which everyone is supposed to embrace; (2) a single, hierarchically organized party, composed of a passionately dedicated elite, which is completely commingled with—or superior to—the official governmental apparatus; (3) a technologically conditioned near-complete monopoly of the means of violence; (4) a parallel monopoly of the means of mass communication, used to disseminate the ideology; (5) a system of lawless, terroristic police control which employs the above monopolies and modern scientific psychology to full advantage. Friedrich stressed the twentieth-century technologies, the single ideologically committed party, and the emphasis on mass politicization, which separate modern totalitarianism qualitatively from earlier kinds of despotism and dictatorship.[2]

It was no doubt inevitable that historians and other writers should

1. Herbert J. Spiro, "Totalitarianism," *International Encyclopedia of the Social Sciences* (New York: Macmillan, 1968), 16:106–07. The first edition of this famous encyclopedia, published in 1934, contained no entry under the word "totalitarianism."
2. "The Unique Character of Totalitarian Society," in *Totalitarianism*, ed. idem (Cambridge: Harvard, 1954), pp. 47–60.

[3]

seek the roots of this twentieth-century phenomenon in the ideologies and social movements of earlier times. One of the most imposing of these attempts has been undertaken by J. L. Talmon, Professor of Modern History of the Hebrew University of Jerusalem, in two weighty tomes of a projected three-volume set.[3] It was Talmon who first introduced the concept of "totalitarian democracy," and he may serve here as principal spokesman for all those writers who link Marx and Engels to the "totalitarian-democratic" tradition, or who identify the two men more generally with totalitarianism.

Talmon finds the origins of modern totalitarianism, paradoxically, in the same current of eighteenth-century ideas that gave rise to modern democracy. He argues that two distinct types of democratic thought, liberal and totalitarian, were implicit in the Enlightenment and were separated from each other in the centrifuge of the French Revolution. Both currents affirm the supreme value of liberty, but the former "finds the essence of freedom in spontaneity and the absence of coercion," while the latter "believes it to be realized only in the pursuit and attainment of an absolute collective purpose." Liberal democrats conceive "politics to be a matter of trial and error" and "political systems as pragmatic contrivances of human ingenuity"; they also leave room for nonpolitical dimensions of human endeavor.[4] Conversely, the totalitarian-democratic current rests on an "assumption of a sole and exclusive truth in politics" and "postulates a preordained, harmonious and perfect scheme of things," a predestined future for mankind which is "treated as a matter of immediate urgency, a challenge for direct action, an imminent event." Ultimately, such an outlook can recognize "only one plane of existence, the political." Talmon posits three stages in the early growth of totalitarian democracy which provide the framework for his first volume: the eighteenth-century "postulate" (principally in Rousseau); the Jacobin "improvisation" during the Reign of Terror; and the ultimate "crystallization" in the conspiracy of Gracchus Babeuf. Throughout, Talmon is concerned not only with doctrines and actions but with identifying a "state of mind, a way of feeling, a disposition . . .

---

3. *The Origins of Totalitarian Democracy* (New York: Praeger, 1960) and *Political Messianism: The Romantic Phase* (New York: Praeger, 1960). Other notable attempts include: Karl R. Popper, *The Open Society and its Enemies* (Princeton: Princeton, 1950); Norman Cohn, *The Pursuit of the Millennium* (Fairlawn, N. J.: Essential Books, 1957); and Hannah Arendt, *The Origins of Totalitarianism,* 2nd ed. (New York: Harcourt, Brace, 1958).

4. *Totalitarian Democracy,* pp. 1–2.

best compared to a set of attitudes engendered by a religion,"—in a word, a totalitarian mentality.[5]

In Rousseau, Talmon sees the grandfather of totalitarian democracy. Beginning from the common eighteenth-century postulate that there exists a natural harmonious order for human society, Rousseau added the dangerous notion that there also exists a collective disposition, or "general will" to realize this perfect order. It could be achieved, he thought, by releasing the traditional restraints on popular self-expression, that is, by popular sovereignty. But since Rousseau posited his general will in metaphysical terms—by definition what is objectively good for the community—he was obliged to allow that it would not always conform to the expressed will of the majority. "Of themselves," he declared in *The Social Contract*, "the people always desire what is good, but do not always discern it. The general will is always right, but the judgment which guides it is not always enlightened."[6]

The problem for Rousseau was, then, to specify the conditions under which the populace could be relied upon to recognize its own best interest, to will, in actuality, the general will. These conditions included for him the absence of political parties, which he distrusted as vehicles of disunity and special interests. Indeed, there should be no "partial society" of any kind to distract the individual from devotion to the common interest. Moreover, in one of his most notorious passages, Rousseau declared: "Whoever refuses to obey the general will shall be constrained to do so by the whole body; which means nothing else than that he shall be forced to be free." Rousseau sanctioned the death penalty for extreme cases.[7] In Talmon's final evaluation, Rousseau's confused ideas at best justified an unlimited tyranny of the majority; at worst they justified an attempt by those who "knew" the general will to impose it forcibly on the reluctant masses—the Jacobin dictatorship.[8]

Talmon holds the Reign of Terror to have been a practical "improvisation" of totalitarian democracy, which came into existence by stages, partly as an ad hoc response to the extremities of foreign and civil war, but "at the same time, it corresponded to, and was the consequence of, a fixed attitude of mind of its authors," the totalitarian mentality.[9] Starting from the purest Rousseauian intentions (expressed in the stillborn

5. Ibid., pp. 2, 11.
6. Henry J. Tozer, trans., bk. 2, chap. 6.
7. Ibid., bk. 1, chap. 7; bk. 2, chap. 5; bk. 4, chap. 8.
8. *Totalitarian Democracy*, pp. 43–49.
9. Ibid., p. 122.

democratic Constitution of 1793), the Jacobin leaders desired only to be agents of the general will. But with a "monumental self-deception and *naïveté*,"[10] they saw it necessary to suppress opinions in conflict with the general will, that is, with themselves. The entire apparatus of the Terror—revolutionary tribunals, press controls, representatives on mission, the insatiable guillotine—was conceived, not as an infringement on democracy, but as its emanation. So Robespierre asserted: "The terror is nothing other than justice, prompt, severe, inflexible; it is thus an emanation of virtue; it is less a particular principle than the consequence of the general principle of democracy, applied to the most pressing needs of the country."[11] With the prohibition of all political meetings save those of the Jacobins, an effective one-party dictatorship was established: it was "no mere tyranny of a handful of men," Talmon urges, but "rested on closely knit and highly disciplined cells and nuclei in every town and village," an incipient totalitarian party.[12]

From the beginning, the Jacobin leaders conceived their dictatorship as temporary emergency government to meet the grave crises of war and rebellion; it would naturally give way in time to the democratic self-government of the people under the Constitution of 1793. But increasingly they sensed that they represented only a militant minority in a sea of mass indifference and hostility. Increasingly it seemed necessary, before dismantling the dictatorship, to prepare the people for democracy by further purges of antisocial elements and by governmental programs to educate and enlighten the masses while suppressing the stultifying influence of religious superstition. The Terror ceased to be merely defensive and took on positive preparatory tasks in an effort to remold man himself to make him fit for the Republic of Virtue. The interventionist economic policies of the regime derived from urgent wartime needs, to be sure, but similarly reflected a Jacobin desire to "restore" the greater degree of socioeconomic equality needed to insure a united popular will in the future polity. In this fashion the Jacobins pointed toward the communist crystallization of totalitarian democracy.[13]

The Reign of Terror burned itself out in less than a year: Robes-

10. Ibid., p. 133.
11. Charles Vellay, *Discours et Rapports de Robespierre* (Paris, 1908), p. 332, as quoted in Talmon, *Totalitarian Democracy*, p. 115.
12. *Totalitarian Democracy*, p. 127.
13. Ibid., pp. 132–64.

pierre found himself on the guillotine, and more conservative elements drew up the new Constitution of 1795, which eliminated universal suffrage and reintroduced, in the Directory, rule by a propertied elite. The bulk of the population, probably relieved to see the Terror end, accepted the new oligarchy with passive resignation. But among the more militant Jacobins, a small cluster around Gracchus Babeuf drew certain tough-minded conclusions from these events. These conclusions all rested on a central premise, the lesson of Ninth Thermidor: that the French population was not yet mature enough for the Republic of Virtue. The wealthy still placed their own avarice ahead of the common good; and the masses were still too mired in indolence and superstition to recognize their own interest or resist the oligarchy of wealth. As Babeuf declared, "The majority always belongs to the party of routine and immobilism; it is unenlightened, fossilized, apathetic."[14]

The Republic of Virtue—perfect democracy under the Constitution of 1793—remained the motivating vision and ultimate goal of the Babouvists, but they now concluded that since the masses were too backward to create it themselves, it would have to be established for them by the enlightened few. The chosen vanguard must act on behalf of the general will and overthrow the hated Directory, undoing the Ninth Thermidor. "It belongs to the most virtuous and courageous few," proclaimed their leader, "to take the initiative in the enterprise of revenging the people."[15] Elementary prudence dictated that the courageous few organize themselves secretly, but the need for secrecy in turn precluded any democratic organizational structure; the vanguard party would be led from the top down by Babeuf and a self-appointed Secret Directory Committee.[16]

When the requisite preparations for an insurrection had been completed, the secret committee would summon forth the vanguard to overthrow the existing regime. They hoped to have at least the immediate support of the Paris working class, among whom they attempted a limited prior agitation, but they did not conceal from themselves the fact that their insurrection would be a minority undertaking, *for* the

14. Victor Advielle, *Histoire de Gracchus Babeuf et du Babouvisme* (Paris, 1884), 1:42, as quoted in Talmon, *Totalitarian Democracy*, p. 207; see also pp. 170–72, 208.

15. *Copie des Pièces saisies dans le local que Babeuf occupait lors son arrestation—Haute Cour de Justice*, 170, pièce 61, liasse 7, as quoted in Talmon, *Totalitarian Democracy*, p. 209.

16. *Totalitarian Democracy*, pp. 222–26.

masses, but not *by* the masses. Moreover, on the morrow of the revolution, the Babouvist leaders saw no alternative but to appoint themselves heads of a provisional government, a "dictatorship of the insurrection,"[17] composed of the same half-dozen men who had formed the party's secret committee. The goal of democratic elections under the Constitution of 1793 would have to be postponed until conditions could be established that would permit the people's virtue to express itself correctly. To create these conditions was precisely the function of this constituent dictatorship: it must remove "the influence of the natural enemies of equality" and restore to the people "the unity of will necessary for the adoption of Republican institutions."[18]

The dictatorial enterprise would have three interrelated tasks. First, it must ruthlessly destroy the old institutions of oppression, as well as the people associated with them, and indeed all those who actively opposed the new order of things. Article 12 of Babeuf's projected "Acte d'insurrection" decreed: "All opposition will be crushed at once by force; those who oppose will be executed." Heads must "fall like hail," declaimed Rossignol, one of Babeuf's lieutenants.[19] Second–and this was Babeuf's distinctive communist conclusion–the new regime must establish the necessary socioeconomic foundation for the Republic of Virtue by eliminating private property and establishing an exact equality of conditions. Each man would contribute the produce of his labor to the common store and would be entitled to withdraw from it only his equal share. No selfish material interest must stand between the individual and his devotion to the community. Finally, the dictatorship would have to control the press and the educational system so as to banish old prejudices and instill among the people the virtue and enlightenment necessary for the exercise of their sovereignty.[20]

No rigid time limit was set for the accomplishment of these tasks, but Babeuf evidently thought a period of about one year would suffice. In any event, "the sovereign power was to be rendered to the people only gradually, and according to the progress of the new ways." Ultimately,

17. *Pièces saisies,* 173, pièce 61, liasse 7, as quoted in Talmon, *Totalitarian Democracy,* p. 215.

18. Philippe Buonarroti, *Conspiration pour l'égalité dite de Babeuf* (Brussels, 1828), 1:138–39, as quoted in Talmon, *Totalitarian Democracy,* p. 216.

19. Buonarroti, *Conspiration,* 2:168; Paul Robiquet, "L'Arrestation de Babeuf," *Le Révolution Française* (Paris, 1895), 28:296; both quoted in Talmon, *Totalitarian Democracy,* p. 220.

20. Talmon, *Totalitarian Democracy,* pp. 187–95, 216, 232–33.

when "the people should enter the peaceable enjoyment of equality . . .
it would be able to exercise in all its plenitude the right of deliberating on its laws as consecrated in the Constitution of 1793."[21]

Such were the hard conclusions Babeuf drew from the failure of the
first Reign of Terror. The groping improvisations of Robespierre found
their final development, their crystallization, in the doctrines and conspiracy of Babeuf, which justified a fully totalitarian one-party dictatorship to create the preconditions for ideal democracy. Talmon does not
doubt the democratic intentions of these men; indeed, absolute sincerity
of intentions belongs to the totalitarian mentality, along with a fanatical
intolerance of all disagreement and an infinite capacity for self-deception. No doubt they genuinely believed the dictatorship would be self-
less and temporary.

Babeuf's conspiracy was nipped in the bud, its organizer executed in
1797, but his fanaticism and his core ideas—the vanguard party, minority revolution, one-party educational dictatorship, wholesale terror
and reeducation, forcible leveling—were passed on by the way of his
follower, Philippe Buonarroti, to Louis Auguste Blanqui, perhaps the
most famous of nineteenth-century French revolutionists.[22] Moreover,
in Talmon's view, they passed from Blanqui to Marx and subsequently
to Marxist parties all over the world. Marxism has been, he asserts, "the
most vital, among the various versions of the totalitarian democratic
ideal." Or, in his second volume: "Marx is entirely within the totalitarian-democratic tradition."[23] It is this proposition which will shortly
be tested.

Talmon does not make it entirely clear whether he considers *all*
streams of socialist thought to be totalitarian. In places he seems to say
this,[24] and in his second volume, dealing with the first half of the nineteenth century, he expressly includes not only Blanqui and Marx, but
Claude-Henri de Saint-Simon and his followers, as well as Charles
Fourier, Victor Considérant, Etienne Cabet, Théodore Dézamy, and
Johann Gottlieb Fichte. Yet elsewhere he suggests that modern-day So-

21. Buonarroti, *Conspiration*, 1:313, as quoted in Talmon, *Totalitarian Democracy*, p. 233; cf. p. 229.

22. Talmon, *Totalitarian Democracy*, p. 177; idem, *Political Messianism*, pp.
168–76.

23. *Totalitarian Democracy*, p. 249; cf. pp. 252–53; *Political Messianism*, p.
205.

24. *Totalitarian Democracy*, p. 12.

cial Democrats belong with liberals and conservatives in holding to an "empiricism in politics" as against the "absolutism" of the Communists.[25] And among early socialists he does not treat systematically or attempt to classify such figures as Pierre-Joseph Proudhon, Louis Blanc, Wilhelm Weitling, Moses Hess, Robert Owen, or any of the Chartist leaders. Surely Louis Blanc, at least, and most of the Chartist leaders would belong to the school of "empiricism in politics."

Especially because Blanc came out of the Jacobin tradition, it might be instructive to document his attachment to the values of liberal, rather than totalitarian, democracy.[26] He looked forward to the attainment of a democratic government and became one of the founders of the Second French Republic in 1848. At the same time, he opposed any new reign of terror or Blanquist-style educational dictatorship.[27] During the revolutionary period he repeatedly counseled patience and played a restraining role among radical elements of the Parisian working class; for this he was hated by the Blanquists, and the feeling was mutual. Far from desiring forcibly to homogenize the popular will, Blanc favored a system of proportional representation to give voice to different minority interests. He wanted civil liberties written into the constitution and a supreme court to defend them. In pure libertarian consistency he even surpassed the official liberals themselves when, in 1848, he voted against the law exiling Louis Napoleon from France simply because he was the Bonapartist pretender. And he expected to achieve socialism, not by violent or forcible expropriation, but through the gradual and peaceful competition of private enterprise with his "social workshops," state-created but self-governing producers' cooperatives. He anticipated no resistance from the propertied classes and saw no need for coercive measures.[28] Thus, a Jacobin political heritage and attachment to so-

25. Ibid., p. 258.

26. The most recent and useful biography of Blanc is Leo A. Loubère, *Louis Blanc* (Evanston: Northwestern, 1961).

27. Talmon does mention in passing Blanc's "visions of a revolutionary dictatorship" (*Political Messianism*, p. 451; cf. p. 427), apparently referring to an incident in March 1848 when Blanc proposed to his colleagues in the Provisional Government a postponement of elections for two months and "dictatorship" by the Provisional Government until then. Alarmed by menacing counterrevolutionary demonstrations, and strongly pressured from the other side by the Blanquist faction, Blanc nonetheless dropped this proposal immediately when Lamartine refused to go along. At worst it marks a momentary aberration from his otherwise consistent opposition to Blanquist ideas. See Loubère, *Louis Blanc*, pp. 95–97.

28. See Loubère, *Louis Blanc*, especially chaps. 3, 4, and 9; vote on Napoleon, p. 26.

cialist egalitarianism–common to Blanc and Blanqui, and to Marx as well–need not inevitably produce a totalitarian program. It would seem that the socialist movement, like the democratic movement, has had its "liberal" and "totalitarian" wings from the early days.

This distinction in the socialist camp between tough-minded totalitarian democrats like Blanqui, and more tender-minded democrats like Blanc, can be extended to Germany where the two principal pre-Marxian socialists, Wilhelm Weitling and Moses Hess, provide a rough parallel. Though not so organized a thinker or conspirator as Blanqui, Weitling learned his socialism largely in the French master's camp and helped to establish the conspiratorial League of the Just among German artisans resident in Paris. He may have taken part in Blanqui's classic insurrection of 1839. Weitling's advocacy of dictatorship was embarrassingly personal: "I see a new Messiah," he wrote in his principal work, *Garantien der Harmonie und Freiheit* (1842), "coming with the sword, to carry into effect the teachings of the first. By his courage he will be placed at the head of the revolutionary army, and with its help he will crumble the decayed structure of the old social order."[29] He explained later to his comrades in the league: "If we call for communism by revolutionary means, then we must have a *dictator* who rules over everything. The *dictator* should not have more than anyone else; we can only allow him this position if he works for the general good."[30] Weitling left little doubt that he had himself in mind for the job.

By contrast, the otherworldly "communist rabbi," Moses Hess, though not at all political like Blanc, preached a tender-minded socialism that was to be achieved through moral persuasion alone, without recourse to dictatorship or any form of coercion. Hess conceived socialism to be the logical and necessary fruition of man's ethical development—the elevation of his fraternal instinct—which could be realized as soon as everyone attained the requisite level of understanding. He saw no need to capture state power or overcome bourgeois resistance:

29. As quoted in Karl Kautsky, *The Dictatorship of the Proletariat* (1919; reprint ed., Ann Arbor: Michigan, 1964), pp. 17–18. The principal biographies of Weitling are Carl Wittke, *The Utopian Communist: A Biography of Wilhelm Weitling* (Baton Rouge: Louisiana State, 1950); and Waltraud Seidel-Höppner, *Wilhelm Weitling: Der erste deutsche Theoretiker und Agitator des Kommunismus* (Berlin: Dietz, 1961).

30. "Diskussionen im Kommunistischen Arbeiterbildungsverein in London: 18. Februar 1845–14. Januar 1846," in *Der Bund der Kommunisten: Dokumente und Materialien,* vol. 1, *1836–1849,* ed. Institut für Marxismus-Leninismus (Berlin: Dietz, 1970), 1:231.

No social class would be so heartless as to leave its fellow men in misery if it had the means to meet their need. We find daily that precisely within the possessing class—no doubt because it is simultaneously the educated class—our attempts at the basic improvement of society find the deepest sympathy.[31]

The rich would voluntarily renounce their wealth; a community of goods and absolute equality would be established. Though manifestly inspired by a chiliastic vision of what he even called the "New Jerusalem," Hess did not draw the tough-minded conclusions of Blanqui, nor did he fancy *himself* the messiah, as did Weitling. Thus, chiliastic longing—common to all three, and to Marx as well—need not inevitably produce blind intolerance or apocalyptic visions of heads falling like hail.

Yet when Talmon comes finally in his second volume to grapple with Marx, he casts this prime antagonist "entirely within the totalitarian-democratic tradition" precisely—and almost exclusively—on grounds of chiliastic longing. Drawing material from Marx's earliest communist writings (1843–1844), he asserts that "the original inspiration of Marx was the Messianic postulate," namely belief in "the imminence of some apocalyptic transformation in the world." The elaborate economic arguments were devised later "to justify the Messianic expectation."[32]   Talmon evidently saw no need to examine Marx's conceptions of revolution or of the role of the party, or the meaning he gave to the phrase "dictatorship of the proletariat." The messianic postulate alone suffices to prove his totalitarian-democratic mentality.[33]

Despite the brilliance of his core insight, Talmon maltreats his own concept of totalitarian democracy through scattershot application.[34]

31.   Opening announcement of *Gesellschaftsspiegel* 1 (1845):1. Also see the major biography of Hess, Edmund Silberner, *Moses Hess: Geschichte seines Lebens* (Leiden: Brill, 1966), pp. 216–17, 227; John Weiss, *Moses Hess: Utopian Socialist* (Detroit: Wayne State, 1960), pp. 18, 34, 42–43.

32.   *Political Messianism*, pp. 204–05. Enigmatically, Talmon devotes less than a chapter to Marx, the putative father of the "most vital" current of totalitarian democracy. One cannot help feeling that, in the middle of his monumental researches, Talmon realized the inadequacy of his basic conceptual categories and so skimmed over Marx as quickly as possible.

33.   Some respected nontotalitarian authorities perversely find the messianic element in Marx's thought to be an attractive and praiseworthy feature: see Paul Tillich, *The Protestant Era*, abridged ed. (Chicago: Chicago, 1957), pp. 173–74; Erich Fromm, *Marx's Concept of Man* (New York: Ungar, 1961), pp. 64–69.

34.   Helpful critiques of Talmon's ideas as applied to the *philosophes* may be

One is either a totalitarian or not, and the merest hint of millennial aspirations or self-righteous certainty brings down the damning epithet. But surely even in the Christian tradition one recognizes infinite shadings of chiliastic longing, ranging from the blandest nod toward the Second Coming doctrine to the most concrete, immediate, and fanatical expectations. May not the same be said of the socialist tradition? And it cannot be simply the conviction of one's own rightness (which nearly everyone shares), but the willingness to tolerate differing ideas that separates the fanatic from the nonfanatic.

Further, even in extreme cases, if impatient chiliasm and bigoted self-righteousness suffice to define the totalitarian mentality, then we have had totalitarians throughout the ages, and the word becomes nothing more than a synonym for fanatic. If the concept of totalitarian democracy is to have a more specific meaning, in line with Friedrich's broader definition of totalitarianism, it would seem preferable to restrict its application to those who, while professing ultimate democratic intentions, draw Babeuf's grim conclusions from the central premise of mass backwardness: namely, the need for a vanguard party, a minority revolution, an educational dictatorship by an elite possessing a monopoly of the means of coercion and communication, wholesale terror, and mass politicization. Such a program can be called totalitarian without robbing the word of its distinctive twentieth-century meaning; it is the program Talmon recognizes as "crystallized" totalitarian democracy.

The belief that Marx and Engels embraced these Babouvist-Blanquist prescriptions for minority revolution and totalitarian dictatorship is, of course, extremely widespread, especially since the Bolshevik Revolution. Even among scholarly authorities, from liberals like Talmon and Isaiah Berlin to socialists like George Lichtheim, from ex-Communists like Bertram Wolfe to Leninists like Stanley Moore, the claim is repeated again and again that Marx and Engels accepted the above package of Blanquist ideas down through 1850, or at least during 1850.[35] The prime —though not exclusive—concern of this volume will be to test that claim,

found in Alfred Cobban, *In Search of Humanity* (London: Cape, 1960), pp. 182–85; and Peter Gay, *The Party of Humanity* (New York: Knopf, 1964), pp. 279–82.

35. Isaiah Berlin, *Karl Marx: His Life and Environment*, 3rd ed. (New York: Oxford, 1963), pp. 186–92; George Lichtheim, *Marxism: An Historical and Critical Study* (New York: Praeger, 1961), pp. 61, 122–29; Bertram D. Wolfe, *Marxism: One Hundred Years in the Life of a Doctrine* (New York: Dial, 1965), pp. 21, 151–64; and Stanley Moore, *Three Tactics: The Background in Marx* (New York: Monthly Review, 1963), pp. 11–33.

to ascertain whether Marx and Engels ever belonged to the Blanquist tradition, the tradition of "crystallized" totalitarian democracy.

For the time being, it will serve the purpose of introduction to review the negative evidence of a relationship between Marx and Engels and the spokesmen of this tradition. In the 1840s, Marx and Engels cultivated the acquaintance of virtually all the major French socialist leaders but, although Blanqui was perhaps the most famous of their number, there is no record that the two men ever sought to contact, correspond with, or meet the senior revolutionist. There was an obvious opportunity in the spring of 1848, when Blanqui was released from prison and Marx and Engels also took up a brief residence in Paris.[36] Blanqui's name is not so much as mentioned in Marx and Engels' correspondence or in any of their writings prior to 1850, save for one fleeting (and inconsequential) reference in a news story published in the *Neue Rheinische Zeitung* in July 1848.[37] Marx and Engels' unpublished notebooks of this period contain no reference to Blanqui, and their surviving libraries hold no writing of Blanqui prior to 1880.[38] The two men certainly became acquainted with Blanquist secret societies in Paris and London during the early 1840s, but both expressly refused to join them, as we will see later.[39]

Babeuf and Buonarroti, both already dead, were ignored by Marx and Engels almost as cavalierly. The younger men were definitely familiar with Buonarroti's famous *Conspiration pour l'égalité dite de*

36.   Maurice Dommanget, *Les idées politiques et sociales d'Auguste Blanqui* (Paris: Rivière, 1957), p. 377. Dommanget cites two other opportunities in later years, when Blanqui visited London in 1860, and when Marx visited Paris in 1869 (pp. 386–87, 391). Dommanget's several books on Blanqui establish him as the foremost—if least critical—biographer. Other useful studies include Alan Spitzer, *The Revolutionary Theories of Louis Auguste Blanqui* (New York: Columbia, 1957); and Samuel Bernstein, *Blanqui* (Paris: Maspero, 1970).

37.   Karl Marx and Friedrich Engels, *Werke*, 39 vols. (Berlin: Dietz, 1956–68), 5:143 (hereafter cited as *Werke*). For negative evidence, see the *Personenverzeichnis* of the appropriate volumes of the *Werke*. Curiously, Blanqui's brother, the respectable bourgeois economist, Jérôme-Adolphe Blanqui, is mentioned several times in the early writings of Marx.

38.   Unpublished *Exzerpthefte* examined by author in Marx-Engels Nachlass, Internationaal Instituut voor Sociale Geschiedenis, Amsterdam. For the surviving libraries, see Institut für Marxismus-Leninismus, *Ex Libris Karl Marx und Friedrich Engels: Schicksal und Verzeichnis einer Bibliothek* (Berlin: Dietz, 1967), pp. 35, 211–28.

39.   See *Werke*, 14:439; Karl Marx and Friedrich Engels, *Selected Works*, 2 vols. (Moscow: Foreign Languages, 1951), 2:313 (hereafter cited as *Selected Works*); and below, pp. 90–91, 112.

Babeuf (1828), although they nowhere saw fit to discuss it at length.[40] Prior to 1850, Babeuf's name appears fourteen times in their writings; Buonarroti's, only four. (In the same period Louis Blanc's name appears more than fifty times.)[41] All the citations but two are passing historical-factual references to the older men's role as forerunners of the modern proletarian movement; sometimes they include an appreciative adjective. The two more serious allusions are unambiguously negative. In an 1843 article describing socialism on the Continent for his English readers, Engels had kind words for almost all the leading schools but dismissed Babeuf's conspiracy in one sentence: "The Communist plot did not succeed, because the then [*sic*] Communism itself was of a very rough and superficial kind, and because, on the other hand, the public mind was not yet far enough advanced."[42]

The second reference appears in the *Communist Manifesto* itself, in a seldom quoted passage at the beginning of the section on utopian socialism. Referring to the "writing of Babeuf and others," the *Manifesto* declared:

> The first direct attempts of the proletariat to attain its own ends, made in times of universal excitement, when feudal society was being overthrown, these attempts necessarily failed, owing to the then undeveloped state of the proletariat, as well as to the absence of the economic conditions for its emancipation, conditions that had yet to be produced, and could be produced by the impending bourgeois epoch alone. The revolutionary literature that accompanied these first movements of the proletariat had necessarily a reactionary character. It inculcated universal asceticism and social levelling in its crudest form.[43]

Rough and superficial, crude and reactionary, premature and doomed to failure—these sentiments scarcely suggest a profound influence of

---

40. Engels referred to it in an 1843 article (*Werke*, 1:482); see also Arthur Lehning, "Buonarroti's Ideas on Communism and Dictatorship," *International Review of Social History* 2 (1957):282.

41. Calculated from the *Personenverzeichnisse* of the appropriate volumes of the *Werke*.

42. "Progress of Social Reform on the Continent," in Karl Marx and Friedrich Engels, *Historisch-kritische Gesamtausgabe*, ed. D. Ryazanoff, 11 vols. (Frankfurt, Berlin, Moscow: Marx-Engels-Lenin Institut, 1927–33), I, 2:436 (hereafter cited as *MEGA*).

43. *Selected Works*, 1:58.

the Babouvists on Marx and Engels. Indeed, the total absence of any direct positive evidence linking Marx and Engels to the Babouvist-Blanquist tradition would appear to throw a difficult burden of proof on the proponents of this hypothesis.

The alternative hypothesis advanced below is that among the currents of early socialism, between tough-minded elitists like Babeuf and Blanqui and tender-minded democrats like Blanc and Hess, Marx and Engels represented a third distinctive combination—they were tough-minded democrats.

{2}

Marx's Political Education

THE PURPOSE OF THIS and the following two chapters is not to offer a general biography of Marx and Engels in their early years, which has been done often enough, but to analyze the development of their political ideas, to expose as much as possible the sources of those ideas and the influences on their evolution. Both men went through three distinct phases in their political education. Marx came from a liberal monarchist background, moved left with the Young Hegelians into the democratic-republican camp toward the end of his university years, and became a communist at twenty-five. Engels' family upbringing was rigidly conservative, and he had already rebelled against it in his teens, embracing a fiery revolutionary variety of the democratic-republican outlook, until at the age of twenty-one he metamorphosed once again into a communist. In the light of the dichotomies posed in the previous chapter, it will be particularly interesting to ask whether Marx or Engels espoused a "liberal" or "totalitarian" version of the democratic ideal during the middle phase, and how conversion to communism affected these previously held democratic convictions. Marx's political education was intellectually the more complex and requires a lengthier exposition.[1]

1. Among the host of general biographies of Marx, perhaps the most useful are Isaiah Berlin, *Karl Marx: His Life and Environment,* 3rd ed. (New York: Oxford, 1963); Franz Mehring, *Karl Marx: The Story of His Life,* trans. Edward Fitzgerald (1935; reprint ed., Ann Arbor: Michigan, 1962); and Boris Nicolaievsky and Otto Maenchen-Helfen, *Karl Marx: Man and Fighter,* trans. Gwenda David and Eric Mosbacher (Philadelphia: Lippincott, 1936). The last named has been republished —too late for use here—in a complete edition that includes the scholarly apparatus omitted in the original edition (London: Allen Lane, 1973). Another late publication is David McLellan, *Karl Marx: His Life and Thought* (New York: Harper, 1973). The most exhaustive treatment of Marx's early years may be found in Au-

[17]

Liberal Monarchist Upbringing

Insofar as it is possible to ascertain with meager direct evidence, Marx's earliest political ideas seem to have derived from his father, with whom he enjoyed an unusually close and warm relationship.[2] The elder man was born in 1782, the second son of the rabbi of Trier. On both sides of his family, Hirschel Marx was descended from generations of rabbis, and his older brother, Karl's uncle, would later assume the paternal office in Trier. For some reason Hirschel broke this family tradition, choosing for himself a different career and a different way of life. Perhaps the rupture stemmed from his situation as a younger son, or from his father's death when the lad was sixteen, but almost certainly it was related to the decisive political event of his youth—the arrival of the French revolutionary armies in Trier in 1794. French occupation brought the dissolution of the ancient ecclesiastical state of Trier and its subsequent incorporation into metropolitan France, where it would remain for two decades, to the end of the Napoleonic era in 1815. Most importantly for the adolescent Hirschel Marx, the arrival of the French brought legal emancipation for the Jews, making it possible to contemplate a career, a whole life, outside the Jewish ghetto, an assimilation into the larger gentile society.

Whatever higher education Hirschel Marx received must have been in French-controlled schools. His later library contained almost as many French titles as German, and he was described by his granddaughter as a "real eighteenth-century Frenchman, who knew his Voltaire and Rousseau inside out."[3] He abandoned the religion of his forefathers for the rationalist deism of the Enlightenment. "You know I am anything

---

guste Cornu, *Karl Marx et Friedrich Engels: Leur vie et leur oeuvre*, 3 vols. (Paris: Presses Universitaires, 1955–62). An excellent shorter treatment in English is David McLellan, *Marx Before Marxism* (New York: Harper, 1970).

2.   Karl Marx retained a warm remembrance of his father and always carried a picture of him that would be buried with Marx in 1883 (see *Werke*, supp. vol. 1 [Ergänzungsband 1, hereafter cited as EB 1], p. 661). On Hirschel Marx, see Cornu, *Karl Marx et Friedrich Engels*, 1:53–60; and especially Heinz Monz, *Karl Marx und Trier* (Trier: Neu, 1964), pp. 128–46. Monz has published an expanded version of this book—too late for use here—under the title *Karl Marx: Grundlagen der Entwicklung zu Leben und Werk* (Trier: Neu, 1973).

3.   Reminiscence of Eleanor Marx in *Neue Zeit* 16 (1898):5. On Hirschel Marx's library, see Heinz Monz, "Die soziale Lage der elterlichen Familie von Karl Marx," in *Karl Marx 1818–1968: Neue Studien zu Person und Lehre* (Mainz: Hase und Koehler, 1968), pp. 79–83.

but a fanatic," he would later write his son, but he urged Karl to remain faithful to a "pure belief in God," like "Newton, Locke, and Leibnitz."[4] He also embraced the liberal political ideals of the Enlightenment and may have had a hand in founding the Literary Casino Society of Trier, established during the French years by liberal members of the town's educated elite. In any event, it was as a French citizen that Hirschel Marx entered the practice of law in government service at the Trier High Court of Appeal (*Oberapellationsgericht*), a position he would hold for the rest of his life, though his employers would change in 1815.

It is known that the elder Marx welcomed the arrival of the Prussian armies in January 1815 with enthusiasm. In a later epistle to his son, he would go so far as to suggest that Karl compose an ode in celebration of Prussia's role in the final defeat of Napoleon, for the emperor's success "would have placed mankind, and the intellect especially, in everlasting chains."[5] A great many originally pro-French Rhinelanders had gradually turned against France as Napoleon's demands for money and conscripts grew ever more oppressive. Jews had special reason for disillusionment, since Napoleon's Decree of March 1808 had withdrawn many of the gains of their recent emancipation. Conversely, Prussia's attractiveness rose under the liberal reform ministries of Stein and Hardenberg, which produced—among other things—a Jewish emancipation decree in 1812. With high hopes, Hirschel Marx addressed an appeal to the new Prussian Governor-General von Sack, on behalf of his "co-religionists," requesting that the Napoleonic edict be dropped so that Jews in the Rhineland might enjoy full civil rights. If some Jews were guilty of inordinate usury, let them be punished by strong general laws against this abuse rather than by special discriminations against Jews. "A just monarch," he wrote expectantly, "will grant general laws when it is necessary to eliminate general vices."[6]

Alas, this supplication fell on deaf ears. The Prussian monarch, Frederick William III, abandoned his liberal pretensions in perfect rhythm with the reduction of French power. Not only did he leave the Napoleonic Decree in effect, but he applied a further, specifically Prussian, restriction which excluded Jews from state service. The exclusion threatened the elder Marx personally, but it evidently did not turn him

---

4. Letter of November 18, 1835, *Werke*, EB 1:617.
5. Letter of March 2, 1837, ibid., pp. 627–28.
6. As quoted in Arnold Künzli, *Karl Marx: Eine Psychographie* (Vienna: Europa, 1966), pp. 39–40.

against his new employer. For the sake of form, he allowed himself to be baptized in the Lutheran Church, adopted the Christian name Heinrich, and thus was able to retain his position at the Trier court. This final and seemingly humiliating break with his past was probably eased for Marx by his assimilationist desires and by the fact that his private religious beliefs, strictly speaking, were neither Jewish nor Christian. Eventually he would have his entire family "converted" to nominal Lutheranism. In 1813 Marx had married Henriette Pressburg, the daughter of a Dutch rabbi, and in the early Restoration period she bore him nine children. Karl Marx, the eldest surviving son, was born in May 1818. He was baptized with the other children in 1824 and confirmed in 1834 at the age of fifteen.[7]

Also in 1834 there occurred in Trier an incident which helps to bring the political ideas of the elder Marx into sharper focus. Among the political ripples that crossed the Rhine in the wake of the French July Revolution was a campaign of banquets in southern Germany organized by prominent liberals to encourage the development of parliamentary government. On Prussian territory only the Literary Casino Society of Trier dared to put on a similar banquet, and Heinrich Marx, now a leading member, was the featured speaker of the evening. The banquet was called in January 1834 specifically to honor Trier's liberal deputies to the Rhenish provincial diet (*Landtag*) at a time when conservatives in the Berlin government were calling for its dissolution. Although the recently revived provincial diets of Prussia had no national function, possessed no real legislative power, and represented the medieval estates rather than the people directly, they were feared by reactionaries as the entering wedge of liberal parliamentarism. Their fear was obviously the elder Marx's fervent hope. Seeking the protection of royal support, he heartily praised the monarch "to whose magnanimity we are indebted for the first institutions of popular representation. In the fullness of his omnipotence he arranged that Diets should assemble so that truth might arrive at the steps of the throne." Liberal institutions through royal generosity was the theme that carried Marx down to his concluding thought: "So let us look confidently forward to a serene future, for it rests in the hands of a worthy father, an upright king, whose noble heart will always remain open and well-disposed to the just and reasonable wishes of his people."[8]

7. Künzli, *Psychographie,* pp. 40–43.
8. Text of entire speech in Monz, *Trier,* p. 88; English translation taken from

Newspapers as far away as Paris carried reports of the banquet and of Marx's speech, and it thoroughly alarmed the Prussian authorities, especially when, in another session a week later, some wine-emboldened club members broke out the old tricolor and sang the *Marseillaise*. The Berlin government cracked down, placing the group under police surveillance and opening high treason proceedings against the ringleaders (but not against Marx). There is no evidence to confirm the widely repeated story that Marx then hastily repudiated his own speech, but neither does the evidence show that he opposed or resisted the crackdown in any way.[9] Somehow never disenchanted by his brushes with Junker reaction, Heinrich Marx remained for the rest of his life an enthusiastic supporter of the Prussian monarchy, seeing it not as a conservative but as a liberal institution. In the aforementioned letter to his son, written near the end of his life, he suggested a poetic theme that would be "full of honor for Prussia" and would reveal "the genius of the monarchy." The defeat of Napoleon provided such a theme. "Only the hybrid liberals of today could idolize a Napoleon. Under him, truly no one dared even to think aloud what is daily written without hindrance in Germany and especially Pr[ussia]."[10]

Thus, to his eldest son, Heinrich Marx bequeathed a political philosophy born of the French Enlightenment which espoused the characteristic early-nineteenth-century liberal program of equality before the law, freedom of expression, and a constitutional monarchy in which the dynasty would share power with an elected legislature representing at least *Besitz und Bildung*, the propertied and educated classes. It was equally characteristic that this paternal liberalism abjured revolution and Jacobin republicanism in favor of compromise, patience, and even resignation, with an unbelievably naive faith in royal generosity and the reformability of the Prussian system. The young Karl Marx evidently embraced this political outlook until after his father's death in 1838. His later rejection of liberalism may well have involved an unconscious rejection of his father, as Künzli's psychological study suggests. Proud and rebellious by nature, Karl very likely felt ashamed of his father's

---

Nicolaievsky and Maenchen-Helfen, *Marx*, pp. 9–10. For the political ideas of the elder Marx, see especially Heinz Monz, "Die rechtsethischen und rechtspolitischen Anschauungen von Heinrich Marx," *Archiv für Sozialgeschichte* 8 (1968):261–83.

9. Story repeated, e.g., in Berlin, *Marx*, p. 28; but see documented analysis in Monz, *Trier*, pp. 88–90, 144–45.

10. Letter of March 2, 1837, *Werke*, EB 1:628–29.

meek silence in the wake of the Casino affair. His own response to it—
as we will see—was quite different. All his adult life, Marx would show
the utmost disdain in politics for meekness, servility, and moralistic
naiveté—precisely the character traits of his father.[11] But at the deepest
level, the political values of his father's generation survived intact in
the adult Marx: belief in the fundamental equality of man and in his
perfectibility, in the progress of human institutions through history, in
reason and science as the keys to the enigma of man's destiny, and in
the ethical imperative to commit one's life to the betterment of mankind. In this sense, Marx always remained a child—a bastard child, some
would argue—of the Enlightenment.[12]

The influence of liberal political ideas was reinforced in the youthful
Marx by his association with another older man, his neighbor and future father-in-law, Baron Ludwig von Westphalen. An appointee of
Hardenberg, Westphalen belonged to the reform-minded element in
the Prussian high civil service. His father had been ennobled for service
to the duke of Brunswick, and his English mother was descended from
the dukes of Argyle. Westphalen himself also began service in Brunswick, but transferred his loyalty to Napoleon when the area was re-
organized into the Kingdom of Westphalia in 1807. His independent
spirit, however, resisted Napoleon's later oppressive policies, and he was
in prison when the allies recovered the territory. Hardenberg was impressed by the highly cultured and competent administrator, and sent
him to Trier in 1816 as government councillor (*Regierungsrat*) charged
with the delicate mission of easing the town's integration into the Prussian governmental system.[13] So it was that Westphalen, then in his six-
ties, took up residence in Trier, joined the Casino Society, came to know
his neighbor, Heinrich Marx, and to befriend the latter's gifted son.
Karl would later recall the many happy hours he spent tramping
through the picturesque woods and hills around his hometown deep in
conversation with the older man. It is known that Westphalen, among
other things, introduced the youth to the teachings of Saint-Simon, although the significance of this encounter should not be exaggerated.
Marx's imagination may well have been fired by Saint-Simon's vision of

11. Künzli, *Psychographie*, pp. 47–50; cf. Berlin, *Marx*, p. 28. See Heinrich
Marx's praise of resignation as a virtue, *Werke*, EB 1:631.

12. Berlin, *Marx*, p. 30; Monz, "Anschauungen von Heinrich Marx," p. 274.

13. On Westphalen see Monz, *Trier*, pp. 156–67; Franz Mehring, "Die von
Westphalen," *Neue Zeit* 10 (1892):481–86, 513–18.

technological progress in a rationally planned society, of man's progressively developing mastery over the forces of nature and over his own institutions, but neither Saint-Simon nor Westphalen drew specifically socialist conclusions from this vision, nor did Marx seriously consider socialism until several years later. The basic thrust of Westphalen's political influence on the adolescent Marx must have been liberal monarchist, in the spirit of the Stein-Hardenberg reforms and the Casino Society, and seemingly in this spirit Marx would dedicate his doctoral dissertation to "my dear fatherly friend, . . . who greets every forward step of the times with the enthusiasm and prudence of truth and with that sun-bright idealism . . . which never recoils before the deep shadows of retrograde ghosts."[14]

The third influence shaping the political mind of the youthful Marx worked in consonance with the other two. After his primary-school education, Karl was enrolled in the Friedrich Wilhelm *Gymnasium* of Trier, which he attended from 1830 to 1835, taking his diploma at the age of seventeen. Ancient, medieval, and modern history he learned from the school's director, Hugo Wyttenbach, a Kantian liberal who was a cofounder of the Casino Society and a close friend of Heinrich Marx's. Surviving police reports suggest an unusually liberal atmosphere at the Trier *Gymnasium:* subversive literature was discovered in one student's possession in 1833; another student was jailed the following year for writing revolutionary verse; Wyttenbach and two of Marx's other teachers had police dossiers. A showdown occurred in 1834 in the wake of the Casino Society banquet when the government threatened to dismiss Wyttenbach. In the end they appointed a reactionary instructor named Loers to share the directorship with him. In his first recorded political act, and much to the embarrassment of his father, Karl Marx conspicuously omitted the customary last visit to Loers when he graduated in 1835, while making it known that he intended to write a poem in honor of the martyr Wyttenbach.[15]

Marx's final school examinations give us our first direct insight into the mind of the seventeen-year-old boy. The best known, "Reflections

---

14. "The Difference between the Democritean and Epicurean Philosophy of Nature" (1841), in Norman D. Livergood, *Activity in Marx's Philosophy* (The Hague: Nijhoff, 1967), p. 59. Livergood has included an English translation of Marx's entire doctoral dissertation in this study.

15. *Werke,* EB 1:617–18; Monz, *Trier,* pp. 92–109; and Nicolaievsky and Maenchen-Helfen, *Marx,* pp. 11–14.

of a Youth on Choosing a Career," glows with the humanist ideals of the German Enlightenment which Marx imbibed from his mentors. Whereas animals have a narrow sphere of activity prescribed by nature, the Deity assigned man "a general goal, to ennoble mankind and himself, but left it up to him to seek the means by which he can attain this goal." We must be guided in the choice of a career by the "welfare of humanity" and "our own fulfillment," which are compatible goals: "Man's nature makes it possible for him to reach his own fulfillment only by working for the perfection and welfare of society at large."[16] In a more secularized form these sentiments would remain at the heart of Marx's ethic throughout his life. A second prescribed essay on the "Union of Believers with Christ" reveals the same humanist and deist conceptions: it treats the subject of union in purely ethical terms of individual self-realization, with no reference to heaven or immortality and no mention of any organized church.[17]

A third examination essay, written in Latin, dealt with the reign of Augustus and has obvious implications for political thought. Recently it has been interpreted as showing Marx's early penchant for "dictatorship," which he allegedly preferred "over any other form of government as leading to the greatest happiness."[18] Most biographers have ignored this essay, perhaps because it is less coherent and thoughtful than the others, but perhaps also because of Marx's hesitating approval of the Roman emperor. He placed Augustus midway in a process of historical degeneration between the virtuous simplicity of the Republic and the unmitigated tyranny of Nero. After constant civil strife had torn the Republic to pieces, Augustus stepped in with an overriding purpose, "to rescue the state." He gathered all power in his own hands and deprived the citizens of Rome of "all freedom, even the semblance of freedom," but he did not "misuse his power" and exercised it with "leniency." Marx concluded reluctantly that Augustus' principate was best suited to his unfortunate time, for in a period of civil strife, "one ruler

---

16.   Karl Marx, *Writings of the Young Marx on Philosophy and Society*, trans. and ed. Loyd Easton and Kurt H. Guddat (Garden City: Doubleday, 1967), pp. 35, 39 (hereafter cited as *Writings*); translation modified—RNH; see original German, *Werke*, EB 1:591, 594). See also McLellan, *Marx Before Marxism*, pp. 35–38.

17.   *Werke*, EB 1:598–601; Henry P. Adams, *Karl Marx in His Earlier Writings* (1940; reprint ed., New York: Russell and Russell, 1965), pp. 13–16.

18.   Robert Payne, *Marx* (New York: Simon and Schuster, 1968), p. 38.

can bring the people to freedom better than a free republic."[19] There is no reason to infer any special dictatorial predilection from these sentiments. They include a distant admiration of the Roman Republic, a recognition of the need for monarchical authority to restrain the centrifugal forces of civil society, and a reluctant approval of extraordinary power for extraordinary times. All these ideas were characteristic of German liberalism in this period and might just as well have been uttered by Wyttenbach or by Marx's own father.[20] Throughout the essay Marx speaks of Augustus as "princeps" or "imperator," not as "dictator." It is easy to forget that the youth was raised in a monarchist tradition.

It had long been resolved in the Marx family that Karl should have a university education, and his father encouraged the lad to study law and plan a legal career on the paternal model. Thus in October 1835, Karl set off for the University of Bonn, closest to Trier. He spent his first student year in an ambitious program of study, which did not prevent him from enjoying the drinking and carousing characteristic of student life there, or even from fighting a duel. Nothing is known of his political ideas or activities during that year. Indeed, overt political activity was scarcely possible in the heavy police-state repression that descended on Bonn in the wake of an unsuccessful attempt by a group of young radicals to overthrow the Frankfurt Diet in April 1835. But Marx's active role in the University Poets' Club probably betokens more than his growing fascination with the muse, if we judge by the amount of police interest in the group and by the number of its members, besides Marx, who subsequently involved themselves in left-wing politics.[21] During the summer of 1836, after his year at Bonn, Marx became secretly engaged to Jenny von Westphalen, his childhood sweetheart and daughter of his "fatherly friend," Ludwig von Westphalen. Jenny was a beautiful young noblewoman, four years his senior; socially it was a most felicitous alliance for the middle-class converted Jew. The prospect of this marital responsibility, combined perhaps with mild chastisement

19. Translated here from German in *Werke,* EB 1:595–97; see original Latin version in *MEGA* I, 1/2:168–70.

20. For example, see the elder Marx's justification of extraordinary royal power in the then current Cologne church-state dispute, *MEGA* I, 1/2:231–33.

21. Including Fenner von Fenneberg, Karl Grün, and L. F. C. Bernays; see Cornu, *Karl Marx et Friedrich Engels,* 1:67–70; Nicolaievsky and Maenchen-Helfen, *Marx,* pp. 15–20.

by his father for his Bonn frivolities, seems to have given the eighteen-year-old Marx a new seriousness of purpose as he set off the following autumn for the more somber atmosphere of the University of Berlin.

Young Hegelian Radicalization

The ensuing five years of study at Berlin were crucially important in Marx's intellectual growth. His interest would be distracted from legal studies first by poetry and then, increasingly, by philosophy. Initially repelled by the system of Hegel then dominant at the university, he soon found himself "more and more chained to the current world philosophy from which I had thought to escape."[22] He joined forces with the Young Hegelians of the so-called Doctors' Club, whose most militant members were at that time moving leftward in a radicalization that would lead them by 1841 to outright atheism and outright republicanism.

It is a misfortune that from this key period there remain only the most meager fragments of direct evidence. We have, from Marx's own hand, a solitary letter to his father, a collection of flamboyant poetry, some notes for his doctoral dissertation, and of course the dissertation itself, on a seemingly obscure topic in Classical Greek philosophy. These sources are particularly disappointing to anyone interested in Marx's political development. Young Engels' verse fairly explodes with political indignation, but Marx's poetic efforts—though psychologically interesting—remain entirely introspective in the romantic tradition.[23] Even Marx's legal studies, as revealed in the letter to his father, concerned the "metaphysics of law" rather than its more political aspects.[24] And his dissertation, while more related to his own emerging philosophy than used to be thought,[25] shows just as little political concern.

Yet the intensely political writing which would immediately follow Marx's university years, in the *Rheinische Zeitung* period, cannot have emerged from a perfect vacuum. We know that early in 1838 he collaborated in a project initiated by his ailing father, to write a pamphlet

22. Letter to his father, November 10, 1837, *Writings*, p. 48.
23. Reproduced in *MEGA* I, 1/2:3–92; on psychological significance, see suggestions of Künzli, *Psychographie*, pp. 148–69.
24. Letter to his father, November 10, 1837, *Writings*, p. 42.
25. See excellent introductory essay accompanying Livergood's translation in *Activity in Marx's Philosophy;* also see McLellan, *Marx Before Marxism*, pp. 52–68.

that would defend the position of the Prussian government in the church-state conflict then brewing with the Catholic archbishop of Cologne.[26] This abortive collaboration may be regarded as a last filial gesture of devotion to the paternal belief in liberal constitutional monarchy. The elder Marx died in May 1838; for the next few years the controlling influence on Marx's political ideas would come from the Young Hegelians of the Doctors' Club.

Hegel had been dead for five years when Marx arrived in Berlin, and his followers were divided into two schools. The conservative school professed to see in the established state and church of Prussia the highest expression of Hegel's World Spirit, the culmination of all human history. Using Hegel's famous maxim, they argued that these existing institutions must be rational (that is, rationally necessary and justified) precisely because they were actual (that is, they actually existed as the product of historical evolution). A younger group of Hegelians, repelled by this smug glorification of the status quo, argued that the world-historical process was not yet finished. Its culminating goal, the rational order of society, still lay in the future; it could be discerned philosophically but had not yet become actual. They quoted the other half of the master's maxim, that what is rational is actual (that is, must *become* actual). To help history along required a philosophy of action, or *praxis*, as urged particularly by August von Cieszkowski, who suggested that action, for Young Hegelian philosophers, should consist of criticizing existing reality according to the rational ideal.[27]

In his legal studies, Marx had already confessed to his father that he "was greatly disturbed by the conflict between what is and what ought to be."[28] Thus was he drawn to the Young Hegelians, who shared his disquietude and who provided a philosophical yardstick for measuring the "is" against the "ought to be." Marx's notes of this period set down the differences within the Hegelian camp and reveal his attraction to the liberal faction. "The liberal party," he wrote, "makes real progress, because it is the party of the Concept," whose *praxis* is criticism:

26. See *MEGA* I, 1/2:231–33.
27. Cieszkowski's principal writing on the subject was *Prolegoma zur Historiosophie* (Berlin, 1838). On the young Hegelians generally, see Sidney Hook, *From Hegel to Marx*, 2nd ed. (Ann Arbor: Michigan, 1962); David McLellan, *The Young Hegelians and Karl Marx* (New York: Praeger, 1969); and William J. Brazill, *The Young Hegelians* (New Haven: Yale, 1970).
28. Letter to his father, November 10, 1837, *Writings*, p. 42.

The theoretical mind, having become free in itself, turns into practical energy, . . . turns against worldly actuality which exists outside it. . . . The *practice* [praxis] of philosophy, however, is itself *theoretical*. It is *criticism* which measures individual existence against essence, particular actuality against the Idea.[29]

By measuring existing actuality against the "Idea," the ideal yardstick of reason, Marx and his friends evidently hoped to undermine the status quo and prepare the ground for the realization of the Idea, which Hegelians believed to be the goal of the historical process.

The Young Hegelians commenced their critical offensive with a concerted attack on the religious prop of the existing order, traditional Christianity. David Friedrich Strauss led the first wave with his *Life of Jesus* in 1835, and the assault reached its crescendo with Ludwig Feuerbach's *Essence of Christianity,* published in 1841. Marx soon shed the deist beliefs in which he had been reared in favor of the Feuerbachian humanist atheism that he would retain the rest of his life.[30] Toward the end of his university years, he began to participate more actively in this polemical battle: he apparently collaborated with Bruno Bauer in an anonymously published satiric pamphlet, supposedly written by a devout Christian, attacking the "atheist and Antichrist" Hegel.[31] Marx intended to continue this collaboration with Bauer after graduation by following him to the University of Bonn and there publishing with him a new periodical to be titled *The Archive of Atheism.* But a governmental crackdown on religious dissent in 1841 put an end to Marx's plans and turned his attention more directly to political questions.

Among the liberal Hegelians at the University of Berlin were a few whose interests, from the beginning, were primarily political rather than religious. The most distinguished of this group was Eduard Gans, professor of law and favored disciple of the old master. A supporter of the French July Revolution and known advocate of an English-style constitutional monarchy, Gans' eloquence attracted a wide university audience. Marx is known to have attended his lectures on criminal law,

29. "Notes to the Doctoral Dissertation," ibid., pp. 61–63.
30. See Marx's notes rebutting the standard rationalist proofs for the existence of God, ibid., pp. 64–66. On the development of Marx's religious views, see Charles Wackenheim, *La faillite de la religion d'après Karl Marx* (Paris: Presses Universitaires, 1963).
31. *Die Posaune des jüngsten Gerichts über Hegel den Atheisten und Antichristen* (Leipzig, 1841).

where Gans applied the weapon of criticism—apparently with surgical skill—in a dissection of the Prussian law codes, weighing each paragraph assiduously against the demands of reason. His influence on Marx can be seen especially in the latter's own legal criticism in the *Rheinische Zeitung* period, as we will observe, although one can also detect there the influence of Gans' professional rival at Berlin, Karl von Savigny, whose conservatively inspired lectures on the history of law doubtless nettled the young student, but whose painstaking attention to the genesis and historical evolution of legal institutions provided Marx with another useful model of critical analysis.[32]

Personally closer to Marx was Adolf Rutenberg, the Young Hegelian whom Marx described to his father as "my most intimate friend in Berlin," and who first introduced the Trier law student into the Doctors' Club in 1837. Rutenberg was an old *Burschenschaftler*, a veteran of the student movement that had hurled its defiance at the 1815 Restoration. He had spent substantial periods of his life in Prussian jails and now made his living as a political journalist, trying his literary skill against the censor to give veiled expression to his liberal views.[33] Marx's penetrating intelligence and caustic wit compensated for his youth in the Doctors' Club, most of whose members were several years his senior. He found his most permanent friend in Karl Friedrich Köppen, a young history instructor who published a biography of Frederick the Great in 1840 and dedicated it to "his friend Karl Heinrich Marx of Trier." In what he called a "spiritual resurrection" of Frederick, Köppen drew pointed contrasts between the liberal reforms of the enlightened monarch and the narrow-minded repressiveness of the present regime. Speaking for the Young Hegelians, he rhapsodized:

> Frederick was our Moses. . . . What can never perish is his immortal spirit, the spirit of the Enlightenment, of freedom of thought and belief, the spirit of equity, the high consciousness of the mission of the state, which alone can guide Prussia in the path of truth. . . . As for us, we swear to live and die in that spirit.[34]

32. Cornu, *Karl Marx et Friedrich Engels*, 1:85–89; Berlin, *Marx*, pp. 67–69; and Joseph O'Malley, "Editor's Introduction," in Karl Marx, *Critique of Hegel's 'Philosophy of Right'* (Cambridge: Cambridge, 1970), pp. xx–xxi.

33. Letter to his father, November 10, 1837, *Writings*, p. 48; Nicolaievsky and Maenchen-Helfen, *Marx*, p. 34.

34. *Friedrich der Grosse und seine Widersacher* (Leipzig: Wigand, 1840), pp. 171–72.

Most likely Marx, like Köppen, remained faithful to the principles of liberal monarchism until 1840, despairing of the old Frederick William III but looking hard to see the profile of a new Frederick the Great in the visage of the crown prince. A contemporary observer in the summer of 1840 characterized the Doctors' Club as "thoroughly devoted to the idea of constitutional monarchy."[35]

When the crown prince did ascend to the throne as Frederick William IV, on the death of the old king in June 1840, he soon quashed all hope that he would be a new philosopher-king. His personal outlook inclined him not at all toward the Enlightenment or liberal reform, but toward a nostalgic medievalism characteristic of the conservative wing of German romanticism. He inaugurated his reign with a few well-meant gestures but soon followed them with a series of repressive measures cracking down on religious and political dissent and victimizing the Young Hegelians particularly. It was this bitter disappointment with the new monarch, combined with the prospect of a long reign, that finally destroyed their monarchism. Köppen once again set about to write a "spiritual resurrection," this time of the Jacobin Republic of 1793![36]

Together with Köppen and other radical spirits, Marx now moved rapidly leftward in a group calling itself "Friends of the People" and described by Arnold Ruge as "the philosophical Mountain" of the Hegelian spectrum.[37] Marx had personal grounds as well for turning against the monarchy: it was precisely Frederick William's new wave of repression that brought about Bruno Bauer's dismissal from the University of Bonn, thwarted Marx's own aspirations for a position there, and forced cancellation of their jointly projected *Archive of Atheism*. With doctorate in hand and hoping to be married, Marx found himself in 1841 suddenly obliged to search about for a career other than the academic one he had planned. He soon found his new vocation in political journalism and intended in one of his first articles to announce his conversion to republicanism. The article was never published and unfortunately has not survived, but Marx described it in a March 1842 letter to Arnold Ruge as "a critique of Hegel's natural right insofar as

35. As quoted in Nicolaievsky and Maenchen-Helfen, *Marx*, p. 39; see also McLellan, *Young Hegelians*, pp. 22–24.
36. Marx to Arnold Ruge, May 1843, *Writings*, pp. 208–09; Cornu, *Karl Marx et Friedrich Engels*, 1:165–69.
37. Nicolaievsky and Maenchen-Helfen, *Marx*, pp. 39–41.

it concerns the *inner constitution.* The heart is a polemic against *constitutional monarchy* as a thoroughly self-contradictory and self-negating hermaphrodite. *Res publica* is not to be translated into German."[38] In this earliest surviving direct statement of political conviction, we see that Marx has moved unambiguously from the liberal monarchist into the republican camp. Only the restrictions of censorship prevent the translation of *res publica* into *Republik.*

Democratic Republican Editor

Marx was a noncommunist democratic republican for about two years. He had rejected monarchism, as we have seen, by the beginning of 1842 (if not before), and by the end of 1843 he would embrace communism. The two-year period between coincides very largely with Marx's journalistic work for the newly established Cologne weekly, *Rheinische Zeitung:* he began his first article in April 1842, was appointed editor in October, and remained editor until the final suppression of the paper by the Prussian government in March 1843. Apart from editorial notes and short polemical skirmishes, Marx wrote twelve substantive essays during this period, ten of which appeared in the *Rheinische Zeitung* and two in Arnold Ruge's *Anekdota.*[39] Rather than describe each article in a narrative sequence—the customary procedure —it seems more profitable to use the entire pool of writing as a source in resynthesizing the principal tenets of Marx's democratic faith. Such a reconstruction may answer the question whether Marx belonged in this period to the liberal or the totalitarian wing of the democratic tradition.[40]

Fully one third of the writing under consideration is devoted to defending freedom of the press. This comes as no surprise if one remembers Marx's thwarted career plans, his continuing needs as an active

38. *Werke,* 27:397.
39. These essays may be found in *Werke,* 1:3–199; EB 1:405–19, 426–30, 434–36.
40. The most extensive narrative accounts are Cornu, *Karl Marx et Friedrich Engels,* 2:1–105; and McLellan, *Marx Before Marxism,* pp. 72–101. Treatments of Marx's views on particular topics during this period may be found for politics in Werner Maihofer, "Recht und Staat im Denken des jungen Marx," in *Karl Marx 1818–1968,* pp. 165–239; for law in Christoph Schefold, *Die Rechtsphilosophie des jungen Marx von 1842* (Munich: Beck, 1970); and for ethics in Eugene Kamenka, *The Ethical Foundations of Marxism* (New York: Praeger, 1962), pp. 17–47.

journalist and editor, and the ever-growing governmental campaign of repression against political and religious dissent. But the emphasis on a free press also reflects deeper concerns which can guide us toward Marx's underlying philosophical conceptions and political values. Early in his reign Frederick William IV issued a royal instruction modifying the censorship law of 1819, supposedly to relax it. Marx's first journalistic venture was a closely reasoned analysis of this instruction, exposing it as a fraud actually more restrictive than the old law itself. With ruthless delight he picked apart the ambiguities contained in limiting adjectives, as for example when the king declared: "Censorship shall not impede any serious and restrained pursuit of truth"; or "Nothing will be tolerated which opposes the Christian religion . . . in a *frivolous* and *hostile* manner."[41] The censor, Marx was quick to point out, is free to decide himself what is serious, restrained, frivolous, or hostile.

The culmination of the instruction, and of Marx's defense of free expression, came with the section on political criticism. "It is an *absolute* requirement," the monarch declared, "that the *tendency* of the criticism of governmental measures be well-intentioned and not spiteful or malevolent."[42] Marx retorted that the old law did not even mention "tendency," did not attempt to judge a writer's intentions. Under the new interpretation, on the contrary:

> The writer is subject to the *most horrible terrorism, to jurisdiction based on suspicion. Tendentious* laws, laws without objective norms, are laws of terrorism, such as those created by Robespierre because of emergencies in the state and by Roman emperors because of the rottenness of the state. Laws that make the *sentiment* of the acting person the main criterion, and not the *act as such,* are nothing but *positive sanctions* of *lawlessness.*

No just law may punish a motive as opposed to an act:

> A law like that is *not a law of the state* for the *citizenry,* but a *law of a party against another party.* The tendentious law cancels the equality of the citizens before the law. . . . It is not a law; it is a *privilege.* . . . In an *ethical state the view of the state is* subordi-

41. As quoted by Marx in "Comments on the Latest Prussian Censorship Instruction" (1843), *Writings,* pp. 70, 75.
42. As quoted by Marx, ibid., p. 79.

nated to its members, even if they *oppose an organ of the state* or the *government*.

Here Marx unambiguously set limits to the power of government in an "ethical state," limits which sanction the right of opposition and recognize "the sacredness and inviolability of subjective conviction."[43]

Marx held that the royal instruction, because it focused on sentiments and intentions, abandoned all objective norms and placed intolerable power in the hands of the censor, whose personal and arbitrary whims would govern all decisions. The censor becomes "prosecutor, lawyer, and judge in one person."

> The essence of censorship is thus based on the haughty conceit of a police state concerning its officials. The public is not given credit for having a sound mind and a good will to do the most simple thing. But even the impossible is to be possible for the officials.

In reality, of course, the officials have their own interests to look after and become merely a self-interested "party against another party" within the body politic. "The *real* cure" for censorship, Marx concluded, "would be the *abolition of censorship*. It is a bad institution, and institutions are more powerful than men."[44]

In other articles Marx developed further thoughts on the subject, and especially on the cure. He reiterated the arbitrariness of all prior censorship: "It can avert no danger greater than itself." Under such censorship, only underground writings are truly free, and "the people became accustomed to regard what is lawless as free, freedom as lawless, and what is lawful as unfree. Thus censorship kills the very spirit of the state."[45] Rather than the censorship law, Marx advocated a *press* law, guaranteeing freedom of expression and presumably making the press answerable only for libel, and then only after publication. Twice he pointed to the United States, where freedom of the press "in its purest and most natural form" enjoyed the protection of such press laws.[46] Unlike the conservative spokesmen whose arguments he was rebutting,

---

43. Ibid., pp. 79–81.
44. Ibid., pp. 91–92.
45. "Die Verhandlungen des 6. rheinischen Landtags . . . Debatten über Pressfreiheit" (1842), *Werke*, 1:60, 64.
46. Ibid., pp. 55–64; specific references to the United States, pp. 58, 63.

Marx saw no danger in diversity of opinion, but regarded it as natural that a politically mature nation would have a press representing the various "doctrines of the people and its parties." "Only where the elements of the popular press," he urged, "maintain their unfettered, independent, and *one-sided* development, and manifest their independence in diverse organs, can a 'good' popular press be formed, i.e. one which unites harmoniously within itself all the *real* elements of the *popular spirit*."[47] Alternatively, he ended another article with the pithy observation: "Without parties there is no development, without division, no progress."[48] Even after becoming a communist, Marx never repudiated these early articles in which he defended freedom of expression with such fervor and wit. Indeed, in 1851, he had them all republished in book form without altering their substance in even the smallest detail.[49]

The issue of a free press pervaded Marx's writings of 1842–1843, not merely because of his practical needs as a journalist and editor, but because of his Young Hegelian view that the press had a central and lofty mission in contemporary society. Journalism was *praxis* for the philosopher, no mere trade or commercial enterprise. The press was to become the prime vehicle of philosophical criticism for measuring actuality against the ideal. It obviously required no censorship, for critical reason is a self-correcting instrument:

> True censorship, founded in the essence of free press itself, is *criticism;* it is a self-generating tribunal. Censorship is criticism as a government monopoly. But criticism loses its rational character when it becomes not open but secret, not theoretical but practical, not above party but itself a party, operating not with the sharp blade of reason but with the dull scissors of arbitrary power.[50]

Thus the sharp blade of critical reason must be wielded openly, independent of any state control, but it must also stand above party and

47. "Das Verbot der 'Leipziger Allgemeinen Zeitung'" (1843), *Werke*, 1:153, 155.

48. "The Leading Article in No. 179 of the *Kölnische Zeitung*" (1842), *Writings*, p. 130.

49. *Gesammelte Aufsätze von Karl Marx* (Cologne, 1851); see Maximilien Rubel, *Bibliographie des oeuvres de Karl Marx* (Paris: Rivière, 1956), pp. 11–12, 91.

50. "Debatten über die Pressfreiheit," *Werke*, 1:55; critique of commercial journalism, ibid., pp. 70–71.

private interests. It must take a position in society between the government and the citizens as an element "which is *political* without being official and bureaucratic, an element which at the same time represents the citizen without being directly involved in private interests."[51] Such a press is "the open eye of the people's intellect, . . . the verbal bond that links the individual to the state and the world, . . . the mirror of the mind in which a people sees itself, and self-examination is the first condition of wisdom."[52]

The "wisdom of the world" for Marx was philosophy, the activity of applying free reason. Philosophical analysis of what exists could produce an understanding of what ought to be. "The critic can . . . develop out of the special forms of existing reality the true reality of that which ought to be, of that which is reality's final aim."[53] Thus human institutions as they ought to be could be discovered by extracting from imperfect existing institutions their inner rational principle, their ideal essence. Marx as a moral philosopher found the "ought" implied within the "is"; he believed the ideal could be derived from the actual, essence from existence. Ethical values for him were not products of speculative fancy or subjective caprice, nor yet of divine commandment or natural law, but were binding logical inferences from the nature of reality itself. Marx never clarified the exact process by which the "ought" could be extracted from the "is," nor did he explain why or how existing reality inherently "aims" to achieve "true reality." Both ideas came from Marx's Hegelian education, which taught that imperfect reality reveals through its own historical development a rational essence, or ideal form, toward which it is supposedly striving.[54]

For Hegel himself the essence or concept of reality became divorced from specifically human concepts and acquired an existence of its own as the Absolute Idea, an impersonal force guiding the development of the universe in a quasi-divine manner. Marx followed the Young Hegelians, especially Feuerbach, in rejecting this aspect of the master's teaching in favor of the view that essences are *human* conceptions, and that historical development is the unfolding of *human* self-conscious-

51. "The Defense of the Moselle Correspondent" (1843), *Writings*, p. 145.
52. "Debatten über die Pressfreiheit," *Werke*, 1:60–61.
53. Letter to Arnold Ruge, September 1843, *Writings*, p. 213 (translation modified—RNH; see original German, *Werke*, 1:345).
54. See *Writings*, pp. 95, 98–100, 122–26; also O'Malley, "Editor's Introduction" to *Critique*, pp. xxi–xxv; Kamenka, *Ethical Foundations*, pp. 32–36 and passim.

ness rather than of some ethereal Absolute Idea.[55] Humanity of course
has its own essence. "Is there no *universal human* nature," Marx asked
rhetorically, "just as there is a universal nature of plants and heavenly
bodies?"[56] What distinguishes man from plants and heavenly bodies is
reason, which enables him to rise above a mere animal existence and
choose his own fate, to be free in the Kantian sense of self-determination
as opposed to external control, autonomy as opposed to heteronomy.
"Freedom is surely the species-essence [*Gattungswesen*] of all thinking
beings," Marx wrote; it is "the natural gift of the universal sunlight of
reason." To achieve and exercise this power of self-determination, to
make real what is potential within him, is the essential destiny of man,
the object of all his striving. "Freedom is so much the essence of man
that even its opponents make it real as they struggle against its realization. . . . No man fights freedom; at most he fights against the freedom
of others."[57] Thus the liberation of man from any form of external control, outside his own will—be it by God, the natural environment, or
other men—was the moral goal of human history in Marx's Young
Hegelian philosophy.

If philosophy as theory revealed the essence and destiny of mankind,
it remained for philosophy as *praxis* to criticize existing human institutions by this standard. "There is no state, no marriage, no friendship
that completely corresponds to its concept," Marx declared, and "world
history decides whether a state is so much at odds with the idea of the
state that it no longer deserves to continue."[58] As a journalist, the philosopher becomes prosecuting attorney in this tribunal of world history.
But he speaks after study, appeals to reason not passion, teaches rather
than dogmatizes, welcomes the test of being doubted, and promises
only the truth. In this period Marx still shared the extraordinary Young
Hegelian faith in the unassisted power of ideas: merely sounding the
Joshuan trumpets of criticism would suffice to shatter the walls of the
status quo. Existing institutions would presumably refashion themselves
of their own accord, once held up to the piercing light of their own
essence. From all this follows the manifest importance for Marx of a
free press, the vehicle of philosophical *praxis,* itself already "one reali-

55. Kamenka, *Ethical Foundations,* pp. 23–25.
56. "Leading Article," *Writings,* p. 118.
57. "Debatten über die Pressfreiheit," *Werke,* 1:54, 47, 51; Kamenka, *Ethical
Foundations,* pp. 26–31.
58. "On a Proposed Divorce Law" (1842), *Writings,* pp. 140–41.

zation of human freedom," and the principal instrument for achieving general emancipation.[59]

Putting his early legal training to good use, Marx singled out jurisprudence as his special province for critical analysis. He cut away at prevailing legal philosophies that opposed his own rationalist doctrine of essences. Thus true laws, laws properly so called, are those that conform to the essence of law and cannot be made by the arbitrary will of an absolute monarch:

> The legislator . . . must consider himself a naturalist. He does not *make* laws; he does not invent them; he only formulates them. He expresses the inner principles of spiritual [*geistigen*] relationships in conscious, positive laws. The legislator would have to be accused of gross arbitrariness if he permitted his whims to replace the nature of things.[60]

If the will of the legislator does not necessarily make a true law, neither does the sanction of custom and tradition. Reflecting the influence of his mentor, Eduard Gans, Marx inveighed against the conservatively minded historical school of law: laws of long standing may only reflect long-standing oppression, "the law of arbitrary power."[61] Most customary laws are really privileges enjoyed by particular groups and hence not true laws at all. To be valid a law must be universal, applying equally to every individual.[62] The only sanction Marx recognized for law was its conformity to reason, which somehow could uncover the inherently necessary "inner principles of spiritual relationships" implicit in "the nature of things."

These relationships, of course, form the fabric of human society, and philosophy is able to "develop the state from reason in human relations." "Philosophy demands that the state be the state of human nature," that is, that society conform to man's essence and serve his essential needs.[63] In this period Marx used the word "state" (*Staat*) to mean the entire body politic, the whole of society politically organized, the

59. "Debatten über die Pressfreiheit," *Werke*, 1:50; *Writings*, pp. 124–25.
60. "Divorce Law," *Writings*, p. 140; cf. *Werke*, 1:112.
61. "The Philosophical Manifesto of the Historical School of Law" (1842), *Writings*, pp. 96–105.
62. "Verhandlungen des 6. rheinischen Landtags . . . Debatten über das Holzdiebstahlsgesetz" (1842), *Werke*, 1:115–16.
63. "Leading Article," *Writings*, pp. 128, 127.

polity, as opposed to the narrower sense of state as just the institutions of government, which Marx called "government" (*Regierung*) and regarded as merely an "organ of the state" (*Staatsorgan*).[64] Reason in human relations argues that men cannot attain their goal of self-determination as isolated individuals, as hermits, but only in concert, by combining their separate talents in organized society. Thus the state is in its essence "a free association of moral human beings . . . aiming at the actualization of freedom."[65]

But moral human beings realize that in society they must limit their own freedom where it infringes on the freedom of others. Only an absolute despot could indulge his every whim, and everyone else would have to be his slave. *Rational* freedom can be achieved in society if each individual acts so that the maxim of his act could be a universal rule, that is, according to Kant's categorical imperative. And indeed, true laws are nothing but such universal Kantian rules; they do not restrict rational freedom, they *establish* it. "Laws are not rules that repress freedom any more than the law of gravity is a rule that represses movement. . . . Laws are rather positive and lucid universal norms in which freedom has attained an impersonal, theoretical existence independent of any arbitrary individual. A statute book is the people's bible of freedom."[66] In this sense, Marx could elaborate his definition of the state, the ideal body politic, as "the great organism in which legal, ethical, and political freedom has to be actualized and in which the individual citizen simply obeys the natural law of his own reason, human reason, in the laws of the state."[67]

With this basis of understanding, Marx criticized those Prussian laws that seemed most at odds with the rational essence of law. It may be argued that his highly philosophical approach served him better for exposing existing abuses than for defining his positive counterproposals, which were sometimes disappointingly vague. And doubtless the impartial voice of reason, when speaking through him, tended to ratify Marx's own prior views: thus customary law was declared an abomination when it legitimated the privileges of hereditary rank, but became the very embodiment of reason when it sanctioned the wood-gathering

64. See n. 43 above (original German, *Werke*, 1:15); cf. *Werke*, 1:158–59; EB 1:419.
65. "Leading Article," *Writings*, p. 118.
66. "Debatten über die Pressfreiheit," *Werke*, 1:58. See Schefold, *Rechtsphilosophie*, pp. 54, 70–71; Kamenka, *Ethical Foundations*, pp. 24, 34.
67. "Leading Article," *Writings*, p. 130.

rights of the poor.[68] All in all, Marx used his journalism to affirm the principles of German and European liberalism in a version now expressly democratic and covertly republican. In the administration of law, for example, he identified himself clearly with the liberal practices he saw established in Britain and France, but only just beginning to emerge in Prussia: the independence of the judiciary from executive power, the right to public trial, the importance of due process and a rational gradation of punishments, and the separation of juridical functions. In Prussian criminal proceedings, he lamented, the "judge, prosecutor, and defense lawyer are *one person*. This contradicts all findings of psychology. But the official is above psychological laws."[69]

Thus rational legal principles might be abused by the government itself, as we also saw where censorship punished intentions rather than acts; they might be abused in another way, however, by private interests within society. In a lengthy article Marx dealt with the Rhenish diet's deliberations on a legislative proposal that would deprive the rural poor of their customary right to gather fallen wood on private estates. The landowning interests represented in the diet wanted to make such wood-gathering a criminal offense and wanted the forest owner to control the setting of compensation and even to receive the fines due the state. Through this utter debasement of legislation, Marx acidly observed, the landowners would make a profit on each transgression! Such a bill, if enacted, would "degrade the state into the instrument of private interest." Many writers have taken this article to mark the inception of Marx's theory of government as an instrument of class domination.[70] But this is a rash inference: Marx was well aware that the diet had no genuine control over legislation, much less over the other prerogatives of the real government—the royal despotism. As we will see shortly, Marx's emerging view of existing governments did not yet contain the notion of class domination.

In dealing with the formulation of law, Marx combined his strict

68. "Holzdiebstahlsgesetz," *Werke*, 1:115-19. Kamenka finds Marx's positive proposals disappointingly vague (*Ethical Foundations*, pp. 33–36).

69. Concerning independence, *Werke*, 1:62; public trial, ibid., 27:399–400; due process, ibid., 1:145; gradation, ibid., p. 114; quotation on separation of functions, "Prussian Censorship Instruction," *Writings*, p. 91.

70. "Holzdiebstahlsgesetz," *Werke*, 1:126. Writers include W. A. Turetski, *Die Entwicklung der Anschauungen von Marx und Engels über den Staat* (Berlin: VEB, 1956), pp. 18–19; Adams, *Marx in His Earlier Writings*, p. 64; but supporting my view see Jakob Barion, *Hegel und die marxistische Staatslehre* (Bonn: Bouvier, 1963), p. 118.

rationalism with an unquestioning belief in popular sovereignty. True law will emerge only when "law is the conscious expression of the will of the people, created with and through it."[71] Implicitly assumed was his faith that the people, given the choice, would will the rational, that is, laws that would not be arbitrary but would express those "inner principles of spiritual relationships" implicit in "the nature of things." The problem which so exercised Rousseau and his totalitarian-democratic disciples concerning possible differences between the "will of all" and the "general will" did not engage Marx's attention; perhaps the Prussian people were as yet so remote from exercising legislative power that the possibility never occurred to him.

There existed, to be sure, the provincial diets representing Prussia's eight provinces, but they had purely advisory powers, could meet only on royal summons, and were still organized in medieval estates (princes, knights, burghers, peasants) in which the large landed interest predominated. The proceedings were not even made public, which prompted Marx to comment in his first *Rheinische Zeitung* article: "To the mystery of government shall there be added a new mystery of representation? . . . A representative who has been withdrawn from the consciousness of his constituents does not represent at all."[72] During 1842, Frederick William IV called upon these provincial diets to elect committees from among their own members to gather in Berlin as the United Committees of Estates, charged with advising the monarch in the levying of new taxes. Marx attacked this sham parliament on several grounds: the principle of aristocratic hereditary right was still mixed with the principle of election; property ownership and church membership were still qualifications; urban communities were grossly underrepresented; but above all representation was still organized by separate estates which conceived their function as defending their own corporate interests against the alien power of the government. In Britain and France, Marx argued (with less than complete accuracy), deputies do not speak for estates but "are elected as representatives of the people." "Because of their peculiar composition, the provincial diets are nothing but a society of special interests which have the privilege of making good their *special requirements* against the state."[73]

71. "Divorce Law," *Writings*, p. 141.
72. "Debatten über die Pressfreiheit," *Werke*, 1:44.
73. "Die Beilage zu Nr. 335 und 336 der Augsburger 'Allgemeinen Zeitung' über die ständischen Ausschüsse in Preussen" (1842), *Werke*, EB 1:416, 419.

Instead of this system, weakly representing special interests before a remote and all-powerful crown, Marx proclaimed it his goal "to transform the mysterious, priestly being of the [Prussian] state into an open, lay being, belonging to all and accessible to all, to transform the state into the flesh and blood of its citizens."[74] As against the representation of landed property and moribund estates, he put forth his own demand

> for a conscious representation of the people's intelligence, which does not advance special requirements against the state, but whose highest requirement is to advance the state as its own deed, as its own state. . . . Representation must not be the representation of anything other than the people itself, must be conceived only as *self-representation*, as an action of the state. . . . Representation must not be viewed as a concession to defenseless weakness, to impotence, but as the self-confident vitality of the highest power. In a true state there is no landed property, no industry, no gross matter which as raw elements could make a bargain with the state; there are only *powers of the spirit* [geistige Mächte]. . . . Not the *unfree thing* but *free man* dominates.

Thus Marx did not oppose representation as such, as some have maintained, but only the representation of property instead of men. Neither did he look forward to a complete homogenization of opinions and interests, but only to the disestablishment of estates whose sole function was to defend their own corporate interests. He suggested the formula: "differences within the unity, but not different unities."[75]

From the passages quoted above it is clear that Marx wanted the popular will to permeate the executive as well as the legislative branch of government. While he could criticize the diets more or less freely, the censorship obliged him to be quite circumspect in the area of royal power. We know that Marx was a principled republican at this time, but open advocacy of a republic was forbidden. He could venture so far as to encourage Hanover liberals to struggle, not merely for a restoration of their revoked Constitution of 1833, but for "a fully new state form corresponding to a deeper, more matured, and freer popular con-

---

74. "Verbot der 'Leipziger Allgemeinen Zeitung,' " ibid., 1:158–59.
75. "Ständischen Ausschüsse in Preussen," ibid., EB 1:419, 410; see also pp. 408, 416, and *Writings*, pp. 213–14. For a contrary view, see Kamenka, *Ethical Foundations*, pp. 37–47.

sciousness."[76] In the case of Prussia, however, he could deal only in metaphors, demanding the transformation of the state into a "lay being" or into "the flesh and blood of its citizens." When accused anyway of trying to undermine the monarchical principle, Marx defended himself before the authorities in February 1843: "The 'Rh. Z.' never expressed a special preference for any *particular state form*. Its concern was with a *moral and rational commonwealth* [Gemeinwesen]; it viewed the demands of such a commonwealth as demands that could and must be realized under *every* state form."[77] Such public equivocation should not obscure the underlying commitment to a republic that Marx expressed privately both before and after the period of his editorship. Thus in May 1843, shortly after the suppression of the *Rheinische Zeitung,* he wrote to Arnold Ruge of their common struggles in a reform movement that had sought to obtain "the results of the French Revolution, thus in the final analysis a republic."[78]

Similarly, Marx could not openly call for a separation of church and state, but he did point out the anomaly of Prussia's situation: "Once a state includes a number of confessions with equal rights, it cannot be a religious state without violating particular confessions." Does not Christianity itself, he asked teasingly, "above all separate church and state?"[79] In the then current dispute between the government and the Catholic archbishop of Cologne concerning mixed marriages, Marx sided with the claims of the state, but he nonetheless opposed the arbitrary and illegal imprisonment of the archbishop; his article on this subject was entirely suppressed by the censor.[80]

Within the executive branch of government the character of the bureaucracy attracted Marx's special attention and would form the key element in his emerging theory of government. Already in his writing on the need for a free press Marx had argued that bureaucrats as cen-

76.   "Die 'liberale Opposition' in Hannover" (1842), *Werke,* EB 1:388.
77.   "Randglossen zu den Anklagen des Ministerialreskripts" (1843), ibid., p. 422.
78.   Letter to Arnold Ruge, May 1843, *Writings,* p. 209. For earlier expression of republicanism, see n. 38 above.
79.   "Leading Article," *Writings,* pp. 126–27.
80.   *Werke,* 27:405–06; Mehring, *Marx,* pp. 40–41; and Cornu, *Karl Marx et Friedrich Engels,* 2:22–23. When his divorce essay was criticized as hostile to Catholicism, Marx replied in a February 1843 editorial note: "This article drew a sharp separation between the realm of the state and that of the church. . . . From that fundamental principle clearly enunciated by the author it follows self-evidently how little he could have intended any sort of calumny against the Catholic church, whose independence rather he demands of the state" (*MEGA* I, 1/2:142).

sors depart from official governmental neutrality and become a party in societal conflict. This basic perception was expanded in his last major article for the *Rheinische Zeitung*, dealing with the distress of the small Moselle winegrowers. Victims of the new competition that had come with the creation of the German Customs Union in 1834, the doomed vintners had appealed to the government for relief. The responsible government agencies had responded sluggishly and inadequately, offering nothing concrete except a temporary tax moratorium. When the unfortunate vintners continued to complain and criticize governmental inaction, the bureaucrats became defensive and repressive. Although Marx had no clear remedy to offer, his sympathies lay entirely with the small vintners of his home district and, within the limits of an increasingly severe censorship, he assailed the bureaucracy.

Even with the best of will, he wrote, the bureaucrat must resent bad conditions in his district and feel that any inquiry constitutes a challenge to his own efficiency and integrity. He will tend to minimize the trouble and place the blame outside his competence on private individuals or on misfortune. His superior will accept his word against that of the distressed persons themselves, and thus is born a "*bureaucratic* reality next to the actual reality." His superior may well have been his predecessor in the same district and also will resent any implication of malfeasance. In this fashion the bureaucracy acquires an interest of its own, separate from and largely hostile to that of the population it administers:

> If the official charges that the private individual is elevating his private interest into the interest of the state, so the private individual may charge that the official debases the interest of the state into his own private interest, an interest from which all others are excluded as laymen, so that even the clearest reality appears illusory to him as against the reality presented in the official reports, . . . so that only the official sphere of activity seems to him to be the "state," against which the world lying beyond that sphere seems the object of the state, in which all community concern and insight are lacking.[81]

As it had in the case of censorship, the bureaucracy here emerged as a self-interested party within society.

81. "Rechtfertigung des Korrespondenten von der Mosel," *Werke*, 1:186, 185 (this portion of the article not translated in *Writings* selection cited in n. 51 above).

Such a conclusion was bound to have corrosive effects on the remnants of Hegelian thinking in Marx's attitude toward government. According to Hegel's view, the institutions of government—and the bureaucracy, par excellence—stood above the passions and selfish interests of civil society, restraining them and uniting their energies on behalf of the entire community. The bureaucracy was supposed to be the "universal class," selflessly and incorruptibly devoted to the whole. It was Marx's central insight of this period, clinched by the final suppression of his own newspaper in March 1843, that governmental institutions, even if not corrupted by private interests, acquire a self-interest of their own in opposition to civil society. From this understanding Marx would begin to draw radical conclusions in the summer of 1843.

Criticism versus Revolution

With the final stifling of the *Rheinische Zeitung* in March 1843, Marx's journalistic career in Germany came to an end. In the same month he wrote to Arnold Ruge of an "impending revolution," the first clear approval of revolution that can be found in his writings.[82] Surely this temporal coincidence can be no accident. Until the suppression Marx had hoped, albeit with increasing pessimism, for the reform of the old order. Although a principled republican in this period, he was not—like Engels and most mid-nineteenth-century republicans—a principled revolutionary as well. One can search his writings in vain to find any force envisaged as the agency of change other than the pure force of ideas, the Joshuan trumpets of criticism.

Marx's entire journalistic activity, it will be remembered, was founded on the idea that *praxis* for the philosopher was criticism, to hold existing institutions up before the piercing light of reason and expose their deficiencies. His evident belief was that criticism would produce self-reform, that the authorities would take this journalistic chastisement to heart and set their own house in order. Significantly, many of Marx's articles addressed themselves to the authorities directly, in the second person, rather than to the public at large. He urged them to understand that "a legal development is not possible without

82. *Writings,* p. 204. In one earlier article Marx did refer to the fate of Charles I in England as a kind of threat, suggesting what could happen if the existing regime failed to reform itself (*Werke,* 1:51). See also Cornu, *Karl Marx et Friedrich Engels,* 2:236; Nicolaievsky and Maenchen-Helfen, *Marx,* p. 52.

a development of the laws."[83] One may see in all this the lingering influence of the Enlightenment, of Marx's father, and especially of the Young Hegelians, expressed in the hope that rational men would naturally prefer a rational order once it had been pointed out to them. Marx's developing perception that the authorities themselves had vested interests to defend—revealed with such crude finality in their suppression of his newspaper—put an end to this hope for self-reform and pushed Marx from the position of reform democrat to that of revolutionary. Only after the weapon of criticism had been gagged did he turn, in his own phrase, to the criticism of weapons.[84]

There are other evidences as well of Marx's essential moderation in this period. Although he collaborated with the socialist Moses Hess in the editorial chores of the *Rheinische Zeitung*, Marx began an article (never published) disavowing the latter's belief that the state itself would one day disappear: "Philosophy must seriously protest when it is confused with imagination."[85] Striking a similar note, Marx did publish in October 1842 an article publicly dissociating his newspaper from communist ideas. Such ideas should be "criticized only after long and deep study," he wrote, precisely because they are impossible of realization and thus constitute a "real *danger*" if they capture the hearts of men. Communist aspirations amount to "a rebellion of man's subjective wishes against his objective *understanding*."[86]

While in Cologne, Marx was constantly bombarded from Berlin with draft articles written by the most extreme Young Hegelians, now calling themselves the *Freien* (Free Ones), who were currently flirting with communist and anarchist ideas and advertising themselves through provocative antics designed to *épater les bourgeois*. Many of these articles fell victim to the censor, Marx wrote to Ruge, but "I permitted myself to dispose of at least as many, because [Eduard] Meyen and his entourage sent us piles of world-overturning scribbling, empty of ideas and written in a slovenly style, the whole tinged with a little atheism and communism (which the gentlemen have never studied)." Marx shrugged off their ensuing protests: "They are quite unable to realize

83. "Anklage des Ministerialreskripts," *Werke*, EB 1:423; second-person usage in, e.g., ibid., 1:112 and *Writings*, pp. 77–78.
84. See Nicolaievsky and Maenchen-Helfen, *Marx*, pp. 52, 61–62; Kamenka, *Ethical Foundations*, pp. 24–25.
85. "The Centralization Question" (1842), *Writings*, p. 108.
86. "Communism and the Augsburg 'Allgemeine Zeitung'" (1842), *Writings*, pp. 134–35.

that, in order to save a political newspaper, we can abandon a few Berlin windbags who in any event think of nothing beyond the concerns of their own clique."[87] Eventually, he broke off all relations with the group, and it was because he believed Engels to be one of their number that Marx snubbed him on the occasion of their first meeting late in 1842. In another letter Marx contrasted the *Freien* unfavorably with the liberal businessmen who provided the main support for the *Rheinische Zeitung;* he characterized the latter as "liberal-minded practical men who have undertaken the troublesome task of struggling for freedom step by step within constitutional restraints."[88] Marx as editor was himself engaged in this same task.

Most writers who see in Marx a totalitarian mentality studiously avoid the period of the *Rheinische Zeitung.*[89] It is not hard to understand why. Marx owed his primary intellectual debts to Feuerbach, Hegel, Fichte, and Kant—to the tradition of classical German humanism. Not a shred of evidence exists to link Marx as yet with Blanqui or Babeuf. The central ideas of totalitarian democracy simply cannot be found in Marx's writings of the *Rheinische Zeitung* period: there is no concept of an organized vanguard party, no call for revolution of any sort, no mention even of the word dictatorship, no invocation of terror in any form, and no expressed desire to silence differing opinions. On the other hand, his devotion to the goal of human freedom, conceived as self-determination, the cardinal importance he attached to freedom of expression, his profound respect for law as a human need, his concern for an appropriate separation of powers even in a democratic state, and his passionate defense of the claims of individuals against those of the government bureaucracy—all these would seem to place Marx safely within the tradition of liberal democracy.

It is doubtless true that Marx believed in an ideal, fixed order of society, rational and harmonious, whose coming he felt to be near, but so did many other nontotalitarian liberals and democrats of his era. One may argue that a Rousseauian concept of the general will underlies his political philosophy of 1842–1843[90] (although Marx did not use

87. Letter of November 30, 1842, *Werke,* 27:411, 413; see Mehring, *Marx,* pp. 44–47, 93; Cornu, *Karl Marx et Friedrich Engels,* 2:85–90.
88. Letter to Dagobert Oppenheim, August 25, 1842, *Werke,* 27:409–10.
89. See J. L. Talmon, *Political Messianism: The Romantic Phase* (New York: Praeger, 1960), p. 205; Robert C. Tucker, *Philosophy and Myth in Karl Marx* (Cambridge: Cambridge, 1961), p. 102; and Künzli, *Psychographie,* pp. 173–75.
90. See Kamenka, *Ethical Foundations,* pp. 24, 34, 37–47.

the term and mentions Rousseau himself only three times), but his version of the general will was not incipiently totalitarian. Although Marx opposed representation by estate, he did not share Rousseau's aversion to representation as such. And although he inveighed against the pursuit of selfish interest at the expense of the community, he exhibited none of Rousseau's hostility toward parties as such. (Indeed, his maxim, "Without parties there is no development, without division, no progress," ought to be a continuing embarrassment to present-day Communist regimes.) Thus, Marx's concept of harmony in a rational society was not so rigid as to exclude all possibility of division or dissent and, whatever his belief in the imminence of its arrival, he did not draw totalitarian conclusions regarding permissible means.

Marx's letter to Ruge of May 1843 is probably his last precommunist writing and deserves extensive quotation as a fitting conclusion to this chapter. Ruge had reacted to Marx's March prophecy of "impending revolution" with a profoundly depressed lamentation concerning the "eternal submissiveness" of the German people; he played with the idea that "man is not born to be free." Marx, now unemployed and facing the prospect of exile, had every reason to share Ruge's pessimism, but nonetheless found some ground for hope:

> Freedom, the feeling of man's dignity, will have to be awakened again in these men. Only this freedom, which disappeared from the world with the Greeks and with Christianity vanished into the blue mist of heaven, can again transform society into a community of men to achieve their highest purpose, a democratic state.
>
> The people, though, who do not feel themselves to be men, grow attached to their masters, like a herd of slaves or horses. The hereditary masters are the purpose of this whole society. . . . They stand where their feet have grown, on the necks of these political animals that know of no other destination than to be attached to the masters and subject to them, to be at their disposal.
>
> The world of the Philistine is the *political animal kingdom,* and if we have to recognize its existence, we simply must acknowledge the status quo. Centuries of barbarism created and formed it, and now it exists as a consistent system, whose principle is a *world dehumanized.* . . .
>
> Despotism's only idea is contempt for man, dehumanized man, and this idea further has the advantage over many others of being

fact. A despot always sees men as degraded. He sees them drown for him in the mud of common life from which they again and again emerge like toads. . . .

Once one has reached the threshold of the political animal kingdom, no further movement and no other withdrawal are possible than to leave its basis and enter the human world of democracy. . . .

And if I do not despair, it is only the desperate situation of the present that fills me with hope. . . . I have only to call your attention to the fact that the enemies of Philistinism, in other words all thinking and all suffering men, have arrived at an understanding for which formerly they lacked the means. . . . The existence of a suffering mankind that thinks and of a thinking mankind that is suppressed must necessarily become unpalatable and indigestible for the passive animal kingdom of Philistinism.[91]

Thus Marx acknowledged the immaturity of the masses that so discouraged Ruge (and that earlier had led Babeuf to totalitarian conclusions), but he was now beginning to glimpse a remedy built into the developing situation itself. That remedy must occupy our attention in the next chapter.

91. *Writings*, pp. 206–11; Ruge's comments quoted by the editors, p. 204.

⟨[3]⟩

Marx's Conversion to Communism

THE PERIOD IMMEDIATELY FOLLOWING the suppression of the *Rheinische Zeitung* was extraordinarily eventful for Marx: in personal life it included a new career decision, marriage, and emigration from his native land; in intellectual development it saw his endorsement of revolution as a means, a major reckoning with Hegel, and—most significantly—conversion to communism.

With the demise of his newspaper early in 1843, Marx decided immediately to leave Germany. "It is unpleasant," he wrote Ruge, "to perform menial service even in the cause of freedom, and to fight with needles instead of clubs. I have grown weary of the hypocrisy, the stupidity, the brutality of the authorities, and of our own bowing, cringing, backbending, and verbal hairsplitting. Well, the government has released me. . . . In Germany there is nothing more I can do. Here one can only be false to oneself."[1] After considering various alternatives, he began arrangements with Ruge for the publication the following year of a new periodical which they would edit jointly in Paris. In the meantime, Marx finally married his childhood sweetheart, Jenny von Westphalen, in June 1843 and spent five months with her (June through October) at her family's summer home in Bad Kreuznach, located on a small tributary of the Rhine not far from Mainz. In this idyllic setting, and freed from his editorial chores, Marx undertook to reexamine his major political and philosophical assumptions.

Marxist convention has long held that the master became a communist only in Paris and announced his conversion when he first called upon the proletariat to undertake "the emancipation of mankind" in his article, "Toward the Critique of Hegel's Philosophy of Law: Introduction,"

---

1. Letter of January 25, 1843, *Werke*, 27:415.

[49]

printed in the inaugural issue of Marx and Ruge's *Deutsch-Französische Jahrbücher* in February 1844.[2] This convention rests upon a myth, partly suggested by Marx and Engels themselves, which confuses scientific discovery and moral commitment.[3] The Paris "Critique" did indeed first disclose the "scientific" law that assigned the proletariat its historic role in the realization of communism, but it is now clear that Marx's moral commitment to communism as an ideal antedated his emigration and was in fact the net result of his Kreuznach ruminations. There in the summer of 1843, Marx reached the conclusion that the ultimate emancipation of mankind could be achieved only in a society organized without a state, social classes, or private property.

The redating of Marx's conversion is principally the work of Shlomo Avineri, who has made his case in a brilliant analysis of Marx's hitherto obscure Kreuznach manuscript on Hegel.[4] This manuscript has been recently published for the first time in English translation under the title *Critique of Hegel's 'Philosophy of Right,'*[5] and will hereafter be called the Kreuznach *Critique* to distinguish it from the Paris "Critique" bearing an almost identical title. The Kreuznach document constitutes a close paragraph-by-paragraph assessment of Hegel's major work in political philosophy, set down by Marx in critical notes. It may be the first draft of a book—never to be finished—of which the Paris "Critique" was intended to form the introduction. First rediscovered and published in 1927, the Kreuznach manuscript is written in the murkiest Hegelian jargon and has only recently received the scholarly attention it deserves. Whatever its fearsome inscrutability, it represents, as Avineri says, "the most systematic of his writings on political theory," as well

2. Paris "Critique" appears in *Writings*, pp. 249–64. Marxist convention perpetuated in, e.g., Franz Mehring, *Karl Marx: The Story of his Life*, trans. Edward Fitzgerald (1935; reprint ed., Ann Arbor: Michigan, 1962), p. 75; Auguste Cornu, *Karl Marx et Friedrich Engels: Leur vie et leur oeuvre*, 3 vols. (Paris: Presses Universitaires, 1955–62), 2:222–28, 251; and Isaiah Berlin, *Karl Marx: His Life and Environment*, 3rd ed. (New York: Oxford, 1963), p. 81.

3. See *Selected Works*, 1:328; 2:311–12.

4. *The Social and Political Thought of Karl Marx* (Cambridge: Cambridge, 1968), see especially pp. 31–40. Unfortunately, however, Avineri ignores the *Rheinische Zeitung* period and, by stressing that Marx was a communist at Kreuznach rather than a "bourgeois democrat," he leaves the misimpression that Marx was *never* a noncommunist democrat.

5. Translated and edited with a splendid introductory essay by Joseph O'Malley (Cambridge: Cambridge, 1970).

as Marx's personal settlement with his Hegelian education, an attempt through Hegel to evaluate existing political institutions, and Marx's first attempt to clarify the relationship between the political and economic facets of society.[6] Many of the ideas expressed in the *Critique* are elaborated—and sometimes stated more clearly—in essays Marx wrote for publication contemporaneously or during the following months: "On the Jewish Question" (written at Kreuznach), the aforementioned Paris "Critique" (begun at Kreuznach and finished in Paris in January 1844), and "Critical Notes on 'The King of Prussia and Social Reform'" (July 1844).[7] These sources will be used together with a handful of surviving private letters to document Marx's emerging communist political philosophy. Of prime importance will be the question whether conversion involved the acceptance of totalitarian ideas.

The Intellectual Setting

Before proceeding, it seems wise to take some account of the intellectual setting and influences that helped to shape Marx's thinking during the Kreuznach metamorphosis. All of his biographers have given prominence to Marx's increasing exposure, while editor of the *Rheinische Zeitung*, to real socioeconomic problems and to proposed socialist remedies. Editorially he had taken up the cause of the victimized Rhenish wood gatherers and the Moselle vintners, expressing an instinctive sympathy for "the poor, politically and socially propertyless masses."[8] But he had offered no clear solutions, especially in the latter case, and later confessed "embarrassment" at having had to discuss "material interests" for which his Hegelian education had not prepared him.[9] Doubtless this embarrassment impelled him toward socioeconomic studies and more serious consideration of the socialist ideas then crossing his path. Although Marx dismissed as amateurish the pink-tinged writings of the *Freien* in Berlin, closer to home he was being exposed daily to the ideas of Moses Hess, who shared the editorial duties of the newspaper, and with whom Marx mooted social issues in weekly gatherings of an in-

6. Avineri, *Social and Political Thought*, p. 41; O'Malley, "Editor's Introduction" to *Critique*, pp. xii–xiii.
7. These essays all included in *Writings*, pp. 216–48, 249–64, 338–58.
8. "Verhandlungen des 6. rheinischen Landtags . . . Debatten über das Holzdiebstahlsgesetz" (1842), *Werke*, 1:115.
9. *Selected Works*, 1:327–28.

formal Cologne discussion group. Hess was more impressed with Marx than vice versa, but the former's sincere socialist idealism must have made some impression on the younger man.[10] When Marx publicly dissociated the *Rheinische Zeitung* from communism, he nonetheless urged in the same article that the new doctrines merited "long and deep study," mentioning specifically the writings of Fourier, Enfantin, Leroux, Considérant, "and above all Proudhon's penetrating work."[11] It is not clear whether he was already digesting this socialist literature himself or knew of it secondhand from Hess and from reading Lorenz von Stein's just published *Der Sozialismus und Communismus des heutigen Frankreichs*.[12]

In any event Marx was not won to communism by the personal influence of Moses Hess (as was Engels) but came to it through solitary reflection. And his reading at Kreuznach did not consist of socialist classics but political theory and history. Marx's biographers have generally failed to appreciate the surprising extent to which the young rebel embraced communism as a means of resolving the *political*—as opposed to socioeconomic—dilemmas of modern society. During his five-month seclusion, Marx read some two dozen volumes and filled 250 pages of his notebooks with excerpts.[13] A few of these works were classics of political philosophy, such as Machiavelli's *Discourses*, Montesquieu's *Spirit of the Laws*, and Rousseau's *Social Contract*, but most of them concerned modern European history, especially the history of the French Revolution. Marx was particularly interested in the republic as a form of government and included a volume on the Republic of Venice, another on the so-called Republic of Poland, and three on the American republic (Tocqueville, Beaumont, Thomas Hamilton). Evidently he was reopening in his mind the question whether, as he had hitherto believed, the republic per se was destined to be the ultimate form of societal organization. For two of his notebooks, Marx prepared

10. Edmund Silberner, *Moses Hess: Geschichte seines Lebens* (Leiden: Brill, 1966), pp. 121–22.
11. "Communism and the Augsburg 'Allgemeine Zeitung'" (1842), *Writings*, pp. 134–35.
12. (Leipzig, 1842); see debate between Avineri, *Social and Political Thought*, pp. 53–54; and Robert C. Tucker, *Philosophy and Myth in Karl Marx* (Cambridge: Cambridge, 1961), pp. 114–16.
13. Unpublished *Exzerpthefte*, Marx-Engels Nachlass, Internationaal Instituut voor Sociale Geschiedenis, Amsterdam; contents summarized in *MEGA* I, 1/2:118–36.

topical indexes of the material excerpted, and his choice of topic categories and the number of entries under each heading reveal a good deal
about his intellectual concerns. Of twenty-six topic headings, those with
the most entries, in rank order, were: "inner sovereignty," "governmental
power," "constitution and administration," "estates general," "constitutional monarchy," "aristocracy," "equalization [of political rights],"
"property and its consequences."[14] Property ranked only eighth, behind a whole series of directly political topics. There was nothing on
capitalism or political economy at all. If Marx's immediate project at
Kreuznach was a reckoning with Hegel's *Philosophy of Right,* he very
understandably armed himself with reading in political philosophy and
history.

Hegel's influential 1821 treatise had attempted to resolve a central
problem in modern political philosophy, a problem posed first and most
sharply by Jean-Jacques Rousseau. The economic institutions of modern society, Rousseau perceived, increasingly sanction for private man
the unrestrained pursuit of his selfish interest without regard for any
larger community. Yet the doctrine of popular sovereignty calls upon
that same man, acting politically as a citizen, to set aside his private interests and concern himself only with the common weal. Can a man
divide himself so neatly into *homme* and *citoyen,* his egoistic private
self and his altruistic public self? This modern dilemma did not exist
in Rousseau's image of the classical polis, the city-state of Greek and
Roman antiquity. There, no separate compartments were recognized
for private and public life: each citizen was entitled and expected to
participate fully in the political life of the community as well as to
identify his private welfare with the welfare of the polis. Captivated by
this image of classical antiquity, Rousseau set about in his *Social Contract* to prescribe the conditions in which modern-day men might once
again spontaneously identify their private interests (*volonté de tous*)
with the general welfare (*volonté générale*). Yet the pessimistic strain
in Rousseau's thought, perhaps the deep fissures within his own person-
ality, led him often to despair whether such a reconciliation could really
be accomplished, and his *Emile* concluded with the unanswered question: How can something right and whole be made of the modern bourgeois?[15]

14. Calculated from *MEGA* I, 1/2:122–23.
15. This way of looking at Rousseau's thought stressed in Karl Löwith, *From*

This unanswered query was taken up by Hegel, who in his youth had absorbed much of Rousseau's admiration for the classical polis. As Hegel perceived it, the modern degeneration from that ideal communal life had begun during the Roman Empire when most men gradually withdrew from active public life to the private concerns of family and work, leaving public affairs to others and thus allowing the state ultimately to become an external and alien force rather than an expression of their own collective will. Following the disappointment of his hope that the French Revolution might somehow restore the classical unity of civil and political life, Hegel developed the essentially conservative view set down in the *Philosophy of Right*.[16] Here egoism is recognized as the necessary and in many respects beneficial foundation of civil society, even though it produces "a battlefield where everyone's individual private interest meets everyone else's." Modern man can tolerate this apparent *bellum omnium contra omnes* because it is tempered by the modern state, exemplified for Hegel then by the Prussian monarchy:

> The principle of modern states has prodigious strength and depth because it allows the principle of subjectivity to progress to its culmination in the extreme of self-subsistent personal particularity, and yet at the same time brings it back to the substantive unity and so maintains this unity in the principle of subjectivity itself.[17]

Thus the task of guarding the public interest, of restraining, reconciling, and elevating all the diverse private wills, of bringing them "back" to substantive unity—this task falls upon the modern state, com-

---

Hegel to Nietzsche: The Revolution in Nineteenth-Century Thought, trans. David E. Green (New York: Holt, 1967), pp. 235–38. Recent scholarship on Rousseau includes: William H. Blanchard, *Rousseau and the Spirit of Revolt* (Ann Arbor: Michigan, 1967); Roger D. Masters, *The Political Philosophy of Rousseau* (Princeton: Princeton, 1968); and Lester G. Crocker, *Jean-Jacques Rousseau*, 2 vols. (New York: Macmillan, 1968).

16.   Jean Hyppolite, "Marx's Critique of the Hegelian Concept of the State," in his *Studies on Marx and Hegel*, trans. John O'Neill (New York: Basic Books, 1969), pp. 108–10. Other authorities on Hegel include Walter H. Kaufmann, *Hegel* (Garden City: Doubleday, 1965); J. N. Findlay, *Hegel: A Re-examination* (New York: Macmillan, 1958); and Z. A. Pelczynski, "An Introductory Essay," in *Hegel's Political Writings*, trans. T. M. Knox (Oxford: Clarendon, 1964), pp. 5–137.

17.   *Hegel's Philosophy of Right*, trans. and ed. T. M. Knox (Oxford: Clarendon, 1962), §§260, 289.

posed (for Hegel) firstly of a monarch whose hereditary position raises him above private and party interests, and secondly of a professional bureaucracy whose exclusive assigned mission is to look after the "universal interests of the community," hence a "universal class." Hegel was much impressed with the achievements of the Stein-Hardenberg civil service and regarded these highly educated and dedicated men as fitting guardians of the common weal. They had renounced the egoism of civil society to devote themselves unselfishly to the service of the whole.[18]

Hegel's state required yet a third institution to mediate between the universal and the particular—the diets or *Stände*, in which representatives of the crown, the bureaucracy, and the estates of the realm met together to harmonize their differences. The third estate still spoke through the old medieval corporations (guilds, professions, municipalities, etc.), which in Hegel's view served usefully to lift the vision of ordinary burghers above their individual needs to the larger concerns of their group. In a parallel process, their representatives in the diets, as they communicated the needs of the burgher estate to the crown, also absorbed the universalism of the latter. Hegel believed that the practice of primogeniture served the aristocratic estate in a similar way: by providing an unassailable economic base to the eldest sons, it allowed them to rise above the egoism of civil society and develop a disinterested concern for the larger interests of their estate and for the universal interest of the community as a whole.[19] Thus did the modern state, in its various manifestations, overcome Rousseau's dilemma, by mediating and transforming the selfishness of individuals into concern for the common weal.

We have already witnessed from a different perspective how Marx became disillusioned, in the real world, with each of Hegel's harmonizing agencies. The august crown, symbol of the state's universalism, was worn in Marx's day by the obscurantist and repressive Frederick William IV. The high-minded Stein-Hardenberg civil servants were transformed into the haughtily indifferent Moselle bureaucrats or into the capricious censors who shut down the *Rheinische Zeitung*. And the mediating diets seemed to him nothing but lobbies for landowning interests which in the Rhenish case even sought to deprive the poor of their piti-

18. Ibid., §§275–86, 291–96; quotation, §205; see also Hyppolite, "Marx's Critique," p. 118.
19. *Philosophy of Right*, §§305–07.

ful wood-gathering rights. Far from transforming and elevating private interests, these institutions for Marx were hopelessly mired in the egoism of civil society, a faithful reflection of that "battlefield" of each against all. Not content merely with a mediation of opposites, a papering over of Rousseau's conflict between *homme* and *citoyen*, Marx struggled to create in his imagination a polity in which state and civil society would be merged in a higher synthesis, in which no distinction would be drawn between private and public interests because they would be identical. Like Rousseau and the younger Hegel, Marx hoped to recapture in modern dress that fundamental unity all three had perceived and admired in the classical polis of antiquity.[20]

As he squared off for the encounter with Hegel, Marx found a powerful ally in Ludwig Feuerbach, whose writings were just then having a major impact on the Kreuznach recluse. In his *Essence of Christianity* (1841) and subsequent essays, Feuerbach had given a Young Hegelian *coup de grâce* to traditional religion, had offered an alternative humanism based on the concept of *Gattungswesen*, and had provided a philosophical tool—the transformative method—for dealing with the old master, Hegel.

Feuerbach explained Christianity, and traditional religion generally, as a projection of human perfections upon an imagined deity. Specifically, men attribute to God the qualities they perceive to be lacking in themselves as isolated individuals: "God is perfect, man imperfect; God eternal, man temporal; God almighty, man weak; God holy, man sinful," etc. What men do not realize, according to Feuerbach, is that the attributes ascribed to the Deity are simply the ultimate capabilities of mankind, when all the diverse talents and qualities of individuals will be blended harmoniously together. If individuals are mortal, the species is immortal; if individuals are weak, the united community of man could have power beyond belief; and so on. "God as the epitome of all realities or perfections is nothing other than a compendious summary devised for the benefit of the limited individual, an epitome of the generic human qualities distributed among men, in the self-realization of the species in the course of world history." When that world-historical process of self-realization is complete, mankind will itself possess all the attributes imputed to God: "As God is, so man *should* be and *desires* to

20.   Hyppolite, "Marx's Critique," pp. 108–10; O'Malley, "Editor's Introduction" to *Critique,* pp. li–lxii.

be."[21] To describe this collective potential of mankind, Feuerbach used the term *Gattungswesen*, translatable in this sense as "species-essence," or "essence of the species," a kind of blueprint of what the human species can become, ought to become, is destined to become.

To worship God amounts to fetishism, for it is to worship the species-essence of mankind. Still worse, the more perfections men project upon the Deity, the more abased they feel themselves. "To enrich God, man must become poor; that God may be all, man must become nothing."[22] In this way, when men created God, they effected an actual schism within themselves, estranging their limited and imperfect selves from their generic self, their species-essence. Instead of realizing the potential of that generic self in their actual lives, they have realized it in fantasy as God and worship it as an alien power over them. To overcome this self-alienation and unite individual men with mankind, Feuerbach believed it necessary first to renounce the God illusion. It is to the study of man himself, the source of that illusion, that men must turn to discover their own proper values, norms, and destiny. Theology must become anthropology. But further, men must abandon their self-centered isolation and enter a community of love with their fellow men, allowing their diverse qualities and talents to mingle together fruitfully in the realization of their joint destiny. "The essence of man is only to be found in community, in the unity of man with man—a unity which nevertheless rests on the reality of the distinction between I and thou."[23] Mankind's destiny is to become an actual *Gattungswesen*, now translatable as "species-*being*," an organic community whose potential has been fulfilled through the loving collaboration of its individual members. And each member may also be called a species-being in that he acts in full consciousness of his species ties, no longer as an isolated, self-centered monad but pooling his unique talents in the group.

21.   *The Essence of Christianity*, trans. George Eliot (New York: Harper, 1957), pp. 33, xvi, 33. Recent studies of Feuerbach and his influence on Marx include: Eugene Kamenka, *The Philosophy of Ludwig Feuerbach* (New York: Praeger, 1970); Klaus Erich Bockmuhl, *Leiblichkeit und Gesellschaft: Studien zur Religionskritik und Anthropologie im Frühwerk von Ludwig Feuerbach und Karl Marx* (Göttingen: Vanderhoeck und Ruprecht, 1961); and Werner Schuffenhauer, *Feuerbach und der junge Marx* (Berlin: Wissenschaften, 1965).

22.   *Essence of Christianity*, p. 26.

23.   *Sämtliche Werke*, 2nd ed. (Stuttgart, 1959), 2:318, as quoted in David McLellan, *The Young Hegelians and Karl Marx* (New York: Praeger, 1969), pp. 109–10.

Feuerbach's atheist humanism, in its Hegelian conceptual framework, had a very substantial influence on the young Marx, clearly visible in the Kreuznach writings and culminating in the now famous Paris manuscripts of 1844. Marx himself poignantly acknowledged this debt in an August 1844 letter to Feuerbach, recently discovered, expressing the

> great admiration and—if you allow me the word—love I bear toward you. . . . You have in these writings—whether intentionally or not I do not know—given a philosophical foundation to socialism. . . . The unity of men with men, which is founded on the real differences among men, the concept of the human species [*Menschengattung*] brought back from the heaven of abstraction to the real world, what is this but the concept of *society!*[24]

Feuerbach not only clarified and reinforced Marx's humanist values but also gave him a philosophical tool for dealing with their common mentor, Hegel. In his "Provisional Theses for the Reform of Philosophy" (1843), Feuerbach applied his critique of religion to Hegel himself, seeing in Hegel's Absolute a substitute God, "man's essence outside man, the essence of thinking outside the act of thinking."[25] The manifestations Hegel attributed to the Absolute are really the deeds of man; Hegel got his subjects and predicates mixed up, and to demystify his philosophy, one must set them right again. "It suffices to put the predicate in place of the subject everywhere, i.e. *to turn speculative philosophy upside down*, and we arrive at the truth in its unconcealed, pure, manifest form."[26] Marx was immediately impressed with the possibilities of this "transformative method," complaining only that Feuerbach "refers too much to nature and not enough to politics."[27] To analyze Hegel's political philosophy with the transformative method was precisely the task Marx now envisaged for himself.

Thus in his Kreuznach retreat, his attention recently drawn to socioeconomic problems, fortified by extensive historical and philosophical reading, and freshly infused with Feuerbach's radiant humanism, the

24.   Letter of August 11, 1844, *Werke,* 27:425; cf. ibid., p. 401; *Writings,* pp. 285, 315–17.
25.   As quoted in Avineri, *Social and Political Thought,* p. 11.
26.   *Kleine Philosophische Schriften* (Leipzig: Meiner, 1950), p. 56, as quoted in Tucker, *Philosophy and Myth,* p. 86.
27.   Letter to Arnold Ruge, March 13, 1843, *Werke,* 27:417.

young Marx set about to grapple with Hegel's *Philosophy of Right*, thereby addressing Rousseau's dilemma concerning the conflict between *homme* and *citoyen* and coming to grips with the real-world dichotomy between the modern state and civil society. As Marx himself expressed it: "The criticism of the German philosophy of right and of the state, which was given its most logical, profound and complete expression by Hegel, is at once the critical analysis of the modern state and of the reality connected with it."[28] In this impressive intellectual enterprise, Marx would ultimately find himself drawing communist conclusions.

The Critique of Hegel and the Modern State

We have already reviewed those elements of Hegel's political philosophy with which Marx would concern himself. Hegel began with his own version of the conventional distinction between the state and civil society. He presented the state as an emanation of the Absolute, as the "actuality of the ethical Idea." And as "actual Idea" the state then "enters upon its finite phase" by "sundering itself into the two ideal spheres of its concept, family and civil society."[29] Here Marx entered the fray equipped with Feuerbach's transformative method: in Hegel's lines he perceived that reversal of subject and predicate that would in time provide the major foundation for his own theory of history and of the state. "The political state cannot exist," he rejoined, "without the natural basis of the family and the artificial basis of civil society; they are its *conditio sine qua non;* but the conditions are established [by Hegel] as the conditioned, the determining as the determined, the producing as the product of its product." On the contrary, the state must be regarded as an emanation of civil society, conditioned by the changing character of that society.[30]

Further, Marx argued, the distinction between state and civil society itself is not a logical necessity inherent in the timeless nature of things;

28. *Critique,* p. 136.
29. *Philosophy of Right,* §§257, 262.
30. *Critique,* p. 9. See also Marx's 1859 recollection that his Kreuznach review of Hegel had convinced him that "legal relations as well as forms of state are to be grasped neither from themselves nor from the so-called general development of the human spirit, but rather have their roots in the material conditions of life, the sum total of which Hegel . . . combines under the name of 'civil society'" (*Selected Works,* 1:328).

rather it reflects a real-world dichotomy which has emerged in modern times. Hegel's ideas are drawn empirically from that modern reality and describe it more or less accurately. But they are drawn unconsciously: Hegel imagines he is working out the logical determinations of the Absolute. "He has presupposed the separation of civil society and the political state (which is a modern situation), and developed it as a necessary moment of the Idea, as an absolute truth of Reason." Hegel is then delighted to "discover" that the real institutions around him are fitting manifestations of the Absolute. "Hegel makes all the attributes of the contemporary European constitutional monarch into absolute self-determinations of the will." Thus "the fact, which is the starting point, is not conceived to be such but rather to be the mystical result," all of which cloaks his "findings" in an aura of profound mystery. Hegel's entire philosophy of right amounts to an elaborate effort—whether conscious or not—to legitimate the existing political order by passing it off as an emanation of the quasi-divine Absolute. Marx was nonetheless willing to undertake the thankless task of demystifying the master's formulations, paragraph by paragraph, because through Hegel he could criticize the modern state itself.[31]

If Hegel was concerned to reconcile the selfish interests of civil society with the universal mission of the state, Marx wanted to assert that no such dichotomy was necessary. A historical argument was in order and, from his current readings as well as from Hegel's own historical conceptions, especially of antiquity, Marx advanced the rudiments of a historical schema that would explain the dichotomy as a passing phenomenon. The schema deserves scrutiny in part because it differs so pointedly from the one he would later work out in collaboration with Engels: the ancient, medieval, and modern periods are differentiated by Marx not according to which social class dominated, but according to the changing relationship between public and private concerns, between political and socioeconomic life.

"The abstraction of the state as such belongs only to modern times,"

---

31. *Critique*, pp. 73, 25, 9; cf. pp. 39–40. Marx's method is well explained for English readers in O'Malley's "Editor's Introduction." Also see Louis K. Dupré, *The Philosophical Foundations of Marxism* (New York: Harcourt, Brace, 1966), pp. 87–97. For more extended treatments of Marx's relation to his mentor, see George Lichtheim, *From Marx to Hegel* (New York: Herder and Herder, 1971); Günther Hillmann, *Marx und Hegel: Von der Spekulation zur Dialektik* (Frankfurt a/M: Europäische Verlagsanstalt, 1966); and Jakob Barion, *Hegel und die marxistische Staatslehre* (Bonn: Bouvier, 1963).

Marx declared, "because the abstraction of private life belongs only to modern times." A purely private life of egoistic indifference to the community would have been inconceivable in the classical Greek polis, except perhaps in a slave. "In Greece, the *res publica* was the real private concern, the real content of the citizen, and the private man was slave, that is, the political state as political was the true and sole content of the citizen's life and will."[32] Apparently this was true (Marx only hints at an explanation) because of the strong tradition of community property shared by the states of antiquity: all landed property was in the last analysis "asserted to be public property." Individual possession could not be separated from the obligations of citizenship, which were the "social nerves of private ownership," its "social and ethical chains."[33] Private needs led necessarily to collaboration in the *res publica* and were inextricably merged with the public interest. Universal participation, in turn, made it possible to conduct public business without a horde of permanent or hereditary officials. "The political state does not yet appear as the form of the material state."[34] The state was simply the citizenry itself in the activity of self-government, and not some alien force standing over civil society.

In the Middle Ages, by contrast, political functions were absorbed into private associations and exercised by estates, guilds, and other corporations, but there was still no separation between public and private life. "Every private sphere had a political character," each corporation, each estate, formed part of the political organism. "The classes of civil society and the political classes were identical because civil society was political society, because the organic principle of civil society was the principle of the state." Universal participation insured that "man was the actual principle of the state, but he was unfree man. It was

32.   *Critique*, p. 32. Marx's use of the word "slave" here is ambiguous: the interpretation given above is fortified by a later passage asserting that in antiquity, "slavery finds its explanation in the rights of war, the rights of occupation: men are slaves precisely because their political existence is destroyed" (p. 111). But almost equally plausible is a figurative interpretation that within each citizen private man was "slave" to public man, as in another later assertion: "With the Greeks, civil society was a slave to political society" (p. 73).

33.   Ibid., pp. 110, 100–01; cf. *The German Ideology* (Moscow: Progress, 1964), p. 33.

34.   *Critique*, p. 32; cf. Hegel's description of the polis in *Hegels theologische Jugendschriften*, ed. Herman Nohl (1907; reprint ed., Frankfurt a/M: Minerva, 1966), pp. 219–29.

therefore the democracy of unfreedom." The medieval caste system confined men to the estate of their birth and resulted in a hierarchy of unblendable groupings, much like the species of the animal world. Such a system denies man's ability to change himself. "It separates man from his universal nature; it makes him an animal whose being coincides immediately with its determinate character. The Middle Ages constitutes the animal history of mankind, its zoology."[35]

Developing his historical schema in his contemporaneous essay, "On the Jewish Question," Marx explained how the seeds of the modern dichotomy between the state and civil society sprouted within medieval society:

The feudal organization of national life did not elevate property or labor to the level of social elements but rather completed their *separation* from the state as a whole and established them as *separate* societies within society. Thus the vital functions and conditions of civil society always remained political, but political in the feudal sense. That is, they excluded the individual from the state as a whole and transformed the *special* relation between his corporation and the state into his own general relation to national life. . . . As a consequence of this organization, the unity of the state . . . likewise necessarily appears as the *special* business of the ruler and his servants, separated from the people.[36]

So began the process in which property and labor were separated from the task of minding the general community business, while, conversely, this task became more and more the special business of the ruler and his servants, that is, the bureaucracy.

Marx saw the process culminating in the civil society produced by the socioeconomic reforms of the French Revolution, which "destroyed all estates, corporations, guilds, and privileges" and thereby *"abolished the political character of civil society.* It shattered civil society into its constituent elements." It brought "the fulfillment of the materialism of civil society . . . the throwing off of the bond that had fettered the egoistic spirit of civil society," and the severing of "the social nerves of private property."[37] Hegel was quite correct to define this trans-

35. *Critique*, pp. 32, 72, 82; see also pp. 106, 109.
36. *Writings*, pp. 238–39 (translation of last sentence modified—RNH; see original German, *Werke*, 1:368).
37. "Jewish Question," *Writings*, p. 239; *Critique*, p. 101; cf. pp. 80–82.

formation with a paraphrase of Hobbes' *bellum omnium contra omnes.*
Its social effect was to "sever all man's species-ties, substitute egoism
and selfish need for those ties, and dissolve the human world into a
world of atomistic, mutually hostile individuals." Thus is man now
"corrupted by the entire organization of our society, lost and alienated
from himself, oppressed by inhuman relations and elements—in a word,
man . . . is not yet an *actual* species-being [*Gattungswesen*]."[38] To these
Feuerbachian allusions we will return presently.

In dialectical relation to the emergence of civil society, the modern
state—"the *special* business of the ruler and his servants"—has evolved
as an institution alienated from the people and standing over it as a
hostile force. Where the "burgher" (egoistic man) is considered to be
a fixed individual without universal concerns, there "the state likewise
in fixed individuals opposes the 'burghers.'" Such a state no longer
speaks for the ideal unity of the people, despite Hegel's illusions, but
becomes a self-interested party. Faithfully reflecting the egoism of
civil society, the ruler and his bureaucrats regard the state as their private property. Thus is completed the dichotomy between civil society
and state which Hegel tries so pathetically to paper over with his elaborate mediations. "Hegel's keenest insight lies in his sensing the separation of civil and political society to be a contradiction. But his error is
that he contents himself with the appearance of its dissolution, and
passes it off as the real thing."[39] Marx now turned his critical blade on
the three specific elements in Hegel's ideal constitution—crown, executive (bureaucracy), legislature (diets)—to expose the pious fraud. Only
the bureaucracy need occupy us in detail, because of its relevance to
Marx's own emerging theory of the state.

With respect to the crown, Hegel had reiterated in his own uniquely
turgid way the standard early modern doctrine that sovereignty rests
solely in the monarch. Marx first taunted his opponent within the context of his own terminology. "What kind of ideality of the state would
it have to be which, instead of being the actual self-consciousness of
the citizens and the communal soul of the state, were *one* person, *one*
subject [?]" Next he thrust deftly to reveal an unperceived implication:
"The state-reason and state-consciousness is a unique empirical person
to the exclusion of all others, but this personified Reason has no content
except the abstraction, 'I will'. *L'Etat c'est moi.*" Finally with a master-
stroke, he disemboweled Hegel's entire argument:

38. "Jewish Question," *Writings*, pp. 247, 231; cf. *Critique*, p. 42.
39. *Critique*, pp. 42, 76.

If the sovereign is the actual sovereignty of the state then the sovereign could necessarily be considered *vis-à-vis* others as a self-subsistent state, even without the people. But he is sovereign in so far as he represents the unity of the people, and thus he is himself merely a representative, a symbol of the sovereignty of the people. The sovereignty of the people is not due to him but on the contrary he is due to it.[40]

With respect to the diets, which Hegel had seen as mediators between people and crown, Marx displayed thoroughness if not deftness in methodically hacking this illusion to bits. In substance, his long argument expanded on two points developed earlier in the *Rheinische Zeitung:* that the diets of Hegel's conception, like their real Prussian counterparts, first are impotent and second represent only entrenched private interests. ("Diets," or *Stände,* may also be rendered "Estates," as in the translation below):

> The Estates are superfluous for the execution of public affairs. The officials can carry out this execution without the Estates; moreover they must, in spite of the Estates, do what is best. Thus the Estates, with regard to their content, are pure superfluity. Their existence, therefore, is pure formality in the most literal sense.
>
> Furthermore, the sentiment of the Estates, their will, is suspect, for they start from the private point of view and private interests. In truth, private interest is their public affairs, not public affairs their private interest. . . .
>
> The Estates are the sanctioned, legal lie of constitutional states, the lie that the state is the people's interest or the people the interest of the state.

They cannot mediate between the extremes of crown and people because these extremes are opposed in essence. Rather they stand, like Buridan's ass, paralyzed between.[41]

If we turn finally to the bureaucracy, we reach the core of Hegel's political thought and of Marx's response to it. The "universal class" played a central role in Hegel's conception of the state, being charged with the "maintenance of the state's universal interest," with harmo-

40. Ibid., pp. 24, 26, 28.
41. Ibid., pp. 64–65, 89, 93.

nizing particular interests and bringing them "back to the universal."[42] This central role is not surprising if Hegel did reflect the realities of early-nineteenth-century Prussia, for that state has been more adequately defined as "bureaucratic absolutism" than anything else.[43] Marx was well aware of Hegel's partiality for bureaucrats and immediately chided him for expanding administrative competence by lumping together the "executive, police, and judiciary, where as a rule the administrative and judiciary powers are treated as opposed." (Even here he mirrored real-life Prussia.) Hegel went so far as to suggest obliquely that state officials made ideally qualified representatives in the diets, which would leave all three branches of government suffused with their spirit. But then, Marx noted acidly, Hegel "is thoroughly infected with the miserable arrogance of the world of Prussian officialdom."[44]

Marx was himself acquainted with that arrogance and, as he warmed to the argument, one hears the echo of his *Rheinische Zeitung* experiences. Neither the classical polis nor the medieval hierarchy of estates possessed a state bureaucracy, Marx urged; it is a modern product and rests squarely upon the separation of state and civil society. And it fully embodies the egoism of the modern state:

> The bureaucracy asserts itself to be the final end of the state. . . .
> The aims of the state are transformed into aims of bureaus, or the
> aims of bureaus into the aims of the state. . . .
>
> The bureaucracy is the imaginary state alongside the real state;
> it is the spiritualism of the state. As a result everything has a double
> meaning, one real and one bureaucratic. . . . The general spirit of
> the bureaucracy is the secret, the mystery, preserved inwardly by
> means of the hierarchy and externally as a closed corporation. . . .
> As far as the individual bureaucrat is concerned, the end of the
> state becomes his private end: a pursuit of higher posts, the build-
> ing of a career. . . .
>
> The police, the judiciary, and the administration are not deputies
> of civil society itself. . . . Rather, they are office holders of the state
> whose purpose is to manage the state in opposition to civil society.
> . . .

42. *Philosophy of Right*, §289.
43. By Hans Rosenberg, *Bureaucracy, Aristocracy and Autocracy: The Prussian Experience, 1660–1815* (Cambridge: Harvard, 1958), especially chap. 9.
44. *Critique*, pp. 41, 124–25; Hegel, *Philosophy of Right*, §§287, 310.

The hierarchy punishes the civil servant to the extent that he sins against the hierarchy or commits a sin in excess of the hierarchy; but it takes him under its protection when the hierarchy sins through him. . . .

In the bureaucracy the identity of the state's interest and the particular private aim is established such that the state's interest becomes a particular private aim opposed to the other private aims.

Thus, in a word, the bureaucracy holds the state "in its possession; it is its private property."[45]

For our purposes the most interesting feature of this analysis is that, like Marx's general historical schema, it contains no notion of class rule. History was not yet for Marx a succession of class dominations, nor did the modern bureaucratic state speak for any social force other than itself. Many writers have been misled by Marx's several efforts in the *Critique* to connect private property and the state. But any careful reading shows the connection to be, not that property owners dominate the state, but that the ruler and his servants own the state as their private property. They are their own masters and serve no interests but their own.[46] Only when Marx began his collaboration with Engels would the class-dominated state transform his thought, as we will discover in the next chapter.

In a sense, Marx's criticism here of crown, bureaucracy, and estates contained nothing that was not already at least implicit in the *Rheinische Zeitung*. What was new in the Kreuznach *Critique*, and precisely what constituted Marx's transition from democratic republican to communist, was the rejection of the modern state per se, *even in its republican form*. To this crucial implication we must now turn our attention directly. Once Marx had grasped the civil society—state dichotomy as the Gordian knot of modern times, he could no longer set his hopes for human self-realization on a mere political transformation that would leave civil society unchanged. Neither could he expect the modern state, no matter how altered, to untie itself the knot in which it was bound. "If the modern state," he wrote in an 1844 article, "would want to transcend the *impotence* of its administration, it would have to transcend the present mode of *private life*. If it wanted to transcend this private life, it would have to transcend itself, for it exists *only* in contrast

45.   *Critique*, pp. 46–47, 50, 52, 48, 47.
46.   See ibid., pp. 100, 107–11.

to that life."[47] Thus Marx had to cut the Gordian knot with a solution that would transcend both the state and civil society in some higher synthesis. Initially he would call this new synthesis "democracy" or sometimes "true democracy," as counterposed to the "republic as merely a particular form of the state."[48] Toward the latter institution he now pointed the merciless blade of criticism.

Marx's extensive reading on republics in general and the American republic in particular obviously convinced him that civil society was not appreciably altered by the simple elimination of the crown. "In the republic as merely a particular form of the state, political man has his particular and separate existence beside the unpolitical, private man. Property, contract, marriage, civil society appear here . . . as particular modes of existence alongside the political state." "The entire content of law and the state is, with small modification, the same in North America as in Prussia. . . . The content of the state lies outside these constitutions."[49] From the American travel impressions of a conservative Englishman, Thomas Hamilton, Marx had excerpted those passages which described growing extremes of wealth and destitution, envy and unrest, weakened respect for property and law—a kind of egoistic nightmare that Hamilton predicted would end in "anarchy and spoliation."[50] The motto of such a society most plainly reads: Every man for himself!

Yet the modern state, and most especially in its republican form, calls upon the individual to set aside this ruthless daily struggle for survival when he acts as citizen and to think only of the common good:

> Civil society and the state are separated. Consequently the citizen of the state and the member of civil society are also separated. The individual must thus undertake an essential schism within himself.

47. "Critical Notes on 'The King of Prussia and Social Reform'" (1844), *Writings*, p. 349.
48. *Critique*, p. 30.
49. Ibid., pp. 30–31.
50. See Thomas Hamilton, *Men and Manners in America* (Edinburgh, 1833), especially pp. 299–310; for Marx's excerpts, *MEGA* I, 1/2:135–36. The significance of this reading for Marx has been emphasized by Maximilien Rubel, "Notes on Marx's Conception of Democracy," *New Politics* 1, no. 2 (Winter 1962):83–85; and by Lewis Feuer, "The Alienated Americans and Their Influence on Marx and Engels," in his *Marx and the Intellectuals* (Garden City: Doubleday, Anchor Books, 1969), pp. 198–209.

. . . In order to behave as actual citizen of the state, to acquire political significance and efficacy, he must abandon his civil actuality, . . . his own actual, empirical reality; for as a state-idealist he is a being who is completely other, distinct, different from and opposed to his own actuality.[51]

Thus Marx arrived through his Hegelian thought structures at Rousseau's classic dilemma, the conflict between private egoism and the expectations of citizenship, between *homme* and *citoyen*.

Further, Marx suggested, individuals mired in the daily struggles of civil society, their actual life, are bound to find something unreal in the occasional acts of citizenship expected of them. The state in general, with its ideal claims of universality, is bound to seem remote and abstract:

Its otherworldly existence is nothing but the affirmation of their own alienation, . . . the religion of popular life, the heaven of its universality in opposition to the earthly existence of its actuality. . . . Monarchy is the fullest expression of this alienation. The republic is the negation of this alienation within its own sphere."[52]

Here Marx formulated Rousseau's dilemma in Feuerbachian terms, applying the latter's critique of religion to the political realm. The idea was only a flash of insight in the *Critique* but would be developed fully in the essay "On the Jewish Question," written at Kreuznach immediately after Marx finished with Hegel.

The "Jewish Question" constituted Marx's open announcement of his conversion, his definitive repudiation of his former republican views, of mere "political emancipation." It began more narrowly as a reply to a Bruno Bauer article which had argued that a Christian state cannot logically grant civil equality to Jews and still remain Christian, but that even a secular state could not do so until the Jews also secularized themselves, that is, gave up their religion. Marx certainly agreed that Jews (like Christians) could not be fully emancipated until they gave up the illusion of religion. But, he argued, Bauer had confused "politi-

51.   *Critique*, pp. 77–78.
52.   Ibid., pp. 31–32 (translation of first sentence modified—RNH; see original German, *Werke*, 1:233).

cal emancipation and human emancipation." Jews can be emancipated politically without having to give up their religion—and should be[53]— as they have been already in North America. In contrast to backward Prussia, with its established church and lingering legal discriminations against Jews, the United States has achieved "political emancipation," which includes a separation of church and state, a relegation of religion to the private sphere. It is a "perfected political state" which "emancipates itself from religion by emancipating itself from the *state religion*, that is, by recognizing no religion and recognizing itself simply as a state. *Political* emancipation from religion is not complete and consistent emancipation from religion because political emancipation is not the complete and consistent form of *human* emancipation."[54]

Thereupon Marx dropped the Jewish question to discuss what really concerned him—the inadequacy of mere political emancipation and the need for universal human emancipation. One point requires emphasis, however: neither here nor later did Marx assert that the former was worthless because it did not include the latter, that the American republic was no more to be preferred than Prussian authoritarianism. "*Political* emancipation is indeed a great step forward. It is not, to be sure, the final form of universal human emancipation, but it is the final form *within* the prevailing order of things."[55] Throughout his life, as we will see, formal democracy without socialism was for Marx not *worthless* but *inadequate*.

In a democratic republic, "man behaves, albeit in a specific and limited way and in a particular sphere, as a species-being, in com-

53.   Several months before, in Cologne, Marx had helped to circulate a petition to the Rhenish Diet supporting the elimination of all remaining legal discriminations against Jews. "As repugnant as the Israelite religion is to me," he wrote Ruge, "still Bauer's view seems too abstract" (*Werke*, 27:418). For details of this incident, see Helmut Hirsch, "Karl Marx und die Bittschriften für die Gleichberechtigung der Juden," *Archiv für Sozialgeschichte* 7 (1967):229–46. On the thorny issue of Marx's alleged anti-Semitism, one should begin with Edmund Silberner, "Was Marx an Anti-Semite?" *Historia Judaica* 11 (1949):3–52; and Shlomo Avineri, "Marx and Jewish Emancipation," *Journal of the History of Ideas* 25 (1964):445–50.

54.   "Jewish Question," *Writings*, p. 223.

55.   Ibid., p. 227; cf. *Critique*, p. 76. In a similar vein, *The Holy Family* (Moscow: Foreign Languages, 1956), p. 149, declared: "States which cannot yet *politically* emancipate the Jews must be rated by comparison with accomplished political states and must be considered as underdeveloped."

munity with other men." The difficulty is, of course, that civil society remains "the sphere of egoism and of the *bellum omnium contra omnes.*"[56] Thus:

> By its nature the perfected political state is man's *species-life* in *opposition* to his material life. All the presuppositions of this egoistic life remain in *civil society outside* the state, but as qualities of civil society. Where the political state has achieved its full development, man leads a double life, a heavenly and an earthly life, not only in thought or consciousness but in *actuality*. In the *political community* he regards himself as a *communal being*; but in *civil society* he is active as a *private individual*, treats other men as means, reduces himself to a means, and becomes the plaything of alien powers. The political state is as spiritual in relation to civil society as heaven is in relation to earth.[57]

Once again Marx formulated Rousseau's dilemma in Feuerbachian terms and then proceeded to draw out the political parallel to the latter's theory of religion.

Both Marx and Feuerbach began from the postulate that men, by their nature, are species-beings, that is, beings who are conscious of belonging to a species composed of others like themselves, and beings who can realize their full human potential only in loving collaboration with those others. What prevents this fulfillment at present is, Feuerbach wrote, men's belief in religion. Perceiving their own imperfections as isolated individuals and not yet conscious of their collective potential, men seek consolation in an imagined God, abase themselves, and worship him as a power standing over them, when he is in reality their own alienated species-essence and represents only a schism within themselves. Marx now saw this phenomenon in politics as well as in religion. For him, however, man's present isolation is not simply a matter of perception but a reality, a product of modern civil society: "egoistic man is the passive and given result of a dissolved society." Equally real is man's debasement: he is "corrupted by the entire organization

---

56. "Jewish Question," *Early Writings*, trans. and ed. T. B. Bottomore (New York: McGraw-Hill, 1964), p. 15 (*Writings*, p. 227). (Here and in a few subsequent cases I find Bottomore's translation smoother or clearer than that of Easton and Guddat; the equivalent page reference in the latter is appended, however.)

57. "Jewish Question," *Writings*, p. 225.

of our society, lost and alienated from himself, oppressed by inhuman relations and elements."[58] In such a society he cannot be an actual species-being; he cannot live in harmonious collaboration with his fellows.

Instead, his species-life appears as an alienation, as a projection upon something external—namely, the modern state. As an alien power this state is most clearly recognizable in its monarchical form, as the king, the Lord Jehovah, before whose authority men must bow down and humble themselves. Such a metaphor did not really fit the democratic republic, however, so Marx substituted the dream of heaven as the specific parallel alienation. Just as religious man imagines a heaven of ideal communal life but which alas has no power over this world's vale of sorrows, so political man creates the republic as an ideal but alas inconsequential expression of his communal life. Here, to be sure, he participates—minimally—as a species-being, but the republic seems to have no power over the vale of civil society: "he is an imaginary member of an imagined sovereignty, divested of his actual life and endowed with an unactual universality." He acts religiously in that he "regards as his true life the political life remote from his actual individuality," just as the Christian regards his eternal life in heaven as his true life.[59] Thus political man has effected a schism not only within himself but also in his institutions. He lives a double life, a real earthly life of egoism in civil society, and an illusory heavenly life of community in the state. Without a change in civil society, the democratic republic must remain little more than a hollow mockery of man's destined fulfillment as a species-being. It remains a mockery, however, not because the bourgeoisie somehow manages still to rule through democratic institutions (the bourgeoisie is nowhere mentioned), but because man's "heavenly" actions as citizen flatly contradict the realities of his daily life.

The gulf between state and civil society manifests itself, Marx continued in the next portion of the "Jewish Question," even in the modern conception of individual rights. All the great French declarations of the revolutionary period spoke of the "rights of man and of the citizen [droits de l'homme et du citoyen]."[60] Why the separation? "The so-

58. Ibid., pp. 240, 231.
59. Ibid., pp. 226, 231.
60. These declarations and constitutions are reproduced in English in John Hall Stewart, ed., A Documentary Survey of the French Revolution (New York: Macmillan, 1951).

called *rights of man*," Marx replied, "as distinguished from the *rights of the citizen*, are only the rights of the *member of civil society*, that is, of egoistic man, man separated from other men and from the community." Marx listed these rights of man according to the declaration that prefaced the Jacobin Constitution of 1793—equality, liberty, security, property. Drawing material from other constitutions as well, he examined each of the four rights and concluded:

> Liberty [Marx used the French *liberté* in the original] is thus the right to do and perform anything that does not harm others. . . . This is the liberty of man viewed as an isolated monad, withdrawn into himself, . . . not based on the association of man with man but rather on the separation of man from man. . . .
>
> The practical application of the right of liberty is the right of *private property*, . . . to enjoy and dispose of one's possessions as one wills, without regard for other men and independently of society. It is the right of self-interest. . . .
>
> "Equality"—here used in its non-political sense—is only the equal right to *liberty* as described above, *viz*., that every man is equally viewed as a self-sufficient monad. . . .
>
> *Security* is the supreme social concept of civil society, the concept of the *police*. . . . Security is the guarantee of the egoism [of civil society].

Thus, Marx summed up, "none of the so-called rights of man goes beyond the egoistic man. . . . Far from viewing man here in his species-being, his species-life itself—society—rather appears to be an external framework for the individual, limiting his original independence."[61]

Clearly Marx had nothing but scorn for the "so-called" rights of man, and he did not discuss individually the rights of the citizen, from which the impression may be drawn that he had at that point rejected individual rights altogether. Such a conclusion would be unwarranted. In this particular polemical context Marx rather took the rights of the citizen for granted, and passed over them hurriedly as "*political* rights that can be exercised only in community with others. *Participation* in the *community*, indeed the *political* community or *state*, constitutes their substance. They belong in the category of *political freedom*, of

61. "Jewish Question," *Writings*, pp. 235–37.

civil rights.[62] These rights were not contemptuously labeled "so-called," like the rights of man. The declaration of 1793, most frequently cited by Marx, included among the rights of "participation" the right of every citizen to vote (article XXIX) and to hold public office (V). Here was equality in its political, as opposed to nonpolitical, sense. Belonging to the "category of political freedom" (*politische Freiheit*, which Marx deliberately contrasted to the French *liberté*, the right to withdraw) were most evidently the rights of free expression and free assembly (VII). As much as Marx scorned the "so-called" rights of man, he would all his life defend the political rights associated with citizenship.[63]

Further analysis suggests an additional refinement. Marx belabored the distinction between human and civil rights much more than the documents did themselves. The French declarations generally named three or four rights (not always the same ones) as belonging to man per se, but made no further separation in their numerous articles. Indeed, Marx had to choose carefully among the various declarations and constitutions before him because no single one would say exactly what he wanted. The original 1789 declaration, for example, expressly included among the rights of *man* "resistance to oppression," which Marx ignored for obvious reasons. The 1793 document linked free expression and free assembly together in the same article with freedom of conscience, although Marx considered the former to be civil rights and the latter to belong with the rights of man. Interestingly, Marx's own treatment of religious freedom showed none of the contempt showered upon the other "so-called" rights of man: he declared, "the *privilege of faith* is a *universal human right.*"[64] Underneath, Marx wanted to dismiss those rights associated in his mind with egoism, and they boiled down to the "practical application" of *liberté*, namely the right to enjoy and dispose of one's possessions without regard for other men. Marx be-

62. Ibid., p. 233.

63. The whole question of rights will be fully discussed in a more appropriate context in volume 2. There has been very little systematic study of this topic: see Iring Fetscher, "Liberal, Democratic, and Marxist Concepts of Freedom," in his *Marx and Marxism* (New York: Herder and Herder, 1971), pp. 26–39; idem, "Marx's Concretization of the Concept of Freedom," in *Socialist Humanism*, ed. Erich Fromm (Garden City: Doubleday, 1965), pp. 260–71; Thomas Sowell, "Karl Marx and the Freedom of the Individual," *Ethics* 73 (1963):119–25; and Susanne Miller, *Das Problem der Freiheit im Sozialismus* (Frankfurt a/M: Europäische Verlagsanstalt, 1964).

64. "Jewish Question," *Writings*, p. 234; cf. *The Holy Family*, pp. 127–29.

labored and abused the distinction between human and civil rights essentially to announce that he no longer believed in private property.

In the conclusion to the main section of the "Jewish Question," Marx returned to the theme of man's authentic nature. Modern society, he suggested, has produced the unfortunate view that men are naturally egoistic and must be forced or cajoled into citizenship. Here, for the first and last time in his pre-London writings, Marx quoted Rousseau—as a horrible example!—to the effect that a legislator seeking to found a nation would have to transform human nature itself, depriving individuals of their solitary independent powers and giving them alien powers that could only be exercised in common. By contrast, Marx viewed authentic man as a cooperative being, a species-being, and saw egoism as a deformation produced by civil society. A true community would not require man to accept *alien* powers but only to exercise his natural ones: "*Every* emancipation is a *restoration* of the human world and of human relationships to *man himself.*"[65] With this understanding of Marx's assumptions and vocabulary, we may appreciate his famous but cryptic finale:

> Human emancipation will only be complete when the real, individual man has absorbed into himself the abstract citizen; when as an individual man, in his everyday life, in his work, and in his relationships, he has become a *species-being;* and when he has recognized and organized his own powers [*forces propres*] as *social* powers so that he no longer separates this social power from himself as *political* power.[66]

"True Democracy"

Was this to be taken as an appeal for communism? Marx nowhere used the word in the "Jewish Question." Many authorities, including those of Communist orthodoxy, have grouped the above call for "human emancipation" with the "true democracy" of the Kreuznach *Critique* as both belonging to Marx's precommunist, transitional period, when he espoused some vague, radical, but still "bourgeois," democracy. He became a communist, so the argument runs, only when he announced in

65. *Early Writings,* p. 31 (*Writings,* p. 241); Rousseau quotation referred to is from *The Social Contract,* bk. 2, chap. 7.
66. *Early Writings,* p. 31 (*Writings,* p. 241).

the Paris "Critique" his discovery that the proletariat was destined to lead mankind to the good society. But the Paris "Critique" in fact does not mention the word "communism" either, and the task there assigned to the proletariat was precisely "universal human emancipation," the same term employed in the "Jewish Question."[67] Close scrutiny of the Kreuznach writings reveals that, whatever so-called scientific "discoveries" he made in Paris, Marx had already undertaken a *moral* commitment to communism as a form of society without private property, social classes, or a state. "True democracy" may indeed be equated with communism.

To document this point, we may review briefly the evidence that Marx wanted "true democracy" to be propertyless and classless, and then turn to our central concern—its statelessness. The Kreuznach writings do not, to be sure, call for the elimination of property and social classes directly, in so many words, but the underlying desire gains clarity in each succeeding document. In the *Critique* itself, Marx limited his discussion of property, following Hegel, to the institution of primogeniture. Where Hegel saw this practice as a guarantee of the disinterestedness of the aristocracy in public concerns, Marx saw it merely as a guarantee of disinterest. For precisely because their property was inalienable through the generations no matter what might befall other people, aristocratic landowners could be indifferent to the larger community. Their property did not give them a vested interest—as in the Greek polis—in the common weal. "Because it is inalienable, its social nerves have been severed and its isolation from civil society is secured." "Primogeniture is . . . the freedom of private rights which has freed itself from all social and ethical chains." In human terms, moreover, the owner of such property cannot use it according to his will; rather it uses him. "Landed property always inherits, as it were, the first born of the house as an attribute linked to it. . . . The subject is the thing and the predicate is the man. . . . The owner of the entailed estate is the serf of the landed property."[68] While restricting his critique to primogeniture, Marx twice noted that this institution is paradigmatic of all private property. He drew no overall conclusion, save for the sarcastic comment: such is "the sovereign splendor of private property, of possession of land, about which so many sentimentalities have recently been uttered and on behalf of which so many multi-colored crocodile tears have

67. Compare *Writings*, p. 221 with p. 260.
68. *Critique*, pp. 99, 100, 106–07.

been shed."[69] It may be argued nonetheless that these seminal thoughts contained the seed of all that Marx would subsequently have to say on the subject of private property.[70]

With respect to classes, we have already witnessed Marx's absolute revulsion at the hereditary caste system of medieval Europe, which appeared to him as "the animal history of mankind, its zoology." The French Revolution, he went on to observe, eliminated these legal estates and their political functions. Political classes became merely social classes, and mobility became more possible; nowadays "money and education are the prevalent criteria" determining social position. But mobility should not be confused with equality. "It is a development of history that has transformed the political classes into social classes such that, just as the Christians are equal in heaven yet unequal on earth, so the individual members of a people are equal in the heaven of their political world yet unequal in the earthly existence of society."[71] The implication seems clear that the transformation that was begun by the French Revolution needs to be completed by applying equality to the "earthly existence of society."

The implication became even plainer in the "Jewish Question." Here Marx developed a set of seductive parallel constructions for his Young Hegelian readers, beginning from their accepted view that man's ultimate self-realization would involve emancipation from the illusion of religion. Marx had stressed that political emancipation only "abolished" religion for the state itself, through disestablishment of the church; it by no means freed the citizens individually from their religious illusions. Only universal human emancipation would accomplish the latter goal. The seductive parallels follow:

The *state* can free itself from a limitation without man *actually* being free from it. . . .

For example, the state as a state abolishes *private property* . . . when it abolishes the *property qualification* for electors and representatives, as has been done in many of the North American States. . . . But the political suppression of private property not only does

69. Ibid., p. 99; paradigmatic, pp. 107, 109. Note also the sentiments on property Marx expressed in his September 1843 letter to Ruge, *Writings*, p. 213.

70. Avineri, *Social and Political Thought*, pp. 27–31; O'Malley, "Editor's Introduction" to *Critique*, pp. lv–lix.

71. *Critique*, pp. 80–82.

not abolish private property; it actually presupposes its existence. The state abolishes, after its fashion, the distinctions established by *birth, social rank, education, occupation,* when it decrees that birth, social rank, education, occupation are *non-political* distinctions; when it proclaims, without regard to these distinctions, that every member of society is an *equal* partner in popular sovereignty. . . . Far from abolishing these *effective* differences, it only exists so far as they are presupposed.[72]

The lesson can scarcely be avoided: universal human emancipation is also required to free man from the real-life "limitations" of private property and class distinctions.

In subsequent writings Marx did not so much change his position as shake off the veils of editorial restraint. The Paris "Critique" already had the proletariat "demanding the *negation of private property,*" and included Marx's most inspired and moving call to arms: "To be radical is to grasp things by the root. But for man the root is man himself. . . . The criticism of religion ends with the doctrine that *man* is the *highest being for man,* hence with the *categorical imperative to overthrow all conditions* in which man is a degraded, enslaved, neglected, contemptible being."[73] The theme of human degradation in modern society was taken up again at length in Marx's now famous Paris manuscripts of 1844, from which scholars have gained a wealth of new insights into Marx's concept of man, man's destiny, and the various forms of his present alienation—wage labor, money, private property, and the division of labor.[74] But the Paris manuscripts are almost totally unpolitical, and to gain some further insight into the "stateless" dimension of Marx's initial vision of communism, we must turn back to the relatively untapped resources of the Kreuznach *Critique.*

Politically, Marx began from the premise that popular sovereignty is the underlying authority of the people themselves to form and reform

72. First sentence, *Writings,* p. 223; remainder, *Early Writings,* pp. 11–12 (*Writings,* pp. 224–25). Also see Marx's polemic against huckstering later in the essay, *Writings,* p. 248.

73. *Writings,* pp. 263, 257–58.

74. *Economic and Philosophic Manuscripts of 1844,* most adequately translated in *Early Writings,* pp. 61–219. It is impossible to cite the abundance of literature dealing with the manuscripts; beginners may start with Erich Fromm, *Marx's Concept of Man* (New York: Ungar, 1961) and seek further guidance from the essays and cited literature in Fromm's *Socialist Humanism.*

their own institutions. He was profoundly disturbed by Hegel's assertion that, even if they wanted to, the people had no right to alter the given monarchical constitution. To Marx that seemed but another example of Feuerbachian man's permitting himself to be ruled by an alien power–an unwanted constitution–that was in reality his own creation:

> Posed correctly, the question is simply this: Does a people have the right to give itself a new constitution? The answer must be an unqualified yes, because the constitution becomes a practical illusion the moment it ceases to be a true expression of the people's will. . . .
>
> Just as it is not religion that creates man but man who creates religion, so it is not the constitution that creates the people but the people which creates the constitution. . . . Man does not exist because of the law but rather the law exists for the good of·man. . . .
>
> Democracy is the resolved mystery of all constitutions. Here the constitution . . . is returned to its real ground, actual man, the actual people, and established as its own work. The constitution appears as what it is, the free product of men.[75]

Marx also expected such a constitution to be the product of a popular revolution. He allowed Hegel's point that, historically, constitutions have gradually changed, "but for the new constitution a real revolution was always necessary." In the development of such a revolution, a constituent assembly would be elected by the people as a special legislature, charged with the task of drawing up a new fundamental law. "In general, when it has appeared in its special capacity as the ruling element, the legislature has produced the great organic, universal revolutions. It has not attacked the constitution, but a particular antiquated constitution, precisely because the legislature was the representative of the people, i.e., of the species-will [des Gattungswillens]."[76]

At the end of the Critique, in a rare reference to contemporaneous political struggles, Marx pointed to the popular movements then agitating in France and Britain for universal suffrage. Here he perceived the crucial effort by the people to win and exercise their sovereignty in a practical sense. The full achievement of that goal would bring world-historic changes:

75. Critique, pp. 58, 30, 29–30.
76. Ibid., pp. 57–58.

It therefore goes without saying that the vote is the chief political interest of actual civil society. In unrestricted suffrage, both active and passive, civil society actually raises itself for the first time to an abstraction of itself, to political existence as its true universal and essential existence. But the full achievement of this abstraction is at once also the transcendence [*Aufhebung*] of the abstraction. In actually establishing its political existence as its true existence civil society simultaneously establishes its civil existence, in distinction from its political existence, as inessential. And with the one separated, the other, its opposite, falls. Within the abstract political state the reform of voting demands the dissolution [*Auflösung*] of this political state, but also the dissolution of civil society.[77]

In this obviously crucial passage, Marx equated the winning of universal suffrage with the end of the old order in Europe;[78] the practical exercise of popular sovereignty would constitute the essential revolutionary act, transcending the dichotomy between state and civil society. The character of this "transcendence" remained, alas, high in the clouds of philosophical abstraction, but we may begin drawing it back toward earth by separating out (according to Avineri's suggestion) three different meanings of the technical Hegelian term *Aufhebung*. In its verb form *aufheben* means simultaneously to abolish (in an old form), to transcend or supersede (that old form), and to preserve (in a higher form).[79] Thus civil society and the state would both be abolished in their old forms and transcended in a higher unity where neither would be distinct from the other. The chief characteristic of the old order, egoism, would disappear in favor of the species life. In civil society this would mean the disappearance of private property—the legal recognition of selfishness—in favor of communal property. In political life it would mean the disappearance of the self-interested state as an institution standing over civil society and alienated from it. But in favor of what?

77. Ibid., p. 121 (translation modified—RNH; see original German, *Werke*, 1:326–27, and compare Easton and Guddat's translation, *Writings*, p. 202).

78. Marx was aware, of course, that universal suffrage had been introduced already in many American states without social revolutionary consequences (see n. 72 above), but in his mind Europe would be different, for reasons that will emerge in the next section.

79. Avineri, *Social and Political Thought*, p. 37.

To say that the old state would "dissolve" is not to say that the polity itself would dissolve, that there would be no arrangements at all for making and carrying out collective decisions. The authentic functions of the old state would be *aufgehoben,* preserved in a higher form. Marx did not want to call these functions "political," or to call the new polity a "state," since both these words smacked of the despised present. On one occasion in the *Critique,* he described the merger which would transcend the state and civil society as a *Gemeinwesen,* equivalent to the French *"commune"* or the English "commonwealth."[80] In another passage he suggested the following terminological distinctions:

> In democracy the abstract state has ceased to be the governing moment. The struggle between monarchy and republic is itself still a struggle within the abstract form of the state. The political republic is democracy within the abstract form of the state. Hence the abstract state-form of democracy is the republic; but here it ceases to be mere political constitution.[81]

If the good society will be organized in the "abstract state-form" of a republic, one is tempted to conclude that Marx was simply playing with words, substituting the grand-sounding "commonwealth" and "true democracy" for the terms "state" and "republic" which he had come to reject. Yet this would not be correct. Marx did not imagine the socialist commonwealth to be merely a conventional democratic republic supervising a nationalized economic system (which became the latter-day social democratic vision). It would be much more radical and requires some effort of imagination for the twentieth-century reader to grasp.

With his characteristic instinct for the jugular, Marx placed the executive branch first on his agenda. "Executive power, in and for itself, has to be the object of popular desire much more than legislative power."[82] Consequently he stressed the need for a thoroughgoing democratization of executive power, and not merely at the top, but at all levels and in all departments. Here was where real power rested in Prussia, after

---

80.   *Critique,* p. 79 (in the manuscript Marx had originally written *Kommune,* and then crossed it out in favor of *Gemeinwesen,* according to the editors of *MEGA* I, 1/1:496). Marx had also used the term once before in the period of the *Rheinische Zeitung:* see above, chap. 2, n. 77.

81.   *Critique,* p. 31.

82.   Ibid., p. 120; cf. p. 54.

all, here was the real "state" that Marx detested and wanted to destroy. He would destroy it in the most radical way: in a word, by eliminating the *profession* of governing. There would be no hereditary monarch, needless to say, but also no professional politicians, professional bureaucrats, professional police, etc. Administration would become the work of everyone instead of being the work of Hegel's so-called universal class. Everyone would mean literally *everyone*, on a part-time or short-term basis; it would not be enough to have only a chance to serve. The chance of every Catholic to become a priest, Marx wryly observed, does not produce the priesthood of all believers. "In a true state it is not a question of the possibility of every citizen to dedicate himself to the universal in the form of a particular class, but of the capability of the universal class to be really universal, i.e., to be the class of every citizen."[83]

In this context, Marx ridiculed the Prussian civil-service examination as something that would be superfluous in a true democracy, where everyone would possess a competent knowledge of public affairs:

In a rational state, taking an examination belongs more properly to becoming a shoemaker than an executive civil servant, because shoemaking is a skill without which one can be a good citizen of the state, a social man; but the necessary state knowledge [*Staatswissen*] is a condition without which a person in the state lives outside the state, is cut off from himself, deprived of air. The examination is nothing other than a masonic rite, the legal recognition of civic competence in the form of a privilege.[84]

It was in this very real and concrete sense that Marx expected the state to "dissolve." It would cease to exist as a separate institution standing over society and run by professionals; public business would become the part-time or short-term activity of ordinary citizens, one activity among many they would pursue.

Marx's ideas on the legislative branch were less original and less developed, but no less radically democratic. He expected that the people would vote on important legislative matters directly, by referendum, which was the sense of his distinction quoted earlier between active and

83. Ibid., p. 50.
84. Ibid., p. 51 (translation of last sentence modified—RNH; see original German, *Werke,* 1:253).

passing voting.[85] But passive voting meant electing representatives who would in turn vote on legislation, and Marx still displayed none of Rousseau's hostility toward representation per se. He called it "the conscious product of civil trust," and in a contemporaneous letter to Ruge contrasted the "representative system" to the "estate system" as the "difference between the control of man and the control of private property" (we are already familiar with his views on the Prussian diets).[86] The control of man was meant seriously: Marx wanted directly elected deputies to be instructed by and bound to their constituents. On the other hand, he expected voters in a true democracy to "share in deliberating and deciding on matters of general concern as the 'all,' that is to say, within and as members of the society"–thus as species-beings and not as self-centered monads.[87] Although Marx did not discuss the judicial branch directly, it is plausible to assume that he wanted it to be elective as well, and that he wanted both the legislature and the judiciary to be deprofessionalized in the same sense as the executive.[88] Career deputies and professional judges would disappear with their executive counterparts.

With these clarifications from the seldom-read *Critique*, the famous and puzzling last paragraph of the "Jewish Question" takes on concreteness. Communist men would no longer separate their own collective power from themselves and turn it over, as alienated "political" power, to the professionals who run an institutionalized state. And their own activities as citizens would no longer be infrequent and unreal, but would become a meaningful part of their daily lives–they would have absorbed the abstract "citizen" back within themselves. It is in this sense that Marx embraced communism to resolve the political as much as the socioeconomic dilemmas of modern society.

Marx nowhere tells us the source of his conception of the ideal polity, a radical democracy without professionals, yet there can be little doubt, for the circumstantial evidence is overwhelming. Marx dropped a rare connecting clue at the end of his above-quoted critique of the Prussian civil-service examination. He appended the final jibe: "No one ever

85.   See n. 77 above.

86.   *Critique,* p. 105; letter to Arnold Ruge, September 1843, *Writings,* pp. 213–14.

87.   *Critique,* pp. 117, 122–23.

88.   Marx would praise the Paris Communards lavishly in 1871 for having accomplished these political goals; see *Selected Works,* 1:470–73.

heard of the Greek or Roman statesmen taking an examination."[89] It would seem that Marx shared with most of his educated contemporaries in Germany an admiration of classical antiquity, and within that variegated civilization he most admired Athens in the age of Pericles (mid-fifth century B.C.). He had noted in the *Rheinische Zeitung,* "Greece and Rome are certainly countries of the highest 'historical culture' in the ancient world. Greece's highest internal development came in the time of Pericles."[90] And indeed, upon reflection, no other political structure in the Western tradition so closely resembles Marx's ideal as Periclean Athens.

"We are called a democracy," Pericles had declaimed, according to Thucydides' report of the famous funeral oration, "for the administration is in the hands of the many and not the few."[91] Important matters, both legislative and executive, had to be resolved by the entire citizenry, exercising its ultimate sovereignty in the frequent open-air assemblies. More routine business was delegated to the Council of Five Hundred, selected annually *by lot* from among a host of candidates elected in the several districts of the city. No person could serve in the council more than twice. All other officials (from tax collectors to generals!) were similarly selected each year by election or by lot and except for generals and certain financial officials could not serve more than once in the same position. There was no permanent, professional civil service, save for a few lower-level functions (clerks, town criers, policemen). Judicial tasks were handled entirely by enormous juries composed of hundreds of "judges," all chosen in the same manner as the council. Alfred Zimmern has estimated that at any given time one-sixth of the Athenian citizenry could be found serving in public office and "eating public bread."[92] Civic competence was expected and assumed in all citizens, whom Pericles praised for adapting themselves to every task "with the utmost versatility and grace."[93]

The core resemblance to Marx's true democracy is simply too striking

89. *Critique,* p. 51; other references to antiquity, pp. 31–33, 108–11.
90. "The Leading Article in No. 179 of the *Kölnische Zeitung*" (1842), *Writings,* p. 115; cf. *Werke,* 1:77.
91. Thucydides, *The Peloponnesian War,* trans. Benjamin Jowett (New York: Bantam, 1960), p. 116.
92. Alfred E. Zimmern, *The Greek Commonwealth,* 5th ed. (Oxford: Oxford, 1931), p. 175 (not including the armed forces). My thumbnail description of the Athenian state is taken from Zimmern's excellent analysis.
93. *The Peloponnesian War,* p. 118.

to be coincidental. Exactly where Marx acquired this admiration for Periclean Athens cannot be ventured; most likely it came by ordinary cultural osmosis from the general veneration given to Greece in early-nineteenth-century German educated circles.[94] What does seem certain, however, is that he could not have acquired it from Rousseau, whose classical model was Sparta and whose hero was Lycurgus, or from the Jacobins, who rather fancied themselves to be Romans.[95] Insofar as Rousseau and the Jacobins were incipient totalitarians, as Talmon argues, it is noteworthy that they avoided Athens as a model while Marx singled it out. To say he admired Athens is not, of course, to say he admired everything about it, or dreamed nostalgically of re-creating the golden age of a simpler society. In *The Holy Family* (1845), Marx would write that Robespierre and his party fell precisely because they confused modern times with antiquity.[96] Periclean Athens served Marx as a general model for the *political* functioning (if he would forgive us the word) of an ideal society, but no more than that. He also used other models from the past—some consciously, some apparently not—to flesh out in his mind various attributes of the "rational" society. But he fully expected that these attributes of past societies could be combined with all the advantages of modern technology, large-scale organization, specialization of skills, etc. In the process of its self-realization mankind would not go back, but onward to develop its full powers. We will return to this vision later, when we have more evidence.

Revolution as the Means

We must still consider the question of means, Marx's strategy for achieving communism. Since this subject will be developed at length in later chapters, we will consider here only Marx's initial views, expressed during the period of conversion itself, at Kreuznach in 1843

94. See Walter Jens, "The Classical Tradition in Germany—Grandeur and Decay," in *Upheaval and Continuity: A Century of German History*, ed. E. J. Feuchtwanger (Pittsburgh: Pittsburgh, 1974), pp. 67–72; for more extensive treatment, see E. M. Butler, *The Tyranny of Greece over Germany* (Cambridge: Cambridge, 1935); Friedrich Paulsen, *Geschichte des gelehrten Unterricht auf den deutschen Schulen und Universitäten*, 2nd ed., 2 vols. (Leipzig: Veit, 1896–97).

95. Rousseau, *The Social Contract*, bk. 2, chap. 7; R. R. Palmer, *Twelve Who Ruled: The Year of the Terror in the French Revolution* (Princeton: Princeton, 1941), pp. 112, 119.

96. Pp. 164–65; see also *Writings*, p. 350.

and Paris in 1844. The obvious question is whether his new radicalism led him implicitly to endorse totalitarian means in the sense discussed above—the vanguard party, minority revolution, educational dictatorship, etc.

We have already witnessed how, by the time he arrived in Kreuznach, Marx had lost faith in the unassisted power of ideas—the Joshuan trumpets of criticism—and now spoke approvingly of an "impending revolution."[97] In the Kreuznach *Critique* he linked that coming revolution to the attainment of universal suffrage, which would dissolve and transcend the antagonisms of modern society. This linkage would be a consistent theme until 1848. For example, in 1845 Marx outlined his still unfinished book on the modern state (alas, it never did materialize) in which the final chapter was titled "Suffrage: the Struggle for the *Aufhebung* of the State and Civil Society."[98] And of course the *Communist Manifesto* itself proclaimed that the "first step" in the revolution would be "to win the battle of democracy."[99] It may seem strange in our own day, especially for Americans, to see universal suffrage linked with the idea of a world-transforming social revolution. Yet it was not at all unusual in early-nineteenth-century Europe, where universal suffrage had been tried only once, in 1792, and had inaugurated the most radical phase of the French Revolution. To conservatives of Marx's time, and even to most liberals, universal voting smelled of the guillotine, committees of public safety, assaults on the established classes, and indeed, if tried again, doubtless a universal assault on private property itself. If these people identified the suffrage with social revolution, it is not surprising that radicals like Marx did too. (Only later would they all discover, to their pleasure or grief, that it might be compatible with existing socioeconomic arrangements.) Moreover, most radical democrats quite plausibly anticipated that universal suffrage could be achieved only by popular revolution, since the existing oligarchies were unlikely to sign their own death warrants. Thus Marx could conceive—as in the citations above—that the winning of universal suffrage would be precisely the act of revolution itself, and would supersede the dichotomy between state and civil society with the reign of "true democracy."

97. See above, chap. 2, n. 82.
98. *Werke*, 3:537 (badly translated in *The German Ideology*, p. 655).
99. *Selected Works*, 1:50. Further evidence of this linkage will be adduced in chap. 5.

Yet certain nagging doubts persist. Did Marx perhaps intend to follow out the Jacobin precedent of elections succeeded by a committee of public safety and a reign of terror, a minority dictatorship resting on a mere show of popular support? At Kreuznach he still treated the attainment of universal suffrage in Britain and France as the general triumph of the people. In the Paris "Critique," completed in January 1844, he first identified the proletariat as the executor of the impending revolution and now emphasized that it would extend to Germany as well—"The *day of German resurrection* will be proclaimed by the *crowing of the Gallic cock.*"[100] In the same passage, however, Marx recognized that "the proletariat is only beginning to appear in Germany." It certainly constituted only a small minority there, and only a somewhat larger minority in France. This observation has given rise to the view that Marx here in effect was advocating minority revolution and its logical consequence, minority dictatorship.[101] The suspicion is heightened by the pronounced chiliastic tone of the Paris essay—Talmon not unjustly calls it "a Messianic document *par excellence*"—which foresaw a grand apocalypse in the immediate future and called upon the just emerging proletariat not only to destroy the existing order but to produce universal human emancipation, the complete overcoming of man's self-alienation, nothing less than the fulfillment of all human history.[102]

These nagging doubts may be assuaged somewhat by the fact that in 1843–1844, Marx nowhere openly called for minority revolution, for a vanguard party, or for dictatorship of any kind. True democracy would appear to follow immediately upon the popular revolution which establishes universal suffrage. Marx showed no partiality for Blanquist secret societies in Paris and, indeed, his repeated assertion that universal suffrage would be the first act of the revolution is flatly incompatible with the standard Blanquist recipe for elections only after a temporary revolutionary dictatorship. Still, how could universal suffrage produce proletarian rule and world-historic changes where the workers are only a minority?

100. Karl Marx and Friedrich Engels, *Basic Writings on Politics and Philosophy,* ed. Lewis S. Feuer (Garden City: Doubleday, Anchor Books, 1959), p. 266. This famous concluding sentence is inexplicably omitted by Bottomore and emasculated by Easton and Guddat, viz. "crowing of the French rooster," *Writings,* p. 264.

101. Stanley Moore, *Three Tactics: The Background in Marx* (New York: Monthly Review, 1963), pp. 14–16.

102. J. L. Talmon, *Political Messianism: The Romantic Phase* (New York: Praeger, 1960), p. 211 and passim.

The paradox can be resolved by a key phrase from the same section of the Paris "Critique"—"the *acute disintegration* of society."[103] Marx first approved of revolution in his letter to Ruge of March 1843; in his next letter two months later he was already linking this revolution to the social dislocation produced by rapid industrialization: "If I do not despair, it is only the desperate situation of the present that fills me with hope. . . . The system of industry and commerce, of property and the exploitation of men leads even more rapidly than population growth to a fissure within present-day society that the old system cannot heal."[104] In the Paris "Critique," Marx expanded on the peculiar kind of misery produced by "the rising *industrial* movement": "For it is not poverty from *natural circumstances* but *artificially produced* poverty, . . . the masses resulting from the *acute disintegration* of society, and particularly of the middle classes [*des Mittelstandes*], which gives rise to the proletariat."[105] By July 1844 Marx was speaking of pauperism as "England's national epidemic," which spreads in "geometrical proportion" as the "necessary consequence of modern *industry*." "In England the misery of labor is not partial but universal, not confined to factory districts but extended to rural districts." The uprising of the Silesian weavers in 1844 portended the same future for Germany.[106]

As Marx became aware of the social dislocation produced by industrialization, he vastly overestimated both the speed and ultimate extent of such pauperization. But he was by no means alone in this miscalculation. Lorenz von Stein, whose aforementioned work first exposed Marx to extended social analysis, himself gave special prominence to the tendency of industrial society toward rapid and extreme polarization. Many conservative writers of this period—to some extent Hegel himself —expressed similar fears about the effects of the factory system.[107] Nor were their fears mere flights of fancy. For Western Europe at large the "Hungry Forties" probably constituted the critical decade in the

103. *Writings*, p. 263.
104. Letter of March 1843, ibid., p. 204; letter of May 1843, ibid., p. 210 (translation modified—RNH; see original German, *Werke*, 1:342–43); see also Cornu, *Karl Marx et Friedrich Engels*, 2:238–39.
105. *Writings*, p. 263.
106. "King of Prussia and Social Reform," ibid., pp. 342–43, 345, 351.
107. Stein, *Sozialismus und Communismus*, pp. 39, 51; Hamilton, *Men and Manners in America*, pp. 299–310; Hegel, *Philosophy of Right*, §§241–45; see also Barion, *Staatslehre*, pp. 100–02; Avineri, *Social and Political Thought*, pp. 54–57.

entire disruptive process of economic modernization. Extrapolating forward from then current trends could scarcely yield anything but the most ominous predictions. Moreover, Marx's own direct, contemporaneous experience tended to confirm a dire prognosis: external competition was pauperizing the small Moselle vintners; estate rationalization was pressing hard on the Rhenish poor by cutting off their traditional wood-gathering rights; and in 1844 the introduction of new machinery had provoked the uprising of the Silesian weavers, immortalized in Heinrich Heine's famous poem.[108] Thus it is quite plausible that he expected the English "epidemic" to spread to the Continent and, by a "geometric" rate of expansion, to produce "universal" pauperism within a few years. As Adam Ulam has observed in hindsight, Marx mistook "the birth pangs of modern industrial society . . . for the death throes of capitalism."[109] It was not until 1850, as we will see, that Marx made an agonizing reappraisal about—at least—the tempo of this change.

Thus the paradox resolves itself: the "acute disintegration of society" would produce a proletarian majority within a few years (insofar as Marx defined the proletariat as the "class that is the dissolution of all classes"—including those peasants and artisans from the old *Mittelstand* who would be uprooted, declassed, and pauperized by the forces of economic modernization);[110] universal suffrage would indeed mean proletarian rule and social revolution. Marx's anticipations of 1843–1844 were without doubt wildly optimistic, as he himself later acknowledged, but they did not include any notion of minority revolution. Even his chiliastic expectations take on a degree of plausibility when the appalling distress of the Hungry Forties and the cataclysmic forebodings of conservative writers are taken into account.

But how could Marx be so confident that the rational order of society would emerge from this chaos of disintegration? How much could really be expected of the uprooted and disoriented masses? Would they not require a vanguard of intellectuals to guide them in their assigned mission? Contrary to some impressions, Marx did have a modest direct acquaintance with the lower classes prior to 1844 (in the Rhineland

108. Readers may be interested in Engels' passing fair translation of "The Weavers" for the *New Moral World*, in *MEGA* I, 4:342.

109. Adam B. Ulam, *The Unfinished Revolution: An Essay on the Sources of Influence of Marxism and Communism* (New York: Random House, 1960), p. 6.

110. See n. 115 below.

and especially in his native Moselle region),[111] but it was certainly in Paris that he first encountered modern urban workers and their organizations. His immediate response was ecstatic, as revealed in his August 1844 letter to Feuerbach: "You should be present at one of the meetings of French workers so that you could believe the youthful freshness and nobility prevailing among these toil-worn people. . . . It is among those 'barbarians' of our civilized society that history is preparing the practical element for the emancipation of man."[112] (Note at the outset that they are prepared not by Marx but by history, that is, the process of capitalist development itself.) About the same time, in his Paris manuscripts, Marx wrote more reflectively:

When communist *artisans* form associations, teaching and propaganda are their first aims. But their association itself creates a new need—the need for society—and what appeared to be a means has become an end. The most striking results of this practical development are to be seen when French socialist workers meet together. Society, association, entertainment which also has society as its aim, is sufficient for them; the brotherhood of man is no empty phrase but a reality, and the nobility of man shines forth upon us from their toil-worn bodies.[113]

Such proletarian associations were crucially important in Marx's revolutionary schema, and not merely—or even primarily—because they defended the material interests of the workers. As they augmented the brute strength of the movement, they simultaneously transformed the consciousness of its individual members. No longer isolated monads, deformed by the crushing egoism of civil society, the workers discovered in association their true selves, their "need for society," and gave up their egoism for the mutuality of the common cause. "The proletariat," Marx would write in 1847, "needs its courage, its self-esteem, its pride, and its sense of independence more than its bread."[114]

111.   Negative impression, Tucker, *Philosophy and Myth,* pp. 113–17; contrary evidence, Avineri, *Social and Political Thought,* pp. 53–57.
112.   Letter of August 11, 1844, *Werke,* 27:426 (as translated by Avineri, *Social and Political Thought,* pp. 140–41).
113.   *Early Writings,* p. 176; cf. *The Holy Family,* p. 113.
114.   "The Communism of the Paper *Rheinische Beobachter,*" *Basic Writings,* p. 269; Avineri, *Social and Political Thought,* pp. 140–49.

Thus the root cause of man's present-day alienation, egoism, was being transcended in proletarian associations. Here, where the worker could actually live as a species-being, the new unselfish socialist man was being created; here was the new society in embryo within the womb of the old; here it was growing in dialectical relation to the disintegration of the existing order.

In this manner, Marx reached the conclusion classically formulated in the Paris "Critique," that the proletariat, not Hegel's bureaucracy, constitutes the "universal class," the class whose task it is to realize the universal need of society,

> a class with *radical chains,* a class in civil society that is not of civil society, a class that is the dissolution of all classes, a sphere of society having a universal character because of its universal suffering, . . . that cannot emancipate itself without emancipating itself from all other spheres of society, thereby emancipating them; a sphere, in short, that is the *complete loss* of humanity and can only redeem itself through the *total redemption of humanity.*[115]

In this process of human redemption, Marx left room for his old weapon of change, philosophical criticism, but no longer as an independent instrument. "The weapon of criticism," he continued in the renowned lines, "obviously cannot replace the criticism of weapons. Material force must be overthrown by material force. But theory also becomes a material force once it has gripped the masses." "As philosophy finds its *material* weapons in the proletariat, the proletariat finds its *intellectual* weapons in philosophy."[116] Thus the task of intellectuals like Marx was educational, to help raise the consciousness of the masses, giving them insight into the cause of their condition and into its necessary solution. But education is by no means identical to direct political leadership: nowhere in these writings is there a call for a vanguard party, or for any party at all, other than the workers' own associations. Marx had an obvious opportunity in Paris to join the League of the Just or some other Blanqui-inspired conspiratorial elite, but he did not. "During my first stay in Paris," he recalled in 1860, "I cultivated personal relations with the leaders of the League [Ewer-

115. *Writings,* p. 263.
116. Ibid., pp. 257, 263.

beck and Mäurer] as well as with the leaders of most of the French secret workers' associations, but without joining any of them."[117]

The crucial point is that for Marx, consciousness would come to the proletariat not *only*, or even *necessarily*, from the outside, from intellectuals like himself. It would emerge from the workers' own spontaneous efforts to cope with the conditions in which they found themselves. Not only does Marx's praise of the French workers' associations testify to this, but even more does his contemporaneous panegyric to the weavers' uprising that had broken out in Silesia:

> The Silesian uprising *begins* precisely where the French and English labor revolts *end*, with the consciousness of the nature of the proletariat. The action itself bears this *superior* character. Not only the machines, the rivals of the worker, are destroyed but also *account books* and titles to property. . . . Not a single English labor revolt has been conducted with equal courage, deliberation, and persistence.
>
> As for the state of education or the capacity for education of the German workers generally, I recall *Weitling's* excellent writings. . . . If one compares the insipid mediocrity of German political literature with this *tremendous* and brilliant literary debut of the German workers; if one compares these gigantic *child's shoes* of the proletariat with the dwarfed, worn-out political shoes of the German bourgeoisie, one must predict an *athletic figure* for the *German Cinderella*. . . . As the impotence of the German bourgeoisie is the *political* impotence of Germany, the talent of the German proletariat—even apart from German theory—is the *social* talent of Germany. . . . Only in socialism can a philosophical people find its suitable practice, thus only in the *proletariat* can it find the active element of its emancipation.[118]

It is safe to assume that the Silesian insurgents never heard of Karl Marx. They developed their own consciousness as the German workers

117. *Herr Vogt, Werke*, 14:439; see also Cornu, *Karl Marx et Friedrich Engels*, 3:5–9.

118. "King of Prussia and Social Reform," *Writings*, pp. 352–53. Marx singles out Weitling in this passage because the ex-tailor was the only significant German socialist writer of that time who actually came from the lower classes. In chapter 5 we will see what Marx thought of Weitling's strategy for revolution.

in general were developing their own talent, without benefit of a vanguard party and quite apart from "German theory"—apart, that is, from the Young Hegelian intellectuals like Marx himself. "German theory" was *helpful* but ultimately *incidental* to the success of the revolution, which would be—as Marx later repeated so often—the *self*-emancipation of the working class.

Thus Marx's conversion to communism, the culmination of his political education, did not carry with it a commitment to totalitarian or elitist means. There can be no question of his chiliastic impatience, so emphasized by Talmon, which led him to exaggerate the real signs of social disintegration. But chiliastic longing has been a recurrent phenomenon in the Western tradition from at least the beginning of the Christian era down to the present day, and it is especially evident in periods of massive social anxiety like the 1840s. It cannot simply be equated with totalitarianism without divesting the latter word of its distinctive meaning. At most this longing creates a *temptation* to employ totalitarian means, and at least to this point, Marx clearly had resisted the temptation.

⟨[4]⟩

Engels' Political Education

IT HAS LATELY BECOME FASHIONABLE in some quarters to treat Engels as the dustbin of Classical Marxism, a convenient receptacle into which can be swept any unsightly oddments of the system, and who can thus also bear the blame for whatever subsequently went awry. No doubt Marx's profounder philosophical conceptions suffered some transformation and vulgarization as Engels tried to disseminate them in later years.[1] But it would be quite unjust to dismiss Engels as a shallow popularizer who misunderstood the system and who himself made no vital contribution to it. His influence on the young Marx is usually acknowledged in the sphere of economics, but what seems to have escaped scholarly notice is the fact that Engels also made a key contribution to the Marxist theory of the state. As we retrace Engels' political education in the following pages, looking once more for evidences of totalitarian democracy, we may also assess the importance of this contribution.

Rebel Democrat

One can count three phases in Engels' political development only in the formal sense that he was reared in a rigidly conservative household. His earliest surviving writings belong already to the second phase, in which he rebelled against parental orthodoxy with an exuber-

---

1. For example, George Lichtheim, *Marxism: An Historical and Critical Study* (New York: Praeger, 1961), pp. 234–58; Iring Fetscher, "From the Philosophy of the Proletariat to Proletarian Weltanschauung," in his *Marx and Marxism*, trans. John Hargraves (New York: Herder and Herder, 1971), pp. 148–81; and Herbert Marcuse, *Soviet Marxism* (New York: Columbia, 1958), pp. 137–38, 142–45.

ant revolutionary republicanism. About the character of his childhood before that rebellion, not a great deal is known.

Like Marx, Engels was an eldest son and born into a comfortable bourgeois family in western Germany during the Restoration period. Engels was two years younger, born in November 1820, and grew up on the other side of the Rhine in the town of Barmen, a locality also just acquired by Prussia in 1815. Barmen was no idyllic backwater of rustic charm, however, but an expanding textile center whose bustling mills and squalid slums gave young Engels an early appreciation of the Janus-faced portent of industrial growth, perhaps the more so because his family owned one of the town's larger factories. The lace and ribbon establishment had been founded by his grandfather back in the eighteenth century, and his own father had extended the family's interests across the English Channel into Manchester through a partnership, the cotton-spinning firm of Engels and Ermen, where the boy was destined to many years of reluctant toil. The senior Friedrich Engels was an able entrepreneur, but apparently also a tyrannical paterfamilias and a strait-laced conservative in politics and religion. Engels would later refer to him as "my fanatical and despotic old man."[2] The boy's mother, as the devout daughter of a Calvinist rector, contributed to the narrow and rigorous pietist atmosphere in which he was reared. At first the senior Engels seems to have intended a legal career in the Prussian civil service for his obviously gifted son and accordingly enrolled the boy, after primary school, in the municipal *Gymnasium* in neighboring Elberfeld. In 1837, however, after only two years, the sixteen-year-old lad was abruptly withdrawn from school and obliged to enter apprenticeship as a clerk in the family business. The *Gymnasium* seems to have awakened Friedrich's intellectual appetites, not for jurisprudence alas, but for poetry and literature and unorthodox political ideas, thus precipitating a serious conflict between father and son over career choices. In contrast to Marx, whose father had encouraged his liberal political and religious development, Engels moved leftward

2. Engels to Marx, March 17, 1845, *Werke*, 27:27. The definitive biography of Engels remains Gustav Mayer, *Friedrich Engels: Eine Biographie*, 2 vols. (The Hague: Nijhoff, 1934), which has been abridged into one volume in its English translation, *Friedrich Engels: A Biography* (New York: Knopf, 1936). For Engels' youth, see Horst Ullrich, *Der junge Engels*, 2 vols. (Berlin: VEB, 1961–66), as well as the already cited double biography, Auguste Cornu, *Karl Marx et Friedrich Engels: Leur vie et leur oeuvre*, 3 vols. (Paris: Presses Universitaires, 1955–62).

as part of an increasingly open rebellion against his "despotic" father. Perhaps for this reason he by-passed Marx's early liberal monarchism altogether in favor of an outright republicanism that exuded unusually strong animosity toward kings and other despotic figures.

Almost certainly Engels first encountered deviant political ideas at the Elberfeld *Gymnasium*, either from schoolmates or perhaps from an instructor. He would later have kind words for a Dr. Clausen, who taught him history and literature and who is known to have had liberal views.[3] During his subsequent apprenticeship, Engels was undoubtedly inspired as well by the radical romantic poet, Ferdinand Freiligrath, who established residence in Barmen in 1837 and who, like the young clerk, was obliged to combine his poetic activities with a drab business career. Although Engels apparently did not become personally acquainted with the older poet at this time, he certainly must have known the "youths from commercial families" who, as Engels wrote in his first published article, "overwhelmed him [Freiligrath] with visits when he came to Barmen, . . . pursued him, praised his poems and his wine, and strove with all their might to drink *Bruderschaft* with someone who had actually published something." In any event, Engels' earliest poetic attempts were plainly modeled after the exotically placed verse of Freiligrath and reflected a parallel alienation from the stultifying atmosphere in which he was constrained to live.[4]

After a year's apprenticeship, the seventeen-year-old Engels was able to arrange a more satisfactory compromise with his father. He secured permission to move to the North Sea port of Bremen, there to continue his tutelage under an old family business friend, Heinrich Leupold, in the linen export trade. During the next three years away from his family the youth matured rapidly, expending a minimum effort on his business chores while taking advantage of the more cosmopolitan climate of the Free City to read voraciously at every opportunity, especially political writings forbidden on Prussian soil. His own letters and writings began to reflect political interests. In a surviving 1839 poem, "Florida," Engels depicted a young *Burschenschaftler* as a tragic "freedom fighter" who suffered imprisonment and exile because of his "striv-

---

3. See *Werke*, 1:427–28; Mayer, *Engels*, 1:20; Ullrich, *Der junge Engels*, 1:9–15.
4. "Briefe aus dem Wuppertal" (1839), *Werke*, 1:428–29; see also pp. 426, 432; EB 2:415. Engels' surviving poems reproduced ibid., EB 2:336–37, 350–52, 510–21; see Mayer's commentary, *Engels*, 1:15–17.

ing for freedom." The black, red, and gold colors of the *Burschenschaft* movement, he reported to his favorite sister, Marie, "are the only colors I can bear," and he proudly displayed them on his purse and pipe tassels.[5] Even his belletristic interests had strong political overtones: it is not accidental that his literary pantheon consisted of Heinrich Heine, Ludwig Börne, and the writers of the Young Germany school, whose political radicalism had earned them the Prussian censor's ban in 1835. After satisfying his curiosity about their writings, Engels defended his heroes in a letter to his boyhood chum, Friedrich Graeber:

> These ideas . . . are not at all demagogic or anti-Christian, as they are branded, but rest on the natural rights of every individual and extend to everything that, under present conditions, contradicts these rights. Among such ideas, above all, are the participation of the people in the work of the state, i.e., constitutionalism, and emancipation of the Jews, elimination of all religious compulsion, of all hereditary aristocracy, etc. Who could be against these things?[6]

Engels concluded that he was "body and soul" a Young German, that he could not sleep nights from thinking of these ideas, and hoped that his friend, then training for the clergy, would not turn against them. He also declared that he had "never been a pietist" and was now inclining toward Christian "rationalism."

Among the writers associated with the Young Germany school, it was Ludwig Börne who influenced the Bremen apprentice most profoundly. Engels' letters and early published writings were filled with increasing admiration for the recently deceased exile, whom he lauded variously as the "heroic fighter for freedom and justice," the "modern Moses," and the "John the Baptist of modern times," and whom he adopted as his mentor in both literary and political matters.[7] Börne was not, strictly speaking, a member of the Young German literary circle, but more an elder statesman. Having grown up a generation earlier in the Jewish ghetto of Frankfurt, Börne—like Hirschel Marx—experienced personally the liberation of the Jews and was able to serve

---

5.   "Florida," *Werke*, EB 2:350–52; letter to Marie Engels, December 6, 1840, ibid., p. 470; see also p. 474.
6.   Letter of April 8, 1839, ibid., pp. 366–67.
7.   Ibid., 1:438; EB 2:50, 395.

as a city official during the Napoleonic period. The Restoration brought dismissal, however, and the beginnings of his politico-literary opposition. He published a periodical, *Die Wage*, in Frankfurt until it ran afoul of the censors in 1821. His liberal views led him to Paris on a number of occasions, and he moved there permanently shortly after the July Revolution in 1830, an exile that would last until his death in 1837.[8]

It was from Paris that Börne put forth his most famous political writings, *Briefe aus Paris*. His initial enthusiasm for the July Revolution quickly soured as he realized how little had actually been changed. He joined the ranks of the radical republican opposition to Louis Philippe and the two hundred thousand plutocrats who now ruled France. He looked forward to the creation of a genuinely democratic republic based on universal suffrage and popular control of the executive, but he regarded all government as a necessary evil, whose prescribed mission should be the preservation of individual rights. "There must be human rights such that no governmental power may destroy, discontinue, or impair at any time, under any circumstances, for the sake of any benefit or to ward off any danger, even when exercised by the poorest street waif in the land." This model liberal democrat, who rejected socialism, nonetheless called for revolution precisely because he was a democrat: "I do not see how the situation can improve except through some kind of new revolution. According to the present electoral law, only the rich—i.e. the aristocratically inclined—can vote and only the rich can be deputies. . . . Only the Chamber can pass laws and naturally will not approve an electoral law that takes power from its hands."[9]

All these sentiments were seconded with characteristic youthful exuberance by Börne's admirer in Bremen. Engels wrote to Friedrich Graeber of his rejection of monarchy and his hatred for kings, especially his own king, Frederick William III, who in 1815 had promised the Prussian people a constitution and then spent the rest of his reign evading the fulfillment of that promise. "I hate him to death," seethed the youth, "and if I didn't despise him so much, that bastard, I would

8. For a recent biography of Börne, see Ludwig Bock, *Ludwig Börne* (Berlin: Rütten und Loening, 1962); for his influence on the young Engels, Ullrich, *Der junge Engels*, 1:100–04; Mayer, *Engels*, 1:43–45 and passim.

9. Ludwig Börne, *Werke* (Berlin, 1911–13), 7:176; 6:102, as quoted in Bock, *Börne*, pp. 222, 205.

hate him more. Napoleon was an angel compared to him." "There is no period," he continued, showing off his reading, "so rich in royal crimes as the one from 1816 to 1830; almost every prince reigning then deserved the death sentence." There was Charles X of France, who had provoked the July Revolution with his attempted royal coup, and Francis I of Austria, "that robot good for nothing but signing death warrants . . . and the patricide Alexander of Russia as well as his worthy brother, Nicholas, whose loathsome deeds need not be recounted—Oh, I could tell you delectable stories of how fond princes are of their subjects—I expect something good only from a prince whose head is sore from the buffetings of his people and whose palace windows are crashing in under the stones of revolution."[10]

In addition to his own king, Engels reserved a special animus for the neighboring Ernst August of Hanover, who had arbitrarily revoked his own country's constitution in 1837 and then dismissed seven liberal Göttingen professors when they protested. Engels composed a poem for this monarch during his private commemoration of the July Revolution in 1839. The inspiration came while he was sailing on the Weser, regarding Hanover on the distant shore, and a storm blew up out of the west, rocking his small boat precariously. In his poem Engels likened the storm to the rising fury of popular discontent also approaching Germany out of the west. He then posed the teasing question to Ernst August: "Speak, do you rest as securely on your golden throne as I in my swaying boat?" The young man's antimonarchist revolutionism derived from the same democratic values as Börne's; Engels was a revolutionary long before he became a socialist and at a time when he still professed Christian belief.[11]

His other dislikes also tend to place Engels squarely within the nineteenth-century democratic tradition. The early Bremen essays lashed out against the remaining legal privileges of the aristocracy, especially primogeniture. (Ever game for a prank, Engels trained his dog to growl fiercely whenever he shouted, "There's an aristocrat.") Sharing the force of his literary invective were the pretensions of the established church and the bigoted self-righteousness of its clerics, personified for

10. Letter of December 9, 1839–February 5, 1840, *Werke*, EB 2:442–43.
11. "Deutsche Julitage 1839," ibid., pp. 410–11. Evidence of Engels' revolutionism, ibid., pp. 92, 410–11, 412; of his Christian belief, p. 435; see also Mayer, *Engels*, 1:46, 90–91.

Engels by his hometown minister, whom he lampooned mercilessly.[12] It is interesting to note that he found nothing attractive in the city-state government of Bremen itself. Here he saw no model self-governing polis, as Rousseau saw in Geneva, but a narrow self-serving oligarchy, in which the legal opposition was equally small-minded and no more deserving of support than the ruling patriciate. Bremen politics helped convince Engels that small states were outmoded and ought to give way to a great unified German nation-state.[13]

The essay "Ernst Moritz Arndt," published early in 1841, was the most political of Engels' Bremen writings and an impressive piece for a youth just turned twenty (when Marx published his first essay in the spring of the following year, he had just turned twenty-four). Here Engels found one thing to admire in Germany's recent past, namely the great national liberation movement of 1813. This event did not appeal to him so much as a liberation from foreign rule: Napoleon's unnatural empire, he thought, was bound to collapse anyway and one should not forget the good things brought by the French—"emancipation of the Israelites, trial by jury, a healthy civil code." Rather, what impressed Engels mightily was "that we armed ourselves without waiting for the all-gracious permission of the princes, yes, that we *forced* the rulers to step forward and lead, in short, that for a single moment we appeared on the stage as the source of state power, as a sovereign people."[14] Unfortunately the appearance was momentary and the princes soon recovered the initiative, restoring the status quo as much as possible to Germany at the Congress of Vienna. Now it was time for the people to reassert itself: "the relationship between rulers and ruled must be ordered in a legal way"; Germans must have "a public life, a developed constitutionalism, freedom of the press"; aristocratic privileges must disappear and there must be "no estates, but citizens having equal rights in a great unified nation."[15] If Engels refrained from demanding a republic openly, it was no doubt because of the censorship restrictions under which he published.

In the same essay Engels took a stand on German nationalism typical

12. On aristocrats, *Werke*, EB 2:62–66, 128–29, 503–04; on clerics, pp. 10, 94–95.
13. Ibid., pp. 88, 433.
14. Ibid., pp. 122, 121.
15. Ibid., pp. 125, 131, 127.

of Young Germany and rather parallel to Mazzini's "liberal" nationalism in Italy. He contrasted the "braggadocio" of the "superpatriots" (*Deutschtümler*) like Turnvater Jahn, whose nationalism was only negative, a hatred of everything foreign, with the "cosmopolitan liberalism" of some south German intellectuals who sought to deny ethnic differences altogether. Striking middle ground and appealing again to Börne's name, Engels prayed that his countrymen might become a "unified, indivisible, strong, and—please God—*free* German people," a people which would recognize, however, that "the development of humanity stands above that of the nation." He hoped that Germans could one day reclaim their lost brethren in Alsace and Lorraine, but they would first have to prove themselves worthy by unifying themselves in a modern constitutional state; patriots should "strive for that, rather than for the extirpation of the French."[16]

The Arndt essay also called for a "synthesis of Hegel and Börne," suggesting the other predominant intellectual influence on the young Engels. If his political and literary values derived from Börne and Young Germany, his religious and historico-philosophical views came from Hegel and especially the Young Hegelian school in Berlin. Engels was not able to break free from the strait jacket of Barmen pietism as effortlessly as Marx shed his early bland deism. His Bremen letters to Graeber reveal a sometimes painful inner struggle through which he moved by stages from Calvinist orthodoxy to a kind of Christian rationalism, and then, under the influence of Strauss' *Life of Jesus*, away from Christianity altogether toward a vague Hegelian pantheism. His curiosity about the Young Hegelians drew Engels' gaze toward Berlin and, after the completion of his Bremen apprenticeship, he chose to perform his year of required military service (1841–1842) in the Prussian capital. There the final step in his religious evolution took place as he was converted by Feuerbach's just published *Essence of Christianity* to the position of atheist humanism he would retain the rest of his life.[17]

During his year in Berlin, Engels was an indifferent soldier—he displayed none of his later interest in militaria—but as usual he devoted every spare hour to study and writing.[18] The chief fruit of this endeavor

16. Ibid., pp. 119, 121, 131, 127, 131; see also Mayer, *Engels,* 1:52–56.
17. *Werke,* EB 2:125. Engels' religious development is best followed in his letters to Graeber; also see Mayer, *Engels,* 1:18–34, 71–80; and especially Karl Kupisch, *Vom Pietismus zum Kommunismus* (Berlin: Lettner, 1953), pp. 11–70.
18. See his letters to Marie from Berlin, *Werke,* EB 2:490–504; Martin Edgar

was a tract attacking Friedrich Schelling, the conservative philosopher appointed to counter Hegel's influence at the University of Berlin. The final paragraphs of Engels' piece bear the heavy imprint of Feuerbachian ideas. With the overcoming of traditional religion, he wrote, the earth which had seemed but a prison now becomes a "splendid royal palace." "Heaven has come down to earth," and the earth "no longer needs to justify itself before unreason which could not understand it; its magnificence and splendor, its abundance, its power, its life are its own justification." "And that favorite child of nature, man, after the long struggles of his youth, returning as a free man after long estrangement to his mother, . . . has also overcome the alienation from himself, the division within his own breast." "He has placed the crown of freedom on his own head," the crown which is "the self-consciousness of humanity." Thereupon Engels concluded with a distinctly un-Feuerbachian political twist, predicting that this freedom would be put into practice after a final "battle of the peoples" against tyranny. "It is our calling . . . to gird our swords round our loins and cheerfully pledge our lives in one last holy war, from which will emerge the thousand-year realm of freedom."[19]

If this enraptured finale sounds an ominous chiliastic note, it must be weighed against Engels' other, more political but less-known, Berlin writings. These writings appeared mainly in the *Rheinische Zeitung* and reveal quickly expanding knowledge and acute political insight; correspondingly Engels' demands for change became more exact and less apocalyptic. An article on South German liberalism, for example, picked apart its shortcomings with considerable dexterity, but ended with a tribute to its real accomplishments, "which truly are not to be despised":

> Above all, it founded a German opposition and thus made possible a political orientation in Germany and awakened parliamentary life; it did not allow the seeds which lay in the German constitutions to decay or die and drew from the July Revolution whatever advantage was to be gained for Germany.[20]

When Engels turned his attention to his own new Prussian monarch, a remarkably perceptive portrait emerged. In contrast to the eminently

Berger, "War, Armies, and Revolution: Friedrich Engels' Military Thought" (Ph.D. diss., University of Pittsburgh, 1969), pp. 13–19.
  19. *Schelling und die Offenbarung* (1842), *Werke*, EB 2:219–21.
  20. "Nord- und süddeutscher Liberalismus" (1842), ibid., p. 248.

modern "Victoria of England, the perfect example of a constitutional queen," Frederick William IV looked backward toward the reestablishment of a genuinely Christian state in Prussia, but understandably shrank from the full consequences of such a revival of medievalism. Thus what he had produced was a *"juste milieu* middle ages":

> Frederick William is not absolutely illiberal or violent in his strivings; God knows he wants to allow his Prussians every possible freedom, but only in the form of unfreedom, of monopoly and privilege. He is no determined enemy of free press, only he wants to grant it as a monopoly of the preferred academic estate. He does not want to abolish or deny the principle of representation, he only dislikes that citizens as such be represented; he is working on a representation of estates, as is already partly carried out in the Prussian provincial diets. In short, he recognizes no general civil and human rights, he recognizes only corporate rights, monopolies, privileges.

Prussian public opinion, Engels continued, now focuses on two demands—a representative constitution and freedom of the press. The king cannot help but yield to the latter and, given that, a constitution will follow within a year. Who knows where things may lead from there, but Prussia's present condition bears a marked resemblance to that of France in . . . (Engels discreetly left the thought unfinished).[21]

Adding his own voice to the demand for a free press, Engels published another article—parallel to Marx's famous journalistic debut—dissecting the ambiguities and contradictions of the existing censorship. Among the points he singled out was §151 of the 1819 Statute, which made it a crime "to excite displeasure and dissatisfaction" with the law code. This was absurd, fumed Engels, and tantamount to forbidding all criticism:

> That is precisely the purpose of all opposition. If I find fault with this legal stipulation, I have precisely the intention of exciting dissatisfaction with it, not only among the people but if possible in the government. . . . I am honest enough to declare forthrightly that, by means of this article, I foster the intention of exciting dis-

21. "Friedrich Wilhelm IV., König von Preussen" (1843), ibid., 1:446, 451, 453.

pleasure and dissatisfaction with §151 of the Prussian Criminal Code.[22]

Evidently the authorities chose to ignore this youthful flippancy. Engels' article, if less definitive than Marx's on the same subject, was no less spirited a defense of the principle of a free press.

Finally, in a short piece on the Prussian judiciary, Engels championed trial by jury and the separation of governmental powers. Conservatives who oppose the former, he noted, begin from the idea that

> no branch of the executive power should be placed directly in the hands of the people, and therefore not the power of the judge. That would be very nice if judicial power were not something entirely different from executive power. In all countries where the separation of powers is really put into effect, judicial and executive power have no connection to each other. Thus it is in France, England, and America; the mixing together of the two powers leads to the most unholy confusion, the ultimate consequence of which would be to unite the police official, the prosecuting attorney, and the judge all into one person. That judicial power is the immediate property of the nation, exercised through its sworn jurors, has long been proven not only from principles but by history as well. It would be superfluous here to reiterate the advantages and guarantees which trial by jury offers.

The judicial conservatives oppose it only because their positions would be threatened and because the "holy letter of the law, the dead abstract justice, would be in danger" if a jury set free some "poor proletarian" who in hungry desperation had stolen a loaf of bread.[23]

These last writings of Engels prior to his conversion to communism make it plain that the democracy he conceived would be liberal rather than totalitarian. By piecing together the scattered bits of evidence, we may define his final political ideal as a democratic republic with a written constitution, recognizing popular sovereignty, equality before the law (including full emancipation of the Jews), a free press together with other civil and human rights, and providing for an appropriate separation of governmental powers, trial by jury, etc.[24] Nowhere in

22. "Zur Kritik der preussischen Pressgesetz" (1842), ibid., EB 2:272–73, 277.
23. "Das Aufhören der 'Criminalistischen Zeitung'" (1842), ibid., pp. 269–70.
24. Although Engels nowhere openly demanded a republic, which the law for-

his presocialist writing is there a call for dictatorship, temporary or otherwise (the word itself is never used), or for a reign of terror, re-education, or any of the other accouterments of Jacobin rule.[25] To be sure, like most early democrats, he expected that these ends could be attained only by force, since existing governments closed off any legal avenue to democracy. But the revolution he anticipated so eagerly would apparently be popular and spontaneous; he devoted no attention, either public or private, to the development of any special vanguard whose task it might be to spearhead the uprising. Whatever temptations his chiliastic impatience may have evoked in his mind, clearly Engels—like his future collaborator—had not yet succumbed.

The Road to Communism

Engels' conversion to communism in the autumn of 1842 seems to have been comparatively abrupt, the product of personal influence rather than long solitary meditation. In any event it left behind no wealth of documentation such as we have for Marx. Only by conjecture can some of the background be reconstructed. We know from Engels' earliest published essay, "Briefe aus dem Wuppertal," that he felt sympathy for the impoverished and degraded factory workers of his native town. There is evidence that this sympathy for the victims of industrialization continued in the Bremen years, and it must have deepened as he read the novels of Dickens and Disraeli, Sue and Sand.[26] In 1842 Engels' Young Hegelian compatriots in Berlin, now calling themselves the *Freien*, generally became more concerned with social questions and the doctrines of socialism. Engels almost certainly read Stein's much-touted account of French socialism when it appeared in Septem-

bade, Mayer (*Engels*, 1:47) and Ullrich (*Der junge Engels*, 1:285–87) seem on safe ground in regarding him as a republican in this period. Engels did dare to describe his hero, Börne, as "*a republican in his very nature*" (*Werke*, 1:438); and in 1843, from the safety of England, he would refer back to his Young Hegelian circle as the "republican party" in Germany, saying they were all "declared Atheists and Republicans" (*MEGA* I, 2:447–48).

25. Engels did express some youthful admiration for Napoleon, mainly as the ruler who brought Jewish emancipation and the Code Napoléon to the Rhineland (*Werke*, EB 2:122, 104, 139–40). Such sentiments were quite typical of Rhenish liberalism in this period (see Jacques Droz *Le liberalisme rhénan, 1815–1848* [Paris: Sorlot, 1940], pp. 196–206), and in any event Engels never suggested any need for a new Napoleon.

26. "Briefe aus dem Wuppertal," *Werke*, 1:417–19; see also EB 2:80–88; Mayer, *Engels*, 1:111.

ber of that year. About the same time he also met Wilhelm Weitling in Berlin, although nothing is known of the interview.[27] It was the other foremost early German socialist, Moses Hess, who claims credit for Engels' conversion.

Following the completion of his military service, Engels yielded to his father's insistence that he move to England to help manage the family cotton factory in Manchester. On the journey there, in October 1842, he stopped in Cologne to meet the staff of the newspaper that had published most of his recent writing. After being snubbed by Marx, who identified him with the irresponsible *Freien*, Engels must have impressed Moses Hess, who spent the following week in intensive discussions with the younger man. Apparently Hess convinced him that communism was the necessary and logical outcome of Hegelian philosophy, especially in its Feuerbachian revision, and that England would shortly lead the way to the New Jerusalem. "We spoke about current questions," Hess reported afterward to his friend Berthold Auerbach, "and he, an Anno I revolutionary, departed from me an enthusiastic communist."[28] Engels was about to turn twenty-two. His conversion did not make him Hess' follower in any narrow sense: he remained much more political and practical than the ethereal, philosophically minded Hess. During the next two years in Manchester, Engels would publish his first essay on political economy and gather material for his first book, a massive empirical study of English working-class conditions.[29] Even more significantly for our purposes, he would immerse himself in English political life, producing no fewer than nine articles on the subject, a body of writing in which Engels developed a coherent theory of the modern state, a rudimentary schema of historical development, and a political strategy for achieving communism.[30]

Engels' early impressions of Britain were undoubtedly colored by

27. A few months later in England, Engels would attempt to arrange a translation of Weitling's book, *Garantien der Harmonie und Freiheit* (Mayer, *Engels*, 1:115–17).

28. Letter of June 19, 1843, in Moses Hess, *Briefwechsel*, ed. Edmund Silberner (The Hague: Mouton, 1959), p. 103; see also Edmund Silberner, *Moses Hess: Geschichte seines Lebens* (Leiden: Brill, 1966), p. 122.

29. "Outlines of a Critique of Political Economy" (1844), *Engels: Selected Writings*, ed. W. O. Henderson (Baltimore: Penguin, 1967), pp. 148–77; the book was published in 1845 as *The Condition of the Working Class in England*, trans. and ed. W. O. Henderson and W. H. Chaloner (Stanford: Stanford, 1968).

30. Most important was a lengthy three-essay set entitled, "Die Lage Englands" (1844), *Werke*, 1:525–92; remaining essays ibid., pp. 454–79.

the expectations Hess had put in his head. The latter's most recent book, *Die europäische Triarchie*, had presented human emancipation as the achievement of three great revolutions: the German Reformation, which had established religious freedom; the French Revolution, which had brought political freedom; and now finally an anticipated English social revolution, which was to achieve social freedom through communism.[31] Thus Engels arrived in Britain looking for signs of fermenting social upheaval. He did not have to look very hard to find them: 1842 had been a depression year with widespread famine in the industrial districts. Manchester itself had been a center of political strikes and rioting only a few months before, largely in connection with the campaign of the Chartists. Originally drawn up in 1838, the Great Charter was conceived as a monster petition to Parliament asking for the full democratization of the English governmental system. Its six points included universal manhood suffrage, secret ballot, equal electoral districts, annual election of Commons, salaries for members of Parliament, and elimination of property qualifications for such members. During the first campaign in 1839, over a million signatures had been collected in favor of the petition, which did not save it from quick oblivion when it finally reached Parliament. The second campaign reached its climax shortly before Engels arrived in 1842: according to the best reckoning, 3,317,702 signatures were collected, representing at least *half* the adult male population of the country, but once again the House of Commons rejected the petition by an overwhelming vote of 287 to 49. While the Charter contained no socialist demands, its mass support came overwhelmingly from the working class and many—probably most—of its leaders were socialists of one sort or another. While some elements favored only peaceful pressure, or "moral force," to back the petition, others urged rioting and "physical force" as the only effective means—hence the disturbances in Manchester, which was a major center of the physical-force wing. Everything seemed to confirm Engels' expectation of imminent social revolution, and he plunged himself into Chartist activities and into intensive study of the English scene.[32]

His earlier view of politics, which pivoted on the drama of despot

31.   (Leipzig: Wigand, 1841); for influence on Engels, see *Werke*, 1:48–88, 550.
32.   On the Chartist movement, see Mark Hovell, *The Chartist Movement*, 3rd ed. (New York: Kelley, 1967); Asa Briggs, ed., *Chartist Studies* (New York: St.

versus people, had to give way to a more differentiated view of contending political forces in a country where the monarch was only a figurehead. Comments on the English Constitution increasingly punctuated his articles and culminated in an extended analysis Engels wrote for his German readers in 1844. Contrary to the conventional belief, he argued, the English Constitution does *not* rest on a balance of powers. The monarchical element survives only as ceremony and veneration: "the power of the crown in practice reduces itself to zero." Not even the Chartists bother themselves about the crown—the ultimate proof of its impotence. Nor do the Chartists concern themselves with the aristocratic element, the House of Lords, which has become an "old people's home for retired statesmen." The struggle over the Great Reform Act in 1832 demonstrated that any desired majority could be manufactured in the upper chamber through the royal power to appoint new peers.[33]

In the English Constitution neither the monarchical nor the aristocratic element predominates, but rather the democratic element, the House of Commons. "In reality the lower chamber both makes the laws and administers them through ministers who are but a committee of that chamber. With this omnipotence of the lower chamber, England would be a pure democracy . . . if only the democratic element were itself really democratic."[34] But the recent experience with the People's Charter had made it clear that Commons cares nothing for majority will. "Is not the lower house a corporation elected purely through corruption and alienated from the people? Does Parliament not continually trample upon the people's will? Does public opinion on major questions have the slightest influence on the government?"[35] Even though the Great Reform Act of 1832 broadened the franchise (still only one of every eight adult males could vote), Commons remains in the hands of the propertied classes. County deputies are essentially picked by the great landowners through their influence over their tenants in the open balloting. Borough deputies represent mainly the well-to-do middle class because of the property qualification and the continuing corrupt electoral practices. "Who really rules in England?—

Martin's, 1960). Figures are from R. R. Palmer and Joel Colton, *A History of the Modern World*, 3rd ed. (New York: Knopf, 1965), p. 467.

33. "Die Lage Englands," *Werke*, 1:572–73.
34. Ibid., p. 574.
35. "Die innern Krisen" (1842), ibid., p. 457.

Property rules. Property enables the aristocracy to govern the election of rural and small-town deputies; property enables the merchants and manufacturers to determine the deputies for the large (and partly also the small) cities."[36] Small wonder, then, that the House of Commons rejected the Charter, for the propertied element "will never relinquish its occupation of the lower house by the approval of universal suffrage, . . . then it would be outvoted by the host of unpropertied people."[37]

Engels went on to expose limitations in the alleged "birthrights" of Englishmen. While the press was undeniably the freest in Europe, it was still constrained by laws on blasphemy, treason, and libel. The right of assembly could be denied at any time by local police, as the Chartists had learned to their dismay. Only the wealthy could take advantage of the habeas-corpus right to go free on bail, as well as the right to be tried by one's peers, since the property qualifications for jurors prevented the poor from being tried by *their* peers. The penal code, even after its recent reform, remained the most severe in Europe; political crimes were generally punished by transportation to penal colonies. Local police and judges constantly abused even these laws in their harassment of the Chartists. The birthrights of Englishmen were guaranteed, it seemed, only for the established classes.[38]

Everywhere he looked, Engels saw a class basis underlying the English constitutional structure. There is nothing in any of his Manchester writings to suggest that such a state might possess an autonomy or a selfish interest of its own, like Marx's state; for him it was purely an instrument of class oppression. It might be noted, however, that Engels was not guilty of some later "vulgar Marxist" crudities. He did not label the existing English oligarchy a "bourgeois democracy," as Horst Ullrich has it, nor did he even conceive it to be the instrument of one class alone; rather he judged England to be ruled jointly—if not too harmoniously—by the aristocracy and the bourgeoisie.[39]

Indeed, the fractious contention between these two partners, so manifest in the recent struggle over the Great Reform Act and in the ongoing conflict over the Corn Laws, suggested a historical progression

36. "Die Lage Englands," ibid., pp. 575–77; see also p. 473.
37. "Englische Ansicht über die innern Krisen" (1842), ibid., p. 454.
38. "Die Lage Englands," ibid., pp. 583–91; cf. pp. 457, 470, 476–77.
39. Ullrich, *Der junge Engels,* 2:155–64. The idea of the class state may conceivably have germinated earlier, as Engels attempted to understand Bremen city politics. See *Werke,* EB 2:433.

in which entrenched aristocratic interests were giving way step by step to those of the rising bourgeoisie. In Parliament the Tories spoke for the aristocracy and the High Church; the Whigs for the industrialists, merchants, and Dissenters.[40] Outside Parliament the proletariat was mustering its forces in the wings under the banners of Chartism. All three social forces were concentrating their energies on control of the House of Commons, which in England meant control of the state as such. It seemed plausible for Engels to conclude that this state, hitherto dominated by the aristocracy, now increasingly controlled by the liberal bourgeoisie, and destined to fall ultimately to the Chartist proletariat—that this state was nothing but an instrument for the use of successively dominant social classes. As Engels himself remembered many years later:

While I was in Manchester, it was tangibly brought home to me that the economic facts, which have so far played no role or only a contemptible one in the writing of history, are, at least in the modern world, a decisive historical force; that they form the basis of the origination of the present-day class antagonisms; that these class antagonisms, in the countries where they have become fully developed, thanks to large-scale industry, hence especially in England, are in their turn the basis of the formation of political parties and of party struggles, and thus of all political history.[41]

Thus did Engels elaborate from his early experiences in Britain a historical schema and a theory of the state quite distinct from what was being worked out contemporaneously by Marx in the seclusion of his Kreuznach retreat.

In Engels' economic studies, on the other hand, which included both the classical economists and their early socialist critics, he reached conclusions quite parallel to those of Marx concerning the "acute disintegration" of capitalist society. His first essay on economic questions stressed a polarizing tendency that seemed to him the necessary consequence of the competitive process itself and was only accentuated by the periodic crises to which the system was liable. "The middle classes must increasingly disappear until the world is divided into millionaires

40. *Werke,* 1:461–63, 468. Engels added that the Radicals spoke for the lower-middle classes.
41. "On the History of the Communist League" (1885), *Selected Works,* 2:311.

and paupers and into large landowners and poor farm laborers."[42] Already, he wrote in another article, "a third, almost a half, of all Englishmen" belong to this class of proletarians, and their numbers "multiply phenomenally." "With the slightest disturbance in trade, a large portion of this class goes without bread; in a major economic crisis the entire class goes hungry. When such conditions set in, what is left for these people but to revolt? Because of its mass, however, this class has become the mightiest in England, and woe to the English rich when it becomes conscious of that fact." Oligarchical intransigence from above, ever widening misery below—these two facts explain the growing strength of the mass Chartist movement. Already it has recruited the bulk of the factory proletariat to its banners and commands a clear majority in Manchester and other industrial cities. Soon the farm laborers in the countryside will also join its ranks.[43]

Engels could never be accused, as Marx has been, of seeing the proletariat only abstractly from Olympian heights as a material force required to realize some philosophical destiny. The affable young man plunged himself into working-class activities, attending meetings by the score, and gained a profound respect for the people he came to know. He repeatedly marveled at "the extent to which the English workers have succeeded in educating themselves." "I have sometimes come across workers, with their fustian jackets falling apart, who are better informed on geology, astronomy and other matters, than many an educated member of the middle classes in Germany."[44] Engels' warmest regard was reserved for the exploited Irish workers, into whose inner circles he was introduced by Mary Burns, the factory girl with whom he had fallen in love and who would be his common-law wife until her death in 1863. "What people!" he exclaimed. "They haven't a penny to lose, more than half of them have not a shirt to their backs, they are real proletarians and sans-culottes—and Irish besides—wild, ungovernable, fanatical Gaels. Nobody knows what the Irish are like unless he has seen them. If I had two hundred thousand Irish, I could overthrow the whole British monarchy."[45] Interestingly,

42. "Outlines of a Critique of Political Economy," *Engels: Selected Writings,* pp. 174, 166; on the development of Engels' early economic thought, see Cornu, *Karl Marx et Friedrich Engels,* 2:304–22.

43. "Die innern Krisen," *Werke,* 1:459; cf. pp. 468, 470–73.

44. *Condition of the Working Class,* p. 272; cf. *Werke,* 1:475.

45. "Briefe aus London" (1843), *Werke,* 1:478. A collection of Marx and Eng-

however, as Engels became more and more involved with the Chartist movement, and though he sympathized with its physical-force wing, he never sought out Feargus O'Connor, the violent, demagogic, and half-reactionary Irishman who was its principal spokesman. Instead he cultivated the cooler-headed revolutionary editor of the *Northern Star*, Julian Harney, who also was more familiar with Continental socialism.[46]

Engels was not attracted to violence for its own sake, but he did consider violent revolution necessary and unavoidable even in England. The Chartist demand for universal suffrage was in effect a demand to let the workers govern the country. To petition Parliament for such a change was equivalent to asking for a legal revolution— "a contradiction in itself and a practical impossiblity." Soon the workers would draw their own conclusions:

A revolution by a peaceful path is an impossibility, and only a forcible overthrow of the existing unnatural conditions, a radical ouster of the titled as well as the industrial aristocracy, can improve the material situation of the proletarians. They are still held back from this violent revolution by their peculiarly English respect for the law; but the conditions in England described above cannot fail shortly to produce general hunger among the workers, and then their fear of starvation will be stronger than their fear of the law. This revolution is an inevitable one for England.[47]

By the end of his stay in England in mid-1844 he was jubilating: "The struggle is already here. The Constitution is shaking in its foundations. . . . In the near future England will be a democracy."[48]

It takes no great acumen to observe in hindsight that Engels was carried away here by his revolutionary desires and, like Marx in the same period, considerably overestimated the rapidity and ultimate extent of the social polarization caused by industrial development. No doubt he also underestimated that "peculiarly English respect for the law." But his vision of proletarian revolution remains clear enough:

---

els' writings on the Irish question has recently been published: *Ireland and the Irish Question* (New York: International, 1972).
46. Mayer, *Engels*, 1:127–28, 139.
47. "Die innern Krisen," *Werke*, 1:460.
48. "Die Lage Englands," ibid., p. 592.

it would be a mass uprising of the pauperized millions against the oligarchy of wealth. It would be, not a minority revolution against democracy, but a majority revolution *for* democracy, a revolution made necessary in the first place by the lack of democratic institutions, of any effective legal modality for political action by the propertyless majority. Thus Engels' conversion to communism did not change his earlier vision of popular revolution but only changed the object of that overthrow—from individual despotism to class despotism.

Engels' commitment of time and energy to the open mass movement for the People's Charter gives sufficient testimony to the democratic character of his revolutionary aspirations, but it is noteworthy that he also expressly rejected the other obvious alternative—a secret, conspiratorial vanguard, the Blanquist short cut to communism. When he first crossed the Channel in late 1842, Engels stayed for a time in London where he became acquainted with some of the recently exiled leaders of the League of the Just, the German-speaking branch of the Blanquist movement. Karl Schapper and Heinrich Bauer had been implicated in Blanqui's classic Paris insurrection in 1839, and now in their new exile—joined by the watchmaker, Joseph Moll—they were trying to win recruits for a London branch of the organization. Engels was impressed by the revolutionary credentials of the trio but nonetheless declined to join. As he recalled many years later: "They were the first revolutionary proletarians whom I met, and however far apart our views were at that time in details—for I still owned, as against their narrow-minded equalitarian Communism, a goodly dose of just as narrow-minded philosophical arrogance—I shall never forget the deep impression that these three real men made upon me, who was then still only wanting to become a man." But when Schapper suggested that he join the league, "I at that time naturally refused."[49]

Although Engels did not elaborate on why such a refusal was "natural," contemporary evidence from 1843 suggests a conscious rejection of the central Blanquist strategy for revolution. In an article describing Continental movements for English socialists, Engels briefly discussed the Blanquist "policy of secret associations" and concluded, "I am not inclined to defend such a line of policy." Later he added, with reference to the Paris insurrection of 1839, "I do not consider such things creditable to any party."[50]

49. "History of the Communist League," *Selected Works*, 2:308, 313.
50. "Progress of Social Reform on the Continent" (1843), *MEGA* I, 2:440; "The 'Times' on German Communism" (1844), ibid., p. 451.

After nearly two years in Britain, Engels returned to Germany in the summer of 1844, stopping off for ten days in Paris to visit the author whose writings in the *Deutsch-Französische Jahrbücher* he admired. This second encounter with Karl Marx sparked an immediate friendship, the beginning of the famous forty-year collaboration between the two men, and resulted in their first joint venture, *The Holy Family*, which would be published the following year. As he continued on to Barmen, Engels resolved to extricate himself as soon as possible from his father's business concerns and rejoin Marx in Paris.

During the next several months, however, from September 1844 to April 1845, Engels lived in his parents' house and occupied himself mainly with writing his book on the condition of the English working class. He also sought to advance the socialist cause more immediately in his own native town, but of course no Chartist movement existed in Germany. On the one hand, the proletariat was not yet sufficiently numerous or politically aware; and on the other hand, an open mass political organization was inconceivable under the existing repressive laws. In such circumstances the temptation must have been much greater to consider revolutionary vanguards and conspiratorial forms of organization. And indeed, many authorities have repeated a claim that, whatever his views on England, at this time Engels thought Germany would come to communism only through the effort of an educated elite. This claim rests on a remark in one of the articles Engels put out for the English press: "There is a greater chance in Germany for the establishment of a Communist party among the educated classes of society, than anywhere else."[51] A more painstaking scrutiny of this article, however, along with Engels' Barmen activities generally, turns up no evidence whatsoever of vanguards or conspiracies, but substantially the same strategy of revolution he applied to Britain.

The article in question discussed two distinct elements in the German communist movement that had separate historical origins. "Philosophical Communism," whose spokesmen were Hess, Ruge, and Marx,

---

51. "Social Reform on the Continent," ibid., pp. 448–49. Elitism claimed by, e.g., Harold Laski, *Harold Laski on the Communist Manifesto* (New York: Random House, 1967), p. 23; Lewis S. Feuer, "Marxism and the Hegemony of the Intellectual Class," in his *Marx and the Intellectuals* (Garden City: Doubleday, Anchor Books, 1969), p. 69; and even by Boris Nicolaievsky and Otto Maenchen-Helfen, *Karl Marx: Man and Fighter*, trans. Gwenda David and Eric Mosbacher (Philadelphia: Lippincott, 1936), pp. 95, 97. Some of these authorities may have been led astray by Mayer's rather misleading summary of the article in question (*Engels*, 1:144–46).

figured as the final inference of Hegelian excogitation and understandably appealed more to the educated classes (hence the remark quoted above). But working-class communism had begun earlier under the inspiration of Weitling and, "being thoroughly a popular party, will no doubt very soon unite all the working classes of Germany" (evidently a hope that the League of the Just would develop into a mass party).[52] Thus Engels had no intention of leaving the workers out; on the contrary, his own efforts in Barmen were directed entirely at reaching the working class and welding together the two historically separated elements which formed the potential strength of German communism. He joined with Moses Hess in creating a new periodical, *Gesellschaftsspiegel*, aimed at the masses; he struggled to organize a working-class "uplift" society, the only associational form permitted by the law; he helped arrange public meetings for this society; he turned out a steady stream of publications and urged Marx likewise to finish and publish his major study of politics and economics. The climax of all this activity came when Engels himself addressed two meetings during February 1845 in neighboring Elberfeld and defied the police with his open advocacy of communism. (One can imagine the everlasting mortification of his father!) Over two hundred people attended the last meeting, and Engels reported to Marx: "People are talking of nothing but communism and we are winning new supporters every day. Communism is a *vérité* in Wupperthal, almost a power already." Unfortunately, he went on, the meetings drew in everyone "from the monied plutocrats to the greengrocers, but not the proletariat."[53] However mixed the results, Engels' methods were clear enough: he used every means he dared to reach the masses with his message; what he did not do was organize an underground conspiracy or fall back upon a parlor socialism for the educated alone.

The text of his speeches has survived and likewise reveals that his expectations for a German revolution were essentially parallel to the English model. He pointed to the same tendencies in German capitalism toward concentration and periodic crises of overproduction, with the same consequent polarization of society and impoverishment for "the great majority of the nation." "Under these conditions the proletar-

52.   "Social Reform on the Continent," *MEGA* I, 2:444–46, 448.
53.   Letter of February 22–26, 1845, *Werke*, 27:20. Engels' other letters to Marx give a running account of his manifold activities: see especially ibid., pp. 6–8, 10, 15–16; also Mayer, *Engels*, 1:205–19.

iat must not only continue to exist, but must continually expand and become an ever more threatening power in our society. . . . The proletariat will finally attain a level of power and insight such that it will no longer submit to the weight of the entire social building which constantly rests on its shoulders, and will demand a more equitable distribution of social burdens and rights; and then—if human nature does not change in the meantime—a social revolution cannot be avoided." But it will not be carried out "overnight and against the will of the nation." From the context of the speech it is clear that Engels expected this cataclysm within a few years, "in a very short time" as he expressed it elsewhere, and thus for Germany even more than Britain he overestimated the speed of industrialization.[54]

Within this vision of impending revolution Engels allowed a certain role for educated members of the propertied classes like himself. For Britain likewise he had suggested that "the more enlightened section of the middle class—admittedly pathetically small at the moment"—might embrace communism.[55] In Germany, as he speculated in several writings, the educated class was less directly tied to profit-making, more disinterested, and hence more receptive to the rational appeal of communism. "There is already a large number of well-to-do and educated people in all parts of Germany who have declared themselves for a community of goods."[56] In these perceived differences between the English and German educated classes lie the roots of the confusion about Engels' alleged elitism, but the only real effect of the differences was the larger number of educated converts he expected in Germany.

Such people might play an educative role in the development of communist forces, but Engels nowhere suggested they should be organized separately or occupy positions of direct political leadership, much less seize power themselves in the name of the proletariat. On the contrary, he made it perfectly clear that their services were ancillary and quite unessential. Whatever help might come from them, he wrote in December 1844, it is "the working classes, who always, and

54. "Zwei Reden in Elberfeld" (1845), *Werke*, 2:536–38, 550, 548; time expectation from Engels' summary of his own speech in "Communism in Germany" (1845), *MEGA* I, 4:345.

55. *Condition of the Working Class*, p. 336.

56. "Beschreibung der in neuerer Zeit entstandenen und noch bestehenden kommunistischen Ansiedlungen" (1845), *Werke*, 2:535; cf. *MEGA* I, 2:448–49; 4:340.

everywhere, must form the strength and body of the Socialist party."[57] Several months later he expressed the same thought even more directly as he gently rebuked the editor of the *Northern Star* for writing that the coming German revolution would be led by middle-class youths. On the contrary, Engels replied, "we do not count on the middle classes at all. The movement of the proletarians has developed itself with such astonishing rapidity, that in another year or two we shall be able to muster a glorious array of working Democrats and Communists— for in this country Democracy and Communism are, as far as the working classes are concerned, quite synonymous."[58] Thus Engels' alleged elitist strategy for backward Germany in 1844–1845 is a pure and simple myth. Like Marx in the same period, Engels conceived communism everywhere to be the self-emancipation of the masses. Democracy and communism were synonymous.

The Classless Society

In later years Engels, like Marx, was reluctant to discuss the specific characteristics of the future society. But in his earliest communist writings—again like Marx—he offers several revealing glimpses of the unabashedly *moral* aspirations he had for humanity before both men donned the protective armor of scientism. These glimpses are doubly valuable since they reflect Engels' own vision before it fell under the shadow of his future collaborator. Insofar as they concern the future polity, the "political" organization of the classless society, it will be useful to review them here.

Only with respect to Britain did Engels expressly discuss the transition to communism following the anticipated revolution to impose the People's Charter:

In the near future England will be a democracy.

But what kind of democracy? Not the kind produced by the French Revolution, which was the antithesis of monarchy and feudalism, but *the* democracy, the antithesis of the middle class and of property. The entire previous development demonstrates this. The middle class and property rule: the poor are without

57.   "Communism in Germany," *MEGA* I, 4:340.
58.   "The Late Butchery at Leipzig—The German Working Men's Movement" (1845), ibid., p. 477.

rights, oppressed and sweated; the Constitution disowns them, the law mistreats them; the struggle of democracy against aristocracy in England is the struggle of the poor against the rich. The democracy toward which England is moving is a *social* democracy.

But mere democracy [*blosse Demokratie*] is not capable of solving social evils. Democratic equality is a chimera, and the struggle of the poor against the rich cannot be fought out on the ground of democracy or of politics at all. Even this stage is a transition, the last purely political means still to be tried and from which simultaneously a new element must emerge, a principle going far beyond all political existence.

This is the principle of socialism.[59]

The political alterations specifically anticipated by Engels during the transition were subsequently described as follows:

As soon as public opinion is solidly behind the House of Commons —as soon as the Commons represent the will of the whole people and not merely of the middle classes—that body will become all-powerful and Queen and Lords will lose even the last trappings of outward authority. . . . An English Chartist is a republican, though he seldom, if ever, uses the term. He prefers to describe himself as a democrat, although he gives his sympathy to republican parties all over the world. Indeed he is more than a republican [*mehr als blosser Republikaner*], because the democracy that he supports is not only political.[60]

The assumption of widespread republicanism among the English lower classes may be another example of Engels' wishful thinking, but more important for our purposes is his equally unhesitating assumption of a social transformation carried out with the support of public opinion, not against it. The political alterations he envisaged here do not go beyond the abolition of the monarchy and the House of Lords. No dictatorship or necessary one-party rule is foreseen, nor any political process other than the enactment of the majority will in a fully democratized House of Commons. The second noteworthy feature of these passages is the new terminology used to distinguish socialist de-

59. "Die Lage Englands," *Werke,* 1:592.
60. *Condition of the Working Class,* p. 259.

mocracy from nonsocialist democracy. After his conversion, Engels could no longer regard a democratic republic per se as the final goal; but neither had he in any way rejected democratic principles. He now saw the democratic republic as a step toward socialism and the political form through which it would be realized, but not as the final goal in itself. "Herein lies the difference between Chartist democracy and all former brands of bourgeois political democracy."[61] These former brands can produce no more than a "chimera" of real democracy, and henceforth Engels would label them *bloss*, meaning "simple" or "mere." His terminology is analogous to the distinction Marx undertook for precisely the same reasons between "true democracy" and the "political republic."[62] Later we will find other parallel separations between "red" and "pale" republicans, "working-class" and "petty-bourgeois" democrats, etc. Thus Marx and Engels' frequent and contemptuous use of phrases like "petty-bourgeois democracy," if the adjective is understood in its *distinguishing* function, implies no contempt for democratic principles per se but only for the inadequacy of political democracy without socialism.

Engels made full use of his international travels and gift for languages to acquaint each national movement for socialism with the ideas and experiments of the others. Thus he described Continental socialism for the English press, and English and American socialism for the German. In the euphoria of his early communist years, and before he was influenced by Marx, Engels' native generosity found much to admire in the various thinkers and communities he described. From his apportionment of praise and blame we can learn a good deal about his own conception of the future polity following the transition period.

It is clear, for example, that Engels expected the state itself ultimately to disappear. His glowing description of Proudhon's ideas included the following political passage:

He gives very important remarks on government, and having proved, that every kind of government is alike objectionable, no matter whether it be democracy, aristocracy, or monarchy, that all govern by force; and that, in the best of all possible cases, the force of the majority oppresses the weakness of the minority, he comes, at last, to the conclusion: "Nous voulons l'anarchie!" What we

61. Ibid., p. 267.
62. See above, chap. 3, n. 81.

want is anarchy; the rule of nobody, the responsibility of every one to nobody but himself.[63]

Whether Engels got this idea directly from Proudhon or by way of Hess, he would henceforth conceive all government to be coercive; the essence of the state lay in its organized coercive power. Therefore even democracy as a form of state, even the rule of the working-class majority would be an evil–though a necessary and defensible one– for it would involve constraining the bourgeois minority to give up its property and power. Once class antagonisms were resolved, however, individuals would presumably internalize elementary social rules to the extent that they would obey them from conviction or habit without the need of any external force.

In several ways Engels stressed the noncoercive principle that for him lay at the heart of communist society. He praised the model communities planned by the French Icarians: "Everything possible is done to secure the liberty of the individual. Punishments are to be abolished." Fourier was lauded for having first established the "unassailable" principle that the diverse talents and inclinations of individuals fit together spontaneously to meet all social needs. "If every individual is left to his own inclination, to do and to leave what he pleases, the wants of all will be provided for, without the forcible means used by the present system of society."[64]

In his Elberfeld speeches Engels contended that capitalist society required a horde of governmental officials to restrain the competitive war of all against all, to prevent forcible crimes against society. "We lay the axe to the *root* of crime–and thereby render superfluous the greater, by far the greater, part of the present activity of executive and judicial authorities." Crimes of passion decline in any event with the progress of civilization, and "crimes against property disappear by themselves where everyone receives what he requires to satisfy his physical and spiritual needs, where social gradations and differences fall away. Criminal justice vanishes of its own accord. . . . [And civil] conflicts that are now the natural consequence of general hostility can then only be rare exceptions, and can easily be settled by arbitrators."[65] One can see this sort of thing already in practice in the American

63. "Social Reform on the Continent," *MEGA* I, 2:442.
64. Ibid., pp. 441, 437.
65. "Zwei Reden in Elberfeld," *Werke*, 2:541–42.

Shaker communities, where there is "not a single gendarme or police-man, no judge, lawyer, or soldier, no prison or penitentiary; and yet everything proceeds in orderly fashion."[66]

The disappearance of these worthies, for Engels no less than Marx, did not mean the disappearance of the polity itself, of all arrangements for making and carrying out societal decisions. What it meant for Eng-els was the disappearance of organized coercion, the essence of the old state. The noncoercive arrangements that would remain Engels preferred to call a "central administration." Its prime function would be to organize production and distribution, tasks which would be sim-ple enough, Engels thought—and he had some experience in these mat-ters—for everyone to learn:

> In communist society it will be easy to become acquainted with production as well as distribution. Since one knows how much an individual needs on the average, it is easy to calculate how much a certain number will need, and since production is then no longer in the hands of private entrepreneurs but in the hands of the com-munity and its administration, it is a small matter to *regulate pro-duction according to needs.*[67]

There can scarcely be any doubt that Engels wanted this administra-tion to be organized according to democratic principles. Virtually his only critical remarks about the different socialist schools were directed at the Owenites and the Saint-Simonians for the antidemocratic and antiegalitarian features of their projects.[68] Conversely, he gave special emphasis to the democratic organization of the Württemberg Separatist community in Zoar, Ohio. "All officials of the society are elected by

---

66. "Kommunistischen Ansiedlungen," ibid., p. 523. For a detailed examination of the sources of Engels' information about American communities, see Lewis S. Feuer, "The Alienated Americans and Their Influence on Marx and Engels," in his *Marx and the Intellectuals*, pp. 164–80.

67. "Zwei Reden in Elberfeld," *Werke*, 2:540, 539.

68. Thus he attributed the difficulties of the English Owenite community of Harmony to external control: "Since the members of the community were not the sole proprietors of the establishment, but rather were governed by the directors of the Society of Socialists which owned it, now and then there developed misunder-standings and discontent." Engels concluded with the hope that soon the commu-nity members would be able to elect their own administrators ("Kommunistischen Ansiedlungen," ibid., p. 531). On the Saint-Simonians, see *MEGA* I, 1:437.

the entire adult membership from among its own number . . . and
can be dismissed at any time by the society." A special five-man council
was also elected "to oversee the other officials and to mediate disputes."[69] This concern for the possible abuse of authority even in the
ideal society appeared again in Engels' approving résumé of a proposal
by Weitling

> to nominate all officers of this administration, and in every partic-
> ular Branch, not by a majority of the community at large, but by
> those only who have a knowledge of the particular kind of work
> the future officer has to perform; and, one of the most important
> features of the plan, that the nominators are to select the fittest
> person, by means of some kind of prize essays, without knowing
> the author of any of these essays; the names to be sealed up, and
> that paper only to be opened, which contains the name of the suc-
> cessful competitor; obviating by this all personal motives which
> could bias the minds of the electors.[70]

One may ignore the particulars of Weitling's idea, since Engels never
came back to it. What is noteworthy in these passages is Engels' evident concern about bias, personal motives, and the possible abuse of
authority in communist society. He does not assume a harmony so
perfect that no safeguards would be needed.

Although Engels was not as explicit as Marx on the point of depro-
fessionalizing public service, he seems to have had this in mind when
he touched on the possible military needs of a communist society in
his Elberfeld speeches. The professional standing army of present-day
society, he argued, was a costly extravagance that would disappear.
No military force would be required for internal peace, and certainly
not for a war of aggression. The only legitimate need might be for
defense against external attack but, instead of a professional army,
"it would be easy to give every able-bodied member of society, in
addition to his other activities, as much training in the real—not parade-
ground—art of weapons as is necessary for the defense of the country.
And imagine, Gentlemen, that the member of such a society in case
of war—which could only break out with an anticommunist nation anyway—would have a *real* fatherland, a real *hearth* to defend, that he

69.   "Kommunistischen Ansiedlungen," *Werke*, 2:529.
70.   "The 'Times' on German Communism," *MEGA* I, 2:452–53.

would fight with an enthusiasm, an endurance, and a courage, before which the machinelike discipline of a modern army would fly apart like chaff." Between 1792 and 1799 the French revolutionary forces had scattered the standing armies of Europe for the mere illusion of a fatherland.[71] There is an evident parallel to Marx in Engels' desire to be rid of the professional army along with professional gendarmes and judges, and in his assumption of several "activities" for each individual in communist society, among which might figure military and other public service.

Finally, Engels' writings of this period reveal a socialism founded upon a humanist conception of man as the creator of his own destiny. Those critics who accuse Engels of debasing Marx and portraying mankind only as a passive and determined object in a mechanistic process of historical development would do well to reread the principal output of his Manchester experience. Whatever its exaggerations and inaccuracies, *The Condition of the Working Class in England* still stands as a moving and formidable indictment of early industrial capitalism. It is based primarily on the moral argument that capitalism dehumanizes its victims, who redeem their humanity when they fight back. "The workers retain their humanity only so long as they cherish a burning fury against the property-owning classes. They become animals as soon as they submit patiently to their yoke, and try to drag out a bearable existence under it without attempting to break free." "The only way in which the worker can retain his self-respect is by fighting against the way of life imposed upon him. It is natural, therefore, that it is when he is taking action against his oppressors that the English worker is seen at his best. It is then that he appears to the fullest advantage—manly, noble and attractive."[72]

Even more explicit, and more Feuerbachian in language, was Engels' essay on Thomas Carlyle, the only contemporary English literary figure he found worthy of recommending to his German readers. Carlyle was justified, Engels allowed, in rejecting an atheism which declared "the universe, mankind, and one's own life to be a lie," but rather than turning back to traditional religion, Engels urged contemplation of

71. "Zwei Reden in Elberfeld," *Werke*, 2:542–43.
72. *Condition of the Working Class*, pp. 129, 242. On Engels' inaccuracies in this work, see Henderson and Chaloner's introduction.

the splendor of the human essence, the development of the species through history, its uncheckable progress, its constant sure victory over the unreason of the individual, its surmounting of everything apparently superhuman, its hard but successful struggle with nature until the final attainment of a free human self-consciousness, the insight of the unity of man with nature and the free spontaneous creation of a new world founded on purely human and ethical conditions of life. . . . Man has only to recognize himself, to measure all conditions of life according to himself, to judge according to his own essence, and to establish the world according to the demands of his nature in a truly human way, and he will have solved the riddle of our time. . . .

If he [Carlyle] had conceived of man as man in all his infinity, he would not have come upon the idea of dividing humanity once again into two heaps—sheep and goats, rulers and ruled, aristocrats and canaille, masters and imbeciles. He would have found the correct social role for talent not in forcible rule but in arousing and pointing the way. Talent must convince the mass of the truth of its ideas and need not bother itself further about the execution which will follow entirely of its own accord. Mankind does not make the transition through democracy in order to return again whence it came. . . . Democracy, to be sure, is only a transition, not to a new improved aristocracy, however, but to genuine human freedom.[73]

This long neglected text may also serve to disclose once again how solidly Engels' egalitarian values were implanted. He carefully renounced the temptation of Carlyle (and Blanqui) to call forth a new elite, even a temporary one, to oversee the construction of the just society. While recognizing differences of "talent," he made it crystal clear that the proper role for the more gifted minority was to arouse and point the way, but not to seize power and rule itself, not to create a "new improved aristocracy." Engels' early communist writings and activities do not betray a single feature of the totalitarian-democratic program for a vanguard party, minority revolution, one-party dictatorship, wholesale terror, and reeducation. No more than Marx was he influenced by the Blanquist tradition.

73. "Die Lage Englands," *Werke,* 1:545–46, 547–48.

Engels and Marx Join Forces—and Theories

In the wake of the last Elberfeld meeting, the police closed in. They prohibited any future gatherings and showed particular interest in the audacious advocate of communism, making it advisable for Engels to flee Germany. It was an emigration he welcomed in any event, for the tension between himself and his "fanatical and despotic old man" had reached the breaking point.[74] In April 1845 he moved to Brussels, where Marx had just taken up residence after his government-ordered expulsion from France, and the two men now permanently joined forces. As we will see, they also joined their separate theories of the state in the chief collaborative work of their Brussels period—*The German Ideology.*

The political education of Engels had involved, in a sense, a longer journey than that of Marx. He grew up in a religiously and politically conservative household instead of a liberal one, but his rebellion against this upbringing came earlier and was more categorical than that of Marx. Thus Engels rebelled as an adolescent, skipped over liberalism completely, became a revolutionary republican by nineteen at the latest, an atheist by twenty, and a communist by twenty-one. The adolescent Marx was less political and more attached to his father; he did not break with his liberal upbringing until after the latter's death, becoming a republican and atheist at twenty-four, and a revolutionary communist only at twenty-five. At the time of his conversion to communism, Engels had neither Marx's maturity of years nor his extensive university education; it is not surprising therefore that his communism rested on a slighter philosophical foundation. Most authorities have also recognized, however, that it rested on a more extensive knowledge of economics and a firsthand acquaintance with modern industrial conditions.[75] Following their separate paths, both men had arrived at essentially the same conception of what the communist polity would be like and how it would be achieved. It would come by political revolution, carried out spontaneously by the pauperized majority of the population after the acute disintegration of capitalist society had polarized the older strata. Both men allowed an ancillary educative

74. Engels to Marx, March 17, 1845, *Werke,* 27:27; see also pp. 18, 26; Mayer, *Engels,* 1:209, 217–19.

75. For the contributions of each man, see *Selected Works,* 2:311–12; Mayer, *Engels,* 1:172–92; and Franz Mehring, *Karl Marx: The Story of his Life,* trans. Edward Fitzgerald (1935; reprint ed., Ann Arbor: Michigan, 1962), pp. 94–97.

and clarifying role for intellectuals, alienated bourgeois like themselves, but neither was influenced by or attracted to the antidemocratic elitism of Blanqui.

The most remarkable difference in the early political ideas of the two men, inexplicably neglected by previous scholars, concerns their conceptions of the state. A handful of writers, to be sure, have made out the puzzling existence of two discrete and not entirely compatible theories of the state in the corpus of writings left by the masters. But only Avineri has guessed—without demonstration—that Engels sired one of them; and no one has undertaken the obvious task of reconstructing the intellectual history of the two concepts.[76]

We have now observed ourselves how Engels produced the more familiar notion we may call the "class state," whose essence is organized coercive power in the hands of the dominant social class. On the other hand, Marx originated the conception we may call the "parasite state,"[77] whose essence lies in its estrangement from the host society that it governs as a self-serving hierarchy of professional administrators. Marx first encountered the state concretely in the form of the bureaucrats with whom he crossed swords in the days of the *Rheinische Zeitung*. His theory of the state was drawn empirically from Prussian experience and gave a central place to the self-interested bureaucracy that formed the core of the Prussian state. Conversely, Engels did not work out a theory of the state until after he left Germany; his concrete encounter was English, as he joined forces with the Chartists to democratize the English Constitution. Here he found a state without a developed bureaucracy, one in which power rested in the hands of the parliament controlled by the propertied classes. The first experience led

76.   Two theories have been perceived by John Plamenatz, *German Marxism and Russian Communism* (London: Longmans, Green, 1954), pp. 135–51; Ralph Miliband, "Marx and the State," in *The Socialist Register 1965*, ed. idem and John Saville (New York: Monthly Review, 1965), pp. 278–96; Robert C. Tucker, *The Marxian Revolutionary Idea* (New York: Norton, 1969), pp. 56–66; and John Sanderson, *An Interpretation of the Political Ideas of Marx and Engels* (New York: Ferhill, 1969), pp. 55–74. Engels' paternity suggested by Shlomo Avineri, *The Social and Political Thought of Karl Marx* (Cambridge: Cambridge, 1968), p. 203, and perhaps also dimly perceived by Cornu, *Karl Marx et Friedrich Engels*, 2:296.

77.   I have taken this label from Marx's later, well-known description of the state of Louis Napoleon in France: "this appalling parasitic body, which enmeshes the body of French society like a net and chokes all its pores" (*Selected Works*, 1:301).

quite plausibly to the conception of a parasite state; the second, to the conception of a class state.

In separating the two theories conceptually, the key point is to recognize that the parasite state does not involve any notion of class rule and indeed seems incompatible with such a notion. Marx's state is its own master and not the mere instrument of some social force external to itself. In the Kreuznach *Critique*, to be sure, Marx had emphasized that the state is a product of civil society and not—as Hegel would have it—vice versa. But when he elaborated this idea, he portrayed the modern state as a product simply of the general egoism of civil society. The state was not used by the bourgeoisie to defend its private property; rather the ruler and his servants regarded the state as *their* private property. One will look in vain for any reference to a "bourgeois state" or to bourgeois domination in the Kreuznach *Critique*.[78] By the time of the Paris "Critique," Marx had identified the proletariat as the final emancipator of mankind, and he also seemed to be moving toward Engels' conception of the state. He set this final drama in a historical context of successive emancipations by different social classes, evidently the fruit of his reading in French history: "In France every class of the nation is *politically idealistic* and experiences itself first of all not as a particular class but as representing the general needs of society. The role of *emancipator* thus passes successively and dramatically to different classes of people." By conceiving itself to represent the whole of society, each successive class can "claim general supremacy" and "seize this emancipatory position and hence the political control of all spheres of society in the interest of its own."[79] These thoughts certainly constitute a step in the direction of Engels' theory, but the stress here still falls upon dramatic "emancipations" rather than extended periods of class domination based on distinctive modes of production. Moreover they are applied to France alone with Germany specifically excepted, save of course for the final proletarian emancipation.

That Marx did not move further and fully embrace Engels' theory can be seen in the remainder of his political writing in Paris. His "Critical Notes on 'The King of Prussia and Social Reform'" still treated

78.   See discussion above, in chap. 3.
79.   *Writings of the Young Marx on Philosophy and Society*, trans. and ed. Loyd Easton and Kurt H. Guddat (Garden City: Doubleday, 1967), pp. 262, 261.

the Prussian state as standing above class antagonisms, looking after its own interests.[80] His chapters in *The Holy Family* contained only brief political thoughts, mainly reiterating the themes of Kreuznach. The French Revolution was surveyed and the period of the Directorate (1795–1799) represented as the "rule" (*Regiment*) of the bourgeoisie. But then Napoleon intervened with the parasite state *par excellence:* "He still regarded the *state* as an *end in itself* and civil life only as a treasurer and his *subordinate* which must have *no will of its own.* . . . If he despotically oppressed the liberalism of bourgeois society—the political idealism of its daily practice—he showed no more pity for its essential *material* interests, trade and industry, whenever they conflicted with his political interests." After the tribulations of the Bourbon "counter-revolution," the bourgeoisie created in 1830 a "constitutional representative state" which it considered as "the *official* expression of its own *exclusive* power."[81] Marx still had not generalized the idea of class rule beyond specific moments in French history. Most significant of all is Marx's January 1845 outline for his still-delayed work on the modern state—the last fragment of his political thinking before Engels' influence became a serious factor—which organized the subject matter entirely in the Kreuznach manner, based on the contrast in modern times between the state and civil society and ending with the struggle to transcend this dichotomy. There is no hint in this outline of a class basis for the state in general.[82] The real merger of the two theories would take place in *The German Ideology.*

When Marx and Engels commenced their serious day-to-day collaboration in Brussels in 1845, curiously each man accepted the other's theory of the state without surrendering his own. The posthumously published manuscript, *The German Ideology,* represented their first truly collaborative work in the sense of being a genuine fusion of thought rather than merely an anthology of separately written essays like *The Holy Family.* And here one finds an attempt—whether conscious or not is impossible to say—to merge the two theories into a congruent whole. The long initial section on Feuerbach contains two passages

80. Ibid., especially pp. 340, 348–50.
81. *The Holy Family,* trans. R. Dixon (Moscow: Foreign Languages, 1956), pp. 166–67; cf. pp. 127–28, 149–58.
82. *Werke,* 3:537. A poor translation of this outline is appended to *The German Ideology* (Moscow: Progress, 1964), p. 655.

that pertain to the question: the first included both theories in the same paragraph without attempting to relate them, as the authors described the origin of the state in the division of labor:

> Out of this very contradiction between the interest of the individual and that of the community the latter *takes an independent form as the State, separated from the real interests of individual and community, and at the same time as an illusory communal life,* but always based on the real bonds present in every family and every tribal conglomeration, such as flesh and blood, language, division of labor on a larger scale, and other interests, *and particularly based,* as we intend to show later, *on the classes already determined by the division of labor, classes which form in any such mass of people and of which one dominates all the others.* (Italics added)[83]

Some thirty pages later Marx and Engels took up, as they had promised, the relation of the state to social classes. They began by reviewing the history of property as a social institution up to the development of modern capital, "pure private property free of all semblance of a communal institution and excluding the state from any influence on its development." They continued, "To such modern private property corresponds the modern state which has been gradually bought by property owners though taxes, has fallen entirely into their hands through the national debt, and has become completely dependent on the commercial credit they, the bourgeoisie, extend to it." Here was Engels' class state in pure form. Abruptly, however, there followed an interposition that, "through the emancipation of private property from the community, the state has become a separate entity beside and outside civil society."[84] Here stood Marx's independent parasite state in apparent contradiction to the preceding sentences.

The attempt at fusion ensued as a distinction of successive historical periods. "The independence of the state is found today only where no one section of the population can attain control over the others. This is the case particularly in Germany."[85] Somewhat later the idea was developed further:

83. *The German Ideology,* from portion translated by Easton and Guddat in *Writings,* p. 425 (cf. Moscow translation, p. 45).
84. *The German Ideology, Writings,* pp. 469–70.
85. Ibid.

During the epoch of absolute monarchy . . . the special sphere which, owing to division of labor, was responsible for the work of administration of public interests acquired an abnormal independence, which became still greater in the bureaucracy of modern times. Thus, the State built itself up into an apparently independent force, and this position, which in other countries was only transitory—a transition stage—it has maintained in Germany until the present day.[86]

In other countries, then, this independent absolutist state was presumably overthrown or "gradually bought" by the bourgeoisie and transformed into its instrument of class oppression.

The fusion was neat enough. Henceforth Engels' theory of the class state would be used for the principal periods in the Marxist historical schema—feudal, bourgeois, and anticipated proletarian—while Marx's theory of the parasite state would be used for the "abnormal" intervening period of absolutism (and later, as we will see, for Bonapartism as a similar phase between bourgeois and proletarian rule). In subsequent writings, inspection reveals that each man immediately assimilated the other's theory for the appropriate historical stages without abandoning his own.[87] *The Communist Manifesto*, of course, presented only the class state, declaring that political power is "merely the organized power of one class for oppressing another" and that "the executive of the modern State is but a committee for managing the common affairs of the whole bourgeoisie."[88] This most famous of Marx and Engels' writings did not mention the parasite state at all, which undoubtedly helps to explain why that idea has remained less widely known. By no means had it been forgotten, however, and it would reappear especially in the 1850s as a conceptual tool for understanding the Bonapartism of Napoleon III, and for understanding Oriental despotism as a kind of early sidetrack in the history of mankind.[89]

86. *The German Ideology* (Moscow translation), p. 208.
87. For Engels, see *MEGA* I, 4:494–95; 6:253–54; *Werke*, 4:44, 50. For Marx, see *The Poverty of Philosophy*, ed. C. P. Dutt and V. Chattopadhyaya (New York: International, n.d.), pp. 145–46.
88. *Selected Works*, 1:35.
89. These ideas will be taken up at an appropriate place in volume 2. Marx's ideas on Bonapartism appear especially in *The Eighteenth Brumaire of Louis Bonaparte* (1852), *Selected Works*, 1:221–311; his ideas on Oriental despotism emerge in the recent anthology of writings edited by Shlomo Avineri, *Karl Marx on Colo-*

Most important for our purposes is the critical necessity of using *both* theories simultaneously in the effort to comprehend Marx and Engels' vision of the future polity after the proletarian revolution. We must postpone detailed consideration of this subject until volume 2, when we have the full body of evidence, but in barest outline it may be noted that Marx's parasite state would be more or less immediately transcended (*aufgehoben*) as professionalism in government gave way to popular self-administration. But Engels' class state would linger for a while in the form of organized coercive power—the nonprofessional workers' militia—required to constrain the restorative efforts of the expropriated bourgeoisie. As such a need gradually disappeared, the class state of the proletariat would "wither away" or "die off" (*absterben*).[90] Only if one grasps that the word "state" has two distinct meanings can one make sense of the many confusing and contradictory things Marx and Engels have said, especially about the Paris Commune.

Their vision of the ultimate classless society likewise included *both* states in negation: it would have no institution of government separate and estranged from the people, and it would have no organized coercive force, for none would be needed. Human emancipation and full human freedom would be attained when no external or coercive power existed, and when the *res publica* became the part-time collaboration of all the people rather than the full-time profession of a special body of coercers. Marx and Engels both allowed for the nonprofessional delegation of authority but insisted on the democratic election of all such officials and appropriate safeguards for their continual accountability, particularly the right of recall. This very radical conception of democracy was linked with a still more radical aspiration (which we will also examine later) to transcend the division of labor altogether. Thus Marx and Engels' version of democracy goes as far beyond today's conventional parliamentary republic as it does beyond the professional one-party dictatorships of the present-day Communist world. However much one might like further details and specifications, and however rashly optimistic one may find their aspirations for mankind, there can be no real question of Marx and Engels' profound democratic conviction.

---

nialism and Modernization (Garden City: Doubleday, 1968), in which Avineri's introduction is particularly helpful.

90. In still another flash of insight, Avineri has noticed that only Engels used the word *"absterben,"* while Marx used *"aufheben"* or sometimes *"auflösen"* (*Social and Political Thought*, pp. 202–03).

Conviction is also the proper term in this connection because, contrary to the myth inspired by Marx and Engels themselves and perpetuated in all "orthodox" Marxist scholarship, both men came to communism out of ethical conviction, not out of scientific discovery. Engels' version of the myth asserted that, after the "discovery" of the proletariat, "communism now no longer meant the concoction, by means of the imagination, of an ideal society as perfect as possible, but insight into the nature, the conditions, and the consequent general aims of the struggle waged by the proletariat."[91] Scientific inevitability had replaced simple moral aspiration. Yet the biographies of the two men make it perfectly clear that both had passionately committed themselves to the "concoction" of an ideal society before they "discovered" that the proletariat was destined to bring it about. Marx had come to communism, as we have seen, out of deep ethical revulsion against the selfishness of modern society and the modern state. Not until Paris did he identify the proletariat as the bearer of communism, and not until considerably later could he present an even remotely convincing "scientific" explanation of the contradictions in capitalism which made the change inevitable. Similarly Engels undertook a moral commitment to communism under the influence of Moses Hess before he journeyed to England and studied firsthand the processes of capitalist development. It is precisely because all this is so that the early writings of both men are so valuable in reconstructing their underlying moral ideas. After 1845 the descending mask of scientism would increasingly obscure—though it never entirely concealed—the profound commitment to humanist and egalitarian values that remained throughout as the ethical foundation of Classical Marxism.

91. "History of the Communist League," *Selected Works,* 2:312.

⟨5⟩

Strategy I:
Proletarian Majority Revolution

WE HAVE OBSERVED how Marx and Engels, in their initial communist writings, envisaged the attainment of communism by means of a spontaneous revolution, carried out by the masses themselves as the result of their own self-maturation, without any need for elite assistance or totalitarian-democratic devices. Of course, it would be rash and unhistorical to assume that this pristine early vision remained absolutely unchanged during the rest of their long and eventful lives. Between 1845 and 1850, as Marx and Engels gained more experience with the diversity of radical strategies and as they were caught up in the revolutionary events and disappointments of that period, their own ideas on revolutionary strategy also developed. The simplicity of their early vision gave way to a more differentiated strategy, or set of strategies, which incorporated a number of new ingredients. Among these new ingredients were four that have about them an odor of totalitarianism, to wit: (1) the creation of the Communist League, which bore the earmarks of a classic vanguard party; (2) a policy of "permanent revolution" for less-developed countries that seemingly would eventuate in minority rule; (3) repeated calls for red terror against the enemies of the revolution; and finally in 1850 (4) an official united front with the Blanquists together with an open demand for a dictatorship of the proletariat.

On the face of it, Marx and Engels would appear to have embraced the central principles of totalitarian democracy. It is for this reason that many authorities have decided the two men were Blanquists, or at least strongly influenced by Blanquism, in the period before 1850,

[132]

or in any event during 1850. Stanley Moore, who has made the most systematic attempt to classify Marx and Engels' strategies in their historical evolution, concludes that during the entire early period to 1850, "their revolutionary tactics were primarily influenced by the tradition of Babeuf, Buonarroti, and Blanqui." Just as reformist Social Democrats would draw their inspiration from the later period of the masters' lives, so Lenin and the Communists of the twentieth century drew their inspiration from the blood-and-thunder revolutionism and elitism of the 1848 period.[1]

In the remainder of this volume we will concern ourselves in one context or another with the four issues listed above—the seemingly Blanquist innovations—as we reconstruct the evolution and differentiation of Marx and Engels' revolutionary strategy from 1845 to 1850. The approach used will combine the narrative biographies begun in the preceding chapters—so essential to providing historical context— with a topical analysis of the issues themselves. In this chapter we will move in time from Marx and Engels' 1845 Brussels collaboration to their reappearance in Germany just after the outbreak of the 1848 revolution; topically we will examine the articulation of their basic vision of proletarian majority revolution, together with the first major complication—the creation of the Communist League.

The Democratic Revolution

The importance of historical context may be immediately appreciated if one thinks of the assumption evident in the works of so many philistine critics of Marx that advocacy of violent revolution is undemocratic per se. Taking for granted the existence of democratic institutions, of a legal road to power, these critics suppose that all proponents of revolution must necessarily be elitists who lack the patience to win majority support for their views or who have no faith in the masses at all. Whatever their claim to speak for the people, such revolutionists construct vanguard parties or guerrilla armies and justify minority revolution, political terror, and totalitarian dictatorship. A *genuine* popular movement would have no need of these expedients; it could simply vote itself into power. Hence, in the philistine view, if Marx and Engels advocated violent revolution, they could not have been democrats at all.

1. Stanley Moore, *Three Tactics: The Background in Marx* (New York: Monthly Review, 1963), p. 22; see other authorities cited above, chap. 1, n. 35.

If one drops the initial unhistorical assumption, the entire frame of reference changes. Marx and Engels lived most of their lives in the predemocratic era of European history, under conditions that made it quite impossible for a working-class movement, even one embracing a sizable majority, to achieve power legally. Prior to the 1870s all the governments they encountered—save the transitory revolutionary governments of 1848—were despotisms or oligarchies of one variety or another. It is important to understand that Marx and Engels did not associate bourgeois rule with democracy ("bourgeois democracy") in this epoch, at least in Europe. Rather, they generally sought to *contrast* "working class democracy and middle class liberalism."[2] In 1847, Engels characterized liberal bourgeois rule as follows:

In European lands it has taken the form of constitutional monarchy. In these constitutional monarchies the voters are only those who possess a certain amount of capital; that is to say, the voters are only the bourgeois. These bourgeois voters elect the deputies, and the bourgeois deputies, having the right to refuse [to vote] taxes, elect a bourgeois government.[3]

Not so greatly exaggerated was Marx's famous *Manifesto* description of such a regime as "but a committee for managing the common affairs of the whole bourgeoisie."[4] Very likely he had in mind the current French July Monarchy, where only the richest two hundred thousand people, or approximately 3 percent of the adult male population, met the astronomical property qualification for voting, and where peaceful efforts to broaden the franchise met with governmental indifference or repression.

While some European democrats renounced violent revolution even under these circumstances, most did not, and precisely *because* they were democrats. Thus Marx and Engels' advocacy of popular revolution to overthrow the repressive oligarchies of wealth did not set them apart from the principles of democracy but, on the contrary, placed

---

2. "Address of the German Democratic Communists of Brussels to Mr. Feargus O'Connor" (1846), *MEGA* I, 6:25.
3. "Principles of Communism," in *Birth of the Communist Manifesto*, ed. Dirk J. Struik (New York: International, 1971), p. 175.
4. *Selected Works*, 1:35.

them squarely in the mainstream of the mid-nineteenth-century demo-cratic tradition. Only much later in their lives, in the period after 1870, did the two men have a chance to see universal suffrage combined with parliamentary government in Western Europe, and they re-sponded to these innovations in a manner one would expect of prin-cipled democrats, as we will see in volume 2.

The Blanquist conception of revolution involved a series of grim deductions from the central postulate concerning the political imma-turity of the masses. Among these was the necessity of postponing democratic elections until after a temporary educational dictatorship. In diametric opposition to such views, as we have witnessed, Marx and Engels foresaw a prior maturation of the populace and a revolution whose *first* act would be the establishment of universal suffrage and democratic institutions. Thus in his Kreuznach *Critique*, Marx had per-ceived "unrestricted suffrage" as the instrument that would achieve "the dissolution of this political state, but also the dissolution of civil society," and he returned to the same theme in his 1845 outline for the still-unfinished project, when he identified universal suffrage as "the Struggle for the *Aufhebung* of the State and Civil Society." Engels had developed parallel views in close association with the English Chartists: their democratic demands, he believed, could only be at-tained by revolutionary action, but their victory would establish a "so-cial democracy" and a House of Commons that would incorporate "the will of the whole people and not merely of the middle classes."[5]

Whatever else changed during the period of our present concern, it is safe to assert that Marx and Engels retained this dramatically un-Blanquist faith in universal suffrage. Nowhere did they call for dic-tatorship or suggest the postponement of elections. On the contrary, they positively overflowed with ebullient confidence that the masses were flocking to the communist standards and would be ready for self-government when the revolutionary moment arrived. "Democracy, nowadays that is communism," jubilated Engels at the end of 1845:

Democracy has become a proletarian principle, a principle of the masses. The masses may be more or less clear about this single cor-rect understanding of democracy but they all possess at least the

5. See above, chap. 3, nn. 77 and 98; and chap. 4, n. 60.

obscure feeling that democracy means equal social rights. The democratic masses can safely be counted in the reckoning of communist forces.[6]

In a similar mood in 1847, Marx asserted that Frederick William IV erred in supposing that the common people of Prussia were his loyal supporters: "The real people, the proletariat, the small peasants and populace . . . would first and foremost force His Majesty to grant a constitution with universal suffrage, freedom of association, freedom of the press and other unpleasant things." And can it be imagined that the proletariat, "which more and more is joining with the communist party, will not know how to use freedom of the press and freedom of association"?[7]

In July 1846, Marx, Engels, and their new Brussels comrade, Philippe Gigot, signing themselves "the German Democratic Communists of Brussels," publicly congratulated the English Chartist leader, Feargus O'Connor, on winning a seat in Parliament and went on to speak of " 'a democratic reconstruction of the Constitution on the basis of the People's Charter' by which the working class will become the ruling class in England."[8] In October 1846, while disseminating his own tactical ideas among the German artisans in Paris, Engels defined the proper road to communism as a "forcible democratic revolution."[9] A month later, in an article chastising the French democrat Alphonse de Lamartine for proposing *indirect* elections, Engels appealed to the legendary Constitution of 1793: "The principles, indeed, of social and political regeneration have been found fifty years ago. Universal suffrage, direct election, paid representation—these are the essential conditions of political sovereignty. Equality, liberty, fraternity—these are the principles which ought to rule in all social institutions."[10]

The central contrast with Blanquist strategy appeared again most interestingly in the successive drafts of the *Communist Manifesto*. The earliest version, dating from June 1847 and only recently rediscovered,

6. "Das Fest der Nationen in London," *Werke,* 2:613.
7. "Der Kommunismus des 'Rheinischen Beobachters,' " ibid., 4:202, 194.
8. "Address of the German Democratic Communists," *MEGA* I, 6:25.
9. Engels to the Communist Correspondence Committee in Brussels, October 23, 1846, *Selected Correspondence: 1846–1895,* trans. Dona Torr (New York: International, 1942), p. 2 (translation modified—RNH; see original German, *Werke,* 27:61).
10. "The Manifesto of M. de Lamartine," *MEGA* I, 6:340.

is in Engels' hand and is laid out in catechism form. Asking about the transition to communism, the draft sets forth the following reply: "The first basic condition for the introduction of a community of goods is the political liberation of the proletariat by means of a democratic state constitution [*demokratische Staatsverfassung*]."[11] In his October draft Engels spelled it out even more clearly, as he queried about the course of the impending revolution: "In the first place it will draw up a *democratic constitution* and by means of this establish directly or indirectly the political rule of the proletariat."[12] Both drafts stress democracy not only as the *first* step of the revolution but also in the *literal* sense of democratic political institutions. Thus they clarify Marx's vaguer language when he expressed the same thought in the final version: "The first step in the revolution by the working class, is to raise the proletariat to the position of ruling class, to win the battle of democracy [*Erkämpfung der Demokratie*]."[13] It is a sorrow that Marx did not retain Engels' sharper formulation, for winning the battle of democracy might be interpreted as mere metaphor, compatible with initial dictatorial institutions. But the context of successive drafts, combined with Marx's pronouncements elsewhere, make his underlying meaning clear. Many years later Engels would recall that "the *Communist Manifesto* had already proclaimed the winning of universal suffrage, of democracy, as one of the first and most important tasks of the militant proletariat."[14] Interestingly, Engels remembered more than the *Manifesto* had actually said, but doubtless what it was intended to mean.

As a final text we may scrutinize the often-neglected "Demands of the Communist Party in Germany," drawn up by Marx and Engels on behalf of the Communist League in late March 1848, when news of the revolution then sweeping across their native land made the formulation of specific demands a matter of urgency. The very first of these demands read: "The whole of Germany shall be declared a unitary and indivisible republic." The second was: "Every German, having

11. "Draft of the Communist Confession of Faith," *Birth*, p. 167 (translation modified—RNH; see original German in *Der Bund der Kommunisten: Dokumente und Materialien*, vol. 1, *1836–1849*, ed. Institut für Marxismus-Leninismus [Berlin: Dietz, 1970], 1:474 [hereafter cited as *Bund Dokumente*]). This early draft of the *Manifesto* will be discussed in more detail in chapter 6.

12. "Principles of Communism," *Birth*, p. 180.

13. *Selected Works*, 1:50.

14. "Introduction" (1895) to *Class Struggles in France, Selected Works*, 1:119.

attained the age of 21, . . . shall be a voter and be eligible for public office." The remaining political demands included salaries for representatives and a uniform salary for all ranks of the civil service, universal arming of the people, and a complete separation of church and state, with all churches henceforth to be financed only from the voluntary contributions of their own congregations.[15] Neither here nor anywhere else is there any call to postpone elections and institute a temporary dictatorship. There can scarcely be any doubt that Marx and Engels' faith in democracy survived at least until the onset of the 1848 revolutions.

In part that faith undoubtedly rested on the still-hypothetical assumption that the masses, given the opportunity, would vote the way Marx and Engels expected. And their confidence of mass support for communism rested in turn upon the prediction of the acute disintegration of capitalist society. Between 1845 and 1848 both men devoted the bulk of their study time to economics, or political economy, as it was then called.[16] They gave particular attention to English developments, for therein Europe's future could be perceived, and English developments only seemed to reconfirm their apocalyptic vision. By the time they wrote the *Manifesto* in late 1847, Marx and Engels were able to pinpoint, in exact and succinct phrases, what appeared to them the reasons for the radical social polarization that spelled acute disintegration.

First and foremost, the *Manifesto* asserted, when free competition is viewed as a process over time, the inevitable result is a concentration of ownership, with the less efficient enterprises going bankrupt or bought up by the more efficient. This law of concentration applies not only to industry but also to agriculture and distributive enterprises:

> The lower strata of the middle class—the small tradespeople, shopkeepers, and retired tradespeople generally, the handicraftsmen and peasants—all these sink gradually into the proletariat, partly because their diminutive capital does not suffice for the scale on which Modern Industry is carried on, and is swamped in competition with the large capitalist, partly because their specialized skill

15. *Birth*, pp. 190–92 (translation modified—RNH; see original German, *Werke*, 5:3–5).
16. For evidence of what they were reading, see *MEGA* I, 4:503–15; also Maximilien Rubel, "Les Cahiers de lecture de Karl Marx," *International Review of Social History* 2 (1957):392–420.

is rendered worthless by new methods of production. Thus the proletariat is recruited from all classes of the population.

The bulk of the old petty bourgeoisie—shopkeepers and artisans—are fated, like their peasant cousins, to be dispossessed and declassed by the forces of concentration, and "will completely disappear as an independent section of modern society." Even within the wealthy modern bourgeoisie, one can perceive that "entire sections of the ruling class are, by the advance of industry, precipitated into the proletariat."[17] Second, the fate of the handicraftsmen is shared by virtually all skilled workmen, whose "specialized skill is rendered worthless by new methods of production." As the continuing technological revolution makes old skills obsolete, it requires in their stead only vast agglomerations of unskilled machine tenders. "Owing to the extensive use of machinery and to division of labor, the work of the proletarian has lost all individual character. . . . He becomes an appendage of the machine, and it is only the most simple, most monotonous, and most easily acquired knack, that is required of him." Here Marx and Engels seem to have had in mind especially the fate of the handloom weavers who were displaced during the 1830s and 1840s by the dissemination of the power loom and by the unskilled labor of women and children. Thus workers generally tend to be "more and more equalized, in proportion as machinery obliterates all distinctions of labor."[18] At higher skill levels, the *Manifesto* did not predict complete technological unemployment but did suggest another sort of declassing, as members of the old "free professions" lose their independent status and are put on salary. "The bourgeoisie has stripped of its halo every occupation hitherto honored and looked up to with reverent awe. It has converted the physician, the lawyer, the priest, the poet, the man of science, into its paid wage-laborers."[19] Thus the manifold gradations of preindustrial society give way to a great gray mass of almost undifferentiated wage earners. This tendency of capitalism to replace skilled by unskilled labor is scarcely mentioned by Marx's followers nowadays—for obvious reasons—yet it clearly belonged to the original prognosis.

17. *Selected Works*, 1:39–40, 53, 41. Marx's economic ideas of this period were most systematically expressed in some lectures he gave in December 1847, later published under the title "Wage Labor and Capital," ibid., pp. 74–97.
18. *Manifesto, ibid.*, pp. 39–40.
19. Ibid., p. 35.

Third, capitalism operates under a law of wages which insures that the worker's remuneration will fluctuate around a level just sufficient to provide "the means of subsistence that he requires for his maintenance, and for the propagation of his race."[20] Local variations of supply and demand may permit wages to rise temporarily, but no permanent improvement can occur, not because of biological population pressure as Malthus and Ricardo had presumed, but because the constant proletarization described above will insure a superabundance of competing hands during the expected life span of the capitalist system. Similarly, trade unionism might bring local and temporary gains, not to mention important nonmaterial advantages, but as Engels wrote in 1845, "all these efforts on the part of trade unionists cannot change the economic law by which wages are fixed."[21] Later in their lives the two men would come to modify this stringent view, but prior to 1848 they repeatedly asserted the law of wages in its most literal form.[22] Indeed, they asserted more, namely that the standard of life constituting "subsistence" was itself declining in an absolute way: "Spirits have taken the place of beer, cotton that of wool and linen, and potatoes that of bread. Thus, as means are constantly being found for the maintenance of labor on cheaper and more wretched food, the minimum of wages is constantly sinking."[23] At the same time, "the burden of toil also increases, whether by prolongation of the working hours, by increase of the work exacted in a given time or by increased speed of the machinery, etc."[24] All these hardships blend together in a process of "increasing misery" (*Verelendung*) for the masses.

Finally, these various tendencies are all abetted and accelerated by the recurring crises—the cycle of boom and bust—to which the capitalist system is subject. A depression is an "epidemic of overproduction," inescapable under the existing order because "the conditions of bourgeois society are too narrow to comprise the wealth created by them." The masses who live at subsistence cannot buy back all they produce;

20. Ibid.

21. *The Condition of the Working Class in England,* trans. and ed. W. O. Henderson and W. H. Chaloner (Stanford: Stanford, 1968), p. 246.

22. See, e.g., *Werke,* 4:60, 82–83; *Selected Works,* 1:96. Also see Thomas Sowell, "Marx's 'Increasing Misery' Doctrine," *American Economic Review* 50 (1960):110–20.

23. Marx, *The Poverty of Philosophy,* ed. C. P. Dutt and V. Chattopadhyaya (New York: International, n.d.), pp. 205–06; cf. *Werke,* 6:543–44.

24. *Manifesto, Selected Works,* 1:39.

while vast human needs remain unmet, market demand periodically dries up. Such crises are overcome, to be sure, but only "by paving the way for more extensive and more destructive crises, and by diminishing the means whereby crises are prevented."[25] Each successive depression pushes under additional segments of the middle class and pauperizes larger elements of the working class, multiplying the reserve army of the unemployed.

Putting these trends together and projecting into the future, Engels had pinpointed the net social result in his *Condition of the Working Class:*

Commerical crises would continue and they would become ever more serious and ever more disastrous as industry expanded and the number of workers continued to grow. The working classes— augmented by the continual ruin of the lower middle classes and by the ever-increasing concentration of capital in fewer and fewer hands—would expand in geometric proportion, until the whole nation, except for a few millionaires, would be composed of workers.[26]

Most likely the revolution would come before this ultimate extreme had been reached; in a rare commitment to a specific date Engels in 1845 prophesied the winning of the Charter by 1846–1847 and the end of capitalism by 1852–1853. In a contemporaneous letter to Harney he was even more sanguine: the Charter before the end of 1846 and socialism by 1849. Although subsequent predictions were worded more cautiously and not tied to exact dates, they were scarcely less apocalyptic: Engels greeted the depression of 1847 in a way that leaves little doubt he believed it to be the death knell of capitalism.[27] These time projections are particularly important in establishing the literalness with which both men used the term "geometric" to describe the growth of the proletariat. Thus they could speak in the *Manifesto* as if their

25.   Ibid., p. 38. Marx's thinking on the causes of the business cycle also became far more elaborate in later years, without changing the basic prognosis; see Ernest Mandel, *The Formation of the Economic Thought of Karl Marx,* trans. Brian Pearce (New York: Monthly Review, 1971), pp. 67–78.

26.   P. 334.

27.   Predictions referred to in letter from Harney to Engels, March 30, 1846, *Bund Dokumente,* 1:294; "Die Handelskrise in England" (1847), *Werke,* 4:325–27.

anticipation were already reality: "The proletarian movement is the self-conscious, independent movement of the immense majority in the interest of the immense majority." Thus they could make the equation that "to win the battle of democracy" would be the same thing as "to raise the proletariat to the position of ruling class." Or Engels' version could declare that a "democratic constitution" would produce the "rule of the proletariat." Thus Engels could assert even more plainly in a contemporaneous article that "a necessary consequence of democracy in all civilized countries is the political rule of the proletariat."[28] While Marx and Engels drew these conclusions as plausible extrapolations of existing trends, it is clear that their extensive reading in political economy between 1845 and 1848 only confirmed what they wanted to see. They did indeed mistake the birth pangs of industrialism for the death throes of capitalism. What is important for our purposes, however, is that Marx and Engels' political strategy in the late 1840s rested upon these expectations—however fanciful—of a geometrically multiplying proletariat and an impending economic cataclysm.

While the two men repeatedly predicted violent revolution during this period, they never made any systematic attempt to justify it morally. No doubt they considered the violence of the starving millions against a repressive oligarchy of wealth to be self-evidently justified, and to plead such a case before a hypocritical bourgeoisie whose own strictures against violence were of such recent vintage—it would all be too demeaning. In any event, by this period the two masters had donned their "scientific" armor and were beginning to speak of the proletarian revolution as a kind of social "earthquake" (Marx), a "pure phenomenon of nature" (Engels).[29] One may reasonably ask a seismologist for the probable timing and severity of the next tremor, but it would be absurd to ask him for a moral justification. Among their contemporary revolutionists, however, the Italian republican, Giuseppe Mazzini, felt no such reluctance to tackle the moral issue and formu-

28. *Selected Works*, 1:42, 50; "Principles of Communism," *Birth*, p. 180; "Die Kommunisten und Karl Heinzen" (1847), *Werke*, 4:317. I have translated *"zivilisierten Länder"* literally, although from the context it is clear that Engels meant to include only those countries that were—in today's terminology—"advanced" or "developed."

29. These phrases come from the early 1850s: Marx, "Revelations Concerning the Communist Trial in Cologne" (1853), *The Cologne Communist Trial*, trans. and ed. Rodney Livingstone (New York: International, 1971), p. 64; Engels to Marx, February 13, 1851, *Werke*, 27:190.

lated what is perhaps the classic nineteenth-century justification of democratic revolution:

> Whenever a way remains open to you in a just cause for the employment of moral force, never have a recourse to violence; but when every moral force is seared up, . . . when ideas are put down by bayonets,—then, reckon with yourself: if, though convinced justice is on your side, you are still in a weak minority, fold your arms and bear witness to your faith in prison or on the scaffold—you have no right to embroil your country in a hopeless civil war: but if you form the majority, if your feeling prove to be the feeling of millions, rouse yourselves, and beat down the oppression by force.[30]

Thus Mazzini's moral revolution involved three criteria: a just cause, majority support, and no other means open. We may bear this standard in mind as we attempt to reconstruct Marx and Engels' implicit moral position from the fragmentary comments they left behind.

We have already noted that Marx became an advocate of violence rather later than Engels. He had begun by "struggling for freedom step by step within constitutional restraints," and only when his newspaper was nonetheless silenced did he turn to the criticism of weapons.[31] In *The Holy Family*, Marx reaffirmed the conclusion that "ideas cannot *carry anything out* at all. In order to carry out ideas men are needed who can dispose of a certain practical force."[32] In a contemporaneous article attacking Ruge, Marx declared that "without revolution, however, socialism cannot come about. It requires this political act in so far as it requires destruction and dissolution."[33] A passage in *The German Ideology*, probably from Marx's pen, amplified this theme and introduced a second one: "A revolution is necessary, therefore, not only because the ruling class cannot be overthrown in any other way but also because the class overthrowing it can succeed only

---

30. Giuseppe Mazzini, *Selected Writings*, ed. N. Gangulee (London: Drummond, 1945), pp. 70–71.

31. See above, chap. 2, n. 88.

32. Trans. R. Dixon (Moscow: Foreign Languages, 1956), p. 160.

33. "Critical Notes on 'The King of Prussia and Social Reform' " (1844), *Writings of the Young Marx on Philosophy and Society*, trans. Loyd D. Easton and Kurt H. Guddat (Garden City: Doubleday, 1967), p. 357. Cited hereafter as *Writings*.

by revolution in getting rid of all the traditional muck and become capable of establishing society anew."[34] These three meager texts contain all Marx was willing to say, and they "justify" revolution only in the quasi-scientific sense of showing why "history" requires it. With the Great French Revolution as his model, Marx stressed the necessity of clearing away old institutions and, even more, old habits of thought. Revolutionary activity would be the school of practical experience where the masses would complete the process of their self-education. Marx noted only in passing that nonrevolutionary means were lacking, a theme Engels would take up at greater length.

In his October draft of the *Manifesto*, Engels faced the moral issues more squarely. "Will it be possible to bring about the abolition of private property by peaceful methods?" he asked himself. His answer follows in full:

This is greatly to be desired, and communists would be the last persons in the world to stand in the way of a peaceful solution. Communists know only too well the futility and, indeed, the harmfulness of conspiratorial methods. They know only too well that revolutions are not made deliberately and arbitrarily, but that everywhere and at all times revolutions have been the necessary outcome of circumstances quite independent of the will or the guidance of particular parties and whole classes. But they also perceive that the development of the proletariat in nearly all civilized countries is violently suppressed, and that in this way opponents of communism are working full force to promote a revolution. Should the oppressed proletariat at long last thus be driven into a revolution, then we communists will rally to the cause of the workers and be just as prompt to act as we are now to speak.[35]

Far from embracing Blanquist ideas, Engels here categorically rejected them. Communists expected to join in a revolution undertaken by the masses, but not to make one themselves "deliberately and arbitrarily" through "conspiratorial methods." Moreover, Engels even expressed a moral preference for peaceful means altogether; it was only the oppression by the other side that made them impossible. This might be regarded as a meaningless academic concession under the circum-

34. Ibid., p. 431.
35. "Principles of Communism," *Birth*, pp. 179–80.

stances, except for Engels' brief allusion to the United States, "where the democratic constitution has been established," and where "the communists must make common cause with the party that is utilizing this constitution in the interests of the proletariat and against the bourgeoisie, that is, with the agrarian National Reformers."[36] Thus Engels did not call for revolution against a democratic constitution but only for utilization of the legal rights and freedoms it provided in the interest of the workers. There was no guarantee, of course, that the bourgeoisie would peacefully submit to being ousted legally through a majority vote, but democratic institutions opened up at least the chance.

In Europe that chance did not exist: even the workers' efforts to join together peaceably and express their views were met with forcible suppression by the existing governments. Citing this "oppression kept up by force," Engels noted in one article that the French communists plan on "meeting force by force, and having, at present, no other means, why should they hesitate a moment to apply this?"[37] He seemed to agree with the general moral principle he ascribed to the left-wing Chartists in 1845: "The oppressed has the right to use all means against his oppressor that the oppressor employs against him."[38] During the 1840s this axiom justified violence; turned around, however, it might later justify restraint. If the oppressor, for example, refrained from certain extremes of violence, was not the proletariat obliged to follow suit? We will see in the later writings of Marx, and especially Engels, the recurring idea of such a gentlemen's agreement respecting mutual restraints or "rules" in the class struggle.

Even within the context of the 1840s, however, Engels emphasized the obligation of principled communists, not to *promote* violence in the coming revolution, but to *reduce* it to the unavoidable minimum. In the conclusion to his *Condition of the Working Class* he drew a frightening picture of seething class hatreds, but then added:

As the workers absorb more and more Socialist and Communist elements so the revolution will be less bloody, less violent and less vengeful. In principle . . . Communism rises above the enmity of classes, for it is a movement that embraces all humanity and not

36.   Ibid., p. 188.
37.   "Progress of Social Reform on the Continent" (1843), *MEGA* I, 2:440.
38.   "Das Fest der Nationen in London," *Werke*, 2:615. Perhaps Marx was implying the same thing ibid., 4:199–200.

merely the working classes. Of course no Communist proposes to avenge himself against any particular individuals who are members of the bourgeoisie. . . . English Socialism (i.e. Communism) undoubtedly accepts the doctrine that the individual bourgeois is not, as an individual, responsible for the acts of the middle classes as a whole. . . . Should the proletariat become more Socialist in character its opposition to the middle classes will be less unbridled and less savage. . . . It may be expected that by the time the rising comes the English working classes will understand basic social problems sufficiently clearly for the more brutal elements of the revolution to be eventually overcome—with the help of the appearance of the Communist Party. In this way the tragedy of a 9th of Thermidor may be avoided.[39]

So the role of the party was to hose down the revolutionary fury of the masses! Yet Engels unmistakably identified higher consciousness with greater restraint. Excessive violence should be avoided if only to prevent an excessive reaction, a "9th of Thermidor." Perhaps all this was just for public consumption, but nowhere in his private correspondence did Engels suggest the contrary. In any event, deeds are a better test of sincerity than words, and we will soon have an opportunity to observe whether Marx and Engels, in a revolutionary situation where real lives were at stake, acted to promote violence or confine it to the unavoidable minimum.

Thus, whatever their reluctance to discuss the ethics of political violence, it seems clear that the revolution Marx and Engels had in mind would easily meet Mazzini's three criteria: the proletarian revolution would be a just cause, supported by the majority, where no other means were open. A final note might be added in the interest of historical perspective. The models of revolution before Marx and Engels at this time were the July Revolution of 1830 and of course the Great French Revolution, with its various stages of development. In these prototypes, new governmental authorities were established essentially by street demonstrations in which the violence was neither massive nor of long duration, and was more often spontaneous than organized. Indeed, in nineteenth-century Europe, three days of violent street demonstrations seemed almost a mutually agreed upon standard—as the events

39. Pp. 335–36.

of 1848 would shortly reconfirm—for toppling cabinets and even thrones. While the communist revolution awaited by Marx and Engels would likely meet greater resistance, there is no evidence as yet that they reckoned on organized and sustained violence over a period of years. The Communist revolutions of the twentieth century, which have established new governments through the planned seizure of power by a paramilitary vanguard, or through the organization of vast guerrilla armies in a protracted civil war—these give a thoroughly misleading impression if read back into Marx and Engels' early Victorian expectations.

Marx and Engels' initial vision of spontaneous majority revolution did not change appreciably between 1843 and 1848, and indeed it remained the ideal model throughout their lives. In the philosophical language they had now abandoned, it constituted the *Wesen*, or rational essence, of the communist revolution, however inadequately actual events might align themselves to that blueprint. All subsequent strategies and tactical expedients were but variations on this classical theme.

Dual Origins of the Communist League

The first of these tactical expedients, the Communist League, must be examined in some detail because it enjoys such a wide reputation as a Blanquist conspiratorial group, or as a Leninist-style vanguard party, or both. In fact it was neither of these things, and an adequate history of the league has yet to be written.[40] Such a history cannot be undertaken here, of course, but we will attempt in this chapter

40. The most adequate general account appears in Ernst Schraepler, *Handwerkerbünde und Arbeitervereine, 1830–53* (Berlin: deGruyter, 1972), which deals with a broader subject. The standard Communist history of the last years is Karl Obermann, *Zur Geschichte des Bundes der Kommunisten 1849–52* (Berlin: Dietz, 1955); a more recent, parallel non-Communist treatment can be found in Shlomo Na'aman, "Zur Geschichte des Bundes der Kommunisten in Deutschland in der zweiten Phase seines Bestehens," *Archiv für Sozialgeschichte* 5 (1965):5–82. Concerning the historical roots of the league, there is a corresponding parallel between the Communist account, Werner Kowalsky, *Vorgeschichte und Entstehung des Bundes der Gerechten* (Berlin: Rütten und Loening, 1962); and the non-Communist, Wolfgang Schieder, *Anfänge der deutschen Arbeiterbewegung: Die Auslandsvereine im Jahrzehnt nach der Julirevolution von 1830* (Stuttgart: Klett, 1963).

to draw attention to the distinctly bifurcated roots of the league, as well as to Marx and Engels' conception of its proper function in the period up to its June 1848 dissolution. In chapter 7 we will return to their London association with the revived league in 1849–1852, and finally in chapter 8 we will examine its internal structure and functioning and draw some overall conclusions.

To view the Communist League as a conspiracy or vanguard party under Marx's direction is doubly misconceived: it exaggerates Marx's influence over the majority of league members and underestimates the importance of a social and ideological division that plagued the group from beginning to end. The organization that came into being in 1847 was essentially an uneasy amalgamation of the artisan League of the Just and Marx's circle of intellectual communists then centered in Brussels, and these two elements in the league—radical artisans and renegade intellectuals—never wholly reconciled their differences of background and outlook.[41] By probing into this hitherto neglected tension, it is possible to clear up almost all of what is ideologically problematic in the league's history, including certain paradoxical utterances of Marx and Engels in the two most influential pronouncements they drew up for the organization—the *Communist Manifesto* and the *Circular* of March 1850.

The Marx circle was drawn together during the Brussels period. After Marx and Engels had worked out a common position in 1845 through their intensive reading and collaborative writing, they began to consider how best they might, as Engels put it, "win over the European and in the first place the German proletariat to our conviction."[42] Since both men by now had wide contacts with socialist groups and thinkers in several countries, as well as an unusual command of European languages, they decided to set up a kind of international office in Brussels to link up by correspondence the socialist movements of the various nations. Thus was born early in 1846 the Communist Correspondence Committee of Brussels—in retrospect a modest pilot antici-

41. This tension was first stressed by Boris Nicolaievsky in "Toward a History of 'The Communist League' 1847–1852," *International Review of Social History* 1 (1956):234–52; and idem, "Who Is Distorting History?" *Proceedings of the American Philosophical Society* 105 (1961):209–36. It has now received appropriate emphasis in the writings of Schraepler and Na'aman cited in note 40, but is not yet really acknowledged in Communist historiography.

42. "On the History of the Communist League" (1885), *Selected Works*, 2:312.

pation of the International of the 1860s. The three active Brussels correspondents, Marx, Engels, and Philippe Gigot, stated their purpose in a letter inviting Proudhon to contribute:

The main object of our correspondence will, however, be to keep German socialists in contact with French and English socialists. . . . In this way differences of opinion will come to light; ideas will be exchanged and impartial criticism arrived at. This will be a step taken by the socialist movement on its literary side towards ridding itself of the limitations of nationality. For at the moment of action it is certainly of great interest to everyone to be informed of the state of affairs abroad as well as at home.[43]

Doubtless the Brussels trio hoped these contacts would in the course of time develop into firmer organizational ties. Proudhon himself declined the invitation to participate, but the committee soon established relations with his countryman Louis Blanc, with the Chartist leader Julian Harney, and with the leaders of the League of the Just in Paris and London.[44]

For our immediate purpose it is more important to observe that Marx and Engels also succeeded in drawing into the activities of this committee a number of German intellectuals who would eventually form the core of the Marx circle in the Communist League. In Brussels itself the group included Marx's brother-in-law, Edgar von Westphalen, Engels' old poetic exemplar, Ferdinand Freiligrath, together with Ferdinand Wolff, Georg Weerth, Sebastian Seiler, and Louis Heilberg. It eventually expanded to include Roland Daniels, Heinrich Bürgers, and Karl d'Ester in Cologne, Joseph Weydemeyer in Westphalia, Georg Weber in Kiel, Wilhelm Wolff in Silesia, and Ernst Dronke and to some extent Hermann Ewerbeck in the Paris branch of the League of the Just. Among these men only Wilhelm Wolff could boast humble origins; all had had bourgeois educations and all pursued—or had pur-

43. English translation, accompanied by French original, in Boris Nicolaievsky and Otto Maenchen-Helfen, *Karl Marx: Man and Fighter*, trans. Gwenda David and Eric Mosbacher (Philadelphia: Lippincott, 1936), pp. 115–16; cf. parallel appeal to G. A. Köttgen, *Werke*, 4:20–21.
44. On the development of the committee, see Schraepler, *Handwerkerbünde*, pp. 146–80; Karl Obermann, "Zur Geschichte des Kommunistischen Korrespondenzkomitees im Jahre 1846, insbesondere im Rheinland und in Westfalen," *Beiträge zur Geschichte der deutschen Arbeiterbewegung* 4 (1962):116–43.

sued—bourgeois occupations. Some had collaborated with Marx in the *Rheinische Zeitung;* most would collaborate in the *Neue Rheinische Zeitung.* Whatever the diversity of their original socialist ideas, they all came more and more to accept not only Marx's intellectual leadership but also his guidance in tactical questions. All of these things distinguish them as a group from the artisans who made up the old League of the Just.[45]

In contrast to the committee, the league of course was a formal membership organization, established for ten years and possessing several hundred members, with its main centers in Switzerland, Paris, and London and underground branches in several German localities. For our purposes it is crucial to understand that journeyman artisans, not factory workers, filled out the ranks of the league. Although no full membership records exist, substantial data from police reports show an overwhelmingly artisan composition. One police informer in the early 1840s, for example, named seventy-two members of the Paris group, of whom two were bourgeois intellectuals and seventy were artisans—fifty-three tailors, ten joiners, four shoemakers, and the remaining miscellaneous. A parallel report for Berlin in 1846 named the entire membership of thirty-two—all artisans and again, not a single factory worker.[46] As a protest group, the league expressed the death cry of German handicraft production, not the birth cry of the industrial proletariat.

The active role of artisans in the revolutionary disturbances of 1848 is now increasingly recognized. Far more than industrial workers, artisans took part in violent demonstrations and riots, volunteered in revolutionary militias, organized themselves into protest groups, met in congresses, issued petitions, and generally manifested acute discontent. Nor is the reason hard to uncover: in the first half of the nineteenth century substantial segments of this class—most notably tailors, weavers, shoemakers, and joiners—were displaced or severely threatened by technological and commercial-managerial advances. Rapid population growth and preindustrial economic expansion had swollen their numbers, exacerbating the disaster that set in following the elimination

45.   The best way to follow the development of the Marx circle is in the correspondence of the relevant parties, reproduced in *Bund Dokumente,* 1:317–465. Also see Schraepler, *Handwerkerbünde,* pp. 151–52, 163–68; Nicolaievsky, "Who Is Distorting History?" p. 225; and Na'aman, "Zur Geschichte des Bundes," pp. 8–13. Heinrich Bürgers would break with Marx in June 1848.

46.   These two police reports reproduced in *Bund Dokumente,* 1:116–22, 258–72, along with a shorter one for the London branch, pp. 238–40. Also see Schraepler, *Handwerkerbünde,* p. 53.

in the early nineteenth century of most internal and external tariff barriers and of most guild restrictions on freedom of occupation and enterprise. Artisans now had to face the withering competition of large-scale commercial producers, first from England and then increasingly from within Germany itself. While master craftsmen were hard hit, it seems clear that journeymen suffered the most. In numbers, the ratio of the latter to the former climbed steadily and must have brought home to most journeymen what fate had in store for them—not the traditional mastership as the reward for their labors, but the bleak and uncertain destiny of an unskilled factory hand.[47]

Artisans' responses to their plight were varied, but generally drastic. Some chose emigration, while others wrecked machines and called for the revival of guild powers to thwart or confine commercial-industrial development. But some perceived in the doom of their own class the end of traditional society generally; in an apocalyptic social radicalism they were able to find hope in the midst of despair. This response seemed most frequent among those journeymen who migrated to Paris during their wanderyears and learned of socialist aspirations from their French counterparts. In the sizable community of German artisans resident in Paris, the ideas of Blanqui, Cabet, and Proudhon, and later of Weitling, Hess, and the True Socialists, all blended confusedly together in a doctrinal potpourri.[48]

One desire seemed to be shared nonetheless by all varieties of artisan communism and lay at the root of its continuing tension with Marxism. Reflecting the acute need of the artisans to find some emergency exit from the hellfire of the industrial revolution, the desire expressed itself positively as the wish to establish communism *immediately*, without going through any lengthy preparatory or intermediate stages of development. Whether the emergency exit appeared in the guise of a world-transforming Blanquist dictatorship, an Icarian model community, a Proudhonist self-help association, or one of the German variations of these schemes, all offered the prospect of quick escape from

47. See Theodore S. Hamerow, *Restoration, Revolution, Reaction: Economics and Politics in Germany, 1815–1871* (Princeton: Princeton, 1958); and especially P. H. Noyes, *Organization and Revolution: Working-Class Associations in the German Revolution of 1848–1849* (Princeton: Princeton, 1966).

48. Schieder, *Anfänge der deutschen Arbeiterbewegung;* Schraepler, *Handwerkerbünde,* pp. 29–126. Also see a perceptive article on the French counterparts of these artisans, Christopher H. Johnson, "Communism and the Working Class before Marx: The Icarian Experience," *American Historical Review* 76 (1971):642–89, especially pp. 653–61.

the unbearable present. The artisans' desire expressed itself negatively as a special animosity toward the agent of their plight—the bourgeoisie, along with its commercial values and program of liberal reforms. They understandably had little immediate sympathy for the idea of allying with the bourgeoisie against the old regime in Germany, of helping their archenemy to power and enduring his rule, however temporary. Indeed, they had every reason to be hostile to industrial development per se, and if most communist artisans did not oppose it actively, neither did they conceive it to be in any way a prerequisite for the good society. They instinctively turned to varieties of socialism that, in addition to offering quick escape, radiated a special animus against the bourgeoisie and were either hostile or indifferent to modernization itself. Concerning these twin issues—the proximity of communism and the need for bourgeois-sponsored economic development—the artisans and the Marx circle would never fully understand each other. Marx and Engels, as we will see, insisted that the road to communism lay only through the purgatory of bourgeois rule and economic modernization. There simply was no emergency exit.[49]

We must postpone further consideration of the second issue until chapter 6, but artisan impatience for immediate communism properly concerns us here in its totalitarian-democratic manifestation—namely, in the pronounced Blanquist and Weitlingesque character of the early League of the Just. Among the German artisans who wandered to Paris in the mid-1830s were the journeyman tailor Wilhelm Weitling, the compositor Karl Schapper, and the shoemaker Heinrich Bauer. Although they were influenced there by several strains of French socialist thought, they designed the League of the Just in 1836 mainly after the then standard model for radical groups—the secret conspiratorial society in the tradition of Babeuf, the Carbonari, Buonarroti, and most recently, Blanqui. Engels exaggerated only slightly when he later described the early league as "actually not much more than the German branch of the French secret societies, especially the Société des saisons led by Blanqui and Barbès, with which a close connection was maintained."[50]

49.   On artisan desires, see particularly Noyes, *Organization and Revolution*, pp. 38–46; Johnson, "The Icarian Experience," pp. 669–72 and passim. Marx and Engels' position on these issues will be treated in chapter 6.

50.   "History of the Communist League," *Selected Works*, 2:307; see Schraepler, *Handwerkerbünde*, pp. 40–64.

Even at the outset, however, there were non-Blanquist features. The league came into existence in rebellion against the utterly dictatorial organizational structure of a still older and more purely conspiratorial group—the League of the Despised. As we will see later, in chapter 8, the Just incorporated several democratic innovations into their own organizational statute. And Wolfgang Schieder has recently presented new evidence from police records challenging the common belief that league members took an active part in Blanqui's classic 1839 insurrection.[51] Whether they did or not, their leaders found it expedient to leave France in the police crackdown that followed the abortive rising. Schapper and Bauer moved to London, as we have already observed, while Weitling went to Switzerland, leaving others to take their places in the Paris league. With this diaspora and the evident bankruptcy of the conspiratorial technique, specifically Blanquist ideas began to recede in league circles, inaugurating a process of development away from totalitarian-democratic precepts that eventually would make the organization attractive to Marx and Engels.

In Switzerland, Weitling organized vigorously on behalf of the league and developed further as an independent thinker whose half-religious socialism owed as much to the dissident Abbé Lamennais as to Blanqui. He continued to believe in force, however, and his somewhat muddled concept of revolution, if less conspiratorial, still included the central totalitarian-democratic ingredients of minority uprising and educational dictatorship. His principal writing of this period, *Garantien der Harmonie und Freiheit* (1842), as quoted earlier, contained a blatantly apocalyptic vision: "I see a new Messiah coming with the sword, to carry into effect the teachings of the first. By his courage he will be placed at the head of the revolutionary army, and with its help he will crumble the decayed structure of the old order." Weitling had little patience with elections: "There must be no searching around for a leader, and no fussing about the election of a leader. Whoever is the first to step forward, whoever takes the lead, whoever shows the bravest endurance and places his life in the balance with all the others, he will be leader."[52] There can be little doubt whom Weitling had in mind for this role. During his Swiss period the ex-tailor also worked out his most notorious tactical idea—to recruit an

---

51. *Anfänge der deutschen Arbeiterbewegung*, pp. 54–55.
52. As quoted in Schraepler, *Handwerkerbünde*, p. 72, and above, chap. 1, n. 29.

army of common thieves to act as shock troops in the assault on private property (a sound Fourierist teaching this—each to his own inclination!). Though Weitling's ideas now carried considerable weight throughout the league, no one seemed very happy about this *Diebstahlstheorie*.[53] And when he was arrested and imprisoned by Swiss authorities in mid-1843, Weitling's influence in league circles began to recede further.

Meanwhile in the Paris branch, the exiled physician Hermann Ewerbeck had taken over the reins of leadership, and he personally espoused Cabet's Icarian communism, which renounced force as a matter of principle. During the early forties the ideas of Hess and Proudhon likewise percolated through the Paris group, eventually blending in a brew called True Socialism, whose principal exponent was Karl Grün. All these were varieties of nonpolitical socialism, which renounced not only violence but every political means. The schemes of Weitling and Blanqui faded more and more into the background.[54] Such was the internal situation when Engels moved temporarily to Paris in August 1846 as a kind of emissary of the Brussels Communist Correspondence Committee to see what could be done in the Paris league. There ensued a long series of meetings, discussions, and disputes as Engels fought a two-front polemical battle against the lingering influence of Weitling and Blanqui on the one hand, and the tender-minded socialism of Proudhon, Hess, and Grün on the other. With characteristic precision he defined his own strategy in opposition to both: "to recognize no means of carrying out these [communist] objects other than a forcible democratic revolution."[55] Forcible revolution was anathema to the unpolitical socialists, while the emphasis on its democratic character was aimed at the remaining followers of Weitling. The formula may stand as a classic statement of Marx and Engels' position between tender-minded sentimentalists and tough-minded elitists—they were themselves tough-minded democrats.

As it turned out, the struggle against Weitling's supporters was scarcely more than a mopping-up operation, in which Engels found a willing ally in Ewerbeck.[56] The verbal wrestling with the nonpolitical

53. Schraepler, *Handwerkerbünde*, pp. 78–84.
54. Ibid., pp. 82–84, 186–89.
55. Engels to the Communist Correspondence Committee in Brussels, October 23, 1846, *Selected Correspondence*, p. 2 (translation modified—RNH; see original German, *Werke*, 27:61).
56. Engels' activities in Paris are best followed in his letters to Marx and the

socialists proved a longer and more arduous task, but by the end of October 1846 Engels could report that the formula cited above had triumphed when, after five evenings of marathon debate, the surviving discussants—perhaps more exhausted than convinced—voted thirteen to two in its favor.[57] The Paris league, having repudiated its Blanquist origins, now seemed to accept the Marxist strategy for achieving socialism.

It was in London, however, that the really decisive transformation took place. The headquarters of the league were transferred there in 1846, and the artisan troika of Schapper, Bauer, and Moll became the international leaders of the organization. After their exile to England the three men moved rapidly away from their conspiratorial past. They established ties with the left-wing Chartist Julian Harney and began to perceive in the recruiting success of Chartism the possibilities of mass propaganda and mass organization for a quite different kind of revolution.[58] This movement away from totalitarian-democratic precepts is nowhere better evidenced than in the reception given to Weitling when he came to London in 1845 following his imprisonment in Switzerland.

Most authorities agree that prison upset Weitling's already precarious mental balance, undermining the coherence of his thought and exaggerating his personal messianic impulses.[59] He arrived in London, evidently expecting to resume his old position as chief spokesman for the league, only to find that the organization had outgrown his putschist ideas. In a series of internal discussions (a partial transcript of which has fortunately survived), Weitling argued that propaganda aimed at the next generation was too slow a means: "I believe everyone is ripe for communism, even criminals. . . . Mankind is necessarily always ripe for communism or never will be. . . . Mere propaganda helps not at all." In a later session he continued: "If we call for communism by revolutionary means, then we must have a *dictator* who rules over everything. The *dictator* should not have more than anyone else; we

Brussels Committee, in *Werke,* 27:32–117; on Weitling's supporters see especially pp. 32, 36, 40–41.

   57. Ibid., pp. 60–62; see also p. 98; Herwig Förder, *Marx und Engels am Vorabend der Revolution: Die Ausarbeitung der politischen Richtlinien für die deutschen Kommunisten (1846–1848)* (Berlin: Akademie, 1960), pp. 42–52.

   58. Schraepler, *Handwerkerbünde,* pp. 117–26.

   59. See, for example, Carl Wittke, *The Utopian Communist: A Biography of Wilhelm Weitling* (Baton Rouge: Louisiana State, 1950), pp. 85–91.

can only allow him this position if he works for the general good." Weitling ended his participation in these sessions with a panegyric to Napoleon, whom he seemed to regard as a model dictator and whose communist successor he evidently hoped to become.[60]

Weitling found only one vocal supporter in these discussions—oddly the True Socialist, Hermann Kriege. Among those who spoke against his ideas in successive meetings, Karl Schapper was the most articulate: "If mankind were ripe for communism, it would have been instituted already. . . . We must not force anybody. The great mass must be convinced of the truth [of communism]; then the rest will follow of its own accord." "We must enlighten the people first; otherwise the external destruction will be followed by self-destruction. From history we can see how everything would always end in anarchy and despotism." Weitling's communism "would be just like soldiers in a barracks, and I fear we would thereby get caught in serious conflicts. . . . Everyone must have his full freedom, without impinging on the personal freedom of others." Schapper concluded that "in Weitling's system there is no guarantee of freedom."[61] Thus did the Londoners repudiate their past in favor of a more democratic conception of the road to socialism.

Feeling humiliated in London, Weitling journeyed to Brussels early in 1846, where he fared no better with the Marx circle. In a famous showdown before the Correspondence Committee on March 30, Marx denounced Weitling's call for an immediate—and therefore a minority—communist revolution in Germany, as well as his penchant for wild emotional appeals instead of systematic education. According to Paul Annenkov's eyewitness account, Marx declared that "it was nothing but deceit to rouse the people without giving them a solid basis for their action. By awakening the fantastic hopes just spoken of, Marx continued, one will never save those who suffer, but one will certainly lead them to their ruin." Here Marx was clearly condemning premature violence and putschism. When Weitling defended his own activity and spoke deprecatingly of mere "literary criticism," Marx smashed the table with his fist and shouted, "Ignorance never did anyone any good!"[62] The meeting was over. When Weitling found himself alone

60. "Diskussionen im Kommunistischen Arbeiterbildungsverein in London: 18. Februar 1845–14. Januar 1846," *Bund Dokumente*, 1:218, 231, 237–38.
61. Ibid., pp. 218, 223, 235, 236.
62. Annenkov's account is reproduced in English in Hans Mühlestein, "Marx

again a few weeks later in the committee's vote to censure Hermann Kreige's True Socialist propaganda, he left Brussels; rejected everywhere and feeling persecuted, he soon emigrated to America.[63]

With Weitling gone and his influence in the league apparently eradicated, the organization that both Marx and Engels had expressly refused to join in 1842 and 1844 now became more attractive to them. Conversely, the artisans were now looking for someone to replace Weitling as a literary spokesman for the group, who could articulate their desires before the larger public. In June 1846 the leaders of the league agreed to enter regular correspondence with the Brussels committee, thus establishing the first formal tie between the two organizations whose merger would create the Communist League. In August Engels moved to Paris on the committee mission described above, forging a second link. Still, a good deal of lingering suspicion and bias had to be overcome before any union could be effected. From previous rumors, Schapper confided to Marx in his June 1846 letter, "we had the idea that you wanted to establish some kind of aristocracy of intellectuals [*Gelehrten-Aristokratie*] and rule over the people from your new godly thrones."[64] Though apparently reassured on this point, Schapper continued to stress the social cleavage in subsequent letters, mincing no words about the "arrogance of intellectuals . . . who don't know how to gain the workers' friendship, who repel them instead of attracting them. You *Brussels proletarians* still possess this damned intellectual arrogance to a high degree."[65] Many artisans in London believed that the Brussels group excluded real workers on principle, an unfounded rumor apparently circulated by Weitling.[66] On the other side, one can see particularly in Engels' reports from Paris a sharp impatience with the "appallingly ignorant" artisans of the league, "*Straubinger*," Engels called them, a term perhaps translatable as "journeymen tramps," traditionally artisans who wandered permanently, taking casual labor without ever becoming masters. "I could never have imagined," he wrote in one pessimistic letter, "such sleepy-headedness

and the Utopian Wilhelm Weitling," *Science and Society* 12 (1948): 127–29; cf. Weitling's own account reproduced ibid., pp. 124–25, and Engels' later recollection, *Werke*, 37:117–18.

63. *Werke*, 4:3; Wittke, *The Utopian Communist*, pp. 117–20.
64. Letter of June 6, 1846, *Bund Dokumente*, 1:347.
65. Letter of July 17, 1846, ibid., p. 380.
66. See ibid., pp. 249, 347.

and petty rivalry among these fellows. Weitlingism and Proudhonism are really the most complete expression of the life circumstances of these jackasses and there is nothing to be done about it."[67] Here was the underlying social basis of the tension between artisans and intellectuals that would color the entire history of the Communist League.

For the time being, however, this tension was on the wane, as both sides perceived a broad area of agreement on political issues. Most of all, Marx and Engels had to be convinced that the league had rejected its conspiratorial past. To this end Schapper reported to the Brussels group in his June 1846 epistle:

As concerns conspiratorial plans, we have long gotten over such stupidities; so far conspiracies have helped no one but our enemies, and we are pleased to see that you have the same opinion. We are certainly convinced that it cannot and will not get started without a thorough revolution, but to want to bring about this revolution by conspiracies and stupid proclamations, à la Weitl[ing], is ridiculous. When the revolution of the spirit now beginning has reached its end, the physical one will come by itself, if those in power do not submit. Our task is to enlighten the people and make propaganda for common ownership; you want the same: therefore let us shake hands and work with united strength for a better future.[68]

Schapper now seemed to share exactly Marx and Engels' conception of revolution. Within league ranks themselves, Schapper and his colleagues sent a circular in February 1847 that ended by warning the members sharply against "putsches, conspiracies, weapons purchases, and similar nonsense."[69]

The remaining steps toward merger can best be followed in Engels' own words in his 1885 essay, "On the History of the Communist League":

In the spring of 1847 Moll visited Marx in Brussels and immediately afterwards me in Paris, and invited us repeatedly, in the

67.   Letter of October 23, 1846, *Werke*, 27:66; letter of January 14, 1848, ibid., p. 111; see also pp. 42, 48, 58, 68, 77, 97.
68.   *Bund Dokumente*, 1:347–48.
69.   "Ansprache der Volkshalle des Bundes der Gerechten an den Bund," ibid., p. 457.

name of his comrades, to enter the League. He reported that they were as much convinced of the general correctness of our mode of outlook as of the necessity of freeing the League from the old conspiratorial traditions and forms. Should we enter, we would be given an opportunity of expounding our critical Communism before a congress of the League in a manifesto, which would then be published as the manifesto of the League. . . .

What we previously objected to in this League was now relinquished as erroneous by the representatives of the League themselves; we were even invited to cooperate in the work of reorganization. Could we say no? Certainly not. Therefore, we entered the League; Marx founded a League community in Brussels from among our close friends there [that is, the Correspondence Committee, the Marx circle], while I attended the three Paris communities.

In the summer of 1847, the first League Congress took place in London. . . . Whatever remained of the old mystical names dating back to the conspiratorial period was now abolished. . . . The organization was thoroughly democratic, with elective and always removable boards. This alone barred all hankering after conspiracy, which requires dictatorship, and the League was converted— for ordinary peace times at least—into a pure propaganda society.[70]

Marx likewise recalled in 1877 that "the first entrance of Engels and myself into the secret Communist League took place only on the condition that everything conducive to authoritarian superstitions [*Autoritätsaberglauben*] be removed from the statutes."[71] The rewritten statutes did indeed provide genuinely democratic forms, as we will see in chapter 8: Marx and Engels received no special powers themselves, and in fact the artisans retained full control of the top leadership. What is noteworthy in Marx and Engels' recollections is the common stress they gave to their precondition for membership—the rejection of totalitarian-democratic precepts.

While waiting for their new manifesto to be put together, the artisans in the London branch hammered out among themselves a pre-

70. *Selected Works*, 2:314–15; also see surviving documents related to the merger, reproduced in *Bund Dokumente*, 1:447–630.
71. Marx to Wilhelm Blos, November 10, 1877, *Werke*, 34:308; cf. Marx's 1860 account of the same events in *Herr Vogt*, ibid., 14:438–41.

liminary statement of negative principles, to declare what sort of communists they were *not*. This statement, almost certainly drafted by Schapper, appeared in the first (and only) issue of their new publication, *Die Kommunistische Zeitschrift*, in September 1847. On questions of strategy and underlying political values it matched Marx and Engels' ideas perfectly:

> We are not among those communists who preach everlasting peace here and now while our opponents in every land are girding their loins for battle. We know only too well that, with the possible exceptions of Britain and the United States, we shall not be able to enter our better world unless we have previously and by the exercise of force won our political rights. . . . [But] we are not conspirators who have determined to begin the revolution on such and such a day or who are plotting the assassination of princes.

The statement went on to urge that the workers of all countries unite, "—openly where the laws permit, for our activities need not fear the light of day—secretly where the arbitrary will of tyrants imposes secrecy upon us." Their first main object should be "to establish a democratic State wherein each party would be able by word or in writing to win a majority over to its ideas." The statement elaborated:

> We are not among those communists who are out to destroy personal liberty, who wish to turn the world into one huge barrack or into a gigantic workhouse. There certainly are some communists who, with an easy conscience, refuse to countenance personal liberty and would like to shuffle it out of the world because they consider that it is a hindrance to complete harmony. But we have no desire to exchange freedom for equality. We are convinced . . . that in no social order will personal freedom be so assured as in a society based upon communal ownership.[72]

The rejection of conspiratorial organization and putschism, the expectation of mass revolution, the call for a democratic state as the first— not last—achievement of that revolution, and the desire not to sacrifice

---

72.   English translation included in Marx and Engels, *The Communist Manifesto*, ed. D. Ryazanoff (New York: International, 1930), pp. 291–92, along with Ryazanoff's valuable notes; German version in *Bund Dokumente*, 1:503–08.

liberty in the name of equality, all attest to the thoroughgoing repudiation of totalitarian-democratic ideas among old league members.

To argue that Marx and Engels became Blanquists by joining the league is thus utterly wrong-headed. The merger became possible, not because Marx and Engels had now embraced the principles of conspiratorial revolution but because the conspiratorial revolutionaries had now embraced the principles of Marxism. Whatever its historical antecedents, the Communist League created in 1847 was an expressly anti-Blanquist organization.

The League as a Vanguard Party

If not a Blanquist organization, perhaps the Communist League was nonetheless a vanguard party in the Leninist sense. Certainly it was regarded by Lenin—and by Communist writers ever since—as the very archetype of Bolshevik organizational principles. Yet there is good reason to be skeptical of this claim, as we will see.

Like Blanqui, Lenin wanted the enlightened few to organize themselves as a vanguard and maintain a certain separation from the mass; Lenin never expected the vanguard, however, to make the revolution by itself, without mass support. Only a revolution that had such support and actively involved the masses could possibly succeed. In this sense Lenin was quite correct in his repeated insistence that he was not a Blanquist. He did believe, on the other hand, that the vanguard had to perform certain essential tasks without which the revolution also could not possibly succeed. These tasks included, first, bringing "revolutionary consciousness" to the masses, who on their own would develop at best only a "trade-union consciousness"; and second, preparing and executing the seizure of power itself, not arbitrarily as the Blanquists seemed to have done, but at precisely the "correct" historical moment when mass discontent reached a peak of violent turmoil that would insure the successful destruction of the old regime as well as popular support for the new one. Without this crucial guidance and coordination by the vanguard, the violent turmoil of the masses would be dissipated uselessly, like steam not enclosed in an engine. Both these critical and demanding tasks required that the vanguard recruit selectively, limiting its size *by preference,* so that only full-time, technically competent, and utterly dedicated revolutionaries would be included. Like Blanqui, Lenin insisted that these professionals carry on day-to-day party activity under military discipline in an organized chain of command from the top down. At the same time, however, he advocated a more democratic apparatus for decision-making at periodic intervals, for example, at party congresses, and in the election of leaders. He also demanded secrecy in party matters, although his various remarks on this subject leave it unclear whether he regarded secrecy as an unfortunate, externally imposed necessity or something to be preferred in any event.[73]

In addition to Communist writers, a great many non-Communists have argued that Marx and Engels favored a vanguard party of this sort, at least prior to 1850; other authorities have contended that the masters' contradictory pronouncements come down squarely on both sides of the issue.[74] To get a clear answer it is necessary above all to pose questions in a sufficiently discriminating manner. It is not enough, for instance, to ask whether the league comprised the enlightened few as against the mass, since in the nature of things parties generally have small beginnings and since no socialist party (save perhaps the uniquely structured British Labor Party) has ever succeeded

73. Lenin's organizational ideas are expounded mainly in his two pamphlets, *What is to be Done* (1902), and *One Step Forward, Two Steps Back* (1904). For intelligent commentaries from diverse viewpoints, see Rosa Luxemburg, "Organizational Questions of the Russian Social Democracy" (1904), in *Rosa Luxemburg Speaks,* ed. Mary-Alice Waters (New York: Pathfinder, 1970), pp. 112–30, a sympathetic but devasting critique by a radical Marxist; Alfred G. Mayer, *Leninism* (Cambridge: Harvard, 1957), pp. 19–103, a liberal and scholarly critique; and Ernest Mandel, "The Leninist Theory of Organization," *International Socialist Review* 31 (1970):27–50, a recent Leninist-Trotskyist vindication of considerable merit.

74. Shlomo Avineri stresses the key role Marx expected intellectuals to play in "Marx and the Intellectuals," *Journal of the History of Ideas* 28 (1967):269–78; while Bertram D. Wolfe emphasizes contradictory pronouncements in *Marxism: One Hundred Years in the Life of a Doctrine* (New York: Dial, 1965), especially chapter 11. There is no really definitive treatment of Marx and Engels' views on the nature of the party. Perhaps the best general overview is Monty Johnstone, "Marx and Engels and the Concept of the Party," in *The Socialist Register 1967,* ed. Ralph Miliband and John Saville (New York: Monthly Review, 1967), pp. 121–58. Also see Maximilien Rubel, "Remarques sur le concept du parti prolétarien chez Marx," *Revue Française de Sociologie* 2 (1961):165–76; Kostas Papaioannou, "Le parti totalitaire," *Le Contrat social* 10 (1966):161–70, 236–45; and Horst Bartel and Walter Schmidt, "Zur Entwicklung der Auffassungen von Marx und Engels über die proletarische Partei," in *Marxismus und Deutsche Arbeiterbewegung,* ed. Deutsche Akademie der Wissenschaften (Berlin: Dietz, 1970), pp. 7–101. I have not had access to Ullrich Haufschild, "Partei und Klasse bei Marx und Engels" (Ph.D. diss., University of Frankfurt, 1965).

in mustering more than a minority of the working class into its *member-ship*. All such parties are vanguards in that sense. The discriminating question is whether Marx and Engels wanted the league to remain small *by preference*, confining its numbers to revolutionaries by profession, instead of seeking maximum growth in the open-ended recruitment of all like-minded people. Similarly, it is not enough to ask whether the assigned mission of the league was to raise the consciousness of the masses, since virtually all parties are assigned this mission; one must rather ask whether Marx and Engels conceived the educational role of the vanguard to be *essential* or simply *ancillary* to the mass development of revolutionary consciousness. The pertinent question is: Would the masses develop such consciousness even if the vanguard did not exist? Finally, it is not enough to ask whether the original vanguard would take part in the revolution generally; we must learn whether Marx and Engels assigned it, as a separate organization, the specific task of preparing and carrying out the seizure of power (with or without mass support) in a deliberate, planned coup. The issue of secrecy is undoubtedly important as well, but it is not adequately discriminating since various kinds of parties have adopted secrecy under conditions of persecution and since Lenin was unclear concerning its positive virtues. There are also questions about internal party organization that we will consider later, in chapter 8.

Most casual writers on this topic have contented themselves with the familiar assertions of the *Manifesto*, where Communists are declared to be "practically, the most advanced and resolute section of the working-class parties of every country, that section which pushes forward all others," and "theoretically, they have over the great mass of the proletariat the advantage of clearly understanding the line of march, the conditions, and the ultimate general results of the proletarian movement." These formulations answer none of the more precise questions posed above. It is noteworthy, however, that they occur in a passage which emphasizes the identity of Communists with, not their separation from, the rest of the "proletarian movement." Thus the Communists appear above not even as a party but only as a "section" (*Teil*) of a larger party or cluster of parties, and further: "The Communists do not form a separate party opposed to other working-class parties. They have no interests separate and apart from those of the proletariat as a whole."[75] Although the *Manifesto* does in fact occasion-

75. *Selected Works*, 1:44.

ally refer to the league as a "party," as in the title itself and when contrasting it to other parties, Marx and Engels most often reserve that word for the proletarian movement as a whole, as when they define the immediate aim of the Communists to be "the formation of the proletariat into a class," a goal they had described a few pages earlier as the "organization of the proletariat into a class, and consequently into a political party."[76] Thus the ultimate and ideal party would encompass the entire proletariat, not simply its most advanced and resolute section. The league was pictured as but one element in the many-sided efforts of the workers to organize themselves in such a party.

To move beyond the limited answers available in the *Manifesto*, we may begin with the new statutes of the league, which set down among other things the conditions for membership. The new rules were not drawn up by Marx and Engels personally, but were hammered out at the two 1847 congresses in an effort to revise the old statutes of the League of the Just. Some of the criteria for membership were simply reformulated from the older document: "professing of communism," "revolutionary energy and zeal for propaganda," and "submission to the resolutions of the League." Judged overall, however, the new rules clearly relaxed what was expected of members, most notably by dropping the great oath of secrecy with its accompanying threat of death for betrayal. They also defined more carefully the grounds for expulsion and created a fairer legal procedure for deciding expulsion cases.[77] The only revision known to have been proposed by Marx and Engels themselves permitted league members henceforth to belong to other political organizations as well, so long as these were not "anti-communist"—clearly also a relaxation.[78] There is not a word about professional competence, full-time activity, or the need to limit membership as a deliberate policy. Indeed, once legal conditions made it possible after March 1848, the league began vigorous efforts to found new branches and recruit new members all over Germany. Among the surviving documents of these months, one will search in vain for any suggestion to restrict membership or confine it to professional revolutionaries. League members generally also involved themselves in the

76. Ibid., pp. 44, 41.
77. Compare "Statuten des Bundes der Gerechten" (1836), *Bund Dokumente,* 1:92–98, with "Statuten des Bundes der Kommunisten" (1847), ibid., pp. 626–30. These statutes will be analyzed in more detail in chapter 8.
78. See ibid., pp. 626, 539.

broader, locally established workers' societies then being formed, in keeping with their mission not to form a separate party but to act as the "most advanced and resolute section" of the wider movement.[79]
   Our second question inquired whether this vanguard was conceived to play an essential, or merely ancillary, role in the mass development of revolutionary consciousness. As we have already seen, the initial communist writings of both Marx and Engels suggest the latter alternative, and the writings of our present period simply reaffirm and develop the same view.
   In his *Condition of the Working Class* (1845), Engels devoted considerable space to the step-by-step historical development of consciousness among the English workers. In discouragingly un-Leninist fashion he treated trade unionism as a spur rather than a drag, and then followed the workers' own efforts through peaceable Chartism to the acceptance of violent means ("physical force") and a form of socialism ("not a very highly developed one") before mentioning any vanguard whatsoever.[80] At this point he touched on the only vanguard in sight, the middle-class Owenite Socialists, whose efforts among the proletariat till now he found more a drag than a spur—"their practical achievements have been negligible." He did allow, however, that if the Owenites "come down to earth" they might help develop the still unsophisticated socialist conceptions of the workers, and in fact he foresaw such a trend to "unite Socialism and Chartism, and give an English dress to the principles of French Communism." But the only specific task he assigned to an eventual "Communist Party" was the one reviewed earlier in this chapter—to restrain the vindictive fury of the masses during the revolution itself.[81]
   The Holy Family (1845) pictured consciousness as something arising entirely out of the life situation of the masses themselves:

The proletariat can and must free itself. . . . Not in vain does it go through the stern but steeling school of *labor*. The question is not

---

79. Surviving documents reproduced ibid., pp. 759–92; also see Walter Schmidt, "Der Bund der Kommunisten und die Versuche einer Zentralisierung der deutschen Arbeitervereine im April und Mai 1848," *Zeitschrift für Geschichtswissenschaft* 9 (1961):577–614.
80. *Condition of the Working Class*, pp. 137–39, 241–70; quoted phrases from p. 267.
81. Ibid., pp. 268–70; see n. 39 above.

what this or that proletarian, or even the whole of the proletariat at the moment *considers* as its aim. The question is *what the proletariat is*, and what, consequent on that *being*, it will be compelled to do. Its aim and historical action is irrevocably and obviously demonstrated in its own life situation as well as in the whole organization of bourgeois society today. There is no need to dwell here upon the fact that a large part of the English and French proletariat is already *conscious* of its historic task and is constantly working to develop that consciousness into complete clarity.[82]

Even "complete clarity" now would seem to come without the assistance of a vanguard, which is nowhere mentioned.

In *The Poverty of Philosophy* (1847), Marx lauded trade-union activities particularly, in opposition to Proudhon, as "ramparts for the workers in their struggles with the owners." Not only do such associations defend the workers' material interests, but perhaps even more importantly they stop the former competition of the workers among themselves, ending the egoism of the individual worker in favor of the mutuality of the common cause—a crucial step in the formation of class consciousness. And, far from restricting the workers' horizons, associations lead naturally forward to political action as the proletariat "becomes united, and constitutes itself as a class for itself. The interests it defends become class interests. But the struggle of class against class is a political struggle." The Chartists are cited as a model. Again, no vanguard required. To be sure, Marx had commented earlier on the role of intellectuals: "Just as the *economists* are the scientific representatives of the bourgeois class, so the *Socialists* and *Communists* are the theoreticians of the proletarian class." He referred mainly to utopian thinkers who appear when "the proletariat is not yet sufficiently developed to constitute itself as a class." Once the latter process commences, such intellectuals "have only to take note of what is happening before their eyes and to become the mouthpiece of this."[83] Mouthpieces are doubtless useful, but scarcely indispensable to the real-life growth of the proletarian movement—no more than political economists were indispensable to the real-life development of capitalism.

The German Ideology (1846), written not long after Marx's extensive study of the French Revolution, gave special emphasis to revolutionary

82.   Pp. 52–53; cf. pp. 73, 113, 181.
83.   Pp. 144–45, 106.

activity itself as providing the final levels of illumination, a capstone of practical political education. The book spoke of the emergence of a class which "constitutes the majority of all members of society, and from it arises a consciousness of the necessity of fundamental revolution, communist consciousness, which may of course arise also in the other classes perceiving the situation of this class." There follows the passage quoted earlier in part:

> For the production of this communist consciousness on a mass scale and for the success of the cause itself, the alteration of men on a mass scale is required. This can only take place in a practical movement, in a *revolution*. A revolution is necessary, therefore, not only because the *ruling* class cannot be overthrown in any other way but also because the class *overthrowing* it can succeed only by revolution in getting rid of all the traditional muck and become capable of establishing society anew.[84]

The same theme reappears momentarily in a later chapter: "In revolutionary activity the changing of oneself coincides with the changing of circumstances."[85] Communist writers have insisted quite properly that Marx did not see consciousness arising "automatically" or "spontaneously" out of circumstances themselves, as if no human effort were required.[86] Here Marx stressed the dialectical relationship he perceived between the changing of circumstances and the changing of consciousness; both manifestly require vast human effort. The point is that the required effort is expected to come not from some outside vanguard, but from the masses themselves as they struggle to understand and change the circumstances that grind them down, organizing themselves, learning even from their own mistakes, and in the process changing their own consciousness as well. Marx's reflexive construction sharpens the point: one changes *oneself* in revolutionary activity. Notice also that the emergence of communist consciousness among "other classes" (for example, bourgeois intellectuals) appears above as something quite incidental to the main process.

In the *Manifesto* itself, the initial historical section retraces "the most

84. As translated in *Writings*, pp. 430–31.
85. (Moscow: Progress, 1964), p. 230.
86. For example, Bartel and Schmidt, "Marx und Engels über die proletarische Partei," pp. 33–35.

general phases in the development of the proletariat" and gives prominent mention to the formation of "combinations (Trades' Unions),"
followed by "permanent associations," and finally by the aforementioned "organization of the proletarians into a class, and consequently
into a political party" (that is, a party composed of the entire class).
The process is explained through the "advance of industry," which
"replaces the isolation of the laborers, due to competition, by their
revolutionary combination, due to association." Thus the workers appear to achieve both revolutionary consciousness and organization
without any external help. To be sure, after Marx and Engels noted
that the bourgeoisie, in its own behalf, first calls the workers to political
action, they added:

> Further, as we have already seen, entire sections of the ruling
> classes are, by the advance of industry, precipitated into the prole-
> tariat, or are at least threatened in their conditions of existence.
> These also supply the proletariat with fresh elements of enlighten-
> ment and progress.
>
>   Finally, in times when the class-struggle nears the decisive hour,
> the process of dissolution going on within the ruling-class, in fact
> within the whole range of old society, assumes such a violent, glar-
> ing character, that a small section of the ruling class cuts itself
> adrift, and joins the revolutionary class, . . . and in particular, a
> portion of the bourgeois ideologists, who have raised themselves
> to the level of comprehending theoretically the historical move-
> ment as a whole.[87]

The contributions of renegade bourgeois "ideologists" are thus recognized as helpful but in no way treated as indispensable or crucial to the
larger process of consciousness formation. Neither are the services of
the Communist League itself treated as indispensable, a point Marx
was shortly to prove in the most dramatic possible way.

Our final question concerned the possible role of the vanguard in
executing the seizure of power itself. Here we will have a chance to
measure words against deeds. Marx and Engels repeatedly denied,
to start with, that the league had any purpose beyond organization
and propaganda; they denied particularly that it was supposed to seize

87. *Selected Works,* 1:41–42, 43.

power itself, with or without mass support. Perhaps Marx best expressed these sentiments in his 1853 defense of the league, then on trial for conspiracy against the Prussian state. Defining the organization as a "secret propaganda society," Marx admitted frankly that "the final goal of the League was the *overturning of the social order*," which in turn necessitated a "*political revolution* and this entailed the overthrow of the Prussian State, just as surely as an earthquake entails the overthrow of a henroost." But, he continued, the accused "did in fact proceed from the blasphemous assumption that the present Prussian government would collapse without their having to lift a finger."[88]

Later in his pamphlet Marx made his meaning crystal clear, as he referred to the (unfulfilled) expectation of new revolution in 1849–1850:

There is no doubt that here too the members of the proletarian party would take part once again in a revolution against the *status quo*, but it was no part of their task to prepare for this revolution, to agitate, conspire or to plot for it. They could leave this preparation to circumstances in general and to the classes directly involved. . . .

The "Communist League," therefore, was no conspiratorial society, but a society which secretly strove to create an organized proletarian party because the German proletariat is publicly debarred, *igni et aqua*, from writing, meeting and speaking. Such a society can only be said to conspire against the *status quo* in the sense that steam and electricity conspire against it.[89]

Thus the members of the league fully expected to take part in a new revolution, but it was not the league's business as an organization to plot, conspire, agitate, or prepare for it. Such preparation was properly left to circumstances and classes *in general* rather than to any vanguard group. Marx was reiterating here the conception of revolution Engels had written into his October 1847 draft of the *Manifesto*, namely that "revolutions are not made deliberately" but are "the necessary outcome of circumstances quite independent of the will or the guidance of particular parties."[90]

88. "Revelations," *Cologne Communist Trial*, p. 64; see also pp. 59, 61, 107.
89. Ibid., p. 108.
90. See n. 35 above.

Correspondingly, on repeated occasions Engels also described the league as "a simple organization of communist propaganda, which was secret only because necessity compelled it to be."[91] In 1860 Marx recalled that "the work of the League—propaganda among the workers in Germany—demanded that the secret form be continued," but that outside Germany it founded open workers' educational societies, which assembled libraries and organized classes, discussions, social entertainments, etc. He ended this description of the league's work with the following curious statement: "During the period of the Revolution [of 1848] in Germany its activity expired of its own accord, since more effective ways now stood open for advancing its purposes."[92] Far from considering it the general staff of the proletarian revolution, Marx here seemed to regard the league as superfluous once legal conditions made secrecy unnecessary in the tasks of organization and propaganda.

Of course all this may have been written merely for public consumption, and we will do well now to test Marx and Engels' statements against their actual behavior in the league during the first period of its existence. Scarcely had the new organization been launched than a whole series of revolutions broke out spontaneously in the spring of 1848. Amidst all this revolutionary turmoil it must be stated that Marx and Engels did not mastermind a single seizure of power in any of the three countries where they stayed.

Engels was in Paris until a month before the February Revolution erupted, but his letters to Marx show no anticipation of the event, much less any hand in it. He continued to report on the familiar old concerns: struggling against the lingering supporters of Weitling and True Socialism within the league there, cultivating contacts with French socialist leaders (notably Louis Blanc and Ferdinand Flocon), and pursuing his usual lighter pastimes ("If French girls did not exist," he had written Marx a few months earlier, "life would no longer be worth the effort. Mais tant qu'il y a des grisettes, va!")[93] An article Engels wrote during the February events themselves reveals his genuine surprise, especially at the proclamation of a republic.[94]

91. "Karl Marx" (1878), Selected Works, 2:144; see also pp. 297, 315, and Werke, 21:16.
92. Herr Vogt, Birth, pp. 148–49, except for the last sentence, curiously omitted by Struik, which comes from the original German, Werke, 14:439–40.
93. Letter of March 9, 1847, Werke, 27:80; see also other letters, pp. 93–114.
94. "Revolution in Paris" (1848), ibid., 4:528–30; cf. 603–04.

Once back in Brussels, Engels found his partner similarly engaged in routine work, lecturing the workers' educational society on the subject of free trade and arranging for a projected international congress of democratic organizations.[95] The dramatic news from Paris raised the possibility that Belgium might follow suit, and Marx and Engels worked with the Brussels Democratic Association (of which Marx was vice-president) in a "peaceful but energetic agitation" toward that end. The association met nightly during the crisis, sending a message of fraternal greeting to the new French Republic and demanding locally that the Brussels city government expand and arm the popular civic guard.[96] As foreigners, Marx and Engels remained passive during the street demonstrations of February 27, which proved to be the turning point in the abortive Belgian revolution. Royal troops broke up the demonstrations with quick efficiency, and in the repression that followed Marx was ordered to leave the country. The Communist League as an organization played no part in these events.

The league was, however, busy with internal matters. Anxious to be at the scene of action, the London central committee dissolved itself and, in a move the artisans would come to regret, transferred its authority to the Brussels circle. This word arrived in Brussels just as the police were closing in, leaving the members there only enough time to delegate Marx a "discretionary authority" to constitute a new central committee in Paris as soon as possible. There, the local branch, enlarged by the in-gathering of London and Brussels émigrés, elected Marx president of the league on March 11, in a seven-man central committee that included Engels and Wilhelm Wolff as well. The Marx circle of intellectuals now gained crucial ground vis-à-vis the artisans.[97]

As president, Marx ignored any temptation to overthrow the bourgeois republican government just established in Paris (even though he might have sought assistance from the newly liberated Blanqui),

95. See ibid., 444–48, 601–03; Nicolaievsky and Maenchen-Helfen, *Marx*, pp. 125–32.

96. See the report concerning its activities in Brussels Democratic Association to Julian Harney, February 28, 1848, *Werke*, 4:604–05. Marx himself apparently donated money toward the purchase of weapons for the workers (Schraepler, *Handwerkerbünde*, p. 218). The fullest account of Marx and Engels' role in the Brussels events appears in Oscar J. Hammen, *The Red '48ers: Karl Marx and Friedrich Engels* (New York: Scribners, 1969), pp. 195–200.

97. *Werke*, 4:607; 27:118; Nicolaievsky and Maenchen-Helfen, *Marx*, p. 151; Nicolaievsky, "Who Is Distorting History?" p. 221.

and focused his attention instead on the expected upheaval in Germany. But here again, his actions must seem disappointing to serious revolution-makers, for he bent every effort to thwart the organization of a "German Legion" of émigrés, intended by its founder, Georg Herwegh, to march on the fatherland as a guerrilla army, drawing the masses to its side and triumphantly proclaiming a German Republic. This usually ridiculed undertaking was in fact probably as well conceived as most deliberately initiated guerrilla operations. The Schwarzwald and Odenwald in southwestern Germany were chosen as target areas because heavy overpopulation, oppressive manorial burdens, and the still-living tradition of the sixteenth-century Peasants' Revolt all seemed to insure maximum support from the local population, while militarily the areas offered rugged terrain and maximum distance from the formidable armies of Prussia and Austria. The legion was to be commanded by a handful of renegade former Prussian officers.[98] None of these factors seemed to entice Marx, who condemned the whole expedition as foolhardy adventurism and predicted—correctly as things turned out—that it would meet military disaster as soon as it reached German soil. Instead, Marx urged German exiles to return to their native towns as individuals and there take part in the popular uprising. So, as Herwegh's eight-hundred-man legion departed Paris on April 1 amidst banners and jubilation, some two to three hundred other exiles followed Marx's advice and departed more quietly for their fatherland. The latter group included most of the league's members as well as Marx and Engels themselves, and they all arrived after the decisive uprisings had taken place. The newly organized Central Committee of the Communist League presided over by Marx had played no active role at all in the initial German Revolution.[99]

In fact, Marx carried out only one demonstrably revolutionary act during his tenure as league president, and that concerned internal matters two months later in Cologne. The aforementioned campaign to expand the organization throughout Germany ended in failure. "The League proved to be much too weak a lever," Engels remembered, "as against the popular mass movement that had now broken out."[100]

98. Schraepler, *Handwerkerbünde,* pp. 226–32.
99. See *Werke,* 5:6–7; 27:119, 122–23, 475, 479, 604; *Selected Works,* 2:317–18; Schraepler, *Handwerkerbünde,* pp. 226–38.
100. "History of the Communist League," *Selected Works,* 2:318; see also *Bund Dokumente,* 1:754–92.

Legal organizations sprang up everywhere, and open propaganda via the press now became possible. Marx and Engels themselves became more and more involved with their own vehicle for open propaganda, the *Neue Rheinische Zeitung*, which they did not want to speak merely for "a tiny sect" but for "a great party of action," namely a united front of all German democrats.[101] Further, when the two men arrived in Cologne, they found the league branch there already seriously divided between their own supporters and those of Andreas Gottschalk, who fundamentally opposed the policy of united front. And Gottschalk was not easily to be cast aside. As a physician in the poorer section of the city, he had gathered together a wide following, and he was now in the process of setting up his own legal organization, the Cologne Workers' Society, whose immediate success rather put the league into eclipse. Amidst so many complications, Marx evidently began to find the secret society more an encumbrance than a help in the main task at hand. Without further ado, he jettisoned the Communist League, leaving its artisan members to their own devices and drawing his own circle of intellectual communists into the activity of the *Neue Rheinische Zeitung*.

Exactly what happened remains a point of bitter contention between Communist and most non-Communist scholars, the disputed evidence consisting of the 1854 testimony of Peter Gerhardt Röser, the last president of the Communist League. Röser's sensational testimony, first published *in toto* in 1964, concerned a league meeting during June 1848:

At this meeting there were very vehement debates. Sharp reproaches were made to Dr. Gottschalk concerning the organization of the Workers' Society, and secondly Marx proposed the dissolution of the League. On the first matter Marx and Schapper were agreed; on the second Gottschalk and Marx were for the dissolution of the League. Schapper and Moll demanded absolutely that the League be maintained, and since no agreement could be reached Marx made use of his discretionary authority and dissolved the League. Marx held the continuation of the League to be superfluous because it was not a conspiratorial but a propaganda organization, and under present conditions—since freedom of the

---

101. Engels, "Marx and the *Neue Rheinische Zeitung* (1848–1849)" (1884), *Selected Works*, 2:299. The policy of united front will be discussed in chapter 6.

press and the right of association existed—it could propagandize openly and did not require secrecy.[102]

Communist scholars have not yet found the courage to admit that Marx would so casually abandon the vanguard party and have challenged Röser's credibility, but the weight of evidence and probability both stand against them.[103] In later recollections about the league, as we have seen, Marx himself said that "its activity expired of its own accord, since more effective ways now stood open for advancing its purposes," and he went on to speak of the league's being "reconstituted" (*rekonstituiert*) in 1849, after the counterrevolution revived the need for extralegality.[104] Similarly, Engels recalled that "from the moment when the causes which had made the secret League necessary ceased to exist, the secret League as such ceased to mean anything." He proceeded to refer to the group in the past perfect tense and also mentioned its "re-establishment" (*Neuorganisation*) in 1849.[105] If neither man expressly alluded to the *act* of dissolution, it may well be that they were none too proud of this high-handed and blatantly unstatutory deed, railroaded through over the plaintive objections of the artisan leaders who had nurtured the organization for more than a decade.[106] But perhaps the most convincing evidence of all comes— unwittingly—from the Communist scholars themselves: their massive collection, *Der Bund der Kommunisten: Dokumente und Materialien*, displays dozens of documents linking Marx and Engels to league activities up to June 1848, but thereafter not a solitary *word* until after the

102. Werner Blumenberg, "Zur Geschichte des Bundes der Kommunisten: Die Aussagen des Peter Gerhardt Röser," *International Review of Social History* 9 (1964):89.

103. Nicolaievsky and Maenchen-Helfen first discovered the document and used it in the 1933 German edition of their biography (see *Marx*, pp. 163–64), sparking the controversy that has gathered momentum in the years since World War II. For an up-to-date review of the details, replete with references to all the previous literature, by an authority who himself takes an intermediate position, see Dieter Dowe, *Aktion und Organisation: Arbeiterbewegung, sozialistische und kommunistische Bewegung in der preussischen Rheinprovinz, 1820–1852* (Hannover: Literatur and Zeitgeschichte, 1970), pp. 250–53.

104. See n. 92 above.

105. "History of the Communist League," *Selected Works*, 2:318–19; cf. p. 299.

106. The organizational aspect of the dissolution will be treated in chapter 8.

two men returned to exile in the autumn of 1849.[107] Whatever opinion others might have, Marx and Engels rather pointedly regarded the organization as defunct.

During the first period of its existence, then, the Communist League did not perform the role of a Leninist-style vanguard party in the eyes of Marx and Engels. They made no effort whatsoever to confine its membership to revolutionaries by profession; they regarded the group as helpful but not essential to the growth of revolutionary consciousness among the masses; and they manifestly did not require the organization for any seizure of power. For them it was indeed a "simple organization of communist propaganda," whose utility vanished as soon as better means of agitation became available. That in their eyes the league was not indispensable as the general staff of the proletarian revolution appears most dramatically in the June dissolution. Can anyone imagine Lenin dissolving the Bolshevik party after the February Revolution in 1917 on the ground that a secret organization was no longer required?!

107. Indeed, the *Bund Dokumente* reproduces only two miserable letters from Hermann Ewerbeck to Moses Hess (November 1, 1848, pp. 863–64; and November 14, 1848, p. 868) which purport to show that *anybody* conceived the league to be still in business (see editors' commentary, p. 34).

⦃6⦄

Strategy II:
Alliance of the Majority Classes

IF WE NOW PROCEED chronologically to Marx and Engels' activity in Germany during the revolutionary year 1848, two major topics logically present themselves for analysis: their special strategy for the relatively unindustrialized fatherland, and their advocacy or use of revolutionary violence and terror. These topics relate to the second and third "complications" introduced at the beginning of the last chapter, namely, the policy of permanent revolution and the call for red terror, both of which may suggest prima facie an endorsement of totalitarian-democratic principles.

A Strategy for Backward Germany in 1848

Since 1917, Marx and Engels' strategy for revolution in backward countries has taken on obvious importance. Lenin was a close student of their writings on Germany in the 1848 period, and his disciples in other developing countries have generally followed suit. From the most obvious source, the *Communist Manifesto,* everyone can recall how the concluding paragraphs forecast a certain telescoping of revolutions in Germany that we may label a "permanent revolution" (even though Marx and Engels adopted the term only momentarily in 1850):

> In Germany they [the Communists] fight with the bourgeoisie whenever it acts in a revolutionary way, against the absolute monarchy, the feudal squirearchy, and the petty bourgeoisie.
>
> But they never cease, for a single instant, to instil into the working class the clearest possible recognition of the hostile antagonism

[176]

between bourgeoisie and proletariat, in order that the German workers may straightway use, as so many weapons against the bourgeoisie, the social and political conditions that the bourgeoisie must necessarily introduce along with its supremacy, and in order that, after the fall of the reactionary classes in Germany, the fight against the bourgeoisie itself may immediately begin.

The Communists turn their attention chiefly to Germany, because that country is on the eve of a bourgeois revolution that is bound to be carried out under more advanced conditions of European civilization, and with a much more developed proletariat, than that of England was in the seventeenth, and of France in the eighteenth century, and because the bourgeois revolution in Germany will be but the prelude to an immediately following proletarian revolution.[1]

· If understood literally, this second overthrow would have to be a minority undertaking, since the proletariat in Germany still constituted but a small fraction of the population. Even allowing for a rapid "disintegration" of capitalist society, the time span implied from the "eve" (Vorabend) of the first event to the "immediately following" (das unmittelbare Vorspiel) second would appear far too short for the full social and political development of a majority proletarian class. A number of scholars have drawn the appropriate conclusion that Marx and Engels' vision of permanent revolution in Germany in 1848, though not exactly Blanquist, nevertheless required a second, minority revolution which could only plausibly be followed by some kind of educational dictatorship.[2]

Against such a conclusion, it must be asserted flatly—however outrageous it may seem—that Marx and Engels did not really mean what they appear to say in these world-famous lines. Or to put it more precisely, they employed phrases that were deliberately ambiguous and to a certain extent misleading, phrases that might be interpreted in different ways according to different predilections. The case for such a jolting hypothesis would have to be unusually convincing; the reader may judge for himself as the evidence is reconstructed, block upon

1.   Selected Works, 1:61.
2.   For example, Erik Molnár, La politique d'alliance du marxisme (1848–1889) (Budapest, Akadémiai Kiadó, 1967), pp. 12–13; Stanley Moore, Three Tactics: The Background in Marx (New York: Monthly Review, 1963), pp. 23–24.

block. Allowing for the sake of argument that the *Manifesto* itself may be suspect, let us start off by resynthesizing the masters' views on the subject from other contemporaneous sources.

As a preliminary, it is necessary to note, and then *discount*, Marx's earliest vision of German revolution, the one contained in his Paris "Critique" of 1844. Here the bourgeois revolution was not telescoped but omitted altogether. The idea of a "partial and merely political revolution" was declared utopian and "already antiquated"; only a "radical revolution, universal human emancipation" was "possible in practice" and would arrive "when all the inner conditions are fulfilled."[3] At this time Marx did not yet perceive successive periods of class domination in German history; consequently there was no reason why human emancipation by the proletariat could not follow immediately upon the "acute disintegration" of civil society. Only after 1845, when Marx fully embraced Engels' theory of the state and its accompanying historical schema, did a bourgeois revolution and a period of bourgeois domination become a logical part of Germany's future.

As both men gained concrete experience from living in various industrializing countries (Britain, France, Belgium), and as they probed deeper in their historico-economic studies, it became clearer and clearer that the revolutionary wave expected to traverse Europe in the near future would catch different nations at different stages of development. Suitable strategies needed to be worked out for each country. Only in Britain, with its advanced industrial base, its bourgeois government, and its politically developed proletarian majority— only here was the classical proletarian revolution described in the preceding chapter really on the agenda for immediate realization. It will be remembered that Engels rashly predicted the end of British capitalism by 1852–1853.[4] Like Britain, France possessed a bourgeois government, to be sure, but unlike Britain, it had a *peasant* majority (as Marx and Engels both expressly recognized), since industrialization was not nearly so far advanced.[5] Under these circumstances the two

3. *Writings of the Young Marx on Philosophy and Society*, trans. Loyd D. Easton and Kurt H. Guddat (Garden City: Doubleday, 1967), pp. 260, 262, 264. Cited hereafter as *Writings*.

4. See above, chap. 5, nn. 26 and 27. In April 1848 Engels would wager his brother-in-law twopence that Harney would be British Foreign Minister within two months! (*Werke*, 27:481).

5. See *The Holy Family*, trans. R. Dixon (Moscow: Foreign Languages, 1956), p. 264; *Werke*, 27:477.

men called for an intermediate sort of revolution that will be discussed presently. Finally in Germany, where autocracy still held sway and the proletariat was even weaker than in France, the first logical task was to support the bourgeoisie in carrying through its revolution. So far as is known, Marx first expressed this view during his showdown with Weitling in March 1846. Against the latter's call for immediate communist revolution, Marx insisted that "there can be no question for the time being of realizing communism. It is the bourgeoisie which must attain power to start with."[6]

In an extended analysis of the German scene in 1847, Engels surveyed the condition of the various social classes. Emphasizing in particular the fragmentation and political immaturity of the working classes, he concluded: "The nobility is too decadent, the petty bourgeois and peasants—because of their entire life situation—are too weak, and the workers will not be mature enough *for a long time yet* to be able to come forward in Germany as the ruling class. There remains only the bourgeoisie" (italics added).[7] The bourgeoisie alone is at present capable of mustering mass support and representing the national interest against the existing absolutist regimes. Therefore it must be supported, and indeed even pushed a little. Marx and Engels were well aware of the relative backwardness and political timidity of the German bourgeoisie and already toyed with the idea that it might fail in its historic mission or compromise with the old regimes. But they felt that the very intransigence of those regimes, their unwillingness to compromise at all, must ultimately drive the bourgeoisie in spite of itself to seize revolutionary power.[8]

A period of bourgeois domination was deemed necessary for a variety of reasons, nowhere expressed with such wry humor as in Engels' journalistic coda to the year 1847:

We are no friends of the bourgeoisie, that is common knowledge. But we do not begrudge the bourgeoisie its triumph. . . . Nothing is more obvious than that they are preparing the way for us, for the

6. According to Weitling's report of the encounter (Weitling to Moses Hess, March 31, 1846, translated in Hans Mühlestein, "Marx and the Utopian Wilhelm Weitling," *Science and Society* 12 [1948]:125).
7. "Der Status quo in Deutschland," *Werke*, 4:49–50.
8. See ibid., pp. 496, 502, 517–18; Herwig Förder, *Marx und Engels am Vorabend der Revolution: Die Ausarbeitung der politischen Richtlinien für die deutschen Kommunisten (1846–1848)* (Berlin: Akademie, 1960), p. 292.

democrats and communists; than that they will have *at most several years* wherein to enjoy the fruits of victory before they are themselves overthrown. . . .

Therefore struggle bravely forward, gracious lords of capital. We need you for the present; here and there we even need you as rulers. You must clear away absolute monarchy and the vestiges of the Middle Ages; you must destroy patriarchalism; you must centralize; you must convert all the more or less propertyless classes into genuine proletarians, into recruits for us; you must create with your factories and commerce the material basis that the proletariat requires for its liberation. In recompense for these things you shall be allowed to rule for a short time. (Italics added)[9]

Thus the political task of the bourgeois revolution in Germany was to clear away the thirty-odd princely despotisms, large and small, that were the legacy of the Middle Ages, and create a modern centralized bourgeois government. But a subsequent period of bourgeois domination was also required for economic development, firstly to polarize the older intermediate strata into genuine proletarians, "recruits for us," and secondly to create the material prosperity that a classless society must have.

Premature revolution in a backward country like Germany, by a proletariat that would not be ready to rule "for a long time yet," could scarcely result in a classless society. Engels remarked elsewhere that "there must always be a dominant class controlling the forces of production and a poverty-stricken, oppressed class, so long as there is not enough produced to supply not only the immediate wants of all the members of society, but also a surplus of products for the increase of social capital."[10] In fact, such an untimely revolution would not likely be lasting at all, as Marx pointedly observed in an important 1847 article:

Should the proletariat overthrow the rule of the bourgeoisie [prematurely], its victory would be only transitory, only an episode in the service of the *bourgeois revolution* itself, like Anno 1794, so long as in the course of history . . . the material conditions had not

9. "Die Bewegungen von 1847" (1848), *Werke*, 4:502–03.
10. "Principles of Communism" (1847), in *Birth of the Communist Manifesto*, ed. Dirk J. Struik (New York: International, 1971), pp. 178–79.

yet been created which would render the destruction of the bourgeois mode of production necessary, and thus also the definitive
overthrow of the political rule of the bourgeoisie. The Reign of
Terror in France could only serve, through its mighty hammer
blows, to spirit away the feudal ruins from French soil.[11]

Thus both men stressed the need for a period of bourgeois domination,
certainly lasting "several years," before the next major step could be
taken successfully. And in the passage above, written just two months
before the *Manifesto*, Marx spoke plainly against a premature proletarian seizure of power, against the very telescoping of revolutions
that the more famous document seems to demand.

While urging a certain patience, Marx and Engels offered the consolation that bourgeois rule would bring important political advantages
for the proletarian movement. However inadequate bourgeois rights
might be, they were not—as the True Socialists continually insisted—
entirely sham or devoid of value. A glance at France, Britain, or America would reveal, Marx wrote in 1847, that "the rule of the bourgeoisie
not only gives the proletariat brand new weapons for struggling
against the bourgeoisie, but also creates for it an entirely new position,
the position of a recognized party." In Prussia the workers have no
stake in the mock parliamentary schemes of Frederick William IV,
but the bourgeois revolution would soon create real parliamentary government, along with "trial by jury, equality before the law, . . . freedom of the press, freedom of association, and a genuine system of
representation," all of which "the proletariat will know how to use."[12]
It should be reiterated, however, that Marx and Engels did not expect
these political gains to include universal suffrage in a fully democratic
republic; rather they anticipated that bourgeois rule in Germany would
follow the then standard model of constitutional monarchy with a parliament elected only by substantial property owners. In brief, Germany
would have reached the stage of development of France under the
July Monarchy.

Following an appropriate period of such bourgeois oligarchy, the
next step would still not be proletarian rule pure and simple, as implied
by the *Manifesto*. Rather it would be (as in France) an intermediate

11. "Die moralisierende Kritik und die kritisierende Moral," *Werke*, 4:338–39.
12. "Der Kommunismus des 'Rheinischen Beobachters' " (1847), ibid., pp. 193,
197, 194; cf. p. 22.

sort of revolution described by Engels in 1847 as "the conquest of political power by the proletarians, small peasants, and petty bourgeois" for the "establishment of democracy," together with certain "social reforms" that would be "preparations, passing intermediate stages for the abolition of private property" while not yet attacking it root and branch.[13] Still too weak to rule alone, the proletarian minority would seek allies among the declining urban and rural lower-middle classes, establishing what we may call an "alliance of the majority classes" for the struggle against bourgeois rule. Marx and Engels' attitude toward these declining older strata was curiously ambivalent: sometimes they were pictured as thoroughly reactionary; other times, as moderately progressive.[14] No doubt in reality this diverse and amorphous layer of the population contained some elements that wanted to turn the clock of modernization back, and some that strove to move it forward. Marx and Engels themselves seemed to recognize a dual potential when they characterized the lower-middle classes as "fluctuating between proletariat and bourgeoisie."[15] In any event, the progressive elements among these strata appeared on the political stage as radical republicans (in contradistinction to the overwhelmingly monarchist bourgeoisie): in the terminology of Marx and Engels they were "mere," "pale," or "petty-bourgeois" democrats. And they were invited to join hands with the proletarian red democrats in the coming campaign against bourgeois oligarchy.[16]

That Marx and Engels envisaged such a broad campaign in Germany rather than immediate proletarian revolution is most convincingly demonstrated in their "Demands of the Communist Party in Germany," drawn up on the very morrow of what they assumed to be a successful bourgeois revolution there in March 1848. This seventeen-point program anticipated a new stage of political struggle against the bourgeoisie but nowhere suggested any immediate proletarian revolution or wholesale assault upon private property. Its political demands, as we have already observed, included a "unitary and indivisible republic" based on universal suffrage, a citizens' militia, equal pay for all civil servants, and a separation of church and state. Among the social and economic demands included, some were designed to benefit the broad

13. "Die Kommunisten und Karl Heinzen," ibid., pp. 312–13.
14. Within the *Manifesto* itself, compare the reactionary image in *Selected Works*, 1:42, 54, 56, and 61, with the progressive image on pp. 42 and 60–61.
15. Ibid., p. 53; cf. p. 42.
16. See *Werke*, 4:202, 309–24, 378–79, 424–25, 601–03.

masses of the population in general: universal free education, free legal services, a steeply graduated income tax, curtailment of the right of inheritance, creation of a state bank to issue paper money and regulate credit "in the interest of the people *as a whole*," and nationalization of the entire transportation system with its gratuitous use guaranteed to the "impecunious classes." Specifically aimed at Germany's peasant majority were the demands to abolish "all feudal dues, exactions, corvées, tithes, etc." without compensation, and to have all peasant redemption payments and rents transferred from the landlords to the state. "It is to the interest of the German proletariat, the petty bourgeoisie and the small peasantry to support these demands with all possible energy," the document concluded.[17]

To win support for and carry out this wide-ranging program of political and socioeconomic reforms were obviously not the tasks of an afternoon. One member of the Marx circle, Louis Heilberg, introduced the Seventeen Demands to Moses Hess in a letter which commented that they were "of an absolutely practical-revolutionary, democratic-communist nature and offer exceedingly rich material for journalistic and agitational activity for the next ten or fifteen years; . . . [they] pave the way toward the transition to a communist social order for the generation that follows us."[18] Surely this is a far cry from the *Manifesto*'s "immediately following proletarian revolution." Even more startling is Engels' own October draft of what became the *Manifesto*: "The communist revolution . . . will take a longer or shorter time to develop according to whether one country or the other has a more developed industry, greater wealth, a more important quantity of productive forces at its disposal. The revolution will therefore assume its slowest pace and be most difficult of achievement in Germany."[19]

The implementation of the Seventeen Demands was not conceived, of course, as the final step in the realization of communism. Rather, it would inaugurate a period of further socioeconomic alterations, as more and more "despotic inroads" were made into the rights of private property. During this period, paradoxically, a semiproletarian government would rule over a semicapitalist economy.[20] But presumably

17. See above, chap. 5, n. 15, and *Birth*, pp. 190–92.
18. Letter of April 17, 1848, Moses Hess, *Briefwechsel*, ed. Edmund Silberner (The Hague: Mouton, 1959), p. 189.
19. "Principles of Communism," *Birth*, pp. 182–83.
20. See allusions to this period, ibid.; *Selected Works*, 1:50; and *Werke*, 4:313–14.

the general laws of capitalist development would continue to operate, at least insofar as the number of modern proletarians would continue to multiply. Eventually they would be able to rule in their own right, as a majority, through the already established democratic constitution. Such an expectation seems implicit in the October draft's response to the question: "What will be the course of the revolution?"

> In the first place it will draw up a *democratic constitution* and by means of this establish directly or indirectly the political rule of the proletariat. In England, for instance, where the proletariat is in the majority, the rule of the proletariat will be direct. In France and in Germany, where the majority of the population consists, in addition to proletarians, of peasants producing on a small scale and of lower middle-class citizens, it will be indirect. For the two last-named categories are only now beginning to become proletarians, and their political interests are becoming more and more dependent on those of the proletariat, so that soon they must adapt themselves to the demands of the proletariat. Perhaps this will entail a second fight, but it will result inevitably in the victory of the proletariat.[21]

Unfortunately, the documents of this period offer no further elaboration on the character of this adaptation or the nature of the possible second fight. But one will also look in vain for any call to alter the democratic constitution or impose a dictatorship, to disfranchise certain elements of the population or overrepresent the cities, to outlaw dissident parties or impose a forced collectivization of agriculture. Perhaps, indeed, the experiences of the twentieth century have left us overly suspicious, and Engels only meant that most lower-middle-class people would be drawn to the proletariat of their own accord as they came to perceive the advantages of communism and as industrial development transformed them more and more into proletarians themselves. Some interesting new evidence for this supposition (from 1874) will be reviewed in chapter 9.

To sum up, in all the contemporaneous documents except the *Manifesto* we find the expectation of a protracted process of societal development, probably extending over two decades altogether, and involv-

21. *Birth*, p. 180.

ing *three* rather than two distinct phases of political evolution—from bourgeois domination to the rule of the majority classes to the rule of the proletariat alone—before the final classless and stateless society. One may call this process a "permanent revolution" only in the drawn-out sense Engels employed when he later recalled their 1848 expectation of a struggle "fought out in a single, long and vicissitudinous period of revolution."[22] Or in another recollection:

To us, February and March could have had the significance of a real revolution only if they had not been the conclusion but, on the contrary, the starting point of a long revolutionary movement in which . . . the people would have developed further through its own struggles and the parties become more and more sharply differentiated until they had coincided entirely with the great classes, bourgeoisie, petty bourgeoisie and proletariat, and in which the separate positions would have been won one after another by the proletariat in a series of revolutionary *journées* [*Schlachttagen*].[23]

Such a special drawn-out version of permanent revolution would not necessitate minority revolution or minority dictatorship: indeed, it expressly presupposes that the masses would develop themselves through their own long and vicissitudinous struggles. And this corresponds to the actual policy pursued by Marx and Engels during their stay on German soil; as we will see, they never attempted to call forth a *literal* "immediately following proletarian revolution."

The *Manifesto* stands alone in suggesting such a sequence of events. Surely that invites suspicion and begs us to ask why. The answer almost certainly lies in the tension between artisans and intellectuals introduced in the preceding chapter. As explained there, artisan impatience to find some escape from their doomed world expressed itself positively

22. "Introduction" (1895) to *Class Struggles in France, Selected Works*, 1:113.
23. "Karl Marx and the *Neue Rheinische Zeitung*" (1884), ibid., 2:302 (except for my rendering of "*Schlachttagen*" as "revolutionary *journées*" rather than simply as "battles"). A few paragraphs later, Engels continued: "When later I read *Bougeart's* book on *Marat*, I found that in more than one respect we had unconsciously imitated the great model of the genuine '*Ami du Peuple*' (not the one forged by the royalists) . . . he, like us, did not want the revolution declared finished but continuing in permanence" (pp. 302–03). So far as I have been able to find, this is the only instance in which either Marx or Engels retrospectively used the phrase "permanent revolution" to refer to their own policies of 1848–1850.

as the desire for immediate communism and negatively in an impla-
cable hostility toward the bourgeoisie and all its works. After rejecting
Blanquism, the artisan leaders of the League of the Just had embraced
a seemingly more patient strategy of democratic revolution, but no
scholar seems to have noticed that they did not thereby embrace two
other essentials of the Marxist recipe for communism—a prior bourgeois
revolution and a high level of industrial development. These prerequisites did not appear at all, for example, in the 1845 London discussions
with Weitling, where only lack of enlightenment was cited as having
prevented the introduction of communism to date. And in *all* the subsequent writings of league artisans down to 1848 that have been reproduced in the massive *Dokumente,* there is not a solitary mention of
any necessary industrial base or a word of support for any bourgeois
revolution.[24] Surprisingly, perhaps, one does not find hostility toward
the industrial revolution per se, just indifference. If Weitlingism and
Proudhonism (not to mention True Socialism) indeed represented the
"most complete expression" of artisan desires, as Engels once opined
in a moment of discouragement, then it is most significant that these
doctrines did not accept the Marxist prerequisites either, which helps
explain why the Brussels circle had to mount such a formidable polemical offensive against them.[25] The artisan spokesmen of the league, then,
anticipated no telescoping of revolutions in Germany because they foresaw only one impending upheaval—a democratic revolution to establish
a democratic state, which would then begin immediately to introduce
the community of goods.[26] Under the obvious influence of Brussels,
the central committee once in November 1846 raised the question
of a possible alliance with the petty-bourgeois "pale" republicans, but
not with much enthusiasm.[27] And nowhere is there any artisan suggestion of support for the cause of the high bourgeoisie, not even as late
as the September 1847 *Kommunistische Zeitschrift,* where Marx and
Engels' tutelage is otherwise very apparent.[28]

24. The documents reproduced on the following pages of *Bund Dokumente,*
vol. 1, are of particular interest: 214–38, 347–50, 376–82, 431–36, 436–41, 452–
57, 470–75, 475–87, 501–10, 528–42.
25. See above, chap. 5, n. 67; also Förder, *Vorabend der Revolution,* pp. 42–
52; P. H. Noyes, *Organization and Revolution: Working-Class Associations in the
German Revolution of 1848–1849* (Princeton: Princeton, 1966), pp. 45–46.
26. See especially *Bund Dokumente,* 1:347–48, 452–53, 474, 487, 505–06.
27. Ibid., pp. 432, 435–36.
28. Ibid., pp. 501–10. Significantly, the only contribution to this abortive news-

To understand how the notion of an "immediately following proletarian revolution" then suddenly appeared, when neither artisans nor intellectuals had espoused it hitherto, it is necessary to review the circumstances surrounding the birth of the *Communist Manifesto*. The London artisan leaders had long perceived the need for a "confession of faith," and after the virtual ostracism of their old literary spokesman, Wilhelm Weitling, they began their 1846 overtures to Brussels, where the requisite intellectual and literary talent seemed available. It is noteworthy, however, that they first thought to hold a league congress on the confession of faith without inviting Marx and Engels. Evidently the artisans wanted to reach some agreement among themselves before calling in the outside intellectuals.[29] But then they relented and in February 1847 sent Moll with his historic invitation for Marx and Engels to present their views before the projected congress. Only Engels actually attended.

No transcript has come down to us, but we know that the June congress occupied itself extensively with the confession of faith. Unable to reach any final agreement, the body produced a preliminary draft to be submitted to the local branches for discussion and revision before the final disposition of the matter at a second congress to be held in November.[30] A copy of this June draft has recently been discovered, as noted earlier, written in Engels' hand. In it one finds the older language of justice and rights mingled awkwardly with Engels' hardboiled "scientific" analysis. The fourth question, for instance, asks on what the community of goods will be based:

Firstly, on the mass of productive powers and means of existence generated by the development of industry, agriculture, trade, and colonization, and on the possibility to increase them infinitely by machinery, chemical and other means.

Secondly, on the fact that in the consciousness or feeling of every

---

paper by a member of the Marx circle was "Der preussische Landtag und das Proletariat in Preussen wie überhaupt in Deutschland" (ibid., pp. 511–24), by Wilhelm Wolff, which went out of its way to stress the necessity of a bourgeois revolution.

29. Bert Andréas, *Gründungsdokumente des Bundes der Kommunisten (Juni bis September 1847)* (Hamburg: Hauswedell, 1969), pp. 18–20; Ernst Schraepler, *Handwerkerbünde und Arbeitervereine, 1830–53* (Berlin: deGruyter, 1972), pp. 193–96.

30. "Rundschreiben des ersten Kongresses des Bundes der Kommunisten an den Bund" (1847), *Bund Dokumente*, 1:482–85.

human being there exist certain tenets as indisputable principles.
. . . For instance, each human being is in search of happiness. The
happiness of the individual is inseparably linked to the happiness
of all, etc.[31]

In June, artisan conceptions were still much in evidence.

During the subsequent local discussions in the Paris branch, Engels
remained dissatisfied with this document, as well as with a counter-
draft advanced by Moses Hess. He began afresh and produced his
October version, "Principles of Communism," which undoubtedly reflected Marxist thinking most precisely, and which the two men apparently introduced and defended at the second congress.[32] Again, in the
absence of a transcript, we know only that the November congress
spent ten days debating the various proposals and amendments that
had come from local branches. Whatever programmatic agreement may
have been reached, the various materials were turned over to Marx
and Engels with the famous commission to "draft" (abfassen) a final
version.[33]

But Marx and Engels' later recollections are surely exaggerated in
their implication that the two men had received carte blanche to write
whatever they pleased.[34] The artisans had proceeded painstakingly up
to this point and are not likely to have abandoned all their previous
exertions so casually; or to have turned over the materials of debate
without some reason; or to have agreed to publish the final document
in the name of the league (Marx and Engels did not appear as authors
in the original edition) without some kind of instruction to the draft-
ers.[35] It seems far more probable that the two men were commissioned
to give final polished expression to principles that had been hammered

31.   "Draft of the Communist Confession of Faith," Birth, p. 162. This document was first published by Bert Andréas in Gründungsdokumente in 1969; see
his comments, pp. 20–22; also Herwig Förder and Martin Hundt, "Zur Vorgeschichte von Engels' Arbeit 'Gundsätze des Kommunismus,'" Beiträge zur Geschichte der Arbeiterbewegung 12 (1970):60–85.

32.   English translation included in Birth, pp. 169–89; see Werke, 27:98, 107.
This must be the draft referred to in Marx's confused 1860 recollection in Herr
Vogt (Birth, p. 149).

33.   See Bund Dokumente, 1:654, 624–25.

34.   See various recollections in Selected Works, 1:21, 2:314–15; Birth, p. 149.

35.   Compare comments of various other authorities on this point: Andréas,
Gründungsdokumente, pp. 20–23; Schraepler, Handwerkerbünde, pp. 204–06,
209–212; Struik in Birth, pp. 209–10; D. Ryazanoff in Communist Manifesto (New
York: International, 1930), pp. 180–91; and Carl Grünberg, "Die Londoner Kom-

out in ten days of hard work, or at least to include such principles in their final version, as implied in another—seemingly more accurate—Engels recollection that the *Manifesto* was an "amalgamation" (*Verschmelzung*) of theoretical and working-class communism.[36] While the artisans probably cared little what the two men said on historical and general philosophical issues, it is not likely that they were so obliging on the specific listed demands or on the expectations for Germany about which disagreement had hitherto prevailed. On these points the final version was patently a compromise, a *Verschmelzung*.

Such an interpretation is fortified by other surviving bits of information. In late January 1848 the artisan central committee dispatched an impatient letter to Marx demanding immediate delivery of the final manuscript, or else return of the lent documents, all in a peremptory tone that scarcely betokened abject subservience to the Brussels intellectuals.[37] And although the final version was not subjected to central committee approval, perhaps because of the pressure of time, Schapper himself read over the proofs before publication.[38] In any event, only a thousand copies were printed in the first edition and appear to have been distributed for internal purposes only, suggesting the possibility of subsequent revision.[39] Any such plans were interrupted, of course, by the news that France had become a republic.

With this factual background, if we now inspect the points at issue in the three successive versions of the *Manifesto* that have come down to us, we will discover a near-perfect triad of dialectical development—

Thesis: The June draft foresaw only one revolution in Germany, which would establish a "democratic state constitution" and proceed directly to "such restriction of private property that prepares its gradual conversion into communal property." To be sure, Engels' above-quoted insistence on an industrial base was included, but there is no mention of any bourgeois revolution whatsoever.[40]

---

munistische Zeitschrift und andere Urkunden aus den Jahren 1847–1848," *Archiv für die Geschichte des Sozialismus und der Arbeiterbewegung* 9 (1921):269–70.

36. "Der Sozialismus in Deutschland" (1892), *Werke*, 22:248.

37. "Beschluss der Zentralbehörde des Bundes der Kommunisten, 24. Januar 1848," *Bund Dokumente*, 1:654.

38. "Erinnerungen von Friedrich Lessner an den zweiten Kongress des Bundes der Kommunisten," ibid., p. 625.

39. According to Bert Andréas, *Le Manifeste Communiste de Marx et Engels: Histoire et Bibliographie 1848–1918* (Milan: Feltrinelli, 1963), p. 10.

40. "Draft of the Communist Confession of Faith," *Birth*, pp. 163–69; see especially pp. 167–68.

Antithesis: Engels' October draft, by contrast, gave particular prominence to the need for a bourgeois revolution, reiterating its benefits and calling upon the communists to "rally to the support of the liberal bourgeois party." The struggle against that party could begin thereafter, "as speedily as possible," but in backward Germany the development of communism would "assume its slowest pace and be most difficult of achievement." Two further stages were specifically mentioned, as we have seen—the rule of the majority classes, and the rule of the proletariat alone—before the classless society would finally emerge.[41] Here was Marx and Engels' vision in its purity, before adulteration.

Synthesis: The final published version blended the two earlier ones in a unique alloy. The artisans allowed Marx and Engels the bourgeois revolution they seemed to desire so fervently, but in exchange the latter consented to speed up the overall process. The three stages were reduced to two and linked by the phrase "immediately following," to satisfy artisan impatience. Marx and Engels might think to themselves that, in a document surveying the entire span of human history, "immediately following" could mean anything from a few days to many years. And they could entertain another mental reservation that the ensuing "proletarian revolution" would not be exclusively proletarian in its first stage.[42] No doubt the artisans could have private thoughts of their own about how actively they would fight on the side of the bourgeoisie.

Thus the idea of a permanent revolution, which appeared here in the *Communist Manifesto* for the first time, was neither fish nor fowl; not the real desire of either artisans or intellectuals, but an effort to

41. "Principles of Communism," ibid., pp. 169–89; see especially pp. 188–89, 182–83, 180.

42. One may legitimately ask why Marx and Engels, if they were dissatisfied with the *Manifesto*'s formulations, did not disavow the document or alter its subsequent editions. It must be pointed out, first of all, that the *Manifesto* played no significant role in the 1848 period and thereafter lay largely forgotten for two decades, until Marx's notoriety as champion of the Paris Commune stimulated a certain interest in his earlier writings. Thus only in 1872 did the two men bother to put out a new edition, and in the preface they acknowledged that many points in the piece were "antiquated" but added that "the Manifesto has become a historical document which we no longer have any right to alter" (*Selected Works*, 1:22; cf. p. 29). In the intervening quarter-century it was Bismarck who had reordered German politics, not the Communist League, and it would have been pointless in 1872 to fuss about old "might-have-been's."

compromise two rather different conceptions of future development. Whatever conclusions later Marxists were to draw from this unfortunate *Verschmelzung*, there is no evidence at all that the masters themselves envisaged a minority revolution or minority dictatorship.

Implementation of the Class-Alliance Strategy

We may put this interpretation to a revealing further test by examining Marx and Engels' actual behavior during the only period of their lives when they were, in some sense, *practicing* revolutionaries.

Even before the 1848 revolution, their organizational commitments reveal the strategic priorities described above. In Britain, where real proletarian revolution was on the agenda, Marx and Engels cultivated their contacts with the working-class Chartist movement but saw no need to draw the "petty-bourgeois" Radicals into any alliance. In France, however, the two men made special efforts to forge an alliance with the Social Democratic circle centered on the newspaper *Réforme*, which they believed to speak for the progressive elements among the lower-middle classes. To effect a parallel alignment in Belgium, Marx even joined and became vice-president of the Democratic Association, the Brussels organization of "pale" democrats which played a leading part in the "peaceful but energetic agitation" that almost toppled the Belgian oligarchy in February 1848. Though predominantly Belgian in membership, the Democratic Association was officially international and thus one of Marx and Engels' many commitments to help link up national groupings of socialists and democrats. They supported the 1845 "Festival of Nations" sponsored by Harney in London, as well as the permanent organization, the Fraternal Democrats, which grew out of it; both men spoke at the latter group's 1847 commemoration of the Polish Revolt of 1830. On the eve of the February Revolution itself, Marx and Engels were active in preparations for an international congress of "pale" and "red" democrats.[43] Thus even as they were entering the Communist League, the two men were also busy forging the organizational links of what they hoped would be the alliance of the majority classes.

In fact, when the revolution came, these links proved more important among their political priorities than the Communist League itself. After

43. For details of these various commitments, see the chronology of Marx and Engels' lives included in *Werke*, 4:673–80, as well as the standard biographies.

the failure of the aforementioned efforts to expand the league and create a nationwide workers' party, Marx and Engels undertook something of an agonizing reappraisal of the German situation. Political consciousness was obviously less advanced than the March Revolution at first suggested, and this called for a certain reshuffling of organizational commitments. On the one hand, they were unwilling to expend further energies on the minuscule league, "to preach Communism in a little provincial sheet and to found a tiny sect instead of a great party of action," as Engels later put it.[44] But the other obvious choice, the Cologne Workers' Society, was precluded because its leader, Andreas Gottschalk, strenuously opposed any united front with non-working-class groups and urged a boycott of the impending National Assembly elections.[45] The upshot was, as we saw earlier in a different context, that Marx cavalierly scuttled the Communist League, passed over the Workers' Society, and joined instead the Cologne Democratic Society, which spoke for the local "petty-bourgeois" democrats. He supported the candidates put up by this group in the May elections.[46] But Marx did not ignore the Workers' Society utterly (as some hostile scholars have delighted in asserting): by June he had become the leading figure in a joint committee set up to link the political activities of the Democratic Society, the Workers' Society, and a third smaller artisan group. By August this committee had been commissioned by a regional congress to perform the same functions for the entire Rhineland.[47] Through his subsequent service on this Rhenish District Committee of Democrats, Marx himself personified the exact sociopolitical alliance he was striving to consolidate. From its first appearance in June, the *Neue Rheinische Zeitung* also spoke, not for exclusively communist or working-class causes, but for "the great party of action," the alliance of the majority classes, and carried on its masthead "Organ of Democracy," to symbolize the common goal shared by "pale" and

44. "Marx and the *Neue Rheinische Zeitung*," *Selected Works*, 2:299; cf. *Werke*, 36:598.

45. Gerhard Becker, *Karl Marx und Friedrich Engels in Köln, 1848–1849: Zur Geschichte des Kölner Arbeitervereins* (Berlin: Rütten und Loening, 1963), pp. 47–49; Dieter Dowe, *Aktion und Organisation: Arbeiterbewegung, sozialistische und kommunistische Bewegung in der preussischen Rheinprovinz, 1820–1852* (Hannover: Literatur und Zeitgeschichte, 1970), pp. 149–51.

46. Schraepler, *Handwerkerbünde*, pp. 253–60, 278–79.

47. *Werke*, 5:485–86, 571: Becker, *Kölner Arbeiterverein*, pp. 58–59, 67–68; Dowe, *Aktion und Organisation*, pp. 171–73.

"red" democrats alike. None of these activities suggests anticipation of any immediately following and exclusively proletarian revolution.

In fact, Marx and Engels' spring reappraisal included another highly significant ingredient. They had come back to Germany in the conviction that absolutism was smashed and the bourgeoisie firmly in the saddle. The next step, as indicated by the Seventeen Demands, was to begin putting together the alliance of the majority classes for the campaign *against* bourgeois rule. But it did not take long to discover that the bourgeois revolution was in fact incomplete and stalled, while the Seventeen Demands could not even be *exposed*, much less implemented. "If a single copy of our 17 points were distributed here," Engels reported to Marx during his April visit to Barmen, "as far as we are concerned all would be lost."[48]

Instead of campaigning against the bourgeoisie, therefore, it was still necessary to support it and spur it on to complete the political tasks of its own revolution, namely, the establishment of genuine parliamentary control in the various princely states and the creation of some kind of national government to unify the fatherland. As a consequence of the revolutionary disturbances in March, most of the German rulers—including most importantly the king of Prussia and the Austrian emperor—had appointed new liberal ministries and permitted the election of constituent assemblies to draw up constitutions for their respective states. A parallel National Assembly was simultaneously elected to meet in Frankfurt and draft a constitution that was to unite all these separate states into a new federal structure. But as the smoke of March cleared, it became apparent that the thrones, the princely armies and bureaucracies—the entire executive apparatus of the old regime—remained very much intact, stunned rather than destroyed by the forces of revolution.[49]

In this ambiguous situation it was not clear, either legally or in terms of real power, whether sovereignty rested still with the various princes,

48. Letter of April 25, 1848, *Werke,* 27:126.
49. Standard general histories of the German Revolution of 1848 include Veit Valentin, *Geschichte der deutschen Revolution von 1848–1849,* 2 vols. (Berlin: Ullstein, 1930–31); Jacques Droz, *Les révolutions allemandes de 1848* (Paris: Presses Universitaires, 1957); and Theodore S. Hamerow, *Restoration, Revolution, Reaction: Economics and Politics in Germany, 1815–1871* (Princeton: Princeton, 1958). Not without interest is Engels' own contemporary history, *Germany: Revolution and Counter-Revolution* (1852), recently republished in Friedrich Engels, *The German Revolutions,* ed. Leonard Krieger (Chicago: Chicago, 1967).

with the separate state assemblies, or with the National Assembly in Frankfurt. The very first number of the *Neue Rheinische Zeitung* attempted to bolster the courage of the hesitant Frankfurt liberals on the point at issue:

> The German people won its sovereign status by fighting in the streets of almost all towns in the country, large and small, and especially on the barricades of Vienna and Berlin. It exercised this sovereignty in the elections to the National Assembly.
>
> The bold and public proclamation of the sovereignty of the German people should have been the first act of the National Assembly.
>
> Its second act should have been the drafting of a German constitution based on the sovereignty of the people and the elimination from the conditions actually existing in Germany of everything that conflicts with this principle.[50]

Far from calling for the overthrow of the bourgeois National Assembly, Marx and Engels repeatedly urged it to exercise its sovereign power in a practical way: "Does not the mere existence of a *constituent* National Assembly prove that *there is no* longer any constitution? But if there is no constitution, then there is no government either. And if there is no government the National Assembly must govern."[51]

In particular the National Assembly should take vigorous measures against the restorative efforts of the old regimes, evidenced in the increasingly menacing attempts by reactionary civil and military officials at the local level to disarm the people, curtail the newly won rights of free assembly and free speech, and reimpose the rule of the bayonet:

> A constituent National Assembly must above all be an *active*, revolutionarily active assembly. The Assembly at Frankfurt is engaged in parliamentary school exercises and leaves it to the governments to act. Assuming that this learned gathering succeeds, af-

---

50.   "The Assembly at Frankfurt" (June 1848), in *The Revolution of 1848–49: Articles from the "Neue Rheinische Zeitung,"* trans. S. Ryazanskaya (New York: International, 1972), p. 22.

51.   "The Programmes of the Radical-Democratic Party and of the Left at Frankfurt" (June 1848), ibid., p. 31.

ter mature consideration, in framing the best of agendas and the best of constitutions, of what use is the best agenda and the best constitution if the governments meanwhile have placed bayonets on the agenda? . . .

[The Assembly] only had to oppose authoritatively all reactionary encroachments by obsolete governments in order to win such strength of public opinion as would make all bayonets and rifle butts ineffective against it. Instead Mainz, almost within sight of the Assembly, is abandoned to the arbitrary actions of the army, and German citizens from other parts of the country are exposed to the chicanery of the philistines in Frankfurt. The Assembly bores the German people instead of inspiring it or being inspired by it.[52]

Marx and Engels constantly chided both Frankfurt and the separate state assemblies for their shortsighted timidity and drew examples from English and French history to demonstrate how *real* parliaments controlled the executive branch of government.[53]

Not only did Marx and Engels counsel the Frankfurt liberals on how to inspire popular confidence by defending revolutionary gains, but they counseled the new liberal ministers in Berlin on how to gain peasant support by abolishing all the old despised manorial obligations without compensation. But the bourgeois ministers were hesitant to tamper with property rights, even those of feudal property, and came forth with a meek legislative proposal that prompted Marx to exclaim that "the German revolution of 1848 is merely a *parody of the French revolution of 1789*":

The French bourgeoisie of 1789 never left its allies, the peasants, in the lurch. It knew that the abolition of feudalism in the countryside and the creation of a free, landowning peasant class was the basis of its rule.

The German bourgeoisie of 1848 unhesitatingly betrays the peasants, who are its *natural allies*, flesh of its own flesh, and without whom it cannot stand up to the aristocracy.[54]

52. Ibid., pp. 31–32.
53. E.g., ibid., pp. 63–65; *Werke*, 5:216–17.
54. "The Bill Proposing the Abolition of Feudal Obligations" (July 1848), "*Neue Rheinische Zeitung*," p. 76.

Instead of Marx's trying immediately to win the peasants *away* from the bourgeoisie, he impatiently explained to the liberal ministers what history required of them.

This policy of critical support for the bourgeois revolution, spurring it to completion, had as its corollary the soft-pedaling of more radical demands that were not yet historically appropriate and would only further frighten the liberals into the arms of the old regime. Down to the time of the November counterrevolution, Marx and Engels never called for the overthrow of the liberal ministries in Berlin and Vienna or of the Frankfurt Assembly; they never called for the establishment of a republic and in fact cautioned against raising such an issue prematurely:

> We do not make the utopian demand that at the outset a *unitary indivisible German republic* should be proclaimed, but we do ask the so-called Radical-Democratic Party not to confuse the starting-point of the struggle and of the revolutionary movement with the goal. . . . The final act of constitution cannot be *decreed,* it coincides with the movement we have to put through. It is therefore not a question of putting into practice this or that view, this or that political idea, but of understanding the course of development. The National Assembly has to take only such steps as are practicable in the first instance.[55]

A certain patience was required, and Marx and Engels repeatedly warned their readers, as we will see presently, against rioting and provocative actions.

If conditions were not yet ripe for a republic, it goes without saying that the working class could not expect much immediate relief from its special sufferings. The *Neue Rheinische Zeitung* was almost embarrassingly silent on specifically proletarian demands and carried scarcely any news stories of proletarian organizations and activities. While the newspaper took sides boldly in the French class war that erupted in June, its pages leave no impression (prior to the counterrevolution) of any irreconcilable class conflicts between the workers and the bour-

55. "Programmes of the Radical-Democratic Party," ibid., p. 33 (except I have translated *"einige"* not as "united" but as "unitary," the opposite of a federal republic).

geoisie in Germany.[56] It never mentioned the *Communist Manifesto* or the Seventeen Demands, nor did Marx and Engels make any effort, after their agonizing reappraisal, to have the *Manifesto* reprinted and circulated in their native land. Indeed, when it was subjected to verbal attack on one occasion in front of Marx, the fiery revolutionary swallowed his tongue, remaining silent about his authorship.[57] One can imagine that Schapper and Moll, who had accompanied Marx to Cologne and loyally supported his policy of united front with the "pale" democrats, grew increasingly restive with all this restraint. They had found their natural sphere of activity in the Cologne Workers' Society, where they encountered the hungry faces of real laborers, while Marx hobnobbed with the well-fed educated bourgeois who led the Democratic Society. We will see later how the artisans eventually broke loose and resuscitated the Communist League on their own initiative.

As the revolutionary year unfolded, Marx and Engels' policy of critical support for the liberal bourgeoisie in the completion of its revolution became more and more critical, less and less supportive. The two men saw growing evidence that the German bourgeoisie would welcome back the old regime, sell out its birthright, and abandon its historically assigned tasks. If this happened, they made ready to move on to the next stage of their strategy, as we will see in the following chapter, without the first's ever having been completed. Even as they contemplated this prospect, however, they did not in their gloom conjure up the *Manifesto*'s "immediately following proletarian revolution." Rather they looked for signs of some fresh wave of revolutionary enthusiasm that would engulf the people at large and sweep into power the alliance of the majority classes—peasants, petty bourgeois, and workers. Nowhere is this expectation so pointedly revealed as in a rarely cited speech given by Marx to the Cologne Democratic Society on August 4, 1848. Two weeks earlier the group had been harangued by Wilhelm Weitling, who had just returned from America with his familiar call for immediate communist dictatorship. Doubtless feeling

56.   Noyes has made these points strongly in *Organization and Revolution*, pp. 120–23; also see Boris Nicolaievsky and Otto Maenchen-Helfen, *Karl Marx: Man and Fighter*, trans. Gwenda David and Eric Mosbacher (Philadelphia: Lippincott, 1936), p. 167; Auguste Cornu, *Karl Marx et la révolution de 1848* (Paris: Presses Universitaires, 1948), p. 20.

57.   Reminiscence of the attacker, Hermann Becker, as recounted by Schraepler, *Handwerkerbünde*, p. 285.

compromised by his "fellow" communist, Marx requested equal time. His words were reported in the society's newspaper:

> The dictatorship proposed by Weitling as the most desirable form of government Marx held . . . to be impractical and entirely impossible, since power cannot be organized by a single class. The desire to put the system of a single brain into execution by means of dictatorship deserves to be called nonsense. On the contrary, the [future] government must be composed, like the Provisional Government in Paris, out of the most heterogeneous elements, which must then reach accord through the exchange of ideas on the most expedient mode of administration.[58]

Even the most comprehensive and scholarly Communist collections have discreetly omitted or mangled this remarkable document, in which Marx not only repudiated the dictatorship of a single individual but also that of a class, in cases where the proletariat—as in Germany—was not yet sufficiently developed to form the majority class.[59]

Thus Marx seemingly remained steadfast in his commitment to democratic principles, even in the cauldron of revolution itself, when the temptation to justify a minority coup d'état must have been strong. Both he and Engels certainly expected that the people would develop "further through its own struggles," but neither tried to implement, literally, the *Manifesto*'s immediate proletarian revolution.

Revolutionary Terror and Restraint

If Marx and Engels' policy was patient, in this sense, it is not to be denied that their language grew more and more violent during the course of the revolutionary year. The *Neue Rheinische Zeitung* contains a number of passages invoking red terror that have been quoted again and again—whether approvingly or in horror—by those

58. *Der Wächter am Rhein*, 2. Dutzend, no. 1, August 23, 1848. Attention was first drawn to this document by the redoubtable Nicolaievsky and Maenchen-Helfen, *Marx*, p. 171; further details of this second duel with Weitling are now available in Dowe, *Aktion und Organisation*, pp. 174–75; Schraepler, *Handwerkerbünde*, pp. 287–90.

59. For example, see *Werke*, 5:570; and *Bund Dokumente*, 1:827, which pretends the report to be "garbled."

who interpret Classical Marxism in a totalitarian way. Bertram Wolfe, for example, has alleged that Marx's study of the Great French Revolution led him "to fall in love with terror as an engine of progress," and that this infatuation "reached its apogee in the years 1848–50."[60] Let us examine the major "terror" passages written by Marx and Engels during their year as practicing revolutionaries and then set them against their actual use of political violence during the same period.

We may begin with the passage that occurs in Engels' treatment of the bloody June Days in Paris, the first major setback for the forces of revolution. Most modern historians would probably agree with Marx and Engels' contention that the Parisian workers were deliberately provoked to a showdown by the government's dramatic closing of the National Workshops in the capital city. With this action, Engels wrote, the bourgeoisie had itself "forcibly driven the workers to insurrection," to a *"revolution of despair,"* from which they could scarcely hope to emerge victorious. The result was a cruel massacre in which three thousand insurgents were killed (mostly helpless prisoners) and fifteen thousand more were imprisoned and eventually deported to penal colonies. The proletarian cause in France had received a staggering defeat. As the battle in the streets neared its grim conclusion, Engels defended the insurgents: "With clear consciousness the bourgeoisie is leading a war of extermination against them. . . . The workers will exact a fearful revenge. After such a struggle as these three June Days only *terrorism* is possible, whether it be exercised by one side or the other."[61]

A second invocation of red terror, the most famous one of all, came from Marx's pen during the triumph of the counterrevolution in Austria. Reactionary circles there had found one advantage in the polyglot character of their empire: against the rebellion of one nationality they were able to use troops of another, hostile nationality. But when in October 1848 the Imperial War Minister, Count Theodor von Latour, ordered German troops from Vienna to march against the Hungarian revolution, the Viennese radicals rose up in violent protests that culminated in the lynching of Latour himself by an enraged mob. Using this act as his justification, Emperor Ferdinand I besieged his own

60. *Marxism: One Hundred Years in the Life of a Doctrine* (New York: Dial, 1965), p. 260, n. 14.
61. "Der 24. Juni" (June 1848), *Werke*, 5:127; see also pp. 118, 128–29, and Marx's later characterization, *Selected Works*, 1:147, 149.

capital city with loyal Croatian troops, which eventually subdued die-hard resistance with unspeakable barbarity, restoring the emperor to full power on his own proper throne. Responding to this dread news, Marx bitterly assailed the reactionaries and promised revenge after the ultimate victory of the people:

> We shall then remember this June and October and we too shall exclaim:
> *Vae victis!*
> The purposeless massacres perpetrated since the June and October events, the tedious offering of sacrifices since February and March, the very cannibalism of the counterrevolution will convince the nations that there is only one way in which the murderous death agonies of the old society and the bloody birth throes of the new society can be *shortened,* simplified and concentrated, and *that way* is *revolutionary terror.*[62]

Two months later came the fall of Budapest and the apparent demise of the Hungarian Revolution, as the emperor's loyal Slavic armies moved eastward. This ruthless subjugation of the last major outpost of the 1848 revolution evoked what is undoubtedly the bitterest and most vicious article Engels ever wrote. First he praised the Hungarian resistance by reference to the Jacobins:

> For the first time in the 1848 revolutionary movement, for the first time since 1793, a nation surrounded by superior counterrevolutionary power, has dared to oppose the cowardly counterrevolutionary passion, to oppose the *terreur blanche* by the *terreur rouge.* . . . In Hungary, armed, organized and inspired by Kossuth we find again the mass uprising, the national production of weapons, the assignats, the summary trials of all who block the revolutionary movement, revolution in permanence,—in short, all the main features of the glorious year of 1793.

Engels then turned his wrath upon the executioners, the smaller Slavic peoples of the Austrian Empire who, as soldiers, had provided the brute force of the counterrevolution both in Vienna and Budapest:

62. "The Victory of the Counter-Revolution in Vienna" (November 1848), *"Neue Rheinische Zeitung,"* p. 149.

Among all the nations and petty ethnic groups of Austria there are only three which have been carriers of progress, which have played an active role in history and which still retain their vitality —the Germans, the Poles, and the Magyars. For this reason they are now revolutionary.

The chief mission of all other races and peoples—large and small —is to perish in the revolutionary holocaust. Therefore they are counterrevolutionary.

He proceeded to assert that "this ethnic trash always becomes and remains until its complete extermination or denationalization, the most fanatic carrier of counterrevolution." And in concluding he predicted a general war in which "these petty, bull-headed nations will be destroyed so that nothing is left of them but their names."[63] A second article on the subject ended even more ominously, urging that if the peoples in question betray the broader revolution for their own ethnic advantage, then there should be a "battle of annihilation and ruthless terrorism—not in the interests of Germany, but of the Revolution!"[64]

This is not the place to introduce Marx and Engels' complex opinions on the question of nationality, but it should at least be noted that, both before and after these articles, we can find writings by Engels which allow for and encourage a future national existence for the smaller Slavic peoples.[65] Thus, while there is no excusing this revolting genocidal outburst, still it was clearly a temporary aberration, born in the anguished helplessness of defeat. Even at the time, Engels seemed ashamed at the violence of his own language, for he added, almost apologetically: "And yet these reproaches would be superfluous and unjust if the Slavs had anywhere taken a serious part in the movement of 1848, if they had hastened to enter the ranks of the revolutionary peoples."[66]

63. "The Magyar Struggle" (January 1849), in *The Russian Menace to Europe*, ed. Paul W. Blackstock and Bert F. Hoselitz (Glencoe: Free Press, 1952), pp. 56–57, 59, 63, 67.

64. "Democratic Pan-Slavism" (February 1849), ibid., p. 84.

65. For early 1848, see Werke, 4:509–10, 5:81–82; afterwards, see ibid, 9:27, 34–35. For fuller discussion of this issue, see Roman Rosdolsky, "Friedrich Engels und das Problem der 'geschichtlosen' Völker," *Archiv für Sozialgeschichte* 4 (1964):87–282; Wolfram Swoboda, "The Thought of Marx and Engels on the Question of the Central European Nationalities, 1846–1856," *Austrian History Yearbook* 9 (1974).

66. "Democratic Pan-Slavism," *Russian Menace*, p. 78.

The fourth well-known passage comes from the final red-inked number of the *Neue Rheinische Zeitung* on May 19, 1849, when the reactionary Prussian authorities finally succeeded in suppressing the paper, thus silencing Marx's venomous criticism for the second time in a decade. Defiantly, the Promethean editor challenged the allegations made by the authorities, concluding:

Why then your hypocritical phrases, your attempt to find an impossible pretext?

We have no compassion and we ask no compassion from you. When our turn comes, we shall not make excuses for the terror. But the *royal terrorists*, the terrorists by the grace of God and the law, are in practice brutal, disdainful, and mean, in theory cowardly, secretive, and deceitful, and in both respects *disreputable.*[67]

One or another of these four passages predicting red terror can be found in virtually every Cold War treatment of Marx and Engels' political ideas, generally presented without any historical context as the eternally valid precepts of godless Marxism.[68] If one does look at the historical context, certain common elements stand out immediately. All these invocations of terror came in moments of crushing defeat for Marx and Engels; there are no parallel passages during the forward-moving period prior to the June Days or during moments of optimism thereafter.[69] In 1849 Marx would declare bitterly that the February and March Revolutions had been too "humane," but he never said such a thing in February or March.[70] While the initiative was on their side, both men called for more thoroughgoing institutional change, but not for more brutality or terror. Furthermore, three of the four outbursts quoted above were responses to deliberate and massive *physical* violence employed by the conservative side; interestingly, the bloodless November counterrevolution in Prussia, though it affected the two men more directly, brought no terroristic language in reaction.[71]

67. [Suppression of the *Neue Rheinische Zeitung*] (May 1849), "*Neue Rheinische Zietung,*" pp. 253–54.

68. In addition to the four actual invocations of terror, there are a few other articles in which terror is referred to in one context or another; see *Werke*, 5:379, 403; 6:107, 388–89.

69. See, e.g., ibid., 5:417–19, 453–54.

70. "The Revolutionary Movement" (January 1849), "*Neue Rheinische Zeitung,*" p. 203.

71. See *Werke*, 6:5–12.

In each of the four cases, red terror is promised in retaliation for the white terror just perpetrated, with an implicit invocation of the lex talionis. On one occasion, in April 1849, Engels made the threat quite personal: after the reactionary Prussian government had extradited a seriously ill political refugee to face the Austrian gallows, Engels promised the "Herren Manteuffel, Brandenburg, and associates" that their own extradition had already been arranged, following the next revolution, to face the "vengeful German people."[72] All this calls to mind the maxim Engels had quoted with approval in 1845: "The oppressed has the right to use all means against his oppressor that the oppressor employs against him."[73] If not a very sophisticated ethical principle, neither was the one appealed to by the counterrevolution: "*Gegen Demokraten helfen nur Soldaten*" (Against democrats only soldiers help). Quite legitimately Engels pointed out as early as September 1848 that, from Paris to Prague and from Lombardy to Posen, the conservative armed forces had shed "more blood in four months than 1793 and 1794 combined."[74]

Finally, all the passages predict red terror by a victorious populace at some time in the *future* but call for no terroristic acts in the *present*. It is highly significant that the same final number of the *Neue Rheinische Zeitung* which contained the red-inked promise of terror without excuses also contained a red-inked caution against violence in the here and now: "Finally we warn you [workers] against any putsch in Cologne."[75] As we will see in a moment, this was no isolated appeal for restraint. In their proper context, then, the terror passages reveal themselves as what they really were—impotent cries of rage against the brutal repression of the counterrevolution, threats and visions of retributive justice in the hereafter, curses such as the weak and helpless have always uttered against the unjust acts of the mighty. Even as visions of revenge they seem fairly pale next to their historical analogues, which—like the Revelation of Saint John the Divine—generally tend to linger sadistically over the physical details of retribution.

While the terror passages may offer some insight into Marx and Engels' psychological capability to withstand defeats, they give a seriously misleading picture of their actual policies in Cologne. These policies

72. "Auslieferung politischer Flüchtlinge" (April 1849), ibid., p. 425.
73. See above, chap. 5, n. 38.
74. "Die Polendebatte in Frankfurt" (August 1848), *Werke*, 5:358.
75. "To the Workers of Cologne" (May 1849), "*Neue Rheinische Zeitung,*" p. 266.

would appear to be drawn far more from Engels' other 1845 maxim, that the duty of communists is to reduce revolutionary violence to the unavoidable minimum.[76] As against the four invocations of future terror, Marx and Engels issued during the same year no fewer than nine warnings against putschism in the here and now. Already on June 11, when rumors of a Blanquist-style insurrection during the approaching Whitsuntide prompted the reinforcement of the Cologne garrison, Engels feared the military authorities would impose martial law and disarm the entire citizenry, as they had already done in Mainz and Trier. He wrote:

We warn the Cologne workers earnestly against this reactionary plan. We ask them urgently *not to give the slightest pretext* to the Old Prussian party to place Cologne under the despotism of martial law. We ask them *to let the Whitsuntide pass with especially complete tranquility* and thereby foil the entire plan of the reactionaries.[77]

If Engels had private knowledge of insurrectionary plans, he could scarcely have chosen a more effective argument to combat them.

A second warning against putschism came on July 4 when local authorities arrested the popular Dr. Gottschalk for having publicly urged the introduction of a republic.[78] The most serious crisis came in September, when the appointment of a new, more conservative ministry in Berlin coincided with an uprising in Frankfurt. The tension in Cologne produced arrests on one side, barricade building on the other, and finally the proclamation of martial law with further arrests, prohibitions, and the temporary suppression of the *Neue Rheinische Zeitung*. On the critical day, September 25, Marx moved from meeting to meeting, urging his listeners not to be provoked to violence.[79] In the wake of his resistance to the November counterrevolution, Marx himself was arrested, yet he signed another appeal in the *Neue Rheinische Zeitung* to avoid violence.[80] A fifth warning came on March 14,

76. See above, chap. 5, n. 39.
77. "Köln in Gefahr," *Werke*, 5:62; see Schraepler, *Handwerkerbünde*, pp. 284–86.
78. *Werke*, 5:165.
79. Ibid. pp. 574–75; cf. p. 421.
80. Ibid., 6:38

1849, during what Marx judged to be deliberate provocations by the government.[81] The last major stroke by the counterrevolution began early in May, when the Prussian king dramatically refused the imperial crown offered him by the Frankfurt Assembly and at the same time dissolved the freshly elected legislature in Berlin. In various parts of Germany protests led to a last round of extended fighting. The lack of any serious violence in Cologne at this time may not be entirely unconnected to the three separate warnings Engels printed on May 4, 6, and 8 against such hopeless uprisings.[82] We have already noted the final red-inked admonishment of May 19 when the *Neue Rheinische Zeitung* itself was suppressed. It would seem Marx and Engels were not easily provoked.

Thus, whatever the violence of their dreams of future retribution, when real lives were at stake in Cologne, the two men showed a restraint and tactical cautiousness that would surely scandalize some of their present-day admirers. Indeed, between the excess of revolutionary talk and the paucity of revolutionary deeds, one might be tempted to conclude that Marx and Engels were merely radical windbags with no stomach for the real thing. But this would be a mistaken conclusion too, for on one notable occasion Marx did *not* call for restraint. The occasion was the November counterrevolution of 1848.

Marx's Behavior in the Counterrevolution

Marx will appear alone in this section because his partner was temporarily *hors de combat*. During the September crisis, when martial law was imposed in Cologne, Engels found himself obliged to flee to avoid arrest. He journeyed through eastern France to Switzerland, where he hibernated until it seemed safe to return to the city, in January 1849.

The September crisis itself marked the beginning of conservative recovery in Berlin, and at first Marx thought the moment of the counterrevolution might be at hand. The crisis began as a conflict between the liberal ministry of David Hansemann and the "pale" democratic majority of the Prussian Assembly. The assembly had censured the cabinet for its failure to curb repeated and violent assaults by units of the regular army on various local citizens' militias. In September

81. Ibid., p. 345.
82. Ibid., pp. 468, 471, 475.

the Hansemann Cabinet resigned in protest, giving the monarch the opportunity to make a fresh appointment of ministers. As Marx read the situation, the bankruptcy of hesitant liberalism left Frederick William two alternatives: either he could give in to the assembly majority by appointing a cabinet led by "pale" democrats, or he could defy the assembly with a reactionary cabinet of his own favorites:

> Either a Waldeck government, recognition of the authority of the German National Assembly [in Frankfurt] and recognition of popular sovereignty;
> Or a Radowitz-Vincke government, dissolution of the Berlin Assembly, abolition of the revolutionary gains, a sham constitutionalism or even the United Provincial Diet.

Marx urged the assembly to insist on its sovereign power, but at all costs not to let itself be dissolved. Even the official theory allowed that the king and the assembly shared constituent authority, that they were equal partners:

> If the Assembly and the Crown have *equal rights, then the Crown has no right to dissolve the Assembly.*
> Otherwise, to be consistent, the Assembly would also have the *right to depose the King.*
> The dissolution of the Assembly would therefore be a *coup d'état.* And how people reply to a coup d'état was demonstrated on July 29, 1830, and February 24, 1848. . . .
> If the Assembly wins and succeeds in setting up a Left ministry, then the power of the Crown existing *alongside* the Assembly is broken, then the King is merely a paid servant of the people and we return again to the morning of March 19.[83]

What is interesting in this important September article is that Marx still did not go essentially beyond the bourgeois revolution. While promising popular insurrection as the necessary response to any attempted royal coup, he was still quite willing to countenance a peace-

83. "The Crisis and the Counter-Revolution" (September 1848), "*Neue Rheinische Zeitung,*" pp. 121–23 (July and February were the dates of the French revolutions; March 19 was the day of royal capitulation in the Prussian Revolution of 1848).

ful forward movement that did not go beyond parliamentary control of a monarchical government, one in which the king would be "merely a paid servant of the people." He did not call for the overthrow or defiance of the liberal Frankfurt Assembly but on the contrary expected a Waldeck ministry to recognize its authority and thus help in the creation of an effective government at the national level.

As events unfolded, Frederick William put off the showdown by appointing a dark-horse prime minister, a conservative but conciliatory general, and the counterrevolution was delayed for another six weeks. Finally, taking courage from the example of his brother despot in Austria, the Prussian monarch marched his loyal troops back into the capital city without resistance, appointed a thoroughly reactionary cabinet under Count Friedrich Wilhelm von Brandenburg, prorogued the Prussian Assembly at bayonet point, proclaimed martial law in Berlin, dissolved the citizens' militia, closed all political clubs, reimposed censorship, etc. In early November the counterrevolution descended unambiguously over Prussian soil.

Marx's response was instantaneous: he helped organize a general campaign of tax refusal and immediate preparations for a popular insurrection to overthrow the new government. No sooner had the king appointed the new cabinet and prorogued the assembly than the *Neue Rheinische Zeitung* declared these acts to constitute an illegal coup d'état and called for the new government to be "starved into surrender." "And how can one starve it into surrender? By refusing to pay taxes. . . . *No taxes are due to a government that commits high treason.*"[84] Three days later, on November 15, the Berlin Assembly met in open defiance of its prorogation and voted the same response, giving legal sanction—if one still recognized the authority of the assembly— to the tax refusal campaign. For the next month the *Neue Rheinische Zeitung* carried the exhortation *"Keine Steuern mehr!!!"* (No More Taxes!!!) in huge letters on its masthead, while Marx played a key role in organizing both the local and regional (Rhine Province) tax refusal campaigns. At first he even tried to involve the bourgeois liberals, but when this failed he continued to make special efforts to reach rural areas and enlist the peasant support that would be crucial to success.[85]

84. "Counter-Revolution in Berlin" (November 1848), ibid., pp. 162–63.

85. See ibid., pp. 159, 162, 164; *Werke*, 6:685. For detailed accounts of Marx's activities, see Oscar J. Hammen, *The Red '48ers: Karl Marx and Friedrich Engels*

Marx did not, however, contemplate a merely passive resistance: he fully expected that government efforts to collect taxes would lead to bloody clashes and then general insurrection. Even his initial call for tax refusal included the following additional appeal: "It is the *duty of the Rhineland to hasten to the assistance of the Berlin National Assembly with men and weapons.*"[86] Then, on November 18, the Rhenish District Committee of Democrats, of which Marx was a leading member, issued an appeal for all democratic associations to have three immediate measures taken in every locality: (1) "Since the Prussian National Assembly itself has ruled that taxes are not to be paid, their forcible collection must be resisted everywhere and in every way"; (2) "In order to repulse the enemy the local militia [*Landsturm*] must be organized everywhere"; and (3) government officials who refuse to acknowledge the authority of the assembly should be watched over by "committees of public safety," and similarly recalcitrant local councils should be "replaced through universal popular elections."[87] Marx himself took part in the Cologne committee set up in accordance with the third measure and called for the ouster of the city council when it refused to endorse tax refusal. His own demands would have gone even further: appointed government officials who refused allegiance to the assembly should not merely be watched over but ousted and declared "traitors," their duties to be assumed by the "provisional committees of public safety, whose orders alone are to be regarded as legally binding."[88]

That Marx understood all this as an open call for revolution is evident from the letter he sent Engels a few days later: "Our paper is agitating constantly with the call for insurrection [*Emeute*] but circumnavigates the penal code in spite of all subpoenas. It is presently very much in vogue. We also put out placards every day. *La révolution marche.*"[89] The placards had to do with Marx's efforts to help organize

---

(New York: Scribners, 1969), pp. 342–46; Becker, *Kölner Arbeiterverein*, pp. 162–65.

86.   "Counter-Revolution in Berlin," *"Neue Rheinische Zeitung,"* p. 163; also see "Ein Brief von Karl Marx zur Steuerverweigerungskampagne," *Beiträge zur Geschichte der deutschen Arbeiterbewegung* 7 (1965):672.

87.   "Appeal" (November 1848), *"Neue Rheinische Zeitung,"* p. 168 (translation modified—RNH; see original German, *Werke*, 6:33).

88.   "Ein Erlass Eichmanns" (November 1848), *Werke*, 6:32; also see pp. 37, 683–84; Hammen, *The Red '48ers*, p. 346.

89.   Letter of November 29, 1848, *Werke*, 27:131.

the local militia and win over the regular garrison soldiers. Through placards and other means, the regulars were invited to fraternize with the militiamen and not allow themselves to be used against the populace. This effort did not have much success, nor could arms be obtained for the irregular forces, which left the garrison commander firmly in control of the city throughout the crisis.[90] Despite Marx's confident letter to Engels, the revolution did not "*marche*"; in fact, it did not materialize at all.

Because of his signature on the November 18 appeal, Marx was himself arrested on November 20 and eventually tried by jury in February 1849 on the charge of "incitement to rebellion." In his long and brilliantly conceived defense speech, Marx did not deny the charge but boldly cried, *tu quoque*: "I do not understand how he [the public prosecutor] dares to invoke against us laws which the Crown itself has trampled in the dirt. If the Crown makes a counter-revolution, the people has the right to reply with a revolution. . . . This was our right and our duty."[91] The attempted resistance of November 1848 proved to be the only insurrection Marx ever personally tried to call forth during his entire life, and his action would appear to fall safely within the limits accepted in the democratic tradition. At least the Cologne jury thought so: not only did it find Marx innocent, but it gave him a special vote of thanks for his informative remarks.[92]

It should be emphasized that Marx had tried to evoke the widest possible popular resistance rather than terrorist violence by a disciplined minority. The appeal of November 18 had called for the replacement of local councils by popular election, not by any self-appointed radical dictators. Marx even acted to restrain the more impetuous elements in the Cologne Workers' Society, insisting on the need for combined action with the democrats.[93] And when the tax refusal campaign failed to catch hold, and armed revolution failed to materialize, Marx did not attempt any measures of violent despair but went grimly back to his editorial desk at the *Neue Rheinische Zeitung*, exchanging the

90. Schraepler, *Handwerkerbünde*, pp. 323–24; see also *Werke*, 7:123; 21:198–99.
91. "The Trial of the Rhenish District Committee of Democrats" (February 1849), "*Neue Rheinische Zeitung*," pp. 227, 246; cf. *Werke*, 21:200–01.
92. Isaiah Berlin, *Karl Marx: His Life and Environment*, 3rd ed. (New York: Oxford, 1963), pp. 177–78.
93. Dowe, *Aktion und Organisation*, p. 208; Becker, *Kölner Arbeiterverein*, pp. 164–65.

sword once more for the pen. After the successive victories of the counterrevolution, Marx wrote on November 30, "nothing remained for democrats but to retreat as honorably as possible and to defend foot by foot, in the press, in public meetings, and in parliaments, the terrain that can no longer be held."[94] Even in this crushing defeat, Marx did not attempt a policy of minority terrorism. Whatever dreams he may have had of popular vengeance in the future, he did not claim any right to take revenge himself in the present.

Initially Marx had seen signs that the counterrevolution would drive the bourgeoisie "once more into the *arms of the revolution, into the arms of the people*,"[95] a last ember of hope for the classic bourgeois revolution in Germany. But that ember soon died: with a few mild protests the bourgeois liberals quickly settled down to accept the royal coup, many seemingly grateful that the "authorities" would now deal with the threat of "anarchy" from the left. The liberal majority of the Frankfurt National Assembly even went so far as to declare "null and void" the tax refusal decree of its sister assembly in Berlin. More than anything else, this act snapped Marx's critical support of the bourgeois revolution. Stormily he announced that this declaration actually "has nullified the Frankfurt Parliament":

> We therefore declare that the German Parliament is guilty of high treason. Nay, we do it too much honor; we impute to it a political importance which it has long since lost. The severest judgment has already been passed upon it—disregard of its rulings and total oblivion.[96]

Two weeks later Marx summed up the entire development in Germany since the March Revolution in his noted article, "The Bourgeoisie and the Counterrevolution," and drew some crucially important conclusions from the failure of the bourgeois revolution:

> The German bourgeoisie developed so sluggishly, timidly and slowly that at the moment when it menacingly confronted feudalism and absolutism, it saw menacingly pitted against itself the pro-

94. "Die revolutionäre Bewegung in Italien" (November 1848), *Werke,* 6:79.
95. "Counter-Revolution in Berlin," *"Neue Rheinische Zeitung,"* p. 159.
96. "The Assembly at Frankfurt" (November 1848), ibid., p. 170 (translation modified—RNH; see original German, *Werke,* 6:43).

letariat and all sections of the middle class whose interests and ideas were related to those of the proletariat. . . . From the first it was inclined to betray the people and to compromise with the crowned representatives of the old society. . . .

The French bourgeoisie began by emancipating the peasants. Together with the peasants it conquered Europe. The Prussian bourgeoisie was so preoccupied with its *most narrow,* immediate interests that it foolishly lost even this ally and turned it into a tool of the feudal counter-revolutionaries. . . .

The history of the Prussian middle class, and that of the German middle class in general between March and December shows that a purely *middle-class revolution* and the establishment of *bourgeois rule* in the form of a *constitutional monarchy* is impossible in Germany, and that the only alternatives are either a feudal absolutist counter-revolution or a *social republican revolution.*[97]

With this final abandonment of the bourgeois revolution, with this first open and direct call for a social republic, Marx inaugurated a new, more radical phase in his strategy for revolution in Germany. Up until now, if his words were sometimes violent, his actual policies showed considerable restraint, with no inclination to call forth the immediate minority revolution of the proletariat that seems implicit in the concluding paragraphs of the *Communist Manifesto.* Whether in the bitterness of defeat he would now pull out all the stops is the question that must occupy us in the following chapter.

97. (December 1848), *"Neue Rheinische Zeitung,"* pp. 184, 199, 202.

❧[7]❧

A Strategy of Minority Revolution?

IN THE PERIOD between December 1848 and August 1850, the policies of Marx and Engels became more extreme than ever before or after, and the two men appeared unambiguously to have embraced—at least temporarily—the central doctrines of totalitarian democracy. While still in Germany, in the period after the counterrevolution, their political strategy began from the premise that the bourgeois revolution had failed; the bourgeoisie itself now stood on the side of reaction and was no longer politically progressive. In effect the two men moved to the second phase of their class-alliance strategy without the first phase's ever having been completed. In itself this constituted a radical innovation which logically implied the possibility of leaping over an entire period of historical development. Then in April 1849, Marx and Engels dramatically broke with the "pale" democrats, attacking their old allies more and more stridently and emphasizing the need for independent proletarian organization. Skipping stages seemed to require a conscious minority revolution, with all its consequences.

After being driven into exile again in the summer of 1849, Marx and Engels pushed this strategy to even further extremes and apparently applied it to France as well: they began for the first time to use the phrase "permanent revolution"; they called more specifically than ever before for a policy of terrorism; they undertook a united front with the French Blanquists in a super-secret society; and they began—also for the first time—to demand a "dictatorship of the proletariat." It would appear that defeat and exile had warped their perspective in a way no one has analyzed more succinctly than Marx himself in an 1875 recollection:

[212]

The violent suppression of a revolution leaves a powerful imprint upon the minds of those involved, especially if they are torn away from their homes and cast into exile. So that even people with steady personalities may lose their heads for a longer or shorter period. They can no longer keep pace with the march of events. They refuse to admit that history has changed direction. Hence the playing around with conspiracies and revolutions which compromises the cause they are serving no less than themselves.[1]

Of course Marx did not think he was describing himself, but many later scholars have drawn such a conclusion.[2] Postponing the question of proletarian dictatorship until chapter 9, let us examine the other issues as they arise chronologically.

German Strategy in 1849

The roots of Marx and Engels' new German strategy extend back to June 1848. Up until that time, as we have seen, the two men anticipated a period of bourgeois rule in Germany that would last at least "several years"; the development of communism would "assume its slowest pace" there because of the country's backwardness. In early June they had even warned against the temptation "to confuse the starting-point of the struggle and of the revolutionary movement with the goal."[3] But the apparent inability of the German bourgeoisie to push its half-revolution of March through to a conclusion, combined with the bloody June setback of the general European revolution in Paris (and Prague), led Marx and Engels to contemplate an acceleration of their strategic timetable.[4] They began looking about for signs and instrumentalities of radicalization, hoping that a fresh revolutionary wave might save Germany from an otherwise inevitable relapse into despotism.

With the model of the Great French Revolution never far from their

---

1. "Postscript" (1875) to *Revelations Concerning the Communist Trial in Cologne,* in *The Cologne Communist Trial,* trans. and ed. Rodney Livingstone (New York: International, 1971), p. 131.
2. See authorities cited above, chap. 1, n. 35.
3. See above, chap. 6, n. 55.
4. See, e.g., *Werke,* 5:64–65, 79.

consciousness, the two men first thought they had discovered an answer in external conflict. In 1792–1794, war against the conservative monarchies of Europe had driven revolutionary France progressively to the left, partly because reactionary elements at home tended to side with the invading enemies, making defeat tantamount to counterrevolution, and thus faintheartedness tantamount to treason. More and more extreme measures seemed to be called for in an effort to mobilize the nation's utmost war potential and save both the country and the revolution. And so in 1848, a war against the remaining bastion of reaction, Czarist Russia, might have a parallel radicalizing effect on western Europe, especially on Germany. From the beginning of the revolution, Marx and Engels anticipated what actually transpired in 1849—that Russia would intervene militarily against the revolutionaries on her Western flank. Increasingly after the June Days, the two men saw such an intervention as a *positive* opportunity: "If the Russians rush in from the east to aid the Prussian dynasty, the French will rush in from the west to aid the German people. . . . The Germans will ally themselves with the French and, united with them, wage a war of the west against the east, of civilization against barbarism, of republic against autocracy."[5] Here was the first veiled suggestion that war might produce a republic in Germany. By mid-July the two men had grown absolutely rhapsodic about the energizing effects of a war against czarism whose by-products would naturally include the liberation of Poland:

> Only *war with Russia* is a war of *revolutionary Germany,* a war which can wash away the sins of the past, in which Germany can gain its manhood, in which it can defeat its own autocrats, and— as befits a people shaking off the chains of a long ignoble slavery —promote the cause of civilization by the sacrifice of its sons, and free itself at home by liberating abroad.[6]

In such an ennobling conflict, one that was deemed inevitable in any event, Marx and Engels did not appear at all fussy about which side fired the first shot. Certainly they exhibited a degree of bellicosity dur-

5. "Drohung der Gervinus-Zeitung" (June 1848), ibid., p. 105; see also pp. 42, 79, 82.
6. Marx, "Die auswärtige deutsche Politik und die letzten Ereignisse zu Prag," ibid., p. 202; cf. Engels on the same theme, ibid., pp. 334–35.

ing this period that cannot be found in their other writings, either before or after.[7]

While the call for a 1793-style war against Russia continued throughout the next several months, by September 1848 a second possible radicalizing agency had turned up—the prospect of a new revolution in France. A little later we will examine Marx and Engels' perceptions of the French scene in some detail; for now suffice it to say that the June violence was followed by progressive infringements on basic civil rights that ultimately left the Republic, in their eyes, little more than a hollow shell, particularly as far as the workers were concerned. The entrenched bourgeois government seemed prepared to jettison even universal suffrage, and thus was not likely to let itself be voted out of power. Its increasing unpopularity raised the likelihood, however, of a new upheaval in which the alliance of majority classes could start afresh, making good the errors of February by combining democratic political structures with an effective program of social reform and controls over the capitalist system. Essentially it was the "intermediate" revolution in a second, improved edition, with its political goal now labeled a "democratic social republic" to distinguish it from the existing martial-law republic of the bourgeoisie. Such a popular resurgence in France would have a catalytic effect on the rest of Europe, or so it seemed to Engels: "Before reaction can be destroyed in Italy and Germany, it must be routed in France. A democratic social republic must first be proclaimed in France and the French proletariat must first subjugate its bourgeoisie, before a lasting democratic victory is conceivable in Italy, Germany, Poland, Hungary and other countries."[8]

Thus, by the time the November counterrevolution had snuffed out Marx and Engels' last hopes for a successful bourgeois revolution in Germany, the two men were ready with an alternative strategy for a more radical revolution, sparked by either war with Russia or a new French rising, or both. So it was that Marx's above-quoted article, "The Bourgeoisie and the Counterrevolution," ended with the appeal for a "social republican revolution." And the *Neue Rheinische Zeitung* greeted the new year with the stinging declaration: "The table of con-

7. This point particularly emphasized by Bertram D. Wolfe, *Marxism: One Hundred Years in the Life of a Doctrine* (New York: Dial, 1965), pp. 24–29.
8. "Mediation and Intervention: Radetzky and Cavaignac" (September 1848), *The Revolution of 1848–49: Articles from the "Neue Rheinische Zeitung,"* trans. S. Ryazanskaya (New York: International, 1972), p. 109.

tents for 1849 reads: Revolutionary rising of the French working class, world war."[9]

The shrillness of this greeting should not obscure the basic socio-political assumptions of the new strategy for Germany. In essence Marx and Engels moved back (or forward?) to the Seventeen Demands, which had assumed the bourgeois revolution to be over. Politically, it will be remembered, this program called upon the majority classes —the peasants, urban petty bourgeois, and workers—to create a democratic republic, and what the *Neue Rheinische Zeitung* now openly reiterated after November was exactly the same demand for a jointly created democratic republic.[10] Nowhere in its pages can one find any call for independent proletarian revolution or dictatorship. On the contrary, united action with the "pale" democrats acquired even greater relevance, as Marx and Engels made clear by their support of the candidates put up by the Cologne Democratic Society in the Prussian elections of January 1849. Special exertions were required to counter the inclination of Gottschalk's followers within the Cologne Workers' Society to put up their own independent candidate. Marx urged them to realize that such a move would only divide the opposition vote and "allow our common enemy, the absolute monarchy, to triumph." For the moment it was not necessary to advance working-class candidates; "plain democrats, even liberals, would be sufficient" if they opposed the present regime.[11] This argument succeeded in winning the society's endorsement of the Democratic candidates, while on the other side Marx went so far as to publish an article openly asking for the support of the bourgeois liberals.[12]

The tactic seemed vindicated when the candidates made a clean sweep in Cologne, and democratic forces emerged with greater electoral strength all across the country. Jubilantly Marx proclaimed that "the petty bourgeoisie, peasants, and proletarians have emancipated

9. "The Revolutionary Movement" (January 1849), ibid., p. 205; also see *Selected Works*, 2:300–03.

10. See *Werke*, 6:207, 217, 265, 460, 504–06.

11. "Komiteesitzung des Arbeitervereins vom 15. Januar 1849," ibid., p. 579; also see Boris Nicolaievsky and Otto Maenchen-Helfen, *Karl Marx: Man and Fighter*, trans. Gwenda David and Eric Mosbacher (Philadelphia: Lippincott, 1936), pp. 184–87; Ernst Schraepler, *Handwerkerbünde und Arbeitervereine, 1830–53* (Berlin: deGruyter, 1972), pp. 327–30.

12. "Montesquieu LVI" (January 1849), "*Neue Rheinische Zeitung*," pp. 211–26.

themselves from the big bourgeoisie, the high nobility, and the high bureaucracy":

> Can the petty bourgeois and peasants, and especially the proletarians, find a better form of government to represent their interests than the democratic republic? Are not these classes precisely the most radical, the most democratic, in the entire society?[13]

It would seem obvious that Marx and Engels' abandonment of the bourgeois revolution did not involve an abandonment of democratic demands or democratic values.

Before the election results were known, Marx had published some unusually revealing thoughts on the subject of universal suffrage, as he criticized a rival newspaper for its naive belief in such a thing as the "will of the entire people":

> For the *National-Zeitung* there exists *one* will of the entire people, which is not the sum of contradictory wills but a united and fixed will. How is that?
>
> That is—the will of the majority.
>
> And what is the will of the majority?
>
> It is the will which emerges out of the interests, life situation, and conditions of existence of the majority.
>
> In order to have one and the same will, the members of the majority must therefore have the same interests, the same life situation, the same conditions of existence, or must be temporarily linked together in their interests, their life situation, their conditions of existence.
>
> In plain words: the will of the people, the will of the majority, is not the will of separate estates and classes but of *one single class,* and of those classes and fragments of classes that are socially—i.e., industrially and commercially—subordinated to this ruling class.
>
> "What should we say to that?" Is the will of the entire people the will of the ruling class?
>
> Exactly, and universal suffrage is precisely the compass needle which, perhaps after various deviations, finally points to the class that is called to rule.

13. "Die 'Kölnische Zeitung' über die Wahlen" (February 1849), *Werke,* 6:216–17.

He concluded with the confident prediction: "Wait just a little while and the people will rise up and fell . . . the counterrevolution with *one* mighty blow."[14]

Within the lingering Hegelian structures of his thought, Marx conceived that each successive class was "called to rule" and to emancipate mankind in some degree. During each period of emancipation, history awarded majority support, as it were, to this ruling class, because the masses would perceive the leadership of the chosen group genuinely to advance the interests of the whole society. So it had been in proper bourgeois revolutions, when the masses had provided the muscle for the bourgeoisie in its struggle to break out from the fetters of feudalism. So it would be again when the proletariat was called upon to play its ultimate emancipatory role, but not, perhaps, before the compass needle of universal suffrage registered "various deviations." Among these, Marx must have had freshly in mind the discouraging peasant landslide of a few weeks before that had swept Louis Napoleon Bonaparte into power as president of France. And he also seemed to anticipate that the successful creation of a republic in Germany would dissolve the tripartite class alliance, leaving the more radical proletarian minority at first in opposition to a "pale" democratic government representing the petty-bourgeois and peasant majority. He implied as much when differentiating himself politically from one of the leading "petty-bourgeois" democrats: "Friedrich Hecker might be a good tricolor republican. The real opposition of the *Neue Rheinische Zeitung* will first begin in the tricolor republic."[15] What is important is Marx's confidence that, despite any preliminary "deviations," the lower-middle classes—or whatever "fragments" thereof might still exist —would eventually swing to support the proletarian cause. Here one can still perceive that fundamental and decidedly un-Blanquist faith in universal suffrage, a faith in the capacity of the masses to learn from their own mistaken "deviations," that was so visible in Marx and Engels' writings during the innocent days before 1848.

By-passing the bourgeois revolution meant essentially that the alliance of the majority classes would have to carry out the central political tasks left undone by the weak and fearful German bourgeoisie—

14.   "Die Berliner 'National-Zeitung' an die Urwähler" (January 1849), ibid., pp. 200, 204.

15.   "Der Staatsprokurator 'Hecker' und die 'Neue Rheinische Zeitung' " (October 1848), ibid., 5:443.

the destruction of absolutism and the remnants of feudalism, and the creation of a modern unified nation-state. Marx and Engels did not imagine that capitalism itself as an economic system could be bypassed. It would now develop, to be sure, under certain popular restraints and controls—as suggested in the Seventeen Demands—but nothing they wrote in this period hints at any immediate introduction of communism. On the contrary, Marx's election appeal of January 1849 warned in the following noteworthy terms against the program of guild revival that was the siren song of the counterrevolution:

> We are certainly the last people to desire the rule of the bourgeoisie. . . . But we say to the workers and the petty bourgeois: it is better to suffer in the contemporary bourgeois society, whose industry creates the means for the foundation of a new society that will liberate you all, than to revert to a bygone society, which, on the pretext of saving your classes, thrusts the entire nation back into medieval barbarism.[16]

Thus Marx contemplated skipping historical stages only in the limited sense that others would accomplish the *political* tasks of the bourgeois revolution. In the more profound sense, there could be no skipping the period of bourgeois-sponsored industrial development that was required to lay the necessary material and social foundation for the communist society. To the threatened artisans Marx seemed to be saying: The purgatory of modernization must be endured. There is no emergency exit. Patience.

This was not welcome counsel. Gottschalk probably articulated the sentiments of many radicalized artisans when he lashed out at Marx's appeal:

> We do not know what will become of our revolution. For us there are, apart from the possibility presented by you as necessary, the rule of the bourgeoisie, still other possibilities, for example, a new revolution, a permanent revolution. . . . For us, the party of the revolutionary proletariat who know no middle ground, there is no fear—least of all of a throwback into medieval barbarism.

16. "Montesquieu LVI," *"Neue Rheinische Zeitung,"* p. 225; also see Nicolaievsky and Maenchen-Helfen, *Marx,* pp. 186–87.

For you such a fear exists. Naturally. You have never been serious about the emancipation of the repressed. The misery of the worker, the hunger of the poor has for you only a scientific, a doctrinaire interest. . . . You do not believe in the revolt of the working people, whose rising flood begins already to prepare the destruction of capital, you do not believe in the permanence of the revolution, you do not even believe in the capacity for revolution.[17]

How odd to find Marx in his most radical period accused of not believing in the permanent revolution! And yet if the phrase is used in Gottschalk's sense to mean a continuous revolution aimed at the more-or-less immediate introduction of communism, then the accusation is warranted: The artisans for whom Gottschalk spoke did not seem tempted by the siren song of medievalism, but neither did they propose to "suffer in the contemporary bourgeois society"; they wanted communism *now*, and the slogan "permanent revolution" came to express that impatient desire, as we will see presently.

We may turn next to the apparent rupture of the united front in April 1849. From the January election campaign down through March there had been close collaboration between "red" and "pale" democrats in Cologne,[18] but on April 14 Marx and three other radicals dramatically published their resignation from the Rhenish District Committee of Democrats, asserting that it was too "heterogeneous" in composition and that henceforth they would devote their energies to "a closer union of the workers' societies."[19] Most scholars have concluded from this action that Marx no longer desired a united front, that he now sought independent organization and action by the proletariat alone.[20] Such

17.   *Freiheit, Arbeit*, February 25, 1849, as quoted in P. H. Noyes, *Organization and Revolution: Working-Class Associations in the German Revolution of 1848–1849* (Princeton: Princeton, 1966), pp. 286–87. Gottschalk was unusually inconsistent and vacillating in his political views and could move from permanent revolution to social monarchism within a few weeks, but his popularity with and closeness to the Cologne lower classes probably makes him a good weathervane of their sentiments (see Noyes' comments, ibid., pp. 285–89).

18.   Documented by Gerhard Becker, *Karl Marx und Friedrich Engels in Köln, 1848–1849: Zur Geschichte des Kölner Arbeitervereins* (Berlin: Rütten und Loening, 1963), pp. 218–20.

19.   "Erklärung," *Werke*, 6:426.

20.   Including both Communist authorities like Auguste Cornu, *Karl Marx et la révolution de 1848* (Paris: Presses Universitaires, 1948), pp. 48–49; Erik Molnár, *La politique d'alliances du marxisme (1848–1889)* (Budapest, Akadémiai Kiadó,

a policy would seem to imply minority revolution and dictatorship . . . but let us see.

It is certainly true that Marx became more and more involved in working-class activities as the revolutionary year progressed. We saw that with the dissolution of the Communist League, he initially chose to join the "petty-bourgeois" Cologne Democratic Society, ignoring the Cologne Workers' Society dominated by his rival, Gottschalk. The latter group became linked to the "pale" democrats, however, through participation in the Rhenish District Committee of Democrats, of which Marx was a leading member. While Marx maintained these organizational commitments, the two artisan veterans of the league, Schapper and Moll, chose to join the Workers' Society, where they gradually won support for Marx's views. When Gottschalk was imprisoned in July, Moll was elected to take his place as temporary president. And when Moll was obliged to flee in the wake of the September crisis, Marx himself was elected to the post, which he agreed to accept only "provisionally until the release of Dr. Gottschalk," because of the burden of his newspaper work.[21] Even this newspaper work took on a more proletarian cast as Marx began, after the counterrevolution, to distinguish working-class interests from those of the bourgeoisie, most notably in his April series, "Wage Labor and Capital."[22]

Marx's progressively rising commitment to the workers' cause, independent of the united front, culminated in the April resignation decision, which may also have reflected pressure from rank-and-file members of the Workers' Society, where the united front had become less and less popular.[23] But the immediate and express reason for the decision was the prospect of creating a mass workers' party at the national level. This project, begun earlier in the revolutionary year by Stephan Born with only partial success, was given fresh impetus in January at a Heidelberg congress of workers' societies, where a rival group

---

1967), pp. 54–55; and non-Communist authorities like Schraepler, *Handwerkerbünde*, pp. 337–42; Nicolaievsky and Maenchen-Helfen, *Marx*, p. 194. But also see contrary views of authorities cited in n. 27 below.

21. "Protokoll der Komiteesitzung des Kölner Arbeitervereins am 16. Oktober 1848," *Werke*, 5:501; also Becker, *Kölner Arbeiterverein*, pp. 90, 145–46.

22. English translation in *Selected Works*, 1:74–94.

23. A contemporaneous report of the resignation declared that it had been turned in "at the wish of the Workers' Society" (Schraepler, *Handwerkerbünde*, p. 339); cf. Noyes, *Organization and Revolution*, pp. 287–89.

decided to link up with Born's organization. This resulted in the call for an all-German congress of workers' societies to be held at Leipzig in the spring for the purpose of launching, in effect, a nationwide workers' party.[24] Needless to say, Marx welcomed these developments and wanted the Cologne Workers' Society to participate in the projected congress and affiliate with the new organization. Hitherto, the Cologne group had supralocal ties only to the regional and national organizations of the "pale" democrats, since no socialist or working-class organization had existed at these higher levels. The first step was obviously to dissolve the old links to the regional and national democratic organizations, which the Cologne Workers' Society did on April 16, following Marx's example two days earlier.[25] The second step was to create a regional organization of workers' societies for Rhineland-Westphalia: to this end the Cologne group invited all workers' societies in the two provinces *"which adhere resolutely to the principles of a social democracy"* to send delegates to a regional congress in Cologne on May 6, as a preliminary to the national Leipzig congress.[26] The Cologne gathering was held just as the last act of the revolutionary year began and, with the complete repression that followed, no national congress could be attempted.

Marx's April resignation really indicated a move to strengthen the "red" democrats' position within the united front, not to rupture the front itself. Until then, proletarian weakness had made it necessary, in his opinion, for local workers' societies to affiliate at the regional and national levels in the organization of their more powerful alliance partner. Now they were strong enough to maintain their own independent organization, a nationwide workers' party. But there was nothing to prevent such a party from collaborating, as before, in united-front actions with the "pale" democrats.[27] The subsequent policy of the Cologne Workers' Society showed no abrupt change in this respect. Two weeks after its alleged "rupture," the society passed a resolution censuring its former president, Gottschalk, for having—among other

24. Noyes, *Organization and Revolution*, pp. 290–306.
25. *Werke*, 6:584; Becker, *Kölner Arbeiterverein*, pp. 237–55.
26. "Mitteilung über die Einberufung des Kongresses der Arbeitervereine," *Werke*, 6:587–88; see also p. 584.
27. See concurring judgments on this point by Becker, *Kölner Arbeiterverein*, pp. 234–36; and Oscar J. Hammen, *The Red '48ers: Karl Marx and Friedrich Engels* (New York: Scribners, 1969), p. 380.

things—slandered the Democratic Society candidate, Franz Raveaux, during the recent electoral campaign, and for having identified Marx unjustly with Raveaux's political views when Marx was in fact only recommending that "red and pale democrats had to unite together against the howlers" of the right.[28] Neither did the "rupture" prevent the *Neue Rheinische Zeitung* from continuing to publish Wilhelm Wolff's long series of articles which analyzed agrarian injustices in a major effort to attract peasant supporters.[29] But the most convincing evidence that Marx and Engels had not abandoned the united-front policy can be found in their behavior during the final spasm of revolutionary violence in Germany.

In April 1849, the Frankfurt Assembly at long last completed work on the national constitution and presented it to the Prussian monarch, Frederick William IV, with the invitation to become German emperor, ceremonial head of the new national government. After his famous arrogant refusal to accept a "crown from the gutter," the more resolute democrats attempted to *force* him and the other German princes, by means of parliamentary pressure, popular demonstrations, and the ultimate threat of violence, to accept the constitution anyway. The princes, led by Frederick William, responded by closing down assemblies, imposing martial law, and generally crushing the remnant forces of revolution in an exercise of overwhelming military force from May through July 1849.

Marx and Engels could not enthusiastically encourage this foredoomed and highly paradoxical quasi-revolutionary campaign, undertaken mainly by principled *republicans* but aimed at forcing a Prussian *monarch* (whom all cordially detested) to accept an imperial crown that he did not even want. The two men would give advice to the insurgents, Engels would even fight, but they remained nonetheless somehow aloof and emotionally disengaged. If such an effort were to be made, it should be for more worthy aims: the National Assembly, Engels wrote on May 2, should "*proclaim civil war*" and "*if it comes to a decision, a unitary and indivisible German republic.*" But he despaired that the Frankfurters would muster such courage. And as violence broke out in the Rhineland during the following days, Engels repeatedly warned the Cologne workers *against* putsches and provoca-

28. "Beschluss der 1. Filiale des Kölner Arbeitervereins," *Werke*, 6:585.
29. "Die Schlesische Milliarde," which ran from March 22 through April 24; see comments of Schraepler, *Handwerkerbünde*, p. 341.

tions.[30] He still believed the "pale" democrats were only playing at revolution. An insurrection in Elberfeld on May 10 finally convinced Engels that developments might turn serious, and he hurried off to the town where he had once attended school.

His own ideas on the tactics of insurrection can be found classically expressed in his 1852 résumé of these events:

> Now, insurrection is an art quite as much as war or any other, and subject to certain rules of proceeding, which, when neglected, will produce the ruin of the party neglecting them. . . . Firstly, never play with insurrection unless you are fully prepared to face the consequences of your play. Insurrection is a calculus with very indefinite magnitudes the value of which may change every day; the forces opposed to you have all the advantage of organization, discipline, and habitual authority; unless you bring strong odds against them you are defeated and ruined. Secondly, the insurrectionary career once entered upon, act with the greatest determination, and on the offensive. The defensive is the death of every armed rising; it is lost before it measures itself with its enemies. Surprise your antagonists while their forces are scattering, prepare new successes, however small, but daily; keep up the moral ascendancy which the first successful rising has given to you; rally those vacillating elements to your side which always follow the strongest impulse, and which always look out for the safer side; force your enemies to a retreat before they can collect their strength against you; in the words of Danton, the greatest master of revolutionary policy yet known, de l'audace, de l'audace, encore de l'audace![31]

Engels arrived in Elberfeld to find the insurrection in the hands of a Committee of Public Safety dominated by "pale" democrats. Against the committee's inclination merely to defend the town against the inevitable Prussian attack, Engels vainly urged that the "insurrectionary career" had been entered upon and the only defense was to expand the rising to neighboring areas, to follow Danton's injunction.[32]

30. "Der preussische Fusstritt für die Frankfurter" (May 1849), Werke, 6:460; warnings, ibid., pp. 468, 471, 475.
31. Germany: Revolution and Counter-Revolution, in The German Revolutions, ed. Leonard Krieger (Chicago: Chicago, 1967), pp. 227–28; cf. p. 206.
32. From Engels' later account of these events, Die deutsche Reichsverfas-

At the same time he reassured the suspicious committee about his own intentions, declaring that in Elberfeld "he wished to occupy himself purely with military matters, and to stand entirely apart from the political character of the movement at hand, since at this time only a black-red-gold movement was possible, and any step against the Reich Constitution must be avoided."[33] Although Engels did occupy himself with purely military matters, he never quelled the anxiety of the committee that he might forgetfully proclaim a red republic, and on May 14 it formally requested him to leave the town, *"in full recognition of his efforts,"* but *"because his presence might give rise to misunderstandings as to the character of the movement."*[34] Meekly, Engels returned to Cologne, demonstrating thereby a clear desire not to impair relations with the "pale" democrats and not to push the insurrection farther to the left than it would go.

With Marx's expulsion from Prussia a few days later and the simultaneous suppression of the *Neue Rheinische Zeitung* on May 19, the two men journeyed southward to Frankfurt, where they vainly urged acquaintances in the National Assembly to organize a serious revolutionary offensive by calling upon the sympathetic Badenese and Palatine armies to march to Frankfurt in support of the constitution. The whole effort could be saved from disaster only by seizing the military initiative. The assembly, however, was disposed to remain nonviolent in its pressure. Marx and Engels continued their journey south, offering the same advice to the insurrectionists in Baden and the Palatinate, but the latter were disinclined to think beyond the defense of their own territories. Marx also urged the provisional governments here to abolish outright all remaining manorial burdens on the peasantry as the only way to secure active rural support, but again without success.[35] In all these situations, Marx and Engels pursued the same recognizable policy: they made no attempt whatsoever to call forth independent working-class insurrections aimed directly at achieving communism;

---

sungskampagne (1850), *Werke*, 7:123–24, 128–30; also see Martin Edgar Berger, "War, Armies, and Revolution: Friedrich Engels' Military Thought" (Ph.D. diss., University of Pittsburgh, 1969), pp. 30–41.

33. According to Engels' contemporaneous report, [Elberfeld] (May 1849), *Werke*, 6:501.

34. As quoted by Engels, ibid., pp. 501–02.

35. Hammen, *The Red '48ers*, 399–401; Molnár, *La politique d'alliances*, p. 63; *Werke*, 7:133–35, 143.

they did not try to undermine the "pale" democratic campaign or push it to the left in a political sense; rather they implored all democrats who would listen to seize the military initiative and press forward, lest the insurrection be doomed (as they feared) by the timidity and defense-mindedness of its own leaders.

Finally convinced that the south Germans were in fact doomed, Marx went off to await more promising developments in Paris, while Engels stayed behind in south Germany, not wanting "to miss the chance for a bit of military education, and mainly because the *Neue Rheinische Zeitung* had to be represented, *honoris causa*, in the army of Baden and the Palatinate."[36] He served for several weeks as adjutant to August von Willich, commander of one of the more disciplined and formidable volunteer corps, and survived four engagements with the Prussian army before his unit was forced across the Swiss frontier. From his experience in this campaign for the Reich Constitution, Engels seems to have drawn two principal conclusions. Firstly, he acquired what would be a lifelong respect for real military power, combined with a parallel disdain for barricade romanticism and the kind of disorganized military amateurism he saw around him in the spring of 1849.[37]

Secondly, he became convinced that the "pale" democrats who had led the campaign, the urban petty bourgeoisie in general, were at least as cowardly and unreliable in a revolution as the liberals of the high bourgeoisie had been. They could not be counted on for much help in the fresh revolutionary struggles that lay just ahead. He summed up these sentiments in his memoir of the campaign:

The history of all political movements since 1830 in Germany, as well as in France and England, reveals to us this class: always boastful, full of high affirmations, sometimes even extreme in its phrases as long as no danger is visible; fearful, grudging, holding back as soon as the slightest threat looms up; astounded, apprehensive, vacillating as soon as the movement it has begun is picked up and taken seriously by other classes; betraying the whole movement for the sake of its petty-bourgeois existence as soon as there

36. *Die deutsche Reichsverfassungskampagne,* ibid., p. 161; see also ibid., 27:509.
37. Berger, "War, Armies, and Revolution," p. 53; see Engels' various comments in his memoir of the campaign, *Werke,* 7:109–97.

comes a struggle with weapons in hand; and finally in consequence of its irresolution always particularly swindled and maltreated as soon as the reactionary party has won.[38]

Thus Engels' confidence in the "pale" democrats of the petty bourgeoisie sank to nearly zero as a result of the campaign for the Reich Constitution. As it happened, Marx had a somewhat parallel experience with their French counterparts during these same weeks—presently to be reviewed—and both men would consequently exhibit for the next year or so a special distrust of and hostility toward the petty-bourgeois democrats that will help to explain the last, most radical refinements of their class-alliance strategy, made during their London exile in the period 1849–1850.

Revolutionary Illusions of 1850

In August 1849, Marx had been in Paris only three months when another governmental expulsion order drove him to London, the city where he was destined to spend the rest of his life. Engels joined him there in November, and the two men busied themselves with refugee relief work, together with the creation of a new monthly, the *Neue Rheinische Zeitung—Revue*. There were several signs that they now took a still more extreme political stand: they rejoined the Communist League and established formal ties with a vanguard of French Blanquists, and they called for "permanent revolution," for a "dictatorship of the proletariat," and for a policy of deliberate terrorism. Although this ultraradical period lasted less than a year, until September 1850, it must be scrutinized in some detail because all four apparently totalitarian-democratic "complications" now appear simultaneously together.

In hindsight it is easy to see that the revolutionary wave of 1848 had passed, but in the bitterness of defeat and exile, Marx and Engels could accept this only by positing the existence of a second revolutionary wave directly behind the first. Desperately they grasped at straws, signs that an international war, a new rising in France, an English economic crisis, or some combination of these developments might rekindle the fires of revolution. Scanning the news for their new monthly

38. *Die deutsche Reichsverfassungskampagne, Werke*, 7:112; cf. *The German Revolutions*, p. 128–29.

in January 1850, Marx and Engels saw hope that Russia might provoke a war with Turkey because of the Porte's refusal to turn over fugitive Hungarian revolutionaries. In their far-fetched scenario, such a conflict would "necessarily" expand into a "European war," with Russia sending troops into Germany to add an "energetic" coup de grace to the counterrevolution, and thence on to Paris, "the ultimate center of the revolution." Britain could scarcely stand aloof at this point, and her economic power would make it possible to strangle the czarist regime within six months. Once again the two men conjured up the prospect of progressive western Europe fighting off reactionary czarism and revolutionizing itself in the process.[39]

With much greater tenacity, they clung to the illusion that a new economic depression stood just around the corner and would catapult first Britain, and then all Europe into new revolutionary storms, just as the depression of 1847 had precipitated the whirlwind of 1848. They predicted confidently that Britain's "colossal forces of production" would quickly outstrip available world markets, "perhaps by spring, at the latest in July or August [1850]."[40] Such an economic crisis, Engels asserted two months later, would make a revolution in Britain "inevitable" and would "speedily lead to the political and social ascendancy of the proletarians."[41] All wishful thinking, no doubt, but those authorities who would make Blanquists out of Marx and Engels in 1850 have not troubled to look any further into the specifically *English* dimension of this revolutionary illusion. It shows no trace of conspiracies, vanguards, or dictatorships.

Having taken up residence in London, Marx and especially Engels reestablished old ties with Julian Harney, who was just then in the process of displacing the half-reactionary Feargus O'Connor as principal spokesman of the Chartist movement.[42] Although with hindsight we know that Chartism was actually dying, Marx and Engels did not, and they demonstrated by their encouragement of Harney a readiness even in 1850 to support an open mass movement where such was legal-

39. "Revue," *Werke*, 7:215–16; cf. 27:515; *Selected Works*, 1:150, 193.
40. "Revue," *Werke*, 7:220; cf. pp. 292–95, 231, 239–43.
41. "The Ten Hours Question" (March 1850), *Democratic Review* (reprint ed., London: Merlin, 1968), p. 376 (German translation in *Werke*, 7:231); cf. Marx's parallel sentiments in *Werke*, 27:504.
42. Peter Cadogan, "Harney and Engels," *International Review of Social History* 10 (1965):67–72.

ly possible. Further, when in February the Court of the Exchequer effectively nullified the Ten-Hours Act of 1847, Engels argued most interestingly that the workers' efforts to secure this legislation had still not been in vain:

> The working classes, in this agitation, found a mighty means to get acquainted with each other, to come to a knowledge of their social position and interests, to organize themselves and to know their strength. The working man, who has passed through such an agitation, is no longer the same he was before [sic]; and the whole working class, after passing through it, is a hundred times stronger, more enlightened, and better organized than it was at the outset. It *was* an agglomeration of mere units, without any knowledge of each other, without any common tie; and now it is a powerful body, conscious of its strength, recognized as the "Fourth Estate," and which will soon be the *first*.
>
> Secondly. The working classes will have learned by experience that *no lasting benefit whatever can be obtained for them by others, but that they must obtain it themselves by conquering, first of all, political power.* They must see now that *under no circumstances have they any guarantee for bettering their social position unless by Universal Suffrage,* which would enable them to seat a *Majority of Working Men* in the House of Commons.[43]

In a parallel article for his German readers, Engels spelled out his conclusion even more plainly: "The reestablishment of this bill would make sense only under the rule of universal suffrage, and universal suffrage in England—where two-thirds of the inhabitants are industrial proletarians—means the exclusive political rule of the working class, with all the revolutionary changes in social condition that are inseparable from it."[44] The self-education of the masses through their own struggles, a popular revolution that would establish immediate democratic rule by the proletarian majority, full confidence in universal suffrage—this utterly un-Blanquist prescription for revolution in Britain had not changed one iota since Engels first espoused it in 1842. And yet it must be borne in mind as we proceed that these lines were

43. "The Ten Hours Question," *Democratic Review,* pp. 375–76 (German translation in *Werke,* 7:230); cf. Marx in *Werke,* 7:211–12.
44. "Die englische Zehnstundenbill" (April 1850), *Werke,* 7:241.

written at exactly the moment when Marx and Engels were establishing their united front with the Blanquists.

The final illusion to which Marx and Engels clung in the first months of their exile was more closely related to that united front—their expectation of imminent revolution in France. We have already observed how, ever since September 1848, the two men had counted on a new French rising to reinvigorate the flagging European left. In June 1849, while Engels remained in Germany to represent the *Neue Rheinische Zeitung, honoris causa,* in the campaign for the Reich Constitution, Marx moved to Paris. He had high hopes for a planned showdown on June 13, in which the French left decided to challenge the constitutionality of Napoleon's use of French troops to suppress Mazzini's republic in Rome and to back up their parliamentary assault with massive street demonstrations.[45] The showdown turned into something of a fiasco, which Marx did not hesitate to blame on the pusillanimity of the "petty-bourgeois" democrats who had organized it, echoing Engels' sentiments concerning their south German counterparts. But neither this disappointment nor his subsequent expulsion from France could shake Marx's confidence that a major revolution was due there. He developed his analysis of the French situation at length in the masterful *Class Struggles in France,* written during 1850 for serial publication in the *Neue Rheinische Zeitung—Revue.*[46]

In *Class Struggles,* Marx depicted the history of France since June 1848 as a "series of *defeats,*" a kind of permanent counterrevolution, in which real political power wound up in the hands of the same high financial bourgeoisie that had ruled under the July Monarchy with its landowning allies.[47] Despite its outwardly republican form, the regime had become increasingly authoritarian: its repeated curtailments of the right of association culminated in the complete prohibition of political clubs in March 1849; its growing infringements on the freedom of the press similarly climaxed in the crippling press law of May 1850; and a president with the ominous name Napoleon was granted special state-of-siege (martial-law) powers that permitted outright physical

45. See ibid., 27:137; *Selected Works,* 1:178–83.

46. See *Werke,* 27:140. *Class Struggles in France* is reproduced in *Selected Works,* 1:109–220. Ironically, in the original serial publication, the final installment came after Marx's dramatic shift of August 1850 and abruptly reversed the prognosis of immediate revolution (see especially pp. 208, 220).

47. *Selected Works,* 1:128, 190–91.

force to be used almost without check.[48] Even universal suffrage itself—capstone of the republican constitution—survived only so long as it produced safe conservative majorities. After the threatening leftist victories in the March 1850 by-elections, it too was thrown aside as the government reverted to property qualifications and undisguised class rule. By this action the bourgeoisie openly confessed, according to Marx, *"our dictatorship has hitherto existed by the will of the people; it must now be consolidated against the will of the people."*[49] A government which thus obliterated the most elementary political rights obviously could not be voted out of power—it had to be overthrown.

In *Class Struggles*, needless to say, the proletariat moved to center stage as the principal agent of this impending overthrow, the most resolute enemy of Napoleon's sham republic. Recovering from the disastrous defeat of June 1848, the radical workers had put forth Francois-Vincent Raspail as their presidential candidate in December. Although his vote was insignificant in the Napoleonic landslide, this electoral effort represented for Marx "the first act by which the proletariat, as an independent political party, declared its separation from the democratic party." (It compared with Marx's roughly parallel separation in Cologne in April 1849.) The widening political repression, however, forced the workers underground into secret societies, which "grew in extent and intensity in the same degree that the *public clubs* became impossible." And the secret societies were generally Blanquist in inspiration, led by his lieutenants to be sure, since *l'enfermé* himself was again languishing in solitary confinement. Thus Marx concluded:

> The *proletariat* rallies more and more round *revolutionary Socialism*, round *Communism*, for which the bourgeoisie has itself invented the name of *Blanqui*. This Socialism is the *declaration of the permanence of the revolution*, the *class dictatorship* of the proletariat as the necessary transit point to the *abolition of class distinctions generally*.[50]

The movement of the most militant French workers into Blanquist secret societies in 1849–1850 goes a long way to explain Marx's desire for a united front (as it does his very first use here of the term, "dic-

48. Ibid., pp. 153, 156, 169–70, 184, 213–14.
49. Ibid., p. 207.
50. Ibid., pp. 160, 186, 203.

tatorship of the proletariat," to be examined in detail in chapter 9). Marx had established contacts with these societies during his three-month stay in Paris in 1849 and developed even closer contacts thereafter with exiled Blanquist leaders in London, as we will see shortly.[51]

For now, we need only observe that Marx's desire to work with the Blanquists did not lead him to endorse their prescription for minority revolution and educational dictatorship in France. *Class Struggles* declared that at the outset of the February Revolution the relatively small French proletariat "was still incapable of accomplishing its own revolution." Provoked to violence in the June Days, its premature struggle was doomed: "Its immediate, avowed needs did not drive it to engage in a fight for the forcible overthrow of the bourgeoisie, nor was it equal to this task." The following spring, the proletariat "was not yet enabled through the development of the remaining classes to seize the revolutionary dictatorship," and thus it would have been folly for the workers to have attempted an independent rising during the June 13 challenge to Napoleon, "to repeat uselessly the June days of 1848." In diametric opposition to Blanqui's ideas, Marx observed that "the French proletariat, at the moment of a revolution, possesses in Paris actual power and influence which spur it on to a drive *beyond its means*" (italics added).[52] By contrast, he reemphasized the need to await the political maturation of the majority classes, to find provincial support for the leadership of radical Paris:

> The French workers could not take a step forward, could not touch a hair of the bourgeois order, until the course of the revolution had aroused the mass of the nation, peasants and petty bourgeois, standing between the proletariat and the bourgeoisie, against this order, against the rule of capital, and had forced it to attach itself to the proletarians as their protagonists.[53]

The French peasants (who comprised two thirds of the population by Marx's own reckoning) and the urban petty bourgeois had both supported the initial February Revolution of 1848. Then, needlessly

---

51. *Werke,* 27:137; Nicolaievsky and Maenchen-Helfen, *Marx,* p. 200; and Maurice Dommanget, *Les idées politiques et sociales d'Auguste Blanqui* (Paris: Rivière, 1957), p. 377.

52. *Selected Works,* 1:136, 149, 176, 181, 137.

53. Ibid., p. 137.

alienated by the provisional government's imposition of new taxes, they had voted for relatively conservative candidates in the April 1848 National Assembly elections, giving the first impulse to the permanent counterrevolution. The political immaturity, not to say gullibility, of these same classes produced the overwhelming vote for Louis Napoleon in the December presidential election, and then for a preponderance of royalist deputies in the May 1849 assembly elections.[54] But Marx's response to these repeated evidences of mass immaturity was not to call for educational dictatorship by an enlightened elite; rather he pointed to the pressure of circumstances through which he expected the masses to educate themselves.

This pressure of circumstances included not only the increasingly heavy political repression which deprived the masses of their hard-won rights, but also the shortsighted economic policies of a callous bourgeois government. Shopkeepers and other urban petty bourgeois were seriously affected when the moratorium on debt and rent collection, in force since the February Revolution, was lifted; peasants were especially antagonized by the restoration of the wine tax. Moreover, the natural processes of capitalist development drove these classes more and more to the wall, as was particularly visible in the case of the peasant majority, whose recurrently subdivided plots were falling ever more hopelessly into debt, mortgaged in the banks owned by the bourgeoisie. Thus, Marx concluded:

The individual capitalists exploit the individual peasants through *mortgages* and *usury;* the capitalist class exploits the peasant class through *state taxes.* The peasant's title to property is the talisman by which capital held him hitherto under its spell, the pretext under which it set him against the industrial proletariat. Only the fall of capital can raise the peasant; only an anti-capitalist, a proletarian government can break his economic misery, his social degradation. The *constitutional republic* is the dictatorship of his united exploiters; the *social-democratic,* the *Red* republic, is the dictatorship of his allies. And the scale rises or falls, according to the votes that the peasant casts into the ballot box. He himself has to decide his fate. . . . Most understandable was the language of the actual experience that the peasant class had gained from the use of the

54. Ibid., pp. 135, 140–46, 159–60, 173–74.

suffrage, were the disillusionments overwhelming him, blow upon blow, with revolutionary speed. *Revolutions are the locomotives of history.*[55]

This radicalization of the lower-middle classes, their self-education —as Marx would see it—had already manifested itself in the assembly elections of May 1849, which despite their monarchist majority also produced a substantially larger left opposition than the 1848 elections. Since then a December by-election had returned a *Montagnard* from the traditionally reactionary rural Département du Gard, and most significantly, "social-democratic" candidates swept several by-elections in March 1850.[56] The latter election had evoked the liquidation of universal suffrage. Thus, notwithstanding the imposing might of the counterrevolution, *Class Struggles* remained optimistic:

Little by little we have seen peasants, petty bourgeois, the middle classes in general, stepping alongside the proletariat, driven into open antagonism to the official republic and treated by it as antagonists. *Revolt against bourgeois dictatorship, need of a change of society, adherence to democratic-republican institutions as organs of their movement, grouping round the proletariat as the decisive revolutionary power—*these are the common characteristics of the *so-called party of social-democracy, the party of the Red Republic.*[57]

From all this it is evident that despite his new ties to the Blanquists and his rhetoric of "permanent revolution" and "dictatorship," Marx's strategy for revolution in France really had not changed very much. He nowhere talked of any conspiratorial seizure of power or postponement of elections. He simply updated the same old vision of popular revolution by the alliance of majority classes aimed at the creation

55. Ibid., pp. 153–54, 194–96, 198. Marx and Engels' view of peasants and peasant politics is explored by Henry Mayer, "Marx, Engels and the Politics of the Peasantry," *Etudes de Marxologie*, ed. Maximilien Rubel (Paris: Institut de Science Economique Appliquée, 1960), 3:91–151; Dieter Hertz-Eichenrode, "Karl Marx über das Bauerntum und die Bündnisfrage," *International Review of Social History* 11 (1966):382–402; and Oscar J. Hammen, "Marx and the Agrarian Question," *American Historical Review* 77 (1972):679–704.

56. *Selected Works*, 1:109, 206–07.

57. Ibid., p. 201; cf. pp. 149, 153, 174–77.

of a democratic republic, now dubbed "social-democratic" or "Red" to distinguish it from the martial-law republic of Napoleon. He stressed that the popular movement adhered to "democratic-republican institutions" and sought to restore "freedom of the press, right of association," etc.[58] How such a democratically structured rule of the masses could be conceived a "dictatorship" must remain a mystery for the time being. Labels aside, the strategy sounds much the same as the one Marx applied to France before the original February Revolution, much the same as the one he applied to Germany after the November 1848 defeat of the bourgeois revolution. The only difference of substance, again parallel to German policy after April 1849, is Marx's emphasis that this time round the proletariat should not fall under the shadow of the "pale" democrats, providing muscle without real direction; this time the proletariat should be organized as an independent force, the militant core around which the declining classes would rally. "This time the *proletariat* . . . [would be] *at the head of the revolutionary league.*"[59]

There is abundant evidence that Marx and Engels suffered in this period from the endemic disorder of exiled revolutionaries—delusions of new upheavals erupting everywhere, brought on, as they saw it, either by international war, economic depression, or a precipitant French tremor. There is no convincing evidence, however, that the two men now embraced a specifically totalitarian-democratic recipe for revolution in Britain or France. But what of their homeland, what of Germany?

Revival of the League and the March Circular

Virtually all authorities have derived Marx and Engels' German policy in 1850 from the most accessible source, the March 1850 *Address of the Central Committee to the Communist League,* more commonly known as the March *Circular.* Drawn up by the two men on behalf of the central committee, into whose narrow circle they had been readmitted, the *Circular* took the form of a secret instruction to the local branches of the league and is undoubtedly the most extreme pronouncement in the entire corpus of Marx and Engels' writings. Anticipating the next round of political upheaval, it called upon the proletar-

---

58. Ibid., p. 202.
59. Ibid., p. 205; see Molnár, *La politique d'alliances,* pp. 91–99.

iat "to make the revolution permanent" by seizing power after the "momentary rule of the bourgeois democracy," in a coup that—if understood literally—could only be the work of a minority. It further called for the maintenance of secret organization; for attempts to establish dual institutions of government during the first phase, including a separate workers' paramilitary force; for the deliberate promotion of terrorism; for "the most determined centralization of power"; and so forth.[60] Noncommunist writers have generally followed Eduard Bernstein's lead in reporting the strong odor of Blanquism hovering about this document. "The *Circular* of March 1850, bears upon it the stamp of the conspirative tradition of Blanqui," Bertram Wolfe has written. "It is doubtful if there is any other document from the hands of Marx in which Lenin, Stalin, Khrushchev, and Mao Tse-tung could find so much evidence for their claim to be the faithful heirs and so large a heritage to claim."[61]

Neither these writers nor the Communist luminaries mentioned by Wolfe seem to have inquired whether the *Circular* expressed Marx and Engels' real views. It is surely strange that the two most widely quoted and widely reprinted Marx-Engels documents of the 1848 period—the *Manifesto* and the *Circular*—were both issued unsigned, as official pronouncements of an *organization*, and yet are accepted uncritically by almost everyone as representing the *personal* views of the masters. It may be worthwhile to introduce once again the technique employed above in analyzing the final paragraphs of the *Manifesto*. Assuming temporarily that there may be something suspect about the *Circular*, let us begin by reconstructing Marx and Engels' views from other contemporaneous sources.

Unfortunately, this task is not so easy as it was in the earlier case, because the two men had little to say about Germany, publicly or privately, during 1850—their attention seemed to gravitate toward the prior developments they expected in France and Britain. In fact, the only completely unimpeachable source that touches on the subject at hand is the closing section of Engels' memoir, *Die deutsche Reichsver-*

60.   The *Circular* is included in *Selected Works*, 1:98–108.

61.   *Marxism*, pp. 153, 19; see also Eduard Bernstein, *Evolutionary Socialism*, trans. Edith C. Harvey (1909; reprint ed., New York: Schocken, 1961), p. 155; J. L. Talmon, *Political Messianism: The Romantic Phase* (New York: Praeger, 1960), pp. 508–13; and George Lichtheim, *Marxism: An Historical and Critical Study* (New York: Praeger, 1961), pp. 122–29.

fassungskampagne, written in February. Focusing on Baden, Engels drew out the implications of the campaign for the future:

Furthermore, the campaign for the Reich Constitution contributed importantly to the evolution of class antagonisms in those German states where they were not yet sharply developed. Notably in Baden. . . . As soon as the insurrection had broken out, class differences emerged sharply, and the petty bourgeois separated themselves from the workers and peasants. In their representative, [Lorenz] Brentano, they [the petty bourgeois] disgraced themselves for all eternity. They have now been driven to such despair by the rule of the Prussian saber that they will prefer any regime, even that of the workers, to their present oppression; they will take a much more active part in the next movement than in any previous one; but happily they will never again be able to have an independent, dominating role as under the dictatorship of Brentano. The workers and peasants, who suffer every bit as much as the petty bourgeois under the present rule of the saber, have not gone through the last insurrection in vain; they (who in any event have their fallen and murdered brothers to avenge) will see to it that in the next insurrection *they,* and not the petty bourgeois, will take the reins in their hands. And although insurrectionary experiences cannot be a substitute for the development of classes, which is only achieved through the working of big industry over many years [*einen langjährigen Betrieb der grossen Industrie*], nonetheless Baden, by its last insurrection and the consequences thereof, has joined the ranks of those German provinces that will occupy the most important positions in the approaching revolution.[62]

From this isolated source certain important conclusions can nevertheless be drawn. The approaching German revolution was not seen as an exclusively proletarian undertaking, any more than in France, but as the joint effort of the same old alliance of the majority classes. Or not quite the *same* old alliance, for, as in France, Engels expected that this time the workers would play an independent and leading role in the class coalition. Together with the peasants they would prevent a repetition of the fiasco into which they had been drawn by the treacherous leadership of the petty bourgeoisie in 1849. As in *Class*

62. *Werke,* 7:196–97.

Struggles, there is now more stress on the peasants and little confidence in the petty bourgeois, but no suggestion of anything but majority rule. Further, there follows the very interesting declaration that no amount of insurrectionary experience can replace the extended process of industrialization which alone can produce the "development of classes" (that is, a politically mature proletarian majority) that will be the necessary foundation for a purely proletarian government and the full implementation of communism. With such a perspective reaching out over "many years," Engels added that after the defeat of 1849, "the only victor can be a somewhat constitutionalized feudal-bureaucratic monarchy, or a real revolution. And a revolution in Germany can never again be terminated except with the complete rule of the proletariat."[63] Here was a conception of permanent revolution in the special, extended sense we have encountered before—"a single, long and vicissitudinous period of revolution."[64]

Such an interpretation receives added weight from the only other piece of contemporaneous evidence, unfortunately a secondhand report rather than the source itself. The 1854 testimony of P. G. Röser, cited before in connection with the June dissolution of the Communist League, also includes his recollection of receiving a letter from Marx in July 1850, asserting that in Germany "communism could be introduced only after a series of years [*Reihe der Jahren*], that it must pass through several phases, and that it could be introduced at all only by way of education and gradual development."[65] Here again one can speak of permanent revolution only in a very protracted sense. The most impressive evidence of all, however, is precisely what Marx and Engels did *not* say: the phrase "permanent revolution" is expressly endorsed by them only in official *organizational* pronouncements; none of their *personal* writings of this period employs the phrase to refer to their own policy.[66] This fact alone should raise healthy suspicions.

To make any real sense of the March *Circular*, we must go back

63.   Ibid., p. 196.

64.   See above, chap. 6, n. 22.

65.   Werner Blumenberg, "Zur Geschichte des Bundes der Kommunisten: Die Aussagen des Peter Gerhardt Röser," *International Review of Social History* 9 (1964):99.

66.   The organizational pronouncements are in the March *Circular* (*Selected Works*, 1:102, 108), where the phrase is used twice, and the statutes of the Universal Society of Revolutionary Communists (*Werke*, 7:553), to be discussed later in the chapter. Marx also used the phrase once in *Class Struggles* (*Selected Works*, 1:203) to describe the policies of Blanqui. Engels used the phrase on one occasion

to the history of the Communist League, and especially to the tension between radical artisans and renegade intellectuals that was stressed in connection with the *Manifesto*. This tension began to rise again after June 1848 and would ultimately lead to an irrevocable split by September 1850. It would appear that the artisans had been in fact only half-convinced by the example of Chartism and Marx's arguments in favor of a mass movement. With the succession of defeats that followed the glorious spring of 1848, a portion of the artisan element fell back into the older Blanquist patterns of thought.

The first crisis came when Marx dissolved the league by fiat in June 1848, over the strenuous objections of Schapper and Moll, who were not prepared to abandon the principle of secrecy or the organization to which they had given twelve years of their lives. Thereafter, as we have seen, the Marx circle took on the burdens of a daily newspaper, cultivated relations with the bourgeois intellectuals who led the Democratic Society, but more or less ignored working-class organizations and interests until after the counterrevolution. By contrast, the artisans entered the workers' societies that had sprung up in Cologne and elsewhere, often gaining positions of leadership within them. They must have found it increasingly difficult to counter the arguments of the most radical workers, who opposed any united-front policy, demanded immediate action on specifically working-class grievances, and regarded Marx and the group around the *Neue Rheinische Zeitung* as little better than "pale" democrats.[67] During the September repression in Cologne, Moll was obliged to flee the country and decided the time had come to revive a secret organization. Back in London, he found considerable sympathy among old league members, who were discouraged by the third failure of the Chartists to secure parliamentary acceptance of the six-point petition. By the end of the year, the league had been reconstituted in London with a new statute and an exclusively artisan central committee composed of Moll, Bauer, and the tailor Georg Eccarius—all without any prior consultation with or approval by Marx and Engels.[68]

---

many years later to allude to their own policies of the 1848–1850 period (*Selected Works*, 2:302–03), but with the explanation cited above, chap. 6, nn. 22 and 23.

67. Noyes, *Organization and Revolution*, pp. 115–23; Shlomo Na'aman, "Zur Geschichte des Bundes der Kommunisten in Deutschland in der zweiten Phase seines Bestehens," *Archiv für Sozialgeschichte* 5 (1965):8–14.

68. *Bund Dokumente*, 1:851-54; Blumenberg, "Aussagen des Peter Gerhardt Röser," pp. 89–90; and Na'aman, "Zur Geschichte des Bundes," pp. 31–33.

Not that the artisans as yet desired a break: Moll returned to Cologne early in 1849 and, with Schapper's assistance, endeavored to reestablish a branch there that would include Marx and his circle. At the meeting of old league members called to revive the branch, Marx opposed the idea. He argued, according to Röser's recollection, that "under existing conditions, with freedom of speech and of the press, the League was superfluous," and that the remodeled statute moreover "tended toward the conspiratorial." This was the period when Marx anticipated the imminent creation of a nationwide legal workers' party that would work hand in hand with the "petty-bourgeois" democrats against the counterrevolution. The meeting ended in a vote that divided the group basically along class lines: the bulk of the artisans present sided with Schapper and Moll, while all the intellectuals sided with Marx and narrowly carried the majority.[69] In spite of this rebuff, Moll continued on to other localities, reestablishing branches wherever he could.

Meanwhile the efforts to create a nationwide legal party fell victim to the counterrevolution, as did the *Neue Rheinische Zeitung* a short time later. Seemingly, Marx and Engels had been wrong, and when the weary exiles regathered in London in the fall of 1849, the two men were once more admitted to the league's central committee, but not without being obliged to eat a large portion of humble pie, as we will see in the March *Circular.* From the artisans' perspective, it had been a mistake to collaborate with the "pale" democrats, to abandon secret organization, to suppose that moderation would pay off in the step-by-step forward development of the revolution. Their dependence on Marx and Engels further declined when they found a new spokesman, August von Willich, a former Prussian officer turned revolutionary whose adjutant Engels had been in the campaign for the Reich Constitution. Under Willich's influence, the schemes of the exiled artisans became at once more military, more conspiratorial, and more ruthless, as they reverted to an essentiallly Blanquist vision of imposing communism by force through the action of a determined minority. Marx and Engels, on the other hand, were now ready to ac-

69. Blumenberg, "Aussagen des Peter Gerhardt Röser," pp. 90–91; Schraepler, *Handwerkerbünde,* pp. 335–36; and Dieter Dowe, *Aktion und Organisation: Arbeiterbewegung, sozialistische und kommunistische Bewegung in der preussischen Rheinprovinz, 1820–1852* (Hannover: Literatur und Zeitgeschichte, 1970), pp. 252–53.

knowledge the need for a *secret* organization, but still conceived of the league as a revolutionary *propaganda* party, not one that would take responsibility for revolutionary action, let alone hatch dark conspiracies.[70] Similarly, the two men now acknowledged the need for an independent workers' organization that would not fall under the shadow of the "pale" democrats, but—however distasteful it might be— they remained convinced that some sort of collaboration with the democrats would be needed in the immediate future and that the introduction of communism under a purely proletarian government was still a long way off.

The only contemporaneous characterization of this intraleague tension has survived in Röser's recollection of the letter Marx sent him in July 1850, a fragment of which was quoted above, and which may now be appreciated in its full context. Röser remembered Marx's letter,

in which he expressed his anger at Willich and Co., and regretted very much that Schapper had linked himself up with this clique. He said that during the winter of 1849–50, in the London Workers' Society, he had given talks on the *Manifesto* in which he had shown that communism could be introduced only after a series of years, that it must pass through several phases, and that it could be introduced at all only by way of education and gradual development. But Willich and his trash—so Marx called them—had opposed him strongly and had said that it must be introduced in the next revolution, even if it required the power of the guillotine; that the enmity between them was already so great that he feared it would cause a split in the league, since the "General" Willich had taken it into his head to introduce communism in the next revolution by brute force with the help of his brave Palatines and against the will of all Germany if need be.[71]

What separated the two factions is here beautifully set forth as the difference between a democratic conception of communist revolution and a quasi-Blanquist one. And the scornful denunciation of the latter conception appears in a letter Marx wrote during the very months when he is alleged to have embraced Blanquism. Alas, there is no

70. See *Werke*, 8:458–59; Blumenberg, "Aussagen des Peter Gerhardt Röser," pp. 91–92; and Schraepler, *Handwerkerbünde*, pp. 410–14.
71. Blumenberg, "Aussagen des Peter Gerhardt Röser," p. 99.

independent way to verify Röser's remembrance of the letter, but the surrounding circumstances all testify to its general accuracy. The tension between the Marx and the Willich-Schapper factions clearly did not pop up suddenly in August or September 1850, when the English depression failed to materialize, but went back to the June dissolution and the subsequent attempts of the artisans to revive the league, with or without Marx's help. It undoubtedly became more abrasive with the emergence of Willich, who rubbed Marx the wrong way with his purely military notion of revolution and his potential as a rival leader.[72] At the deepest level, however, it was the same tension we have encountered from the outset—the tension between radicalized artisans seeking some immediate escape from the doom of their class and the vision of Marx, which conceived man's ultimate emancipation to lie on the far side of a capitalist purgatory of modernization. It is eminently plausible that this tension, reported by Röser in debates during the "winter of 1849–50," would find some expression in the March *Circular* issued by an internally divided central committee toward the end of that winter.

Unfortunately, we know even less about how the *Circular* was drawn up than in the case of the *Manifesto*. Stylistic analysis would seem to confirm Marx and Engels' authorship, as would Marx's twice-repeated reference to the document "composed [*verfasste*] by Engels and myself." But Engels spoke of the document as "edited [or "revised" —*redigierte*] by Marx and myself,"[73] which may be more accurate in view of the fact that the *Circular* was not issued over Marx and Engels' signatures but as the official pronouncement of a central committee which also included Willich as well as Bauer and Eccarius, artisans who had helped revive the league in 1849 against Marx's opposition. (Moll had been killed in battle during the campaign for the Reich Constitution, and Schapper had not yet returned from German imprisonment.) Whatever the process of formulation, any serious analysis of the *Circular's* final content, with all its ambiguities and contradic-

72.   Gustav Adolf Techow, another officer-turned-revolutionary and a friend of Willich, claimed that Marx once delivered a drunken monologue venting his suspicions of Willich and officers in general, saying they were "always the most dangerous people in a revolution. From Lafayette to Napoleon, nothing but a chain of traitors. *One must keep dagger and poison ready for them*" (as quoted in Carl Vogt, *Mein Prozess gegen die Allgemeine Zeitung* [Geneva: Vogt, 1859], pp. 153–54).

73.   Marx, *Werke*, 9:507; 27:278; Engels, ibid., 21:220 (mistranslated as "composed" in the Soviet-sponsored *Selected Works*, 2:320).

tions, leaves no doubt that it was the work of a committee, an attempt to reconcile or patch over deep fissures within that committee.[74]

The opening passages reviewed the league's activity during the 1848 revolution, neatly circumventing with ambiguous language the touchy issue of whether the organization was really dissolved. But there is nothing ambiguous about the chastisement meted out to those comrades who "believed the time for secret societies to have gone by and public activities alone sufficient," who allowed the movement to come "under the domination and leadership of the petty-bourgeois democrats," and who allowed themselves to be "seduced" into putting up joint candidates with democrats in the various elections.[75] Here most sharply Marx and Engels were obliged to eat humble pie, repudiating before the party public their own vigorously defended policies of 1848–1849. Here is the first convincing evidence of radical artisan participation in the formulation of the *Circular*.

The crucial issue dividing the group was the radicals' desire for an immediate communist revolution versus Marx's insistence on a process extending over many years. The obvious compromise was an exact rerun of the *Manifesto's Verschmelzung*, except that the "treacherous role which the German liberal bourgeois played in 1848 against the people, will in the impending revolution be taken over by the democratic petty bourgeois, who at present occupy the same position in the opposition as the liberal bourgeois before 1848." The radicals allowed what was distasteful to them—an initial collaboration with these "pale" democrats, not within a common organization, to be sure, but in the "struggle against a common adversary [where] no special union is required." They even allowed that after this collaboration had brought down the old regime, "the petty-bourgeois democracy will for a moment [*für einen Augenblick*] obtain predominating influence in Germany."[76] But emphasis then turned to the means by which this "inevitable momentary [*augenblickliche*] rule of the bourgeois de-

---

74. This view first espoused in lonely isolation by Nicolaievsky and Maenchen-Helfen, *Marx*, p. 206, and elaborated somewhat in Nicolaievsky's later article, "Who Is Distorting History?" *Proceedings of the American Philosophical Society* 105 (1961):219–21. The interpretation is now strongly fortified by recent studies emphasizing the artisan-intellectual conflict within the league, even though these writers have not sufficiently reinterpreted the *Circular* in the light of their own findings: see Na'aman, "Zur Geschichte des Bundes," pp. 41–44; Schraepler, *Handwerkerbünde*, pp. 365–68; and Dowe, *Aktion und Organisation*, p. 254.

75. *Selected Works*, 1:98, 105.

76. Ibid., pp. 100, 103, 102.

mocracy" could be made as short and shaky as possible: the workers were advised to arm themselves independently as a "proletarian guard"; "alongside of the new official governments they must establish simultaneously their own revolutionary workers' governments" in the form of municipal committees or workers' societies; and they must harass the petty-bourgeois regime continually, undercutting every proposal for reform by advancing a more radical counterproposal.[77]

On the other hand, the influence of Marx and Engels was recognizable in the instructions given to marshal the strength of the masses *before* any direct assumption of power. League members were urged to help create workers' societies in every locality, to "combine with the rural proletariat," and to convene a congress of the league on German soil as soon as possible to help link up the workers' societies in a single nationwide organization. Elections were anticipated for a new national assembly in Germany, and the workers were called upon to participate, putting up their own independent candidates even where there was no chance of success. The *Circular* declared that "at the beginning of the movement, of course, the workers cannot yet propose any directly communistic measures," and that "it is not in the power of the workers to prevent the petty-bourgeois democrats from" barring their way initially to "the fruits of victory." Thus the *Circular* seemed to anticipate a process of mass organization that could scarcely take place in a "moment," and indeed its penultimate paragraph declared that "the German workers are not able to attain power and achieve their own class interests without completely going through a lengthy revolutionary development [*ohne eine längere revolutionäre Entwicklung ganz durchzumachen*]."[78]

No genuinely Blanquist program would allow for initial petty-bourgeois domination, for an open mass workers' party, for participation in early elections, or for the postponement of "communistic measures" until after "a lengthy revolutionary development." Some twenty years after the March *Circular*, Engels had occasion to criticize a manifesto issued by thirty-three Blanquist exiles in London. Their program had proclaimed: "We are communists because we want to arrive at our goal without stopping at way stations and compromises that only postpone the victory and lengthen the slavery." To this Engels responded:

77.   Ibid., pp. 105, 103–04, 107–08.
78.   Ibid., pp. 102–06, 107, 103, 108 (German from *Werke*, 7:253–54); see also Na'aman, "Zur Geschichte des Bundes," pp. 41–44.

We German communists are communists because we see the final goal clearly beyond all the way stations and compromises created not by ourselves but by historical development. . . . The Thirty-Three are communists because they imagine that as soon as *they* have simply the will to overleap the way stations and compromises, then the matter will be taken care of; and that when the day of action arrives and they take over the helm, then communism will be "introduced" the morning after.[79]

In 1850, precisely this same division separated Marx and Engels from the backsliding artisans in Willich's faction.

While the radicals, like their Blanquist cousins, would have preferred to by-pass all way stations, they were willing to compromise with the Marx faction to the extent of allowing for a *momentary* petty-bourgeois phase. But in the glaring contradiction between this "momentary rule of the bourgeois democracy" and the "lengthy revolutionary development" just three pages later, one may perceive the residual tension underneath the surface. In any event, the central task assigned by the *Circular*, "to make the revolution permanent, until all more or less possessing classes have been forced out of their position of dominance, until the proletariat has conquered state power," could be interpreted by the radicals as a job requiring a few weeks or months, and by the Marx group as the work of many years. The slogan "Revolution in Permanence," used again at the end of the document, had a militant ring, but it was vague enough to cover both conceptions. The phrase itself dates back, of course, to Marat and the Reign of Terror but does not appear to have been current among nineteenth-century French Blanquists (Marx to the contrary), whose conception of revolution did not allow for progressive stages.[80] Neither had Marx and Engels ever employed the slogan, prior to 1850, to describe their own

---

79. "Programm der blanquistischen Kommuneflüchtlinge" (1874), *Werke*, 18:533 (Blanquist program as quoted in German by Engels). Also see Alan Spitzer, *The Revolutionary Theories of Louis Auguste Blanqui* (New York: Columbia, 1957), pp. 157–73; Dommanget, *Les idées*, pp. 152–70; and John Plamenatz, *German Marxism and Russian Communism* (London: Longmans, Green, 1954), pp. 129–35.

80. In *Class Struggles*, Marx attributed the slogan to the French Blanquists, as he did the phrase "dictatorship of the proletariat" (*Selected Works*, 1:203), even though the authorities on Blanquism find no use of either phrase by this school (Spitzer, *Revolutionary Theories*, pp. 170–71; Dommanget, *Les idées*, p. 158). We will inspect the motives behind this strange attribution below in chapter 9.

policies. It appears to have regained currency precisely among those German ultraradicals like Gottschalk and Willich who were half influenced by Marx's idea of historical stages, without having the patience to endure any long delays in the realization of communism. The phrase turned up once more in 1850, in another committee pronouncement apparently drafted by Willich that will be introduced shortly.[81] Thereupon it disappeared from view again as quickly as it had emerged. After the September 1850 split, Willich's faction repudiated all collaboration with the petty bourgeoisie and reverted to a simple one-step revolutionary strategy involving immediate seizure of power and minority dictatorship—hence they had no further need of the phrase.[82] Neither do the surviving records show that the Marx faction ever used it again.

The slogan "Permanent Revolution" can therefore be attributed to Classical Marxism only with the most severe reservations. It was really a compromise slogan, an unfortunate *Verschmelzung* parallel to the *Manifesto*'s "immediately following proletarian revolution"—a deliberate ambiguity designed to mask two drastically opposed conceptions of revolution. To complete the permanent revolution within a few weeks or months would plainly require minority action and dictatorship; to do so over a period of many years need not. The ambiguity, it cannot be emphasized too strongly, lay in the committee pronouncements, not in Marx and Engels' own thought or personal writings. After breaking with the radicals in September 1850, Marx would lament to Engels concerning the burdens of that ill-starred collaboration—"the system of mutual concessions, the halfway positions tolerated for decency's sake, and the duty before the public to bear one's share of ridicule with all those jackasses in the party—all that is over now."[83]

---

81.   Phrase cited in n. 89 below; for Gottschalk's use, see n. 17 above. Nicolaievsky reports that the slogan "kept popping up again and again" among Marx's left opponents in Cologne in 1848–1849 ("Who Is Distorting History?" p. 220, n. 33).

82.   See Karl Wermuth and Wilhelm Stieber, *Die Communisten-Verschwörungen des 19. Jahrhunderts,* 2 vols. (1853–54; reprint ed., Hildesheim: Olms, 1969), 1:244, 266–82, 291–98.

83.   Letter of February 11, 1851, *Werke,* 27:185. As in the case of the *Manifesto,* one may legitimately inquire why Marx and Engels did not repudiate the *Circular* after the split, or alter it in subsequent publication. In this case, the secret document first became public when it was discovered by the Prussian police and played a prominent part in convicting some of Marx and Engels' oldest friends and comrades in Cologne in 1852. To have repudiated the *Circular* for which they were

Thus the two men were perfectly aware of the "mutual concessions" and "halfway positions" contained in the joint pronouncements of 1850. If later authorities uncritically accepted those pronouncements as showing ambiguities in Marx and Engels' own thought, that is simply faulty scholarship.[84]

The only other issue remaining for us to examine in the March *Circular* is its advocacy of terror. The relevant passage will sound familiar, for it has been quoted and requoted endlessly since it first appeared publicly as state's evidence in the 1852 conspiracy trial of the Communist League:

Above all things, the workers must counteract, as much as is at all possible, during the conflict and immediately after the struggle, the bourgeois endeavors to allay the storm, and must compel the democrats to carry out their present terrorist phrases. Their actions must be so aimed as to prevent the direct revolutionary excitement from being suppressed again immediately after the victory. On the contrary, they must keep it alive as long as possible. Far from opposing so-called excesses, instances of popular revenge against hated individuals or public buildings that are associated only with hateful recollections, such instances must not only be tolerated but the leadership of them taken in hand.[85]

As it stands, the instruction flatly reverses Engels' 1845 counsel to hold down violence to the unavoidable minimum, and it is more specif-

---

partly responsible, while their friends languished in jail because of it, would scarcely have been fitting. Thereafter, it was not until 1885 that Engels published the document as an appendix to the reedition of Marx's *Revelations Concerning the Communist Trial in Cologne*. By that time it had become, like the *Manifesto*, a "historical document." Engels did see fit to add a footnote modifying the extreme centralism advocated by the *Circular* and noted in his preface that the petty bourgeoisie would still (in 1885) have to come to power in Germany before the workers could rule in their own right. "Much of what is said there is, therefore, still applicable today" (*Selected Works*, 2:320). He did not specify what was inapplicable.

84. See especially Wolfe, *Marxism*, pp. 160–64; Lichtheim, *Marxism*, pp. 122–23. The "ambiguous legacy" of Classical Marxism is also the theme of Sidney Hook, *Marx and the Marxists: The Ambiguous Legacy* (Princeton: Van Nostrand, Anvil Books, 1955), especially pp. 12, 49.

85. *Selected Works*, 1:103–04 (German original may be compared for syntax in *Werke*, 7:249). On the 1852 conspiracy trial, see the editor's introduction and assembled documents in Karl Marx, *The Cologne Communist Trial*, trans. and ed. Rodney Livingstone (New York: International, 1971).

ic than any of the terror passages in the *Neue Rheinische Zeitung.*
Like the latter, however, it calls for acts of terror in the future, not
in the here and now. One may even sense certain elements of restraint
in the specifications for revenge against "public buildings" (recalling
the Bastille?) and "hated individuals" (recalling the Austrian Minister
Latour?), rather than against the old regime as a whole, or entire political parties, or entire classes. Even in this most bloodthirsty of all the
documents associated with Marx and Engels, there is no advocacy of
one-party rule or governmental suppression of the right of opposition.

In any event, the instruction cannot be accepted as it stands. Even
the awkward syntax of the passage suggests its having been reworked
by several hands, and we cannot know how Marx and Engels would
have expressed themselves without the pressure of the Willich faction.
It would certainly be safer to fall back upon their other writings from
1850 to determine their real views during this most radical period.
Interestingly enough, *none* of these other writings, public or private,
supported a policy of terror, or even mentioned the word at all. On
the other hand, the subsequent pronouncements of the Willich group
went into considerable detail concerning the preparation of proscription lists, prevention of emigration, arrest and punishment of all "enemies of the people," etc.—all of which strongly points to Willich as
the real author, literally or in spirit, of the *Circular* directive.[86] Never
after 1850 did Marx or Engels write anything so strong on the subject
of terrorism, and in fact there are a number of later statements *against*
terrorism which suggest that the 1845 counsel was still remembered
after all, and that the *Neue Rheinische Zeitung* utterances must indeed
be understood as outbursts of rage rather than as a serious policy of
deliberate terrorism.[87]

There can be little question, then, but that the March *Circular* seriously distorts Marx and Engels' views on both the timing of revolutionary development and the use of terror. It would be best to disregard
the document altogether as a source for the political doctrines of Classical Marxism.

86. "Verhaltungsmassregeln für den Bund vor, während, und nach der Revolution," Wermuth and Stieber, *Communisten-Verschwörungen,* 1:294, 296.

87. Probably the strongest post-1850 statement relative to terror is to be found
in Engels' 1873 essay "On Authority" (*Selected Works,* 1:578), which is quoted
below, pp. 315–16. But see his contemporaneous 1874 reservations in *Werke,*
18:532–34. Other statements against a policy of terrorism can be found ibid.,
21:189–90; 31:409, 413; 33:53; as well as in *Selected Correspondence: 1846–1895,*
trans. Dona Torr (New York: International, 1942), pp. 286, 348, 390–91.

United Front with the Blanquists

Marx and Engels' collaboration with the Willich faction of the revived league was not their only association with the proponents of minority revolution in 1850. They also established a formal united-front organization with exiled French Blanquists. If one recalls the circumstances of this period, it is not really difficult to understand the motives of the two men. Driven once again into exile by the superior forces of reaction, after the sublime hopes of 1848, they could not but wish for a second chance and conjure up the prospect of a fresh revolutionary wave. Conditions on the Continent precluded the kind of open mass organization they would have preferred, leaving only the possibility of secret societies. But the secret societies then in existence were either dominated by Blanquists (in France) or powerfully influenced by their ideas (in Germany). If the two men expected to have any influence on radical working-class policies and actions in the anticipated new upheaval, they had little choice but to deal with the secret societies.

The centrality of France to the revolutionary schema dictated in particular Marx and Engels' attempts to establish ties with the prospective leaders of the French proletarian party. Thus the two men socialized with Blanquist émigrés in a New Year's celebration sponsored by the Fraternal Democrats at the end of December 1849; Engels addressed a banquet in February 1850 organized by the same Blanquists in honor of the founding of the Second Republic; and finally in April, Marx, Engels, and Willich joined the exiled lieutenants of Blanqui, Jules Vidil and the artisan Adam, together with the English Chartist leader, Julian Harney, to create the short-lived Universal Society of Revolutionary Communists. Harney may actually have been the prime mover in bringing the group together. It was a "secret society of higher degree" which included only the six leaders of the respective national revolutionary organizations.[88] Its statutes survive in the handwriting of Willich and begin ominously: "The aim of the association is the downfall of all the privileged classes, to subject these classes to the dictatorship of the proletarians by maintaining the revolution in permanence until the achievement of communism, which is to be the last form of the constitution of the human family."[89] Here is the last call

88. Expression of Nicolaievsky and Maenchen-Helfen, *Marx,* p. 209; also see Schraepler, *Handwerkerbünde,* p. 372; and editorial notes in *Werke,* 7:639–41.

89. Translated from French original reproduced in Nicolaievsky and Maenchen-Helfen, *Marx,* p. 209; cf. German translation in *Werke,* 7:553.

for permanent revolution to be endorsed by Marx and Engels, and, together with the reference to proletarian dictatorship (to be discussed in chapter 9), it must be regarded also as a compromise formulation. But Marx and Engels' cautiousness in this united front is probably reflected in the subsequent statutory requirement that all decisions be made by a two-thirds majority. With the support of the more level-headed Harney, they could block any reckless adventure. And the admission of any new member needed the unanimous approval of the original six.[90]

No record survives of *any* decision's being made by the Universal Society during the six months of its existence. In what must be a reference to the group, a June 1850 report of the Communist League's central committee asserted that "the delegates of the Blanqui secret societies are in regular official communication with the League representatives whom they have entrusted with important tasks in preparation for the next French revolution. The leaders of the revolutionary Chartist Party are also in close contact."[91] The preparatory tasks alluded to are probably the same ones described by Emmanuel Barthélemy, another Blanquist leader in London, in a letter to his imprisoned chief:

We have begun jointly with the German communists the drafting of a revolutionary Manual, containing point by point all the measures that the People must take immediately after the revolution to insure its success and to avoid a repetition of what happened in February. Our intention is to reproduce the Manual in a little booklet that we can distribute among the workers. . . . We will also print the Manual in the form of a proclamation to post in the streets of Paris.[92]

Dommanget suggests that this manual may have become the basis for Blanqui's later Manifesto of Doullens. Whether Marx and Engels themselves were among the "German communists" involved in these labors is unknown, but such endeavors would seem more appropriate to Willich's revolutionary tactics.

What *is* known to belong to Marx's literary production during the period of the united front is a most remarkable and neglected book

90. Ibid.
91. *The Cologne Communist Trial*, p. 249.
92. Letter of July 4, 1850, reproduced in Dommanget, *Les idées*, p. 383.

review that may serve to erase any final lingering doubts concerning Marx's alleged Blanquism in 1850. Surveying two books just published by former Parisian police spies, Marx entered upon the most sustained and devastating critique of Blanquist conceptions ever to flow from his pen. He began with historical background:

> We know the inclination of the Latin peoples toward conspiracies, and the role that conspiracies have played in modern Spanish, Italian, and French history. . . . It is known how until 1830 the liberal bourgeoisie stood at the head of conspiracies against the Restoration. After the July Revolution [of 1830], the republican bourgeoisie took its place; and the proletariat, already trained in conspiring under the Restoration, stepped into the foreground as the futile street battles of the conspiracies eventually frightened off the republican bourgeoisie. The *société des saisons*, with which Barbès and Blanqui carried out the *Emeute* of 1839, was already exclusively proletarian. . . . These conspiracies naturally never embraced the great mass of the Parisian proletariat.[93]

Exempting Blanqui himself, Marx then turned his guns on "conspirators by profession, who dedicate their entire activity to conspiracy and who live from it." These self-styled "men of action" lead utterly bohemian lives, "whose only fixed stations are the bistros where the conspirators rendezvous," and whose "unavoidable consumption by the liter" is financed unwittingly by the workers' contributions. Their style of life and conceptions of revolution bear a marked resemblance to those of the police spies sent to infiltrate their ranks:

> A real revolution is just the opposite of the conceptions of police spies, who, like the "men of action," see in every revolution the work of a small coterie. While all the movements provoked more or less arbitrarily by coteries remained nothing more than *émeutes*, . . . the February Republic was brought about necessarily by the circumstances which drove into the streets the masses of the proletariat standing outside the coteries.[94]

93. " 'Les Conspirateurs,' par A. Chenu . . . 'La naissance de la République en Février 1848,' par *Lucien de la Hodde*" (May 1850), *Werke*, 7:271.
94. Ibid., pp. 272, 269–70.

For Marx, then, a real revolution is brought about by "circumstances," not by the plotting of some self-appointed vanguard. He continued:

It goes without saying that these conspirators do not restrict themselves simply to organizing the revolutionary proletariat. Their business consists precisely in forestalling the process of revolutionary development, spurring it into artificial crises, making revolutions extempore without the conditions of revolution. For them the only condition required for revolution is the sufficient organization of their own conspiracy. They are the alchemists of revolution, and they share in every way the deranged notions and narrow-minded fixed ideas of the alchemists of old. They grasp eagerly at new contraptions to achieve the revolutionary miracle: incendiary bombs, explosive devices with magical powers, and rioting that is supposed to have effects all the more wondrous and astonishing the less it has any rational basis. Busy with such plot-mongering, they have no further aim than the next assault on the existing regime and look with deepest disdain upon a more theoretical enlightenment of the workers as to their class interests. . . .

In the same degree that the Parisian proletariat stepped into the foreground as its own party [*selbst als Partei*], these conspirators lost any decisive influence, were dispersed, and found a dangerous competition in secret proletarian societies whose goal was not immediate insurrection, but the organization and development of the proletariat.[95]

It is hard to exaggerate the importance of this rarely quoted document.[96] Indisputably written by Marx, published in his own journal, appearing during the very weeks when the March *Circular* was issued and the Universal Society was being formed, it would appear to eliminate any question that Marx embraced Blanquism in 1850. He scorned the motives, ideas, methods, and effectiveness of such "conspirators by profession," whom he regarded as utterly incapable of producing a real revolution. The ideal party emerges rather as the *entire* proletar-

95. Ibid., pp. 273–74, 275; cf. 28:500.
96. Although discussed already in 1933 by Nicolaievsky and Maenchen-Helfen (see *Marx*, pp. 214–15), this document has been steadfastly ignored by Communist authorities (e.g., Molnár, Bartel and Schmidt) and non-Communist authorities alike (e.g., Lichtheim, Wolfe, Na'aman). It has never been translated into English.

iat organized as such—"selbst als Partei"—and not any vanguard thereof. When governmental repression obliges the workers to join together
in secret, such groups ought to have the same objectives as an open
legal party, namely, the "organization and development of the proletariat," "theoretical enlightenment," something more than simply "immediate insurrection."

During the entire period prior to 1850, Marx and Engels in their
writings ignored the Blanquists almost totally; during the six brief
months of the united front, the latter's conceptions drew the sustained
and withering blast just cited. Surely this can be no accident. Far from
being driven to accept Blanquist ideas in the despair of exile, Marx
was trying here to "straighten out" his new allies, to convert *them* to
Marxist ideas.[97] Just as he saved his choicest strictures for his democratic compatriots before 1849, so now he treated his new partners to that
special frankness reserved for members of the family. One may add
to Marx's devastating review some less direct but contemporaneous
"educational" remarks published by Engels, concerning the tragedy
of radical leaders like Thomas Münzer who take power before conditions are ripe, and concerning the surprisingly parallel reactionary messianism of Thomas Carlyle.[98]

In June 1850 Marx secured a desk in the reading room of the British
Museum—an event sometimes taken as symbolic of the transition from
the young to the mature Marx, from the revolutionary-activist editor
to the scientific-determinist scholar. His eager study of current economic trends, combined with the failure of the anticipated August
depression to materialize, convinced him that "in view of this general
prosperity, in which the productive forces of bourgeois society are flour-
ishing as exuberantly as they possibly can under bourgois conditions,
there can be no talk of a real revolution." Not that he abandoned
the expectation altogether: "*A new revolution is only possible as the
result of a new crisis. But it is just as inevitable as this crisis.*"[99] If
there was no longer any prospect of immediate upheaval, however,

97. Perception of one of the few authorities to stress the significance of the
book review, namely, Hal Draper, "Marx and the Dictatorship of the Proletariat,"
Etudes de Marxologie, ed. Maximilien Rubel (Paris: Institut de Science Economique Appliquée, 1962), 6:37.

98. See *The German Revolutions,* pp. 103–04; *Werke,* 7:259–61.

99. *Class Struggles, Selected Works,* 1:210 (translation modified—RNH; see
original German, *Werke,* 7:440).

there was no longer any need to continue the increasingly fractious collaboration with Willich, whose forces became even more imposing with the return of Karl Schapper to London in the summer of 1850. The famous schism took place at an extraordinary meeting of the league's central committee on September 15. Now that an accurate transcript of the complete proceedings has been discovered and published (in 1956), we can see that the internecine dispute involved not merely the famous contrast between real conditions versus naked will, but also a clear contrast between majority versus minority revolution. Attacking the putschist policy of Willich and Schapper, Marx declared:

In place of the materialist standpoint of the *Manifesto*, they substitute idealism. Instead of real conditions they make naked *will* the driving force of the revolution. What we say to the workers is: You must go through 15, 20, 50 years of civil war in order to change existing conditions, in order to make yourselves fit to exercise power; whereas they say, we must come to power *at once* or we may as well lay ourselves down to sleep. Just as the word "people" was abused by the democrats, so now the word "proletariat" has been degraded to a mere phrase. To make this phrase effective, it would be necessary to declare all the petty bourgeois to be proletarians, and thus in practice represent the petty bourgeoisie instead of the proletariat.[100]

Lucidly expressed here is Marx's idea that the proletarian masses must educate themselves for the exercise of power through their own political struggles, in a process that will take decades to complete. The reference to "civil war" (*Bürgerkrieg*) need not be understood as meaning fifty years of continuous violence; one may recall Engels' characterization of a "long and vicissitudinous period of revolution" in which nonviolent struggles and the gradual maturation of the proletariat would be punctuated from time to time by a "series of revolutionary *journées*."[101] Appearing before the tough "men of action" with a counsel of restraint, Marx would not have wanted to be taken for a sissy.

100. Transcript published by Boris Nicolaievsky in "Toward a History of the 'Communist League' 1847–1852," *International Review of Social History* 1 (1956):249.
101. See above, chap. 6, nn. 22 and 23. In 1853 Marx published an abbreviated version of this speech and altered the text to read "15, 20, 50 years of civil

Schapper counterattacked by suggesting that Marx's star was on the descendent and that the new revolution would call forth fresh leaders. But he also challenged Marx's view of the future with respect to precisely the issues we have been scrutinizing: "I do not share the view that the [petty?] bourgeoisie will come to power in Germany, and I am fanatical about this." He perceived the controversy thusly:

The question at issue is whether we are to chop a few heads off right at the start or whether it is our heads that will fall. In France the workers will come to power and when that happens, we will also come to power in Germany. Were this not the case, I would indeed lay myself down to sleep. . . . When we are in power, we can take such measures as are necessary to secure the rule of the proletariat. I am fanatical about this point.

Thereupon Marx rejoined:

If the proletariat came to power [now], it could not introduce directly proletarian measures but only petty bourgeois ones. Our party can only govern when conditions allow it to carry out its own program. Louis Blanc gives the best example of what is gained by coming to power too soon. Even in France, it is not the proletariat alone that will come to power but the peasants and petty bourgeois as well, and it is *their* measures that will have to be carried out, not the proletariat's.[102]

Marx's chain of reasoning makes little sense except on the assumption of majority rule. And it stands in diametrical opposition to Schapper's "fanatical" insistence on immediate power, even if that would require minority rule and the guillotine.

Particularly interesting in the debate was Marx's twice-repeated assertion that he was only reiterating the stand agreed upon and set forth in the March *Circular*.[103] This fortifies the view that he did not

---

and national wars" (*Werke*, 8:412), evidently believing that such a formulation would be softer and less shocking to the general public (Nicolaievsky, "Toward a History," p. 243). It was the more familiar version until Nicolaievsky published the full transcript of the original speech.

102. Nicolaievsky, "Toward a History," pp. 250–52.
103. Ibid., pp. 249, 252.

radically change his strategy before or after March 1850: for him the "permanent revolution" was meant to signify a process of development that would stretch out into the future some fifteen, twenty, or fifty years, and that the workers must first make themselves "fit to exercise power." With respect to these projections, Röser's testimony adds some tantalizing details:

> Willich and Schapper wanted communism introduced at the present level of enlightenment, if need be by force of arms during the forthcoming revolution. Marx considered communism possible only as a result of education and gradual development; in one of his letters to us [in 1850?] he marked off four phases we had to pass through before its realization. He said the petty bourgeois and the proletariat will march together against the monarchy up to the next revolution. . . . When the petty bourgeoisie takes the helm, the communists will first begin independent activity and opposition. The social republic will follow, then the social-communist, which will finally give way to the purely communist.[104]

Alas, there are no further specifications which might clarify especially the "social-communist" stage.

When this final schism was consummated, Marx carried virtually all the league intellectuals with him, but only a minority of the artisans. Especially among those artisans living a life of exile in London, there was a heavy majority for Willich and Schapper, which adds further weight to the general interpretation advanced here.[105] Schapper himself explained the split by saying "the people who represent the party on the theoretical side have parted company from those who organize the proletariat" and that henceforth there would have to be two leagues, "one for those who work with the pen, and one for those who work in other ways."[106] When the latter went on to create a group of their own, they insured its class purity by excluding all "merely literary elements" on principle (a neat formulation this—it kept

---

104.   Blumenberg, "Aussagen des Peter Gerhardt Röser," pp. 115–16; also see Nicolaievsky, "Who Is Distorting History?" p. 218; Na'aman, "Zur Geschichte des Bundes," pp. 69–70.

105.   Schraepler, *Handwerkerbünde,* pp. 418–20; Na'aman, "Zur Geschichte des Bundes," pp. 72–73.

106.   Nicolaievsky, "Toward a History," p. 250.

out the likes of Marx and Engels while embracing the aristocrat and ex-officer Willich as a proletarian brother).[107] So it happened that after three years of shaky marriage, the radical artisans and the renegade intellectuals went their separate ways.

There remained only to effect a parallel break with the French Blanquists, to liquidate the Universal Society of Revolutionary Communists. Responding to a written inquiry from Adam, Vidil, and Barthélemy in October, Marx and Engels, together with Harney, declared that they had "long since regarded the association of which you speak as dissolved de facto" and sarcastically invited the three Frenchmen to Engels' residence to witness a ceremonial burning of the statutes.[108] This ceremony, if it ever took place, was a fitting coda to the ultraradical period of 1850.

Let us sum up: anyone who wants to ascribe a Blanquist strategy of minority revolution to Marx and Engels is obliged to ignore their entire life work before and after 1850 and to draw evidence from a period of six months when the two men presumably took leave of their senses and embraced the totalitarian-democratic principles they otherwise repudiated. Further, one must avert one's eyes from a very impressive body of contrary evidence even during this period in order to focus on a handful of documents, the most damning of which (the March *Circular* and the statutes of the Universal Society) were manifestly spawned by committees and involved compromise formulations on the key issues. Finally, one must tear these documents from their intricate historical context, place them in the most sinister possible light, and present them baldly as general principles of Marxist strategy applicable to any time, place, and circumstance. However often these tricks are still performed, they are none of them acceptable practices of serious scholarship.

In actuality, Marx and Engels' strategy during the ultraradical period was but a refinement of the one they had had in mind for France prior to February 1848 and for Germany after November 1848. It anticipated a popular revolution against authoritarian government, supported by workers, peasants, and urban petty bourgeois, and aimed at the creation of a democratic republic. Only after an extended period

107. "Ansprache vom 1. Oktober 1850," Wermuth and Stieber, *Communisten-Verschwörungen,* 1:266.
108. Letter to Adam, Barthélemy, and Vidil, October 9, 1850 (English original; retranslated here from German), *Werke,* 7:415.

of time would the proletariat be developed enough to rule alone and implement full communism. The refinement involved three new points: (1) the workers should develop their own independent organizations within the broader alliance of majority classes, so as not to fall under the shadow of the "pale" democrats; (2) as between their two partners, the workers should count more on the peasants and expect quick betrayal from the petty bourgeoisie; and (3) in the absence of political freedoms—and only for that reason—it is necessary to work in and with secret societies and collaborate with their largely Blanquist leaders. Even during the ultraradical period, however, Marx and Engels definitely did not accept the Blanquist prescription for a deliberate seizure of power by a conspiratorial elite, followed by the educational dictatorship of that elite and the immediate introduction of communism, with elections postponed until the classless society was a reality. The two men repudiated these ideas not merely at the time of the September split, but during the ultraradical period itself, most sharply in the hitherto neglected April book review with which Marx balanced the March *Circular*.

After 1850, for the rest of their lives, Marx and Engels would retain the two principal strategies analyzed in these last chapters. For more advanced countries with a working-class majority, like Britain—simple proletarian revolution. For less advanced but still essentially bourgeois countries, like France and Germany—the more complex process beginning with the alliance of the majority classes. In later years, after the appearance of stable democratic institutions in parts of western Europe, Marx and Engels would even allow the possibility of a peaceful and legal assumption of power by the workers. On the other hand, for extremely backward countries with remnants of primitive communist institutions, most notably Russia, they would allow for the possibility of an immediate merging with the classless societies that would have developed in the West. Both these later strategy modifications— the one partly anticipating social democratic ideas, the other partly anticipating Bolshevik ideas—will be taken up in volume 2.

Internal Party Democracy

WE HAVE ALREADY LOOKED AT the Communist League from the outside, as an alleged conspiracy or a vanguard party, asking questions about its assigned historical tasks and relationship to the masses. But there is another way of looking at such organizations, from the *inside,* as autonomous structures, miniature societies with their own arrangements for choosing and dismissing leaders, making "laws," binding members to a certain discipline, and so forth. The character of these internal arrangements, whether they are more authoritarian or more democratic, undoubtedly tells us a good deal about the underlying political values and assumptions of the organizations' founders, leaders, and perhaps members. If one inspects the values and assumptions of early socialist thinkers in such a light, the results are frequently devastating. Some socialists were frankly antidemocratic, of course: Robert Owen never pretended to desire anything but authoritarian leadership for the model communities he established. The dictatorial aspirations of Babeuf, Buonarroti, and Blanqui were faithfully reflected in the dictatorial internal structure of the conspiratorial groups they founded. More complex are the cases of those socialists who opposed authoritarianism publicly, while endorsing it "privately," as it were, for their own organizations. As a prime representative of this type, we may single out Pierre-Joseph Proudhon, especially because his "libertarianism" has been contrasted so often to the alleged "authoritarian socialism" of Marx.[1]

1. Expressions of George Woodcock, *Anarchism: A History of Libertarian Ideas and Movements* (Cleveland: World, Meridian Books, 1962), pp. 118–21 and passim. On the underlying authoritarianism of many early socialists, see Hal Draper, *The Two Souls of Socialism* (New York: Independent Socialist Clubs, 1966); and

As an anarchist, of course, Proudhon did not aim at creating a political party, but his notebooks from our period are filled with dreams and plans for establishing a working-class "association," or cluster of "progressive societies," as he alternately labeled his venture, which would be partly educational institutions and partly functional cells of the new mutualist order in which members would make and exchange goods outside the capitalist marketplace. Proudhon's notebooks, only recently published, have proven a major embarrassment, however, in that the father of anarchism there revealed through countless instructions to himself what it was he really wanted: "Have myself named Director of all these societies." "Once I have taken my place, no one can think of disputing it with me." "The Society must be like a single man, speaking through my mouth. . . . Having proved myself on a number of occasions, I am beyond criticism." "*Take the initiative in everything, that is the only way to remain the Master.*—Despotism is nothing else." "Determine my line of conduct and my plan in advance: utilizing men and sacrificing them as soon as they become obstacles and don't go along any more, or as soon as they want to drag the Society along a false path. —No politics of liberalism." "I worship humanity," he generalized a little later, "but I spit on men."[2] Proudhon's reputation as an antiauthoritarian can scarcely survive these incredible self-exposures.

What about Marx and Engels? Can private desires like these be found in their notebooks or in the letters they sent one another? Did they devise authoritarian statutes for the organizations they helped to mold? Did they seek dictatorial power for themselves within those organizations? These questions take on added significance when one reflects that Marx and Engels regarded workers' associations as embryos of the new society within the old, where the habits and attitudes of socialist man were being formed within the womb of capitalist society. If the two men expected to inaugurate socialism with totalitarian

Lewis S. Feuer, "Marxism and the Hegemony of the Intellectual Class," in his *Marx and the Intellectuals: A Set of Post-Ideological Essays* (Garden City: Doubleday, Anchor Books, 1969), pp. 53–69.

2. *Carnets de P.-J. Proudhon*, ed. Pierre Haubtman (Paris: Rivière, 1960–), 1:76, 283, 284, 278, 270; 2:56. These passages and others have been reproduced by Hal Draper in a devastating critique of Proudhon's "libertarianism": "A Note on the Father of Anarchism," *New Politics* 8, no. 1 (Winter 1969):79–93. Also see the earlier study of J. Salwyn Schapiro, *Liberalism and the Challenge of Fascism* (New York: McGraw-Hill, 1949), pp. 332–69.

dictatorship, surely some sign of these plans or assumptions would turn up in the microcosm, in their prior organizational activity. Conversely, if such activity proved to be in substantial accord with liberal-democratic principles, that would help to confirm Marx and Engels' democratic intentions for the macrocosm.

The Communist Correspondence Committee

The Communist Correspondence Committee of Brussels was the first of three organizations in which Marx and Engels played leading roles during the period of our concern. It was also the most amorphous, since its purpose was only to establish regular communication by letter among socialists in the various countries of western Europe. So far as is known, the committee had no formal organization or even members. Its correspondents kept in touch intermittently with the Brussels center, but they paid no dues and were not bound by any statutes or statement of principles. As the committee's circle expanded, it began to hold occasional meetings in Brussels, attended by local communists as well as those—like Hess and Weitling—who passed through the city on occasion. It is not known what formal structure, if any, these meetings had, but on at least one occasion a vote was taken.[3]

This nebulous association has nonetheless been credited by Marx's hostile biographers as being a "party" which conducted at least two "purges," one of Weitling, the other of the True Socialist Hermann Kriege.[4] Since the term "purge" in our time brings to mind forced confessions, show trials, and executions, it might be instructive to examine the fate of these earliest purge "victims." The first incident, concerning Weitling, has already been recounted above and involved nothing more terrible than some sharp words between two opinionated men. Since the committee was not a membership organization, there could be no question of expelling Weitling, much less of further punishment. The former tailor continued to receive material help from the Brussels group and even attended another meeting a month later, where he

---

3. See above, pp. 148–50; also *Werke*, 4:3. In the broader workers' society Marx helped to organize in Brussels in 1847, he was proud to report to Georg Herwegh: "Here things are discussed in quite parliamentary fashion" (ibid., 27:470).
4. Leopold Schwartzschild, *Karl Marx: The Red Prussian*, trans. Margaret Wing (New York: Scribners, 1947), pp. 140–47; Robert Payne, *Marx* (New York: Simon and Schuster, 1968), p. 132.

freely voted against Marx on the principal item of business discussed.[5] Neither did Marx have any power to expel Weitling from the League of the Just—assuming he wanted to—since he did not yet belong himself. In fact, the artisan leaders of the league wrote to congratulate Marx when they heard of the dispute: "W. W[eitling] cannot tolerate anyone except those who blindly obey his orders, who find no book interesting that he has not written."[6] There was nothing more to the first "purge." If, on this occasion of their first meeting, Marx had not disagreed sharply with Weitling's putschist ideas, doubtless the hostile biographers would have found that even more sinister.

The second incident involved a statement, "Zirkular gegen Kriege," issued by the Brussels committee in May 1846. Hermann Kriege was a young True Socialist writer who in 1845 had emigrated to New York, where he began publishing the *Volks-Tribun* and propagating the doctrines of his school in a particularly effusive and sentimental manner. His specific misdeeds included a sycophantic open letter requesting financial help from American millionaire John Jacob Astor and a call for the free distribution of land to homesteaders on the basis of individual proprietorship. Marx and Engels saw in Kriege an irresistibly vulnerable target in the factional campaign they were then beginning to mount against True Socialism. The "Zirkular," signed by the seven participants of the Brussels committee meeting who had voted for it, solemnly declared that "the tendency represented by the editor, Hermann Kriege, in the *Volks-Tribun* is not communistic," and that it was "compromising to the communist party." It went on to censure his specific errors, especially the "petty bourgeois" land scheme that would only encourage private property. Copies were dispatched to all the committee's correspondents, including one to Kriege himself, which he published along with his own rebuttal.[7] That was the sum total of the second "purge." The pronouncement took the form of a public censure but obviously could not expel Kriege from a communist party that was as yet no more than a confraternity of the mind.

In the same letter congratulating Marx for humbling Weitling, the league artisans suggested that the "Zirkular" was "perhaps too hard" on Kriege, who was young, after all, and "can still learn."[8] Perhaps

5.   See above, pp. 156–57; also *Werke*, 4:3; Ernst Schraepler, *Handwerkerbünde und Arbeitervereine, 1830–53* (Berlin: deGruyter, 1972), pp. 156–57.
6.   Letter of June 6, 1846, *Bund Dokumente*, 1:348.
7.   *Werke*, 4:3–17; Schraepler, *Handwerkerbünde*, p. 161.
8.   Letter of June 6, 1846, *Bund Dokumente*, 1:350.

Marx and Engels may be accused of displaying that intellectual arrogance for which they would become famous in encounters with rival ideologues. But even this should not be exaggerated. A week before the Kriege statement, Marx wrote the cordial letter to Proudhon that was quoted earlier, inviting him to become a correspondent. And the Brussels committee managed to remain on speaking terms with socialist spokesmen as diverse as Cabet and Harney, Hess and Flocon, Schapper and Blanc. Nor should it be assumed that the two "victims" of Marx and Engels' arrogance were necessarily more open minded themselves. One of Kreige's articles espousing the socialist cause had asserted: "Whoever does not support such a party can rightly be treated as an enemy of mankind." The "Zirkular" offered the following notable rejoinder:

This intolerant sentence would appear to contradict [Kriege's teaching of] "devotion to *everyone*," the "religion of love" toward all. But it is an entirely logical consequence of this new religion which, like every other religion, hates and persecutes all its enemies to death. The enemy of the party is predictably transformed into a heretic. Instead of an enemy of the real *party*, whom one *combats* [kämpft], he becomes a sinner against an imagined *mankind*, whom one must *punish* [bestrafen].[9]

Thus Marx and Engels regarded it as legitimate to "combat" ideological "enemies"; they had neither the inclination nor the power to "punish" a "heretic."

The Communist League

The Communist Correspondence Committee eventually merged with the League of the Just in 1847 to become the Communist League. As Marx and Engels drew closer to the League of the Just in the months preceding, they found an organizational structure that had already evolved a considerable distance from its conspiratorial beginnings. The original League of the Despised, founded in 1834, had been patterned as a faithful replica of its Babouvist and Carbonarist parent groups. The founders who wrote its statutes generously provided themselves with full "legislative and executive power" (Art. 39), as well as the right to co-opt their own successors (Art. 41). To them every

9.   *Werke*, 4:13–14; letter to Proudhon cited above, chap. 5, n. 43.

member owed "unconditional obedience" (Art. 40), and they had the right not only to expel but even to pronounce death sentences against "traitors" (Arts. 13, 28, 34, 54). The group had two sets of statutes, one governing the outer organization, and another super-secret set governing the inner core. The various branches of the organization had no control over its leaders and were forbidden any contact with each other (Arts. 13, 23)—they merely received instructions handed down from above.[10]

In 1836 part of the group split off, largely over the issue of its dictatorial structure, and formed the League of the Just.[11] The new organization adopted a statute in 1838 that contained many democratic innovations. The central committee was now elected annually, not by the entire membership, to be sure, but by the leaders of the district in which its seat was located (Arts. 24, 25, 36), leaders who themselves would have been elected by the membership of each local unit (Arts. 15, 21). The central committee retained the right to co-opt one or two additional members to its own body (Art. 27). Its basic function was confined to the execution of "laws" that now had to be passed by a majority of the full membership (Arts. 30, 32, 33), although here too it retained the privilege of legislating "according to its own conviction" where circumstances made the normal procedure "impossible" (Art. 34). Members now owed more limited obedience (Art. 11), and their expulsion could be pronounced only by the local units (Art. 10). However, new members still took a great oath of secrecy and were threatened with death or other punishments if they broke it (Arts. 7, 9). The need for secrecy likewise still prevented the local units from contacting one another (Art. 18). This statute was further revised in 1843, but its essential features remained intact down to the reorganization inspired by Marx and Engels.[12]

If the two men had nourished dictatorial ambitions or had authoritarian values, one would have expected them to encourage a backsliding toward the older conspiratorial principles of organization. But, on

10. "Statuten des Bundes der Geächteten," *Bunde Dokumente*, 1:975–85; Schraepler, *Handwerkerbünde*, pp. 41–43. For an analysis of the function of secrecy and ritual in conspiratorial groups, see E. J. Hobsbawm, *Primitive Rebels* (New York: Norton, 1965), pp. 150–74.

11. See *Bund Dokumente*, 1:89–92; Schraepler, *Handwerkerbünde*, pp. 49–52.

12. "Statuten des Bundes der Gerechten," *Bund Dokumente*, 1:92–98; Schraepler, *Handwerkerbünde*, pp. 52–53. For later revisions, see *Bund Dokumente*, 1:153–54.

the contrary, they insisted on a fuller democratization of the existing statute. Marx recalled in 1877 that "the first entrance of Engels and myself into the secret Communist League took place only on the condition that everything conducive to authoritarian superstitions be removed from the statutes."[13] In June 1847, for the first time in its history, the league called a general congress to which each local unit sent one representative. In addition to its work on the "confession of faith" scrutinized earlier, this congress hammered out a draft of a new statute, which was next submitted to the local units for discussion and amendment, and then returned to the second congress, of November 1847, for final modification and adoption. Both Marx and Engels attended this second congress and seem to have been satisfied with the product of its labors.[14]

The new statute began with a declaration that the purpose of the Communist League was "the overthrow of the bourgeoisie, the rule of the proletariat, the abolition of the old civil society founded on class antagonisms, and the establishment of a new society without classes or private property."[15] The organization retained the basic pyramidal structure of the parent league: the smallest units, called communities (*Gemeinden*), consisted of from three to twenty members each. These members were empowered to elect their own chairman and his assistant, and to admit new members (Arts. 6–8). The communities of a given city or region constituted a circle (*Kreis*), in which the assembled chairmen and assistants sat as the circle committee and elected their own president (Arts. 12–13). This committee had executive authority over the entire area and linked up the communities below with the leading circle above it (Arts. 13–14). Leading circles were located in the principal city of that country or province over which they had jurisdiction (Arts. 16–18), but their governing committees were constituted from their own communities, as in the case of ordinary circles. The leading circles in turn linked the circles with the highest authorities—the congress and the central committee (Arts. 18, 20).

13. See above, chap. 5, n. 71.
14. Details of this procedure reviewed earlier, pp. 187–89; cf. Engels' recollection, *Selected Works*, 2:315.
15. "Statuten des Bundes der Kommunisten," *Bund Dokumente*, 1:626–30 (also printed in *Werke*, 4:596–601; a rather unreliable English translation in Marx and Engels, *The Communist Manifesto*, ed. D. Ryazanoff [New York: International, 1930], pp. 340–45).

The most significant single innovation in the new statute was the provision for annual congresses (*Kongresse*) to serve as the "legislative power" of the league, to keep tabs on the central committee, to set dues, and to sit as a supreme judiciary in expulsion cases (Arts. 21, 30, 33, 38–39, 43). Each circle elected a number of delegates to the congress according to the size of its membership; members of the central committee were also entitled, ex officio, to attend its annual deliberations, where they had voice but not vote (Arts. 31–32, 35). Thus the awkward choice of legislative procedures available to the old league—cumbersome plebiscite or committee fiat—gave way to the system typical cf representative democracies.

The central committee (*Zentralbehörde*) of the new organization found itself more carefully supervised and its powers more exactly circumscribed. Its five members were still elected annually by the circle (or leading circle) committee of the city in which its seat was located (Art. 22), apparently due to the desirability of having all its members living in one place, where they would be well known and where their activities could be checked continually. The committee lost the right to co-opt additional members and could be recalled itself at any time by its own electors (Art. 25). Also, the congress now determined the seat of the central committee and could move it from year to year (Art. 34). The latter body was further obliged to submit an annual report on its activities and expenditures to the scrutiny and approval of the former (Arts. 21, 48). If "questions of general or immediate interest" arose, the committee was required to initiate a "discussion" by the entire membership and if necessary call an extraordinary congress (Arts. 27, 33), but it could no longer legislate under any circumstances. Neither did it have any authority over expulsions. Among the five members of the ruling body, one was chosen president and another secretary, but committee decisions were reached by simple majority vote. Thus the new statute embodied the basic liberal-democratic principles of elective leadership, with carefully limited powers and responsibility to a representative body. There is no hint of dictatorship here, or even the more subtle features of totalitarian democracy.

To avoid police persecution of its Continental branches, some limited elements of secrecy were retained—notably, party names and the rule of no contact between local communities (Arts. 4, 9). But the *mystique* of secrecy was excised by the elimination of the great oath and the threatened punishments (Art. 50), and also by the league's undertaking to print a public manifesto of its aims. The most important conditions of membership, as reviewed in chapter 5, were "professing of communism," "revolutionary energy and zeal for propaganda," and "submission to the resolutions of the League"; and new members had to be accepted unanimously by their community (Art. 2). If a member no longer met the specified conditions of membership, he might be suspended (*entfernt*) by his community or circle committee, but he could be permanently expelled (*ausgestossen*) only by majority vote of the congress itself (Arts. 37–39). There was henceforth no punishment that went beyond expulsion.

We know that Marx and Engels approved the new statute in general, but not—since no minutes of the founding congresses have ever turned up—exactly which stipulations they may have proposed, supported, or opposed. Some new light has been shed on the subject, however, by the recent publication of a document containing two suggestions sent in to the central committee by the Brussels group during the period of local discussion between the two congresses. Neither proposal betrays any sinister intention. The draft statute of June had stipulated that no member could belong to any other "political or national organization." The Brussels group held such a restriction to be "unpolitical, since it robs us of all possibility to influence these organizations."[16] It will be remembered that this was the period in which Marx and Engels were urging a united front with the "pale" democrats. The demand for exclusive loyalty was relaxed in the final version, which forbade membership only in "anti-communist" organizations (Art. 2D). The original draft had also retained an element of the old legislative process by stipulating that all legislative decisions of the congress be submitted to the communities for full membership approval. "If times become revolutionary," the Brussels group objected, "this restriction would cripple all the energy of the congress. We remember that in 1794 the aristocrats put the same demand before the Convention in order to paralyze all action."[17] The argument must have been convincing, for the article in question was deleted from the final version. Note that Marx and Engels were asking for membership confidence in the congress, not the central committee.

16. Brussels suggestions quoted in "Ansprache der Zentralbehörde des Bundes der Kommunisten an den Bund" (September 1848), *Bund Dokumente*, 1:539; draft statutes of June appear ibid., pp. 466–69.

17. Ibid., p. 539.

The November congress also commissioned Marx and Engels, as related earlier, to draw up the public statement of the league's aims,
the document that became the *Communist Manifesto*. While this fact
is repeated in all the standard histories, few writers have mentioned
that Marx and Engels received no special powers or even high offices
in the league as a price for their joining. The June congress designated
London as the seat of the central committee, to which only artisans
were elected—Schapper as president, Moll as secretary, along with
Bauer, Eccarius, and Karl Pfänder. Marx became merely the chairman
of the Brussels circle and Engels, a member of his circle committee.[18]
If, like Proudhon, the two men had desired dictatorial control of an
organization, they certainly did not press for it in the league, nor did
they take the other option of creating their own group from scratch.

Because of its rapid organizational growth and intellectual preemi-
nence, the Brussels circle soon earned the high regard of the London
artisan leaders. "London and Brussels at the present moment form the
pillars for the entire league," the central committee wrote Marx in October 1847.[19] This may help to explain why, with the outbreak of the
1848 revolution, the Londoners suddenly transferred the seat of the
central committee to Brussels. While there was no statutory authority
for such action, the League of the Just had undertaken a similar shift,
establishing a precedent a few years earlier.[20] The London leaders
doubtless felt that a revolutionary organization should be directed from
the scene of revolution, to which they were themselves about to repair.
As we have seen, the Brussels comrades received this commission just
as the police were closing in and hurriedly met on March 3 to transfer
the seat once again to Paris, voting Marx "discretionary power [*dis-
kretionäre Vollmacht*] for the temporary central direction of all league
affairs, with responsibility to the new central committee to be constituted and to the next congress."[21] The new committee subsequently
elected by the enlarged Paris circle was composed of Marx as presi-

18. See ibid., pp. 476, 489, 497.
19. Letter of October 18, 1847, ibid., p. 582.
20. *Werke*, 4:607; Dirk J. Struik, ed., *Birth of the Communist Manifesto* (New
York: International, 1971), p. 148; Schraepler, *Handwerkerbünde*, p. 193.
21. "Beschluss der Zentralbehörde des Bundes der Kommunisten" (March
1848), *Werke*, 4:607; cf. variations in French-language version of this resolution,
reprinted by Dieter Dowe, *Aktion und Organisation: Arbeiterbewegung, sozialistische und kommunistische Bewegung in der preussischen Rheinprovinz, 1820–
1852* (Hannover: Literatur und Zietgeschichte, 1970), p. 139.

dent, Schapper as secretary, together with Bauer, Moll, Engels, Wilhelm Wolff, and Karl Wallau—a near-perfect balance between London and Brussels, between artisans and intellectuals.[22] This central committee moved its seat once more in April to Cologne, where it continued to function actively until the June dissolution. If Röser's testimony is correct, Marx can justly be accused of abusing his office grossly when he used his "discretionary power" to dissolve the league. It is not entirely clear whether he intended to liquidate the entire organization or just the central committee and the Cologne circle upon which it was now based. He seems to have been concerned mainly to rid himself personally of the burden of the league; some of its other branches—in London, Paris, Berlin, and Switzerland—appear to have continued some functions throughout 1848.[23] In any event, the statute did not provide authority for either action, and Marx's special powers, by any reasonable interpretation, had already lapsed with the creation of the new central committee in Paris. Only four members of that committee were present at the June meeting, according to Röser's recollection, while several nonmembers from the Cologne circle also participated, making its statutory position even more dubious.[24] It must be emphasized, however, that Marx abused his "discretionary" authority not to gain dictatorial control over the Communist League but—perversely—to dissolve it.

Whatever the exact formal status of the league during the summer of 1848, Joseph Moll was instrumental in reconstituting a central committee in London at the end of the year, with himself, Bauer, and Eccarius as members. When Marx declined to rejoin the organization early the next year, he argued among other things that the newly revised statute "tended toward the conspiratorial,"[25] and it is worth observing what changes the artisans made in the temporary absence of the intellectuals. The new statement of purpose declared simply in favor of "the introduction of a unitary indivisible social-democratic

22. *Werke,* 27:118.
23. See speculations of Shlomo Na'aman, "Zur Geschichte des Bundes der Kommunisten in Deutschland in der zweiten Phase seines Bestehens," *Archiv für Sozialgeschichte* 5 (1965):25–30; Dowe, *Aktion und Organisation,* pp. 250–53; Schraepler, *Handwerkerbünde,* pp. 266–72.
24. Werner Blumenberg, "Zur Geschichte des Bundes der Kommunisten: Die Aussagen des Peter Gerhardt Röser," *International Review of Social History* 9 (1964):89; see account given above, pp. 172–74.
25. See above, chap. 7, n. 69.

republic" (Art. 1). Members were now forbidden to participate in "any other political organization" (Art. 2), a reversal of Marx's 1847 advice and probably a deliberate repudiation of his united-front policy. The most significant changes concerned expulsion. The painstaking two-stage process of local suspension and congress expulsion was dropped in favor of immediate local expulsion, while the central committee was empowered to expel entire communities (Art. 34). Most ominously, the death penalty was revived for cases of "betrayal" (Art. 33).[26] There would appear to be some justice in Marx's complaint of conspiratorial backsliding, and his refusal to join speaks again in his favor.

It is not clear how Marx and Engels were readmitted to the league's central committee in the latter part of 1849. Apparently the members of all previous central committees, when they turned up in London, were welcomed into the ruling body by its surviving members, Bauer and Eccarius. This would explain the reappearance of Marx and Engels, Pfänder, and eventually Schapper. But the committee had four additional members by the time of the 1850 split—Willich and two London artisans who sided with him, Albert Lehmann and a certain Fränkel, as well as the recent recruit to the Marx circle, Konrad Schramm. Marx himself claimed to have nominated Willich on Engels' recommendation, but we do not know whether the London circle made the decisions, or whether the central committee had resumed a policy of co-optation.[27] In the confusion of the time, no one seems to have observed the statute very strictly. In any event, Marx had the support of six of these ten members as the final crisis approached.

Perhaps having learned something from his high-handed Cologne dissolution, Marx took considerable pains to proceed against the Willich-Schapper faction in a reasonably statutory fashion. At the famous showdown in September, he introduced a three-part motion proposing: (1) that the central committee dissolve itself and transfer its seat to Cologne, where a new committee would be elected, since the "open rebellion" of the Willich-Schapper minority in London would otherwise make a schism inevitable; (2) that the new central committee draft new statutes, since the December 1848 revisions were not everywhere accepted, and two sets of statutes were producing complete "anarchy"; and (3) that the London membership of the league divide itself into

26. "Statuten des Bundes der Kommunisten" (December 1848), *Bund Dokumente*, 1:876–80.
27. See *Werke*, 14:440; Na'aman, "Zur Geschichte des Bundes," p. 36; Schraepler, *Handwerkerbünde*, p. 358.

two entirely separate circles, both acknowledging the new Cologne center, since the two factions could no longer work together within a common framework.[28]

In defending his proposals, Marx pointed out—perhaps with a touch of irony—that the statute of December 1848, revised in his absence, gave the central committee majority the right to dissolve the London circle (which supported Willich) and expel the entire minority: "I do not make such a proposal, because it would bring useless quarrels and because these people are still communists according to their own conviction, even though the views they presently express are anti-communist. . . . I believe I have found the way for us to separate from each other without destroying the party."[29] If Marx had had dictatorial ambitions, expulsion surely would have been the appropriate move, since it would have left him as president of a central committee composed entirely of his own supporters. Instead, he proposed to relinquish his own presidency and transfer control of the organization to Cologne, where he doubtless hoped his friends would prevail, although he could not be sure and certainly could not be present himself. Some weeks earlier, Schapper had made a similar proposal to move the seat of the league to Cologne, and Marx had opposed it.[30] These factors suggest that, contrary to general impressions, Marx's proposals may have been aimed at genuine compromise, not at a split. In any event, they came too late: just before the vote accepting them, Willich and his coterie dramatically walked out.[31]

The new central committee chosen by the Cologne circle included Röser, Bürgers, and Carl Otto, who agreed with Marx on the substantive issue but were independent enough to censure both sides on the procedural question involved:

As for the question of formal legality, it was clear that both parties had abandoned the procedure laid down in the statutes—for according to these they should have appealed to the congress. But

28. From the transcript of the meeting, reprinted by Boris Nicolaievsky, "Toward a History of 'The Communist League' 1847–1852," *International Review of Social History* 1 (1956):248–49.

29. Ibid., p. 250.

30. Karl Wermuth and Wilhelm Stieber, *Die Communisten-Verschwörungen des 19. Jahrhunderts*, 2 vols. (1853–54; reprint ed., Hildesheim: Olms, 1969), 1:269.

31. Nicolaievsky, "Toward a History," p. 252; also see Marx's recollection *Werke*, 9:506–07.

further reflection convinced us that in a sense both parties had acted rightly, for even if a congress had been physically feasible in London at the time, it would inevitably have brought about the complete disintegration of the League.[32]

In the meantime, however, Willich and Schapper had formed their own central committee, based on the London circle, and had expelled the entire Marx faction including the new Cologne central committee. The latter body returned the compliment, and thus two entirely separate leagues were created by the curious process of mutual expulsion.

The Cologne central committee also accepted the responsibility of drawing up a new statute, and it is interesting to note that all of the "conspiratorial" innovations of the December 1848 version were now excised. Participation in other political organizations was once again permitted (Art. 2). Expulsion once again became more difficult, and the central committee could expel entire communities only upon the request of a circle (Art. 4). The death penalty likewise disappeared. New machinery was set up to resolve "disputes" within and between the various units of the organization, as well as between them and the central committee, with the congress acting as the highest court of appeal (Art. 17). The statute did contain one significant sideswipe at Marx: it declared the league "indissoluble, as long as the proletarian revolution has not reached its final goal." These new rules were formally endorsed by the London branch in January 1851, with Marx objecting only to the fuzziness of the initial statement of purpose. Even though his influence over the ideology and tactics of the rump organization was now unchallenged, he sought no change in its basically democratic structure.[33]

Scarcely had these arrangements been completed when the Prussian police began a series of arrests that wiped out the new central com-

32. "Address of the Cologne Central Committee to the Communist League" (December 1850), *The Cologne Communist Trial,* trans. and ed. Rodney Livingstone (New York: International, 1971), pp. 255–56; also see *Werke,* 7:561–65; Blumenberg, "Aussagen des Peter Gerhardt Röser," pp. 106–07; Schraepler *Handwerkerbünde,* pp. 422–25.

33. "Statuten des Kommunistischen Bundes" (December 1850), *Werke,* 7:565–67; Schraepler, *Handwerkerbünde,* p. 427. The Willich-Schapper faction likewise drew up a new statute in November 1850 which retained the artisan position on all the moot questions (see Wermuth and Stieber, *Communisten-Verschörungen,* 1:244–47; cf. p. 294).

mittee, left the entire Cologne branch decimated, and brought league operations all over Germany to a virtual standstill. After this paralyzing blow, nothing remained but for the handful of members exiled in the safety of London to pick up the pieces and resume the role of leadership. For the next year, the Marx circle worked furiously on the legal defense and public vindication of their imprisoned comrades.[34] But a few days after their conviction in November 1852, Marx introduced a motion before a meeting of the London circle to dissolve the league, declaring that "the continuation of the league on the Continent as well is no longer appropriate to the time." Doubtless this action contradicted the statute of 1850, but as Marx explained in his letter to Engels, it merely gave sanction to a dissolution that had already been put into effect by the Prussian authorities.[35]

Throughout the five-year history of the Communist League, one can find no trace in any of Marx and Engels' private writings of the secret autocratic ambitions nourished by Proudhon. Neither do the two relevant statutes reveal anything but straightforward liberal-democratic conceptions. In his actual behavior as league president, Marx's record was certainly blemished, particularly by the June 1848 dissolution, but not in such a way as to suggest personal dictatorial ambitions or totalitarian assumptions.

The Cologne Workers' Society

During the period in 1848–1849 when political freedoms existed in Germany, we have seen how Marx abandoned the secret Communist League in order to devote his political energies to open legal activities —the *Neue Rheinische Zeitung*, the Cologne Democratic Society, and the Cologne Workers' Society. Of these, the first two need not detain us long.

The *Neue Rheinische Zeitung* was not a political organization, of course, and could be passed over entirely, were it not for a half-serious remembrance by Engels in 1884 concerning the structure of its editorial staff: "The editorial constitution was simply the dictatorship of Marx." This characterization turns up like a bad penny in every hostile treat-

---

34. See detailed account with numerous documents in *The Cologne Communist Trial;* also Dowe, *Aktion und Organisation,* p. 279.
35. Motion quoted in Marx to Engels, November 19, 1852, *Werke,* 28:195.

ment of Marx, adduced as final proof of his incurable authoritarianism. Engels' subsequent explanation is generally omitted:

A big daily paper, which has to be ready at a definite hour, cannot observe a consistent policy with any other constitution. In this case, moreover, Marx's dictatorship stood to reason, was undisputed, willingly recognized by all of us. It was primarily his clear vision and sure policy that made this publication the most famous German newspaper of the revolutionary years.[36]

At worst, Marx was guilty of organizing his editorial staff along the lines followed by virtually every other newspaper and business enterprise in the world—what Engels called dictatorship is elsewhere known as management prerogative.

Engels probably chose the word "dictatorship" remembering a specific incident from the early days of the newspaper. One member of the editorial staff, Heinrich Bürgers, had submitted his first article and was distressed when Marx as editor shortened and revised it. As Marx himself recalled, Bürgers "was so incensed that he appealed to universal suffrage. By way of exception, I gave in to this, declaring at the same time that in a newspaper office dictatorship, not universal suffrage, must rule. Universal suffrage [then] declared itself universally against him."[37] Finding himself thus isolated on the editorial staff, Bürgers resigned in protest (though his zeal for democracy did not prevent him from becoming an enthusiastic supporter of Bismarck a few years later). This "dictatorship" over an editorial staff composed of a handful of personal friends, who willingly accepted his authority, can scarcely be taken very seriously if Marx was ready to accept the usual democratic rules in larger, more formally structured organizations.

For almost a year Marx belonged to the Cologne Democratic Society, whose three thousand members elected a committee of twenty-five persons to guide the organization under the presidency of the advocate Karl Schneider II. Marx belonged to this guiding committee and was also chosen by the membership along with Schneider to represent the

36.   "Marx and the *Neue Rheinische Zeitung*," *Selected Works*, 2:300 (translation modified—RNH; see original German, *Werke*, 21:19).

37.   Letter to Ferdinand Lassalle, September 15, 1860, *Werke*, 30:565; also see Boris Nicolaievsky, "Who Is Distorting History?" *Proceedings of the American Philosophical Society* 105 (1961):215, n. 20.

society in the Rhenish District Committee of Democrats. Marx's evident ability to work with these "pale" democrats in an organization he did not control has never attracted much scholarly attention.[38] Secret societies and the clashes of great rival personalities are doubtless more exciting subjects of investigation than a day-by-day collaboration in a democratically structured legal organization.

This may also explain the relative neglect, until recently, of Marx's participation in the Cologne Workers' Society, which merits more of our attention here because of Marx's brief role as its president and because of the changes he inspired in its organizational structure. It will be recalled that the Workers' Society was founded in April 1848 by the popular communist physician Andreas Gottschalk, who had himself elected president at the first meeting. The group functioned partly as an educational society, partly as a political club, and partly as a quasi trade union for the workers and especially journeymen artisans of Cologne. Beginning with three hundred members, it grew to a peak strength of six to seven thousand during the summer of 1848, making it by far the largest political organization in a city that had perhaps twenty-one thousand eligible voters. Its members were originally organized by craft, with each trade choosing one representative for a guiding committee of fifty persons which shared executive power with the president. Gottschalk reserved the right to appoint four secretaries of his own choosing and to edit the society's newspaper.[39]

While Marx initially remained aloof from his rival's organization, Schapper and Moll made it their principal center of activity. Capitalizing on growing resentment against Gottschalk's benign authoritarianism and unpredictable political vacillations, the two men steadily gained influence within the society. When Gottschalk was imprisoned in July 1848, the membership elected Moll as his replacement, with Schapper as vice-president.[40] During the next two months, major steps were taken to politicize the organization and revamp its structure. The

38. Touched on in Dowe, *Aktion und Organisation,* pp. 171–75; also see M. A. Kotschetkowa, "Die Tätigkeit von Marx und Engels in der Kölner Demokratischen Gesellschaft (April bis Oktober 1848)," *Sowjetwissenschaft: Gesellschaftswissenschaftliche Beiträge* (1960), no. 11, pp. 1155–57.

39. Gerhard Becker, *Karl Marx und Friedrich Engels in Köln, 1848–1849: Zur Geschichte des Kölner Arbeitervereins* (Berlin: Rütten und Loening, 1963), pp. 26–38; Dowe, *Aktion und Organisation,* pp. 145–55; Schraepler, *Handwerkerbünde,* pp. 250–51, 272–73.

40. *Bund Dokumente,* 1:820–21; Becker, *Kölner Arbeiterverein,* p. 90.

old craft divisions had already been discarded, and the group henceforth rested on six branch societies (*Filialvereine*), geographically set in the working-class neighborhoods of the city. Each branch elected its own officers, who were then also called together as a committee of twenty-five to oversee the affairs of the whole society. The president lost his special power to appoint secretaries and edit the newspaper. Citywide general membership meetings—hitherto a rarity—were now held once a month to make important decisions and to hear lectures on political topics. A system of regular dues was also instituted. Thus the victory of Marx's supporters in the Workers' Society did not produce dictatorship but rather increased democracy and membership participation, combined with greater efforts at political education.[41]

The society again became leaderless as a consequence of the September crisis, when Moll was obliged to flee the country and Schapper was temporarily jailed. The guiding committee then invited Marx to become president, and their choice was confirmed by the general membership meeting of October 26, which also named Röser as vice-president pending Schapper's release. With mock deference to his rival, Marx agreed to accept the position only "provisionally until the release of Dr. Gottschalk," pointing to the excessive burdens of his editorial post.[42] The *Neue Rheinische Zeitung* defended Gottschalk during his trial, but Marx did not resign when the old president was set free in late December. Gottschalk made some efforts—perhaps shady ones— to recover his former position, but when he sensed that Marx now enjoyed majority support within the organization, he suddenly panicked and left the country.[43] If Marx was unwilling to turn the society back over to his rival, still he must have been serious about the primacy of his editorial obligations. After attending the committee meeting of October 16 to accept the presidential invitation, and the general membership meeting ten days later to be confirmed, he managed to attend only two further meetings during his four months in office, otherwise leaving the affairs of the society in the hands of its vice-president.[44] Such behavior provides scant evidence of dictatorial ambitions.

41.   *Bund Dokumente*, 1:840, 842; Dowe, *Aktion und Organisation*, pp. 177–80.
42.   *Bund Dokumente*, 1:854–58; Becker, *Kölner Arbeiterverein*, pp. 145–46.
43.   See *Werke*, 6:585; Dowe, *Aktion und Organisation*, p. 213; Schraepler *Handwerkerbünde*, p. 325.
44.   Meetings attended by Marx noted in *Bund Dokumente*, 1:865, 896; those chaired by Röser or Schapper on pp. 856, 865, 870, 872, 896, 904, 905.

Marx's term as president did witness increased emphasis on political education, including an extended point-by-point membership discussion of the Seventeen Demands. He encouraged society efforts to agitate among the rural population and establish new branches in the countryside around Cologne.⁴⁵ But internal factional strife came to a head in a controversy with Gottschalk's remaining followers over control of the society's newspaper. After Gottschalk's arrest, the editorship of the newspaper passed from hand to hand until one of his oldest lieutenants, Wilhelm Prinz, assumed the position in October. Prinz remained loyal to his old chief and assisted in the latter's increasingly bitter verbal assault, from his self-imposed exile, on Marx's leadership and policies. In January he went so far as to attack in an editorial the two candidates officially endorsed by the Workers' Society for the Prussian Assembly elections. Marx and the society leadership reacted by creating a three-man editorial committee to read and approve all newspaper copy before it was published, to guarantee "that this organ really represents the interests of the society."⁴⁶ When Prinz defied this editorial committee and published a second attack on the two candidates, the leadership took the final step. They did not attempt to oust Prinz or seize the newspaper; they simply declared that it no longer spoke for the society and proceeded to create a separate organ of their own. Although not formally expelled, Prinz now withdrew from the organization, along with some of Gottschalk's other followers, and began to construct a new splinter group. The schism grew out of the central political issue that had always divided Marx from Gottschalk—participation in elections in a united front with the democrats—and does not appear to have involved any abuse of official power by Marx and his followers. On the contrary, Prinz would appear to have misused his position as editor of the society's official newspaper.⁴⁷

The culmination of Marx's presidency came with the adoption of a new organizational statute at a general membership meeting in February 1849. Marx did not himself serve on the commission that drafted the new rules, but he evidently influenced those who did and approved

45. See ibid., pp. 855, 870, 872–73; Becker, *Kölner Arbeiterverein,* pp. 127–33, 168–69; Dowe, *Aktion und Organisation,* pp. 199–205.

46. "Protokoll der Komiteesitzung des Kölner Arbeitervereins, 15. Januar 1849," *Bund Dokumente,* 1:896.

47. Ibid., pp. 902–04; for details of this conflict, see Becker, *Kölner Arbeiterverein,* pp. 178–95; Oscar J. Hammen, *The Red '48ers: Karl Marx and Friedrich Engels* (New York: Scribners, 1969), pp. 319, 370–74.

the fruit of their deliberations.[48] Moreover, the statute acquired a much wider significance because of the preparations then in motion to link up workers' societies all across the country. Not only was it published in the local society's own newspaper, but as far away as Berlin in Stephan Born's *Verbrüderung*, with the recommendation that other societies look upon the statute as a model. Some four thousand copies of the document were printed separately and distributed far beyond Cologne.[49] Marx, like Born, obviously hoped the statute would serve as a model for an open and legal workers' political organization.

The new statute began from the same structural building blocks that had sustained the old organization. The society was composed of nine branch clubs (*Filialklubs*), based on geographical sections of the city and composed of several hundred members each (Art. 2). Each branch met weekly and elected its own officers; the branches all met together on Mondays in a general membership meeting (Arts. 3–4). The business of the society was administered by a committee composed of the nine branch presidents, together with the newspaper editor and five additional persons elected directly by the membership at large (Arts. 7–8). From among its own number this committee then elected a president, vice-president, secretary, and treasurer (Art. 9). All officers were chosen for a term of merely three months and could be recalled at any time by their electors (Art. 10). New members were accepted by acclamation at branch meetings unless there was some objection, in which case the committee decided after hearing all sides (Arts. 5–6). Upon a branch's written request, the committee could join with the branch secretaries to constitute a court of arbitration to judge complaints raised by one member against another (Arts. 17–18). There was no provision for expulsion at all, much less for more serious punishments. There were no sworn oaths or ceremonial rituals as in the older conspiratorial tradition. Neither were there any expectations of full-time revolutionary activity, technical competence, or quasi-military discipline, as in the later Leninist tradition.[50]

Far from entrenching his position with special prerogatives, Marx took the occasion to resign as president of the Workers' Society, so as to devote his full energies to the *Neue Rheinische Zeitung*. If he had desired dictatorial control or an influential position in the anticipated national workers' party, surely he would have clung to his office

48. *Bund Dokumente*, 1:906, 913–14, 1147.
49. Becker, *Kölner Arbeiterverein*, p. 254.
50. Statute reproduced in *Bund Dokumente*, 1:1148–49.

as a power base and used it as a springboard to national leadership. But he really did conceive his own role to be that of editor, of philosophical critic, and no amount of historical twisting can turn him into a would-be red Napoleon.

So much ink has been lavished on the Communist League that it is worth reemphasizing that Marx abandoned that organization entirely when legal conditions permitted and helped to develop this open mass organization instead. In this sense, the restructured Cologne Workers' Society rather than the league should count as the real culmination of Marx's organizational work in the revolution of 1848, the model proposed for nationwide imitation under conditions of legality, the kind of party that would have come to power in Germany if things had gone as Marx expected. The Cologne model encompassed the bulk of the local working class in a loosely disciplined mass organization, run by the workers themselves without any necessary help from outside intellectuals or vanguards. Here was the proletariat *selbst als Partei*. The model provided for a maximum of membership participation (the ordinary rank-and-filer would attend two meetings a week), and a maximum of control over all leaders (very short terms and instant recallability). Here was Athenian democracy in miniature, the new society developing within the womb of the old.

Retrospect on the "Party"

The Cologne Workers' Society soon fell victim to the counterrevolution, forcing Marx and Engels organizationally back into the secret Communist League. After it likewise fell victim to the counterrevolution in 1852, the two men retreated from that kind of political activity and never again belonged to a secret society. In fact, the *only* organization in which they subsequently played active roles was the International Working Men's Association, an unusually heterogeneous federation of national proletarian organizations that no one could mistake for either a subterranean conspiracy or a closely knit vanguard party. To deal with the International lies beyond the scope of the present volume, but in the decade following the revolution of 1848, Marx and Engels did make occasional retrospective comments about the league and about their conception of the "Party." These statements add corroborative weight to the interpretations advanced here and may serve as a coda to the themes of this chapter.

Since most of the league members in London sided with Willich and Schapper in the September 1850 schism, Marx and Engels were left relatively isolated in the English capital. Feelings of isolation were doubtless increased when Engels was obliged to move to Manchester in November, to work once more in his father's firm. Marx buried himself increasingly in the British Museum, and the two men seemed to lose all interest in their own faction of the league, at least until the wave of arrests in the spring of 1851 temporarily revived their concern. It was in February of that year that Marx and Engels exchanged a pair of letters releasing their pent-up hostilities and revealing some embarrassingly un-Leninist attitudes on the subject of the "Party." Marx began the exchange, in a letter quoted earlier in part:

I am greatly pleased by the public, authentic isolation in which we two, you and I, now find ourselves. It corresponds completely with our position and our principles. The system of mutual concessions, the halfway positions tolerated for decency's sake, and the duty before the public to bear one's share of ridicule with all those jackasses in the party—all that is over now.[51]

These sentiments obviously struck a deep chord in Engels, for he responded immediately, emotionally, and at considerable length:

At last we have once again—for the first time in a long while—an opportunity to show that we do not need any popularity, any support from any party of any country whatever, and that our position is totally independent of such trifles. From now on we are responsible only for ourselves. . . . How do people like us, who flee official posts as from the plague, fit into a "party"? We who spit on popularity, who mistrust ourselves when we begin to get popular, what does a "party" mean to us, i.e., a band of jackasses who swear by us because they think we are the likes of them? In truth, it is no loss if we no longer serve as "the correct and adequate expression" of those narrow-minded dogs with whom the last few years have thrown us together.

A revolution is a pure phenomenon of nature that is governed more by physical laws than by the rules which determine the de-

51. Letter of February 11, 1851, *Werke*, 27:184–85 (translation adapted from Bertram D. Wolfe, *Marxism: One Hundred Years in the Life of a Doctrine* [New York: Dial, 1965], p. 196); see above, chap. 7, n. 83.

velopment of society in ordinary times. Or rather, these rules take on a more physical character in a revolution, the material force of necessity comes more powerfully into the foreground. And, as soon as one appears as the representative of a party, one is drawn into this unremitting natural compulsion. Only by keeping oneself independent, while remaining in *essence* more revolutionary than the others, can one for a time at least maintain one's independence as against the whirlpool, though in the end of course one is drawn in. This position we can and must take in the next such event. Not only no official *government* position, but also as long as possible no *party* position, no committee membership by proxy, no responsibility for jackasses, merciless criticism for everyone, and thus the serenity that all those muttonheads' conspiracies will not carry us along.[52]

Amidst all the invective against the Willich-Schapper faction, one can also perceive Marx and Engels' genuine lack of interest in the sort of power that might come with high party or government positions. Their temperamental preference for the role of independent critics had displayed itself throughout the previous revolutionary period: whatever their changing party commitments, they carefully kept the *Neue Rheinische Zeitung* and the subsequent *Revue* free from any organizational control whatsoever. And so in the future they wanted to be free to dispense "merciless criticism for everyone," presumably even the leaders of the eventual proletarian revolution. What also shines through these letters is Marx and Engels' utter disregard—however highly they prized the organization of the proletariat in *general*—for the indispensability of any *particular* organization. A revolution is a "pure phenomenon of nature," driven on by the "material force of necessity," and not by some indispensable vanguard party.

During the following decade, Marx and Engels' correspondence contained occasional references to "our party," as if they still belonged to some organized group. Inspection of the context in each case reveals one of two special senses of the term "party." In some cases the word is employed informally and narrowly to refer to the small group of renegade intellectuals who clustered around Marx in the 1848 period,

52. Letter of February 13, 1851, *Werke*, 27:190 (translation adapted from Wolfe, *Marxism*, pp. 196–97).

the "Marx party," as Engels labeled it on one occasion.[53] This was the circle drawn together by the Communist Correspondence Committee, which entered the league in the summer of 1847, became the "party of the *Neue Rheinische Zeitung*" during 1848 and 1849, sided with Marx in the Willich-Schapper schism, and—however scattered thereafter—remained tied together by bonds of personal friendship. It was never a formally organized party, of course, at most a faction within the league, more exactly a circle of political friends that perhaps Engels best described on one occasion as "our clique."[54] Only in a flight of unbounded fancy could this circle be identified as the vanguard party of Lenin's conception.

The other sense of the word "party" in the correspondence of the 1850s goes to the opposite extreme and broadly embraces the entire *potential* proletarian movement, even though it was not actually organized in a formal party at the time. This was the sense Marx used in an 1859 letter to Engels, recounting an incident in which some of Willich's old followers evidently challenged Marx's political credentials: "I told them straight out: We had received our appointment as representatives of the proletarian party from nobody *but ourselves.* It was, however, endorsed by the exclusive and universal hatred consecrated to us by all the parties and fractions of the old world."[55]

The most illuminating reference to party in this broader sense, however, came in an 1860 exchange of letters between Marx and one of the earliest members of his circle, the poet Ferdinand Freiligrath. Marx had first written to enlist the poet's help on a particular matter, appealing to him as "an old party friend and an old personal friend."[56] Freiligrath took this as a reference to his active role in the Communist League and replied—apart from the substantive matter at hand—that he was rather relieved to be done with the party. "My nature," he wrote, "and that of every poet, needs freedom! The party is a cage, too, and one sings, even for the party itself, better outside of it than within."[57] Somewhat stung by the poet he had always respected, Marx

53. Letter to Joseph Weydemeyer, April 12, 1853, *Werke*, 28:581; cf. p. 224; 29:573. For discussion of the senses in which Marx and Engels used the word "party," see the authorities cited above, chap. 5, n. 74, especially Johnstone.

54. Letter to Joseph Weydemeyer, April 12, 1853, *Werke*, 28:576.

55. Letter of May 18, 1859, *Selected Correspondence: 1846–1895*, trans. Dona Torr (New York: International, 1942), p. 123; cf. *Werke*, 28:579, 580; 29:432.

56. Letter of February 8, 1860, *Werke*, 30:444.

57. As quoted in Wolfe, *Marxism*, p. 199.

hastened to make his own position clear, saying in essence that by "party," he did not mean *that* party: "First of all I want to observe that, since the 'league' was dissolved on *my motion* in November 1852, I have *never* again belonged—nor do I belong now—to either a *secret* or a *public* association; that therefore the *party* in this entirely ephemeral sense has ceased to exist for me for the past eight years." He went on to relate how on two occasions during those eight years, he had been asked to help in efforts to revive the league. "I replied that I have not been connected with any combination since 1852 and am deeply convinced that my theoretical labors serve the working class more than participation in combinations the time for which has passed." He continued:

And so of the *"party"* in the sense of your letter I have known *nothing* since 1852. If you are a *poet, so I am a critic;* I had my fill with the experiences of 1849–52. The "league," like the *société des saisons* in Paris, like hundreds of other organizations, was only an episode in the history of the party, which everywhere grows up naturally and spontaneously [*naturwüchsig*] from the soil of modern society.

"By party," Marx concluded, "I meant the party in that great historical sense."[58]

Thus a critic needs his independence no less than a poet. Even though dedicated to the party in the "great historical sense," he may also get his "fill" if encaged in a real-life party. Marx obviously still felt no burning personal ambition, here in 1860, to lead a party of his own—vanguard or otherwise—or even to belong to a formally organized group at all. On the contrary, he and Engels abandoned their independence as critics only with the greatest reluctance and for relatively short periods of their lives. Like the exchange of 1851, this rarely cited letter to Freiligrath shows how utterly expendable Marx regarded any *particular* organization. For him the Communist League was but an "episode," one "ephemeral" contribution to the many-sided efforts of the proletariat to organize itself, efforts which require no outside push, because they grow "naturally and spontaneously out of the soil of modern society."

58. Letter of February 29, 1860, *Werke*, 30:489–90, 495 (translation adapted from Wolfe, *Marxism*, p. 200).

❧[9]❧

"Dictatorship of the Proletariat"
—*The Career of a Slogan*

WE HAVE NOW DEALT with three of the four "complications"—the vanguard party, the permanent revolution, the call for red terror—that have given rise to the view that Marx and Engels were totalitarian democrats at least in the earlier part of their lives. And we have also gained a vantage point from which to examine the fourth and perhaps most important topic, the concept that lies at the very heart of the controversy about their political philosophy—the dictatorship of the proletariat. No term in the Marxist vocabulary has become so famous, so provocative, so rich in mutually incompatible interpretations. The diversity of interpretations no doubt stems in part from the fact that Marx and Engels used the term so infrequently and were so miserly in descriptive detail. In the later classic debate on the subject, Lenin was able to regard the concept as "the very essence of Marx's teaching," while Karl Kautsky could dismiss it as a "little expression" (*Wörtchen*) that Marx had dropped once in a letter.[1] Vulgar anti-Marxists have always imagined that Marx had in mind his own personal dictatorship.[2] Since the establishment of the Soviet Union, however, most people have supposed the characteristics of that regime to reflect Marx's concept most faithfully, and both sides in the Cold War have had a vested interest in maintaining that identification, whether accurate or not.

---

1. V. I. Lenin, *The Proletarian Revolution and the Renegade Kautsky* (New York: International, 1934), p. 16; Karl Kautsky, *The Dictatorship of the Proletariat*, trans. H. J. Stenning (1919; reprint ed., Ann Arbor: Michigan, 1964), p. 140.

2. Beginning perhaps with Eduard von Müller-Tellering, *Vorgeschmack in die künftige Diktatur von Marx und Engels* (Cologne, 1850), and reaching down to the latest sensationalist biography, Robert Payne, *Marx* (New York: Simon and Schuster, 1968), p. 12.

If Marx and Engels really stood for a democratically organized party and a democratic majority revolution, as the last chapters have argued, why did they want to follow it all up by dictatorship? What sort of dictatorship did they have in mind? Are their references to the postrevolutionary state really so vague as to allow any interpretation from Eduard Bernstein to Joseph Stalin? Toward the resolution of these questions, the largest step yet taken is to be found in the groundbreaking monograph of Hal Draper.[3] Putting all previous authorities to shame, Draper undertook the obvious task of culling from the whole body of Marx and Engels' writings all uses of the terms "dictatorship of the proletariat," "proletarian dictatorship," or any other combination of the two component ideas. In the forty-odd volumes of material, he found that the term was used in only eleven places—a moral victory, at least, for Kautsky's viewpoint. But more significantly, by arranging the eleven loci in chronological order, he perceived a startling correlation, never noticed before, that unravels most of the mystery surrounding the real meaning of the expression. In seeking to answer the questions posed above, the following chapter builds from the foundation of Draper's brilliant core insight. To examine all eleven loci as a fund of evidence, it will be necessary in this chapter to go beyond 1850 and look at specific incidents in Marx and Engels' later lives.

The Concept of Dictatorship

The word "dictatorship" has undergone a radical shift in meaning since World War I, and to understand Marx's usage of it, one must divest the term of its present-day identification with totalitarianism

3. "Marx and the Dictatorship of the Proletariat," *Etudes de Marxologie*, ed. Maximilien Rubel (Paris: Institut de Science Economique Appliquée, 1962), 6:5–73; abridged version in *New Politics* 1, no. 4 (Summer 1962):91–104. Draper's essay obliges one to acknowledge the mediocrity of all the other literature on the subject: the polemics of Lenin and Kautsky cited in note 1 were intensely partisan and hurriedly written, of course; also see Ernst Drahn, *Marx und Engels über die Diktatur des Proletariats* (Berlin: Die Aktion, 1920); Wilhelm Mautner, "Zur Geschichte des Begriffs 'Diktatur des Proletariats,' " *Archiv für die Geschichte des Sozialismus und der Arbeiterbewegung* 12 (1926):280–83; Sherman Chang, *The Marxian Theory of the State* (Philadelphia: Spencer, 1931); Bertram D. Wolfe, *Marxism: One Hundred Years in the Life of a Doctrine* (New York: Dial, 1965), chaps. 10–11; and Werner Hofmann, "Die Auffassung von der sozialistischen Revolution und der Diktatur des Proletariats bei Marx und Engels und in der kommunistischen Bewegung der Gegenwart," in *Marxismus in unserer Zeit: Beiträge zum zeitgenössischen Marxismus* (Frankfurt a/M: Marxistische Blätter, 1968), pp. 137–53.

and return to the original Roman institution of *dictatura*.[4] In republican Rome, dictatorship was a largely benign form of temporary crisis government, most purely exemplified in the familiar story of Cincinnatus, who, when a Roman army had been trapped by the Aequians, left off plowing to accept his appointment as dictator. He raised an army, defeated the foe, gave up his office, and returned to his plow—all in sixteen days. Perhaps because the Romans had such a deep suspicion of executive authority and had divided and restricted it in so many ways, they found it necessary to revert temporarily to one-man rule in periods of foreign invasion or grave civil strife.

The Roman institution of dictatorship possessed three crucial features not found in the present-day concept. First, it was provided for in the republican constitution itself and expressly designed to preserve that constitution in moments of grave crisis. Only the Senate could decide when such a moment had arrived; then the consuls chose a dictator from outside the ranks of public officialdom. Second, it was a temporary charge, lasting only until the crisis had been met, or in any case no longer than six months. For three hundred years, this iron rule was never violated, although the *dictatura* was invoked on approximately ninety occasions. The normal officials of government remained at their posts and resumed their authority when the dictator stepped down. Only with the decay of republican institutions could Sulla and then Julius Caesar have themselves appointed "dictator for life"; they created dictatorship in the modern sense by destroying it in the traditional republican sense. Third, the classic dictator held extended but not unlimited powers, powers to cope with an emergency but not to be left entirely unchecked. He could suspend laws and issue temporary decrees, but he could neither enact nor repeal permanent legislation. His judicial authority was confined to criminal cases affecting the safety of the state. Within the executive realm, his powers were understandably widest: he had unrestricted military authority to command the armies and to maintain order at home, but he could not declare war himself or spend state funds without the express consent of the senate. And since it was his sacred trust to preserve the constitutional order, he could be legally prosecuted if he attempted to abuse his office or extend its tenure beyond the emergency. Far from being an antithesis

---

4. This shift perceived in the interwar years by Henry R. Spencer, "Dictatorship," *Encyclopedia of the Social Sciences* (New York: Macmillan, 1931), 5:132.

to the republican rule of law, the Romans conceived dictatorship to be its ultimate defense.[5] It is evident that this classical institution has come down to us in two quite different ways. On the one hand, the idea of emergency, or crisis, government survives today in the form of martial law, or its Continental European equivalent, the state of siege. All democratic constitutions provide for such crisis government in one way or another, and it retains most of the Roman attributes: designed to shield the state in times of invasion or civil unrest, its essential function is *preservative;* it involves only a *temporary* suspension of normal governmental procedures and civil liberties; and it provides for *extended* but by no means unlimited executive power. Modern democracies do not choose a private citizen to wield this emergency power, however, but normally bestow it upon the incumbent chief of state and/or his regular military commanders.[6] While we no longer use the Roman name for such crisis government, it follows the spirit of the classical institution most closely. Dictatorship to protect an established, legally constituted government will be called *preservative dictatorship* in the following discussion.

From the Latin word "dictatura," on the other hand, and doubtless from the degeneration of the institution under Sulla and Caesar, we have derived our general term for a government by one person possessed of extraordinary powers. Unlike the model of Cincinnatus, however, modern dictators characteristically destroy preexisting governmental forms along with traditional rights and liberties; they exercise arbitrary and unchecked power; and most importantly, they do so on a continuing or permanent basis. To the extent that such dictatorships also exhibit the kinds of characteristics enumerated by Carl J. Friedrich and summarized in chapter 1, they are often called "totalitarian."[7] While Hitler and Stalin are most frequently cited as models, the concept of totalitarian dictatorship can be extended to include equivalent

5. Clinton Rossiter, *Constitutional Dictatorship: Crisis Government in Modern Democracies* (New York: Harcourt, Brace, 1963), pp. 15–25; Draper, "Dictatorship," p. 7.

6. Rossiter, *Constitutional Dictatorship,* pp. 3–14 and passim; Karl Dietrich Bracher, "Crisis Government," *International Encyclopedia of the Social Sciences* (New York: Macmillan, 1968), 3:514–18.

7. See above, chap. 1, n. 2; see recent rethinking by Carl J. Friedrich, Michael Curtis, and Benjamin R. Barber, in their *Totalitarianism in Perspective: Three Views* (New York: Praeger, 1969).

rule by a small committee or a single elite party. Thus the contemporary notion of dictatorship, despite the name, is far removed from its Roman origins and, for purposes of distinction here, will be called *continuing dictatorship*.

It is this second notion that is most commonly read back into the ideas of Marx and Engels. Actually, as we will see, they anticipated neither a preservative nor a continuing dictatorship, but something that belongs to a distinct third category. In order to appreciate this tripartite distinction, we must return to the historical evolution of the word. Between the collapse of the Roman world and the time of the French Revolution, the term seemed to fall into disuse and, when employed at all, referred only to the historical institution. Thus the strong men of Renaissance Italy were called *"podesta,"* even though their functions paralleled the Roman model in some respects. Machiavelli did not counsel his prince to take the name dictator, but he obviously remembered the Roman institution when he wrote in the *Discourses* "that republics which, when in imminent danger, have recourse neither to a dictatorship, nor to some form of authority analogous to it, will always be ruined when grave misfortune befalls them."[8] In the seventeenth century, Oliver Cromwell established a "protectorate," not a dictatorship. As late as the mid-eighteenth century, Rousseau would still develop his chapter on dictatorship by reviewing the features of the Roman practice, emphasizing its limits and its preservative function, "that the state should not perish."[9] Not until the French Revolution did the Latin word become infused with new meaning.

Because the leaders of that revolution took the Roman Republic as their model, it was perhaps inevitable that the expression "dictatorship" would regain some currency. Even though none of the revolutionary constitutions institutionalized the practice, Girondin and Jacobin leaders revived the word when they began to accuse each other of aspiring to a dictatorship. Robespierre and the Committee of Public Safety did not wield powers expressly called dictatorial, and Robespierre himself, with a level of self-deception accorded only the sincerest fanatics, repeatedly denounced dictatorship out of pure democratic zeal, even as he was being sent off to the guillotine.[10] But two prominent Jacobins did expressly call for dictatorship as a positive good: Saint-Just, who

8.   (Leslie J. Walker translation), bk. 1, chap. 34.
9.   *The Social Contract* (Henry J. Tozer translation), bk. 4, chap. 6.
10.   As reported by Draper, "Dictatorship," pp. 10–11.

said "all revolutions require a dictator to save the state by force"; and Marat, who urged the need of a dictator "to save liberty by violence."[11] This advocacy of dictatorship, not to preserve long-established institutions, but to "save"—or more exactly, to consolidate—a new revolutionary government and the achievements of the revolution, marks a clear, new direction in meaning for the old Roman term.

The new direction found its full expression, of course, in the ideas of the ultra-Jacobin, Gracchus Babeuf, whose call for a "dictatorship of the insurrection" we reviewed in chapter 1. Babeuf, it will be remembered, drew a grim lesson from the Ninth Thermidor, that the masses were still too backward to liberate and govern themselves. It would therefore be necessary for the enlightened few to act in their name, establishing a temporary dictatorship by committee with a threefold mission: to eradicate old institutions and the leaders associated with them, to lay down the foundations—including common ownership—of the new egalitarian order, and to control the education of the masses in the new ways of virtue.[12] This conception of dictatorship shares with the Roman archetype the elements of extraordinary power allotted to one man—or in this case, a small committee—to deal with a temporary emergency. Its overriding purpose is not to preserve, however, but rather to constitute, and hence it may be labeled *constituent dictatorship*. Further, since the tasks of Babeuf's provisional regime were to be entrusted to an enlightened few and would crucially involve the tutelage of the masses, our labeling may be refined into a specific subspecies—*constituent-educational dictatorship*.

No great imagination is required nowadays to see the degenerative potential of such a dictatorship. It cannot possibly have the built-in safeguards of the Roman practice, since there would be no "normal" government to resume authority and check abuses. No matter how sincere the democratic intentions of its leaders, the destructive tasks of the dictatorship would all too likely grow into a blind repression of any and all independent institutions; its program of common ownership, into a system insuring the leaders' control over the economy; and its educational endeavors, into organized brainwashing. With such a degeneration, any temporal limit would surely recede indefinitely into the future, and constituent dictatorship would be transformed into

11. As quoted in J. L. Talmon, *The Origins of Totalitarian Democracy* (New York: Praeger, 1960), pp. 145, 124.
12. See above, pp. 8–9.

continuing dictatorship. This is, of course, exactly the danger of genuinely totalitarian-democratic ideas. In fairness to Babeuf and his conspirators, it might be allowed that the degenerative potential had not been so frequently demonstrated in their time as it has in our own.

In any event, by Marx and Engels' time, the word "dictatorship" might refer to the Classical Roman institution of preservative crisis government or to the more recent Babouvist conception of constituent dictatorship espoused also by Blanqui. But the word had not yet been used to describe *permanent* one-man rule, or continuing dictatorship in the modern sense.

Marx and Engels' Understanding of Dictatorship

It has already been stressed in previous chapters that Marx and Engels did not apply the word "dictatorship" to the rule of the proletariat until March 1850. Prior to that time, they never discussed, or even mentioned in any surviving writing, the Babouvist-Blanquist conception of educational dictatorship, although they must have been familiar with it. Their own vision of communist revolution did not rest on the fundamental postulate of mass immaturity, but rather presupposed the masses' prior self-education. Consequently, they did not require any period of educational rule by an enlightened minority, or any postponement of democratic elections. We have reviewed above their consistent advocacy of immediate democracy, from the beginning of their political careers down to 1850, as well as their conviction that "a necessary consequence of democracy in all civilized countries is the political rule [*Herrschaft*] of the proletariat." Quite plausibly then, in the writings of this early period, they employed the term "*Herrschaft*" rather than "*Diktatur*" to refer to the dominion of the proletariat after the revolution.[13]

Ironically, the word "dictatorship" was pushed into Marx and Engels' active vocabulary, not by Blanqui, but by the general who became Blanqui's arch antagonist in 1848—Louis-Eugène Cavaignac. As the June violence in Paris became threatening, the French National Assembly declared a state of siege and invested Cavaignac formally with a "commissioned dictatorship" to restore law and order in the capital city. This was apparently the first actual revival of the practice, *by name*, since Roman times. Suddenly the term "dictatorship," which

13.   See above, chap. 5, nn. 28 and 12.

Marx and Engels had used on only three occasions in *all* their previous writings,[14] began to punctuate their columns in the *Neue Rheinische Zeitung.* During the following months, it appeared twenty-one times, of which nine referred specifically to the "military dictatorship" of Cavaignac, and six referred to other, parallel "counterrevolutionary" leaders, or to their actions.[15] Thus Cavaignac's literal dictatorship sparked Marx and Engels' frequent use of the word as an abusive epithet, but it also must have set them thinking about its wider implications.

In the remaining six occurrences, the term "dictatorship" was employed for the first time without a pejorative connotation. These are much more interesting for our purposes. They are all to be found in polemics Marx and Engels carried on concerning the exact legal status and powers of the Prussian Assembly then meeting in Berlin. It will be recalled that the two men constantly prodded the various constituent assemblies that had been convened in Germany, urging them to assert popular sovereignty as against the princes' claims of divine right and to assume the powers of government themselves. Above all, they called upon the Frankfurt National Assembly to set up a central government for all of Germany. But, in the meantime, they were perspicacious enough to understand that real power still resided in Berlin, Vienna, and the lesser state capitals. Thus, as citizens of Prussia, they quite naturally focused most of their attention on the Prussian Assembly which had been called in the wake of the March Revolution to draw up a constitution for that state. Until the new constitution would be in effect, there existed some crucial questions of legal competence and political power: Did prerevolutionary laws still have force? Did sovereignty reside in the more-or-less democratically elected assembly or still with the king? Did the king, or the assembly, have the power to appoint and control cabinet ministers? While articulating their position on these questions, it was Engels who first used the word "dictatorship" to describe government during such an interregnum, during what he called a "revolutionary provisional condition" (*revolutionäres Provisorium*).[16]

14. Three uses appear in *Werke,* 1:571; 3:449 (cf. p. 522); 5:84. I have included every grammatical form of the word—noun, adverb, etc.
15. References to Cavaignac: *Werke,* 5:116, 120, 123, 124, 125, 148, 376; 6:366, 386. Other parallel uses, ibid., 5:157 (three times), 402; 6:59, 497. Also note spoken use of word cited above, chap. 8, n. 37.
16. "Vereinbarungssitzung vom 4. Juli" (July 1848), *Werke,* 5:195. The first

The specific issue concerned the Prussian Interior Minister, Friedrich Kühlwetter, who had asserted that a commission from the assembly had no right to question him about his official actions, since that would constitute an interference with the executive branch of government, a violation of the separation of powers. Engels replied testily that the old governmental arrangements, which placed all power in the hands of the king, did not recognize the principle anyway. And a new constitution had not yet been created:

> The revolutionary *Provisorium* consists precisely in the temporary suspension of the division of powers. Either the legislative authority momentarily seizes executive power for itself, or vice versa. It makes no difference whether this revolutionary dictatorship (and it is a dictatorship no matter how sluggishly it may be exercised) lies in the hands of the crown or the assembly, or both together. Herr Kühlwetter may find several examples of all three possibilities in the history of France since 1789.
>
> The *Provisorium* gives . . . the assembly other attributes far beyond the mere right of investigation. It even gives it the right, if need be, to transform itself into a *court of law* and to make convictions in the absence of laws![17]

In a later article, Engels went on to generalize that "as a consequence of this *Provisorium*, everything that serves to secure the achievements of the March Revolution falls within the competence of the assembly."[18] Thus Engels declared dictatorship to be the necessary consequence of the interregnum situation created by any revolution. With the old legal order overthrown and the new one not yet created, there are no commonly acknowledged rules under which to govern, and yet political decisions must nonetheless be made and acted upon. Each side necessarily behaves "dictatorially," that is, outside any framework of commonly acknowledged rules. Notice that such a "dictatorship" may be exercised by a democratically elected assembly, may be sluggish rather than ruthless, and involves only the unavoidable fact of extra-legality.

---

use of the word "dictatorship" in this sense on July 11 leaves little doubt that it was called to mind by Cavaignac's formal dictatorship then in operation.

17. Ibid.

18. "Die Debatte über den Jacobyschen Antrag" (July 1848), ibid., p. 230.

Marx took up the same theme during the Prussian ministerial crisis in September 1848. As explained earlier, the cabinet had resigned after receiving a brusque instruction from the assembly to curb the regular army's frequent assaults on militiamen.[19] The ministers protested against this legislative incursion into the realm of executive prerogative, this violation of the "constitutional principle" of separation of powers. Marx believed that the showdown between crown and assembly was at hand:

"Constitutional principle!" The very gentlemen who are out to save the constitutional principle at any price should realize first of all that, during a provisional condition, it can only be saved at all by energetic action.

"Constitutional principle!" But the vote of the Berlin Assembly, the clashes between Potsdam and Frankfurt, the disturbances, the reactionary ventures, the provocations of the soldateska—have not these things at last shown that, despite all phrase-mongering, we are still on *revolutionary ground*, and the pretense that we have already reached the stage of a *constituted*, an established constitutional monarchy only leads to collisions, which have already brought the "constitutional principle" to the brink of the abyss?

Every provisional condition of state [*provisorische Staatszustand*] following a revolution requires a dictatorship, and an energetic dictatorship at that. From the beginning we reproached [Prime Minister] Camphausen for not acting dictatorially, for not immediately shattering and eliminating the remnants of old institutions. While thus Herr Camphausen indulged in constitutional fancies, the defeated party strengthened its positions within the bureaucracy and in the army, and occasionally even risked an open fight. The assembly was convened for the purpose of agreeing on the terms of the constitution. It existed as an equal party alongside the crown. Two equal powers in one *Provisorium!* . . . It was this very division of powers in a *Provisorium* that was bound to lead to conflicts. . . .

In any unconstituted state of affairs, what matters is only the *salut public*, the public welfare, and not this or that principle. The ministry could avoid the collision of the assembly and the crown

19. See above, pp. 205–07.

only by recognizing itself the principle of public welfare, even at the risk of coming *itself* into collision with the crown. . . . It never hesitated to employ measures of public welfare (*mesures de salut public*), dictatorial measures, against the democrats. Or what else was the application of old laws to political crimes even when Herr Märker [the Justice Minister] had already acknowledged that these articles of the Prussian Code had to be repealed? What else were the wholesale arrests in all parts of the kingdom?

But the ministry carefully refrained from intervening against the counterrevolution in the name of public welfare.

It was this half-heartedness of the ministry in face of the ever more threatening counterrevolution that compelled the assembly *itself to dictate* measures of public welfare. . . .

The resolution of August 9 flouted the constitutional principle, it is an encroachment made by the legislative power on the executive power, . . . it turns the assembly of conciliation into a *National Convention*.[20]

Here in September, Marx echoed what Engels had said in July, that every "provisional condition of state" requires a "dictatorship," that is, a government standing outside any established legal framework. Since unavoidable extralegality is the only criterion, Marx argued—like Engels before him—that even a democratically elected assembly may, indeed *must*, exercise such a dictatorship. The very terminology of this passage betrays the paradigm Marx had before his eyes. He was, of course, a close student of the Great French Revolution and at one time had planned to write a history of the original National Convention.[21] Now he was imploring the Prussian Assembly to imitate its famous predecessor in certain respects, by asserting its own right to speak for the nation, as against royal claims, and by acting boldly to secure the democratic achievements of the revolution. It should justify its actions, given the temporary absence of any established frame-

20. "The Crisis and the Counter-Revolution," *The Revolution of 1848–49: Articles from the "Neue Rheinische Zeitung,"* trans. S. Ryazanskaya (New York: International, 1972), pp. 124–25 (translation modified—RNH; see original German, *Werke*, 5:401–03).

21. See Jean Bruhat, "La révolution française et la formation de la pensée de Marx," in *La pensée socialiste devant la Révolution française*, ed. Société des Etudes Robespierristes (Paris: Clavreuil, 1966), especially pp. 128, 140–41, 166–67.

work of constitutional law, by appealing directly to the public welfare. Doubtless it would be held responsible by the public. These *mesures de salut public*, unavoidably extralegal but representing the will of the majority through its elected legislators, would be dictatorial and democratic at the same time.[22]

Marx emphasized that this democratic "dictatorship" ought to be an "energetic" one and pointed out its obvious tasks—"shattering and eliminating the remnants of old institutions," especially the bureaucracy and the army. Engels' earlier piece had suggested the same field of action, and with more elaboration:

After a revolution, the first necessity is a renewal [*Erneuerung*] of the entire civil and military bureaucracy, as well as a part of the judiciary, especially the public prosecutors. Otherwise the best measures of the central power will run aground on the refractoriness of subalterns. The weakness of the French Provisional Government and the weakness of the Camphausen Ministry have borne bitter fruit in this regard.

In Prussia especially, where a bureaucratic hierarchy in the military and the administration has been perfectly organized for forty years and has ruled with absolute power; in Prussia, where precisely this bureaucracy was the main enemy defeated on March 19, here a complete renewal of the civil and military officials was infinitely more urgent. But the ministry . . . [did] nothing, and thus allowed its old enemies, the bureaucrats, to retain the real power in their own hands.[23]

Thus Marx and Engels equated dictatorial energy with the large-scale replacement of officials necessary in any meaningful democratic revolution that overthrows an old, established authoritarian regime. Nowhere did they call for the physical liquidation of such officials, for heads falling "like hail."[24] Indeed, the two measures of the Prussian Assembly which they expressly identified as "dictatorial" were not even actions to *dismiss*, but only to *control*, royally appointed officials (that is, cabinet ministers). To be sure, Marx and Engels encouraged the arming of the general population and the development of a broadly

22. Cf. Wolfe, *Marxism*, pp. 203–04.
23. "Vereinbarungssitzung vom 4. Juli," *Werke*, 5:191–92; cf. 6:138, 234.
24. Expression of Babeuf's lieutenant, Rossignol, cited above, chap. 1, n. 19.

based popular militia as the ultimate means by which the masses could intimidate or, if need be, defeat the defenders of the old regime. But as a matter of actual record, Marx only called for the use of those weapons on one specific occasion, defensively, in an effort to ward off the November counterrevolution.[25] Neither do the two men appear to have equated dictatorship with the denial of political rights to the opponents of the revolution. At least they never urged such a denial in any surviving writing, public or private, during the 1848 period. They vigilantly defended free speech, free association, and the right to vote—the principal immediate achievements of the March Revolution—without ever attempting to justify any exceptions.[26] In short, what they chose to call dictatorship in 1848 had the same features we would nowadays associate with a provisionally established democracy. It goes without saying that we would not call such a government "dictatorial" but would use a term like "provisional" or perhaps "prelegitimate."[27]

Thus the general revolutionary "dictatorship" advocated by Marx and Engels in the *Neue Rheinische Zeitung* had almost nothing in common with the present-day conception of permanent one-man rule. It will be remembered that Marx specifically denounced Weitling on this point in August 1848: "The desire to put the system of a single brain into execution by means of dictatorship deserves to be called nonsense."[28] Marx and Engels' idea had more in common with the old Roman practice—a temporary exercise of extraordinary power during an emergency—but lacked the central preservative function of the classical institution. It was to be a *constituent* dictatorship, like that of Babeuf and Blanqui, but a constituent dictatorship of a crucially different subspecies. It would not be *educational.* Marx and Engels' conception did not rest on the postulate of mass immaturity: it did not require rule by a self-appointed committee but assumed the authority of a democratically elected constituent assembly; it did not require massive terror and liquidations, since opposition would be less worrisome to a majority government; and for all these reasons it would not require any vanguard control over the press and educational system. Its "dictatorial" (that is, extralegal) character would cease by definition with

25. See treatment above, pp. 205–10; for advocacy of a popular militia, see especially *Werke,* 5:243–52.
26. See, e.g., *Werke,* 5:18, 90–93, 165–68, 175–81, 198–201, 216–21, 229.
27. Latter term suggested by Wolfe, *Marxism,* p. 203.
28. See above, chap. 6, n. 58.

the creation of new permanent institutions of government, of a new legality. This was the conception of dictatorship, it will be argued, that Marx and Engels applied two years later, and thereafter, to the proletarian revolution per se.

The Marriage of Dictatorship and Proletarian Rule

The special definition of dictatorship elaborated in the *Neue Rheinische Zeitung* was not expressly applied at the time to the future rule of the workers. Only in March 1850 did the phrase "dictatorship of the proletariat" for the first time replace the habitual "rule of the proletariat." Even assuming the special meaning of "dictatorship" just described, the shift in terminology obviously requires some explanation, and it is Draper's contribution to have done this in a manner that clears away most of the confusion surrounding the famous slogan. In briefest outline, his thesis is that Marx and Engels agreed to accept the word "dictatorship" favored by the Blanquists in a united-front program drawn up with them in 1850, but that the two men themselves still understood the word to mean the sort of "prelegitimate" democratic government we have just encountered and not the kind of educational dictatorship by a small committee that the Blanquists wanted.

In the entire body of Marx and Engels' writing, encompassing perhaps six or seven million words, the term "dictatorship" (in any grammatical form) is linked to the working class a total of sixteen times, in eleven separate writings.[29] There are in addition two reports of Marx and Engels' having uttered the slogan in spoken remarks. These eighteen uses are neatly clustered, as Draper revealed and as we ourselves will see, in three distinct chronological periods—1850–1852, 1871–1875, and 1890–1893—with roughly a score of years separating each period. During the first two periods, and at no other time, Marx and Engels worked in united fronts with the Blanquists. This double coincidence in time can scarcely be accidental, and we will see how the final uses of the nineties fall into line too, as "a sort of echo of 1875."[30]

Let us begin with the second of the eleven writings, which is actually

29. Draper, "Dictatorship," pp. 29–30. Draper actually counts fourteen uses in the eleven writings: when the term is used more than once in the same sentence or paragraph, he does not count the repeats, as I do. Also we disagree about one particular use, as explained in note 39 below.
30. Ibid., p. 30.

the first occasion on which Marx and Engels associated *their own names* with the call for proletarian dictatorship, and which is simultaneously the clearest expression of the united-front compromise. The reasons that impelled Marx and Engels into this short-lived collaboration have been discussed earlier. The perceived imminence of renewed upheaval, the centrality of France to the revolutionary schema, the impossibility of legal organization, and the established leadership of Blanquist elements among the French secret societies, all convinced the two men to participate in the Universal Society of Revolutionary Communists, organized in mid-April 1850. Its statutes, as reviewed earlier, included a statement of purpose that was evidently drafted by Willich but signed by all six founding members. It read:

[Locus 2]

The aim of the association is the downfall of all the privileged classes, to subject these classes to the dictatorship of the proletarians [*dictature des prolétaires*] by maintaining the revolution in permanence until the achievement of communism, which is to be the last form of the constitution of the human family.[31]

In our earlier discussion of Marxist strategy, we saw how the slogan "revolution in permanence" was employed here and in the March *Circular* as a compromise formulation, a deliberate ambiguity that could be interpreted in one way by the advocates of minority revolution, and in a quite different way by Marx and Engels.[32] In exactly the same fashion, the phrase "dictatorship of the proletarians" must be understood as a compromise and a deliberate ambiguity. The Blanquists had called often enough for dictatorship, but of course they meant dictatorship by a small committee, and—contrary to widespread impressions—they had never before used the expression "dictatorship of the proletariat."[33] Marx and Engels had long urged the "*rule* of the proletariat," but never before had they called it dictatorship. The obvious compromise was to put the two ideas together.

31. See above, chap. 7, n. 89.
32. See above, pp. 245–47.
33. Maurice Dommanget, *Les idées politiques et sociales d'Auguste Blanqui* (Paris: Rivière, 1957), pp. 171, 378; Alan Spitzer, *The Revolutionary Theories of Louis Auguste Blanqui* (New York: Columbia, 1957), p. 176; Draper, "Dictatorship," pp. 15–19.

Doubtless this terminological marriage was made easier for Marx and Engels by the general concept of dictatorship they had elaborated in the *Neue Rheinische Zeitung*. If every government during a revolutionary *Provisorium* is dictatorial by virtue of its unavoidable extralegality, then the anticipated proletarian government must be also. If the bourgeois Prussian Assembly exercised a dictatorship in 1848, then a parallel assembly elected by universal suffrage after a proletarian revolution would also be a dictatorship, . . . a dictatorship of the proletariat.

That Marx and Engels were quite conscious of the difference between the Blanquist conception of dictatorship and their own is most precisely disclosed in an 1874 article by Engels that will be examined below as Locus 7, but which may be previewed here:

From Blanqui's conception that every revolution is a surprise attack by a small revolutionary minority, there follows of itself the necessity for a dictatorship after the success of the venture. This would be, to be sure, a dictatorship not of the entire revolutionary class, the proletariat, but of the small number who have made the surprise attack, and who are themselves previously organized under the dictatorship of one or several individuals.[34]

One could not ask for a more exact distinction. In the 1850 compromise, Marx and Engels conceded use of the term "dictatorship," which cost them little because of their own special definition, while the Blanquists conceded, at least for the record, that the dictatorship would be exercised by the "proletarians," that is, the "entire revolutionary class," and not by "one or several individuals." Among Marx and Engels' own writings of 1850, we have reviewed already the evidence that they did not embrace a Blanquist conception of minority revolution and minority dictatorship. Most weighty was the trenchant critique of conspiratorial revolutionaries that Marx published in April, at the very time the Universal Society was being founded.[35]

If Locus 2 expresses the united-front terminological compromise of April 1850, then Locus 1, published three or four weeks earlier, represents a preliminary effort by Marx to suggest the phrase to the French Blanquists, indeed, to put the words right into their mouths. In this

34. "Programm der blanquistischen Kommuneflüchtlinge," *Werke*, 18:529.
35. See above, pp. 228–38, 250–53; see also Draper, "Dictatorship," p. 37.

work, *Class Struggles in France,* Marx built up to the idea with a veritable deluge of "dictatorships." Hitherto, he had been quite sparing in the use of the word, but it appears seventeen times in the course of *Class Struggles* alone. And it appears in a variety of political settings: proceeding from right to left, there are four references to Cavaignac's dictatorship, nine references to bourgeois dictatorship under the state of siege (which declared the workers *"hors la loi"*), and two references to the awaited popular dictatorship of workers, peasants, and petty bourgeois.[36]

The two last-named uses deserve special inspection. While explaining the growth of popular opposition to the bourgeois "dictatorship" in 1849, Marx spoke of a January reconciliation between the socialists and the *Montagne,* with the result that "the social and the democratic party, the party of the workers and that of the petty bourgeois, united to form the *social-democratic party,* that is, the *Red* party."[37] The third element in the prospective coalition, the peasants, would soon join, for "only the fall of capital can raise the peasant; only an anti-capitalist, a proletarian government can break his economic misery, his social degradation. The *constitutional republic* is the dictatorship of his united exploiters; the *social-democratic,* the *Red* republic, is the dictatorship of his allies."[38] Here the term is obviously employed to refer not to the ultimate, purely proletarian government, but to the more imminent government of the allied majority classes. The second passage—actually prior—seems to refer to the same regime: "the proletariat, forced by the terrible material defeat of June to raise itself up again through intellectual victories and not yet enabled through the development of the remaining classes to seize the revolutionary dictatorship, had to throw itself into the arms of the doctrinaires of its emancipation, the founders of socialist sects" (such as Louis Blanc).[39] Here the proletariat could not "seize the revolutionary dictatorship" without the support of the "remaining classes," the peasants and petty bourgeois.

36. References to Cavaignac, *Selected Works,* 1:151, 155 (twice), 156; to bourgeois dictatorship, 149, 155, 183, 198, 200 (twice), 201, 206, 207; "hors la loi," p. 157.
37. Ibid., p. 175; cf. terminological distinctions on p. 166.
38. Ibid., p. 198.
39. Ibid., p. 176. Draper counts this use, wrongly I think, as a reference to the ultimate dictatorship of the proletariat, not to that of the allied classes ("Dictatorship," pp. 23, 32–33).

There is a disturbing implication in the second passage that, whatever support might come from these latter classes, the proletariat alone would seize and exercise the revolutionary dictatorship. And yet there is no positive evidence that Marx meant anything more than that the proletariat, as the most resolute and politically experienced element in the coalition, would naturally attract the support of the other classes. Among the "common characteristics" he ascribed to the "party of the Red republic" were "adherence to democratic-republican institutions" and the demands for "freedom of the press" and the "right of association." In the passage concerning the peasants just cited in the last paragraph, Marx went on to add: "And the scale rises or falls, according to the votes that the peasant casts into the ballot box. He himself has to decide his fate."[40] One may recall Marx's thought expressed in the *Neue Rheinische Zeitung* that "universal suffrage is precisely the compass needle which, perhaps after various deviations, finally points to the class that is called to rule."[41]

We may now proceed to the last two uses of the word "dictatorship" to be found in *Class Struggles*—the ones that refer unambiguously to the rule of the proletariat per se. The first occurs in the section on the June Days, which according to Marx taught the proletariat the futility of its earlier optimistic reformism:

[Locus 1a]
Only its defeat convinced it of the truth that the slightest improvement in its position remains a *utopia within* the bourgeois republic, a utopia that becomes a crime as soon as it wants to become a reality. In place of its demands, exuberant in form, but petty and even bourgeois still in content, the concession of which it wanted to wring from the February republic, there appeared the bold slogan of revolutionary struggle: *Overthrow of the bourgeoisie! Dictatorship of the working class!* [Diktatur der Arbeiterklasse!][42]

There is no record whatsoever that such a bold slogan "appeared" anywhere in Paris following the June defeat. A far greater likelihood

---

40. *Selected Works*, 1:198; cf. passage cited above, chap. 7, n. 53. Later in this chapter we will review some important new evidence on how Marx thought peasant support might be achieved.
41. See above, chap. 7, n. 14.
42. *Selected Works*, 1:149.

is that Marx, with an eye toward the Blanquist partiality for the word "dictatorship," was "launching the slogan himself," as Draper puts it, in the hope of getting the Blanquists to think in terms of class rule rather than rule by a clique.[43]

The second use fortifies this impression, as Marx described the leftward movement of the workers away from the "doctrinaire Socialism" of Louis Blanc:

[Locus 1b]

The *proletariat* rallies more and more round *revolutionary Socialism*, round *Communism*, for which the bourgeoisie has itself invented the name of *Blanqui*. This Socialism is the *declaration of the permanence of the revolution*, the *class dictatorship* of the proletariat [Klassendiktatur *des Proletariats*] as the necessary transit point to the *abolition of class distinctions generally*, to the abolition of all the relations of production on which they rest, to the abolition of all the social relations that correspond to these relations of production, to the revolutionizing of all the ideas that result from these social relations.[44]

Again, there is no record that Blanqui or his followers ever used the slogan "dictatorship of the proletariat," nor does Marx *quite* make such a claim. Neither had they used the slogan of permanent revolution. Neither is there anything remotely Blanquist about "ideas" resulting from "social relations" that correspond to "relations of production"— all of which is pure unadulterated Marx, of course. Clearly, what Marx was doing was putting words into the mouths of the Blanquists, invigorating his own bland "rule of the proletariat" with the fearsome-sounding "dictatorship," but italicizing and this time doubly emphasizing its class nature, with "*Klassendiktatur* of the proletariat." The proposition must have been clear: if only the Blanquists would accept the notion of class dictatorship instead of clique dictatorship, the road to a united front would be open. The success of this preliminary effort by Marx can be witnessed in the Universal Society's statement of purpose, cited above as Locus 2.

The two remaining loci of the 1850–1852 period are nothing more than echoes of Locus 1. One of the few left-wing newspapers in Ger-

43.   See Draper, "Dictatorship," p. 32.
44.   *Selected Works*, 1:203.

many to survive the counterrevolution for a time was the *Neue Deutsche Zeitung*, published in Frankfurt by Otto Lüning with the aid of his brother-in-law, Joseph Weydemeyer. Weydemeyer, of course, was a key member of Marx's inner circle, and it was probably his influence that induced the True Socialist Lüning to publish, in June 1850, a long summary and review of *Class Struggles in France* that helped bring Marx's views before the German public. In the course of these articles, Lüning allowed that "the aim and final end of all revolutionary movements of the present day is the *revolutionary rule, the dictatorship of the working class.*" He found no fault with the word "dictatorship," obviously drawn from Locus 1, and held that the rule of the workers would be a hundred times more moral and rational than the rule of the Junkers and capitalists. But, he continued, "class rule is always an immoral and irrational state of affairs," and the aim of the revolutionary movement should be "not the transference of rule from one class to the other but the abolition of class differences."[45]

Marx was obviously irritated by Lüning's holier-than-thou True Socialism and fired back a letter to the editor that was published on July 4:

[Locus 3]

To the Editor of the Neue Deutsche Zeitung:

In the feuilleton of your paper for June 22 of this year, you reproached me with advocating the *rule and the dictatorship of the working class* [*die* Herrschaft und die Diktatur der Arbeiterklasse], while as against me you urge the *abolition of class differences altogether.* I do not understand this rectification.

You knew very well that the *Communist Manifesto* (published before the February Revolution of 1848), p. 16, says: "If the proletariat during its contest with the bourgeoisie is compelled, by the force of circumstances, to organize itself as a class, if, by means of a revolution, it makes itself the ruling class, and, as such, sweeps away by force the old conditions of production, then it will, along with these conditions, have swept away the conditions for the existence of class antagonisms and of classes generally, and will thereby have abolished its own supremacy [*Herrschaft*] as a class."[46]

45. *Neue Deutsche Zeitung*, June 22, 1850, as quoted in Draper, "Dictatorship," pp. 38–39.
46. *Werke*, 7:323; see Draper's discussion, "Dictatorship," pp. 39–41.

Although just an echo of Locus 1, Marx's letter is significant for its unhesitating equation of the slogans of the *Manifesto* with the seemingly more stringent formulations of 1850. For the proletariat to make itself the ruling class, or "to win the battle of democracy" as the *Manifesto* declared elsewhere, is here equated with "the *rule and dictatorship of the working class.*" Marx seemed to feel no special explanation was necessary for the term "dictatorship," nor did Lüning. Both men clearly understood dictatorship to mean the rule of an entire class; indeed, it was precisely class rule per se that made Lüning uncomfortable. This obscure letter adds further confirmation that Marx had not altered his views of the character of the postrevolutionary government since the time of the *Manifesto—"Herrschaft"* and *"Diktatur"* had become interchangeable.

Locus 4 is a fainter reecho of Locus 3, as the slogan bounced back and forth across the Atlantic Ocean in 1852. With the ultimate demise of the *Neue Deutsche Zeitung*, Weydemeyer emigrated to New York where he began writing for German-language periodicals. His first article in America was published in the New York *Turn-Zeitung* on January 1, 1852, and bore the title, "The Dictatorship of the Proletariat." It was little more than a condensation of the *Manifesto* and used the key phrase only once, in the final paragraph.[47] Weydemeyer regularly sent Marx and Engels copies of his publications, and it is almost certain Marx received this article, along with at least one other, toward the end of February.[48] This would explain why the famous slogan that Marx had not used in almost two years popped up extraneously in his return letter to Weydemeyer on March 5. The letter contained various materials and suggestions for future articles, such as Marx regularly sent Weydemeyer, including some general observations on the class struggle in modern society. Marx then added:

[Locus 4a and b]

And now as to myself, no credit is due to me for discovering the existence of classes in modern society nor yet the struggle between them. Long before me bourgeois historians had described the historical development of this class struggle and bourgeois economists

47. Reprinted in English translation by Hal Draper, "Joseph Weydemeyer's 'Dictatorship of the Proletariat,'" *Labor History* 3 (1962):208–17.
48. See *Werke*, 28:15, 24, 25, 492, 500, 503; Karl Obermann, *Joseph Weydemeyer: Pioneer of American Socialism* (New York: International, 1947), pp. 35–45.

the economic anatomy of the classes. What I did that was new was to prove: (1) that the *existence of classes* is only bound up with *particular, historic phases in the development of production;* (2) that the class struggle necessarily leads to the *dictatorship of the proletariat* [Diktatur des Proletariats]; (3) that this dictatorship itself only constitutes the transition to the *abolition of all classes* and to a *classless society.*[49]

Toward the end of his letter Marx wrote, "From the above notes take anything you think suitable." Though one of the most widely quoted loci, this use is one of the least illuminating. Marx only repeated the phrase he saw in Weydemeyer's article—itself an echo of previous uses —and added nothing new to its definition. He might just as likely have used the more habitual "rule of the proletariat," had not Weydemeyer's article called his attention to the alternative term.

Thus, born of a desire to create a united front with the Blanquists, the phrase "dictatorship of the proletariat" was used twice in preparatory overtures, once in the compromise itself, once in an echo, and twice in a reecho two years later. Interestingly, the French Blanquists, who had never used the slogan before, did not use it again until the second united front with the Marxists in 1872. Similarly, the Willich-Schapper faction of the Communist League abandoned the slogan after the September 1850 schism. Their subsequent pronouncements called for a "revolutionary dictatorship" by a "Central Committee" that would be chosen by those members of the "armed fourth estate" who had "fought the revolution through." General elections were to be put off until the full attainment of communism.[50] The compromise of 1850 manifestly failed to alter the views of either side. Marx and Engels continued to believe in majority rule by the proletariat, which might be called dictatorship since revolution necessitated temporary extra-legality. The Blanquists and their German imitators continued to believe in an educational dictatorship by a small minority. The ambiguous

49. Letter of March 5, 1852, *Selected Correspondence: 1846–1895,* trans. Dona Torr (New York: International, 1942), p. 57; see Draper, "Dictatorship," pp. 43–46.
50. "Verhaltungsmassregeln für den Bund vor, während, und nach der Revolution," in Karl Wermuth and Wilhelm Stieber, *Die Communisten-Verschwörungen des 19. Jahrhunderts,* 2 vols. (1853–54; reprint ed., Hildesheim: Olms, 1969), 1:296, 297; cf. pp. 272, 274, 291.

and unfortunate compromise slogan, "dictatorship of the proletariat," might have died a natural death at that point, like the other compromise slogan, "permanent revolution," had not the two groupings renewed contact in the aftermath of the Paris Commune.

The Second Blanquist Alliance

During the two full decades between the Universal Society and the Paris Commune, Marxists and Blanquists had little if anything to do with one another, and during that entire period neither side used the phrase "dictatorship of the proletariat." It is precisely this striking temporal coincidence that makes Draper's thesis so convincing. In the 1860s, Marx and Engels collaborated with the Proudhonist trade unionists who figured so prominently in the French section of the International Working Men's Association, but this separated them even more from the Blanquists, who were bitter enemies of Proudhonism. Thus l'enfermé had two of his followers expelled for attending the 1868 congress of the IWA.[51] Personally, Marx and Blanqui managed to admire each other at a respectful distance. On the occasion of Blanqui's return to prison in 1861, Marx wrote in sympathy to Louis Watteau that he had always regarded Watteau's chief as "the head and heart of the proletarian party in France."[52] Marx's son-in-law, Paul Lafargue, was a Blanquist by origin and tried to bring the two men together. In 1869 he wrote Marx, "Blanqui has the greatest esteem for you"; and in 1879 he would balance this with a letter to Blanqui, shortly before the latter's death, saying, "Marx, who has followed your political career with great interest, would be very happy to make your acquaintance."[53] Nonetheless, the two men never actually met, although there were at least three occasions when it would have been quite possible.[54] Both men may have sensed that their mutual respect would be best preserved at a certain distance.

It was the Paris Commune of 1871, or rather the suppression of the Paris Commune, that brought Marxists and Blanquists back into

51.   Charles DaCosta, Les Blanquistes (Paris: Rivière, 1912), p. 18.
52.   Letter of November 10, 1861, Werke, 30:617.
53.   Marx quoted Lafargue in his letter to Engels, March 1, 1869, Werke, 32:264; Lafargue to Blanqui as quoted in Spitzer, Revolutionary Theories, pp. 115–16.
54.   See above, chap. 1, n. 36.

closer contact. Marx's enthusiasm for this abortive municipal revolution, the rebellion of France's radical center against the conservative countryside, found its immortal expression in his contemporary addresses to the IWA, published as *The Civil War in France.* Here he celebrated in glowing phrases the ultrademocratic features of the revolutionary government in Paris that the Blanquist faction among the Communards had deplored and opposed.[55] As soon as the Communal government had been established, the Blanquists tried to introduce a resolution suspending all democratic forms, appointing a dictatorial committee of public safety, and militarizing public life until the national government in Versailles would be overthrown. They gave up the plan only when it became apparent that the other political factions within the Commune would not accept it.[56] Obviously, the decades between 1850 and 1871 had not softened the contrast between the Marxist and the Blanquist conceptions of revolutionary government.

Following the particularly bloody suppression of the Commune, however, the situation changed in a number of ways. Marx and Engels felt an instinctive sympathy for the heroic Communards, quite independent of faction, which found expression in their untiring relief work on behalf of the refugees who streamed into London. Among these refugees were a number of Blanquist militants whom Marx and Engels sensed might now be won over. "A few had attained greater clarity on the essential principles," Engels remembered in 1891, "through [Eduard] Vaillant, who was familiar with German scientific socialism."[57] In particular, the two men were looking for allies in the great factional struggle then mounting to its climax within the International. However much Blanquists and Marxists might be at odds on other issues, they could stand shoulder to shoulder against the anarchist faction of the IWA, against the unpolitical socialism of Proudhon and especially Bakunin. Circumstances had conspired to aid this rapprochement when in April the main Proudhonist leader of the French section and founding member of the International, Henri Tolain, chose to support the Versailles government against the Commune. Indignantly, the Paris

55. *Selected Works,* 1:468–73.
56. See Edward S. Mason, *The Paris Commune* (New York: Macmillan, 1930), p. 509; G. D. H. Cole, *A History of Socialist Thought,* 5 vols. (New York: St. Martin's, 1953–60), 2:166; see also Engels' comments, *Selected Works,* 1:438.
57. "Introduction" (1891) to *The Civil War in France, Selected Works,* 1:436; also see Draper, "Dictatorship," pp. 50–52.

Federal Council expelled Tolain from the IWA, a step happily confirmed by Marx's general council in London.[58] This move against Blanqui's old rival must have made the International more attractive to the Blanquist Communards, as did Marx's relief efforts and courageous public defense of their unpopular cause. Bewildered by defeat and exile, politically adrift in a strange country, these militants now found themselves courted, feted, and welcomed into the IWA. Very likely Paul Lafargue played a key role as intermediary in establishing this second united front, which was cemented in August when Vaillant and other Blanquist leaders were elected on Marx's nomination to the general council.[59]

The feting continued in September, when the general council invited a host of Communard refugees to celebrate the seventh anniversary of the IWA at a grand banquet. The number of Blanquists present can be judged from a report in the *New York World* that the very mention of *l'enfermé's* name "set the whole assembly in motion like an electric shock." It was on this gala occasion that Marx, in his keynote address, revived the slogan that had lain dormant for twenty years. According to the same *World* account, Marx retraced the step-by-step growth of workers' movements, with a predictable culmination:

The last movement was the Commune, the greatest that had yet been made, and there could not be two opinions about it—the Commune was the conquest of the political power of the working classes. There was much misunderstanding about the Commune. The Commune could not found a new form of class government. In destroying the existing conditions of oppression by transferring all the means of labor to the productive laborer, and thereby compelling every able-bodied individual to work for a living, the only base for class rule and oppression would be removed. But before such a change could be effected a proletarian dictature would become necessary, and the first condition of that was a proletarian army. The working classes would have to conquer the right to emancipate themselves on the battlefield. The task of the Interna-

58.   Institute of Marxism-Leninism, ed., *Documents of the First International: The General Council of the First International, 1870–1871: Minutes* (Moscow: Progress, [1964]), p. 355.
59.   Ibid., p. 255; *Werke,* 18:8.

tional was to organize and combine the forces of labor for the coming struggle.[60]

Here Marx all but called the Paris Commune a dictatorship of the proletariat, which it certainly was according to his own understanding of the term,[61] but which must also have sounded an agreeable chord with the Blanquists in the audience. If the English-language report is precise, Marx even used the French form of the word—"*dictature*"— in what was a virtual replay of Locus 1, namely a suggestion to the Blanquists of a slogan that could unite the two schools. This time a special twist can be discerned in the veiled allusion to the "misunderstanding" of the anarchists who supposed that the state could be disbanded forthwith. Counterposed in particular to this prime error of their common anarchist foes, "proletarian dictature" was an ideal slogan for the united front.

The Blanquists obviously caught the hint, for when the IWA factional conflict reached its boiling point at the Hague Congress of September 1872, Vaillant introduced an antianarchist political-action resolution to the effect "that abstention from political action is the negation of the first duty of the working class: the conquest of political power having as its goal making a clean sweep of the old society and creating the elements of the new by the dictatorship of the proletariat."[62] While defending this resolution on the floor, Vaillant employed the slogan again, turning it adroitly against both the Bakuninist and Proudhonist varieties of anarchism, which he labeled respectively "abstentionists out of ignorance" and "abstentionists for political reasons." Thus did he take up the old 1850 slogan to assert the position of his camp against the indifference of the anarchists to the conquest of state power, in this neatly paired antagonism between political and unpolitical socialists, between Marxists and Blanquists on the one side and Proudhonists and Bakuninists on the other. But the common front was destined to last only as long as the common threat. After voting jointly to expel the Bakuninists on a reformulated political-action resolution, the united

60. *New York World*, October 15, 1871, as reprinted in *New Politics* 2, no. 3 (Summer 1963):130–32; German translation in *Werke*, 17:432–33.
61. See discussion above, pp. 291–97. Engels would expressly call the Commune a "dictatorship of the proletariat" in 1891, as we will see later in this chapter.
62. *Internationale et Révolution* (London, 1872), as quoted in Draper, "Dictatorship," p. 55, n. 93.

front was suddenly ruptured when the Blanquists walked out in genuine indignation as a response to Marx's unexpected proposal to transfer the IWA headquarters to New York—in other words, to oblivion.[63] The second collaboration thus endured scarcely longer than the first.

In the period following the rupture, the Blanquist refugees issued two pronouncements that provoked Engels, for the first time in his own name, to write the phrase "dictatorship of the proletariat" in Loci 5 and 7. Locus 7 was a response to the Blanquist program, *Aux Communeux*, issued in 1874. This program included the slogan "dictatorship of the proletariat" along with other evidences of recent Marxist influence but retained the central Blanquist postulate of mass immaturity. Thus it declaimed against the "fraud of universal suffrage" and asserted that by no means must "the revolutionary minority abdicate before the average, distorted opinion of majorities that have been subjected to all of the influences of ignorance and privilege."[64] Obviously, their exposure to Marxism had affected the Blanquists' terminology more than their underlying ideas. Engels reacted to the pronouncement in an extended and much neglected critique, "Programm der blanquistischen Kommuneflüchtlinge," published in June 1874. Here we may appreciate in its larger context the razor-sharp counterposition previewed earlier of the Marxist and Blanquist conceptions of dictatorship:

[Locus 7]

These Blanquists are so called not because they form a group founded by Blanqui—only a few of the 33 signers of this program have ever spoken personally to Blanqui—but rather because they want to be active in his spirit and according to his tradition. Blanqui is essentially a political revolutionist. He is a socialist only through his sympathy with the sufferings of the people, but he has neither a socialist theory nor any concrete practical proposals for social redress. In his political activity, he was mainly a "man of action," who believed that a small and well-organized minority, by attempting a revolutionary surprise attack at the right moment, could raise forth the masses of the people with a few initial successes and thus make a successful revolution. Such a group could

63.   Hans Gerth, ed., *The First International: Minutes of the Hague Congress* . . . (Madison: Wisconsin, 1958), p. 217; see also pp. 212–14, 220, 286.

64.   As quoted in DaCosta, *Les Blanquistes*, pp. 48–49 (translation from Draper, "Dictatorship," p. 56).

be organized, of course, only as a secret society under Louis Philippe, and so there occurred what usually occurs with conspiracies.
The members grew weary of constantly holding back, with empty
promises that action would soon begin, and finally lost all patience,
becoming rebellious and leaving only the alternatives: either to let
the conspiracy fall apart or to let fly without any external justification or signs. So they let fly (on May 12, 1839) and were squashed
in a twinkling. This happened even though the police for once
were entirely unaware of the Blanquist conspiracy; it descended
on them from the clear blue sky.

From Blanqui's conception that every revolution is a surprise attack by a small revolutionary minority, there follows of itself the
necessity for a dictatorship after the success of the venture. This
would be, to be sure, a dictatorship not of the entire revolutionary
class, the proletariat [*der Diktatur, wohlverstanden, nicht der gan-
zen revolutionären Klasse, des Proletariats*], but of the small number who have made the surprise attack, and who are themselves
previously organized under the dictatorship of one or several individuals.

We see, then, that Blanqui is a revolutionary of the preceding
generation.[65]

In criticizing his ex-partners, Engels here proceeded by bold and un-
ambiguous strokes to the heart of what separated them: conspiratorial
revolution and minority dictatorship versus spontaneous mass revolution and majority dictatorship. He referred to the crucial slogan only
to counterpose as sharply as he could the dictatorship of "the entire
revolutionary class" to the dictatorship of "a small revolutionary minority" or of "one or several individuals." He thereby excluded from the
Marxist conception of the workers' dictatorship any notion of rule by
an elite, a vanguard party, a central committee, or a single strong man.
Such ideas, he declared in a tragic lapse of his gift for prophecy, belonged to the "preceding generation."

Engels went on in this remarkable document to criticize the Blanquist refugees for wanting now to "let fly" once again without consider-

---

65. "Programm der blanquistischen Kommuneflüchtlinge," *Werke*, 18:529. Engels mercifully refrained from mentioning that the 1839 pattern repeated itself
again in virtually every detail in the *émeute* of August 1870 (see Spitzer, *Revolutionary Theories*, pp. 153–54).

ing that the French workers "needed a long period of rest" to recover from 1871. He chastised them as well for preparing proscription lists to eliminate their rivals from any new commune, for wanting to suppress religion by decree, for imagining that they could "overleap the way stations and compromises" on the road to communism, and for defending blindly all the shootings, burnings and other "stupidities" perpetrated by the Commune during the torment of its final days.[66] Not wanting to be entirely negative, Engels also made the customary deference to the "revolutionary instinct and lightning resolution of Blanqui," and commended the program on what had been borrowed from the *Manifesto*, "although its translation into Blanquist French leaves a good deal to be desired." "This program shows some progress," he concluded, "the undeniable service of Vaillant." It is "a good sign when French workers adopt correct theoretical principles even though they come out of Germany."[67] In later years, Vaillant did indeed go on to fulfill Engels' desires by leading some of his followers into the French Socialist party and the Second International. It is fitting that Locus 7, the last one relating to the Blanquists specifically, should have been another educational effort to redirect the latter's thinking away from instant revolution, clique dictatorship, and terrorism.

We may now move back chronologically to Locus 5, Engels' 1872 tract on *The Housing Question*, in which he criticized a just-published statement on the issue by a German Proudhonist, Artur Mülberger. In the course of this polemic against anarchism, Engels made a side reference to the first of the two Blanquist pronouncements, *Internationale et Révolution* (1872). Specifically, he wanted to counter Mülberger's claim that the principles of Proudhon generally inspired the French working class. Such a claim obviously overlooked the movement inspired by Blanqui:

[Locus 5a]

When the so-called Blanquists made an attempt to transform themselves from mere political revolutionists into a socialist workers' faction with a definite program—as was done by the Blanquist

66. *Werke*, 18:530–35; see passage cited above, chap. 7, n. 79. Some key portions of this article have been published in English in Marx and Engels, *Writings on the Paris Commune*, ed. Hal Draper (New York: Monthly Review, 1971), pp. 227–30.
67. *Werke*, 18:530, 532, 534–35.

fugitives in London in their manifesto, *Internationale et Révolution*—they did not proclaim the "principles" of the Proudhonist plan for the salvation of society, but adopted, and almost literally at that, the views of German scientific Socialism on the necessity of political action by the proletariat and of its dictatorship [*seiner Diktatur*] as the transition to the abolition of classes and with them of the state—views such as had already been expressed in the *Communist Manifesto* and since then on innumerable occasions.[68]

While making the polemical point that the Blanquists borrowed their ideas from Marx rather than Proudhon, Engels singled out the two points—the need for political action and for a postrevolutionary dictatorship—that were bound to nettle the anarchists most. He used the word "dictatorship" for exactly the same purpose as had Marx and Vaillant the year before—to emphasize what united the political socialists against the unpolitical socialists. As in Locus 3, Engels also equated the word with the demands of the *Manifesto* and the views expressed "since then on innumerable occasions," suggesting that—like Marx—he perceived no dramatic change in his own views on revolutionary government since 1847.

Mülberger had gone on to stress that the housing shortage transcended class lines, affecting all strata of the population. He emphasized this point, he said, because "we have been so frequently and largely exposed to the *absurd* charge of pursuing a *class policy*, of striving for *class domination* [Klassenherrschaft]." Here was another bêtise too tempting for Engels to pass by. He rejoined:

[Locus 5b]
Friend Mülberger thus makes the following points here:
1. "We" do not pursue any "class policy" and do not strive for "class domination." But the German Social-Democratic Workers' Party, just *because* it is a *workers' party*, necessarily pursues a "class policy," the policy of the working class. Since each political party sets out to establish its rule [*Herrschaft*] in the state, so the German Social-Democratic Workers' Party is necessarily striving

68. *Selected Works*, 1:555. Note Engels' comment to Friedrich Sorge in a letter of November 16, 1872: "You will be amused at the little brochure in which Vaillant quite seriously declares all our economic and political ideas to be Blanquist discoveries" (*Werke*, 33:538).

to establish *its Herrschaft*, the *Herrschaft* of the working class, hence "*Klassenherrschaft*." Moreover, *every* real proletarian party, from the English Chartists onward, has put forward a class policy: the organization of the proletariat as an independent political party is the first condition of its struggle, and the dictatorship of the proletariat [*Diktatur des Proletariats*] is its immediate aim. By declaring this to be "absurd," Mülberger puts himself outside the proletarian movement and inside the camp of petty-bourgeois Socialism.[69]

With the fiery slogan fresh in his mind (from Locus 5a), and having repeated *Herrschaft* five times in the same paragraph, Engels seems here to have shifted to *Diktatur* simply for relief, as a synonym. Though quite casually inserted, the term is particularly noteworthy in this passage because of Engels' incidental remark—so jarring to twentieth-century conceptions—that even the Chartists had been striving for a "dictatorship of the proletariat." The six purely democratic demands of the People's Charter were equated in his mind with the revolutionary rule of the working-class majority in England—hence with proletarian dictatorship. No locus yet cited reveals so clearly that Marx and Engels used *Diktatur* as a synonym for *Herrschaft* and assumed, under either label, a democratic governmental structure.

Marx chose the phrase more deliberately in his own contemporaneous polemic against Proudhonism, "Indifference to Politics," which he wrote in Italian. He began the essay with a two-page caricature of the Frenchman's teachings, done with heavy-handed sarcasm:

[Locus 6]

"The working class should not form a political party, and should not, under any circumstances, undertake political action, since to combat the State is to recognize the State, which is contrary to the eternal principles. . . .

"If in the political struggle against the bourgeois State the workers only manage to wrest concessions, they are making compromises, which is contrary to the eternal principles. One must therefore scorn any peaceful movement, as the English and American workers have the bad habit of doing. . . .

---

69. *Selected Works*, 1:556 (*"Herrschaft"* restored to original German for emphasis); Mülberger's words as quoted by Engels.

"If the political struggle of the working class assumes violent forms, if the workers substitute their revolutionary dictatorship [*la loro dittatura rivoluzionaria*] for the dictatorship of the bourgeois class, they are committing the terrible crime of lese-principle, for to satisfy their own base everyday needs and crush the resistance of the bourgeoisie, instead of laying down arms and abolishing the State they are giving it a revolutionary and transient form."[70]

Within the framework of his caricature, Marx smuggled in his standard argument against the anarchist desire to abolish the state immediately. The workers must first seize the state, give it a "revolutionary and transient form," and use it to "crush" (*schiacciare*) bourgeois resistance, before they eventually lay down their arms. This is the *only* locus in which either Marx or Engels pointed to a specifically repressive mission for the dictatorship of the proletariat. (Small wonder Lenin chose the passage for special emphasis in his *State and Revolution*.)[71] One may recall, however, Marx's 1848 assertion that every revolution "requires a dictatorship, and an energetic dictatorship at that," charged with the task of "immediately shattering and eliminating the remnants of old institutions."[72] Here in Locus 6, Marx seemed to be applying this general notion expressly to the rule of the workers.

Engels amplified this theme in a parallel contribution to the Italian socialist press, "On Authority," as he chastised the anarchists for demanding that "the first act of the social revolution should be the abolition of authority":

Have these gentlemen ever seen a revolution? A revolution is certainly the most authoritarian thing there is; it is the act whereby one part of the population imposes its will upon the other part by means of rifles, bayonets and cannon—authoritarian means, if such there be at all; and if the victorious party does not want to have fought in vain, it must maintain this rule by means of the terror which its arms inspire in the reactionaries. Would the Paris Com-

70. In Marx, Engels, and V. I. Lenin, *Anarchism and Anarcho-Syndicalism* (New York: International, 1972), pp. 94–95; Italian original from Marx and Engels, *Scritti Italiani*, ed. Gianni Bosio (Milan: Avanti, 1955), pp. 98–99.
71. (New York: International, 1943), p. 51.
72. See n. 20 above.

mune have lasted a single day if it had not made use of this authority of the armed people against the bourgeois? Should we not, on
the contrary, reproach it for not having used it freely enough?[73]

This passage includes virtually the only approving reference to revolutionary terror to be found in Marx and Engels' writings after 1850.
Engels seemed to be drawing out the implication that the revolutionary
rule of the workers would at first necessarily rest not on law but directly
on force, on the terror that the weapons of the "armed people" would
"inspire" among the reactionaries. All sorts of questions come to mind,
of course, concerning the exact nature of this terror, by whom it might
be applied, against whom, whether there would be any limits or restraints in its application, and so forth—but these queries must be postponed for systematic examination in volume 2. Suffice it to say for
the moment that neither here nor anywhere else did Marx or Engels
call for the wholesale physical extermination of the enemies of the
revolution. Their prognostications always assumed the exertion of force
by a ruling majority over a rebellious minority. With respect to the
Paris Commune, the only specific measure of "terror" they ever proposed was the seizure of the assets of the Bank of France![74] It must
also be noted that Locus 6, the only one alluding to the *functions* of
the dictatorship, spoke of the workers' need "to satisfy their own base
everyday needs and crush the resistance of the bourgeoisie," but not
of any *educational* tasks whatsoever.

Because Marx and Engels stressed the necessity of retaining the state
after the revolution, because they even called it a dictatorship on occasion, they left themselves open to the anarchist countercharge that they
were simply preparing a new despotism to replace the old. Bakunin
exploited this opening to the fullest in his *Statism and Anarchy* (1873),
as we will see in the next section. Thus Marx and Engels had to be
careful to emphasize the transitory nature of proletarian rule and avoid
giving any impression of reverence for the state as such. Here one
finds the motive behind Locus 8, one of the most quoted but least
understood uses, in Marx's 1875 *Critique of the Gotha Program.*

In 1875 the two existing factions of the German socialist movement

73.   *Selected Works,* 1:578.
74.   "The bank in the hands of the Commune—this would have been worth
more than ten thousand hostages," proclaimed Engels (ibid., p. 437). Cf. Marx's
parallel thoughts, *Writings on the Paris Commune,* p. 233.

merged: the more-or-less Marxist followers of August Bebel combined with the followers of Ferdinand Lassalle in a congress at Gotha and drew up a draft program for the united party. Marx and Engels favored the merger but were distressed that so many Lassallean ideas had found their way into the new draft program—including his central demand for state-aided producers' cooperatives and the call for a "free state" with an odd assortment of democratic reforms (universal suffrage, referendum, trial by jury, elimination of lingering restrictions on freedom of the press and association)—that remained deferentially silent on the crucial executive powers reserved in the Bismarckian constitution for the monarch and his chosen ministers. In his *Critique*, originally a private letter to the leaders of the Bebel faction, Marx sharply condemned "this kind of democratism which keeps within the limits of what is permitted by the police and not permitted by logic." "The whole program," he complained, "for all its democratic clang, is tainted through and through by the Lassallean sect's servile belief in the state."[75] If issued without change, this draft program would be a disastrous liability, for, as Engels later recalled, "we were at the time . . . engaged in the most violent struggle against Bakunin and his anarchists, who made us responsible for everything that happened in the labor movement in Germany; hence we had to expect that we would also be saddled with the secret paternity of this program."[76] Hence Marx's effort, seconded by Engels in a separate letter to Bebel, to have the draft program revised.

Both men began the political section of their criticism with a dissection of the unfortunate expression "free state." Actually the term "free people's state" (*freier Volksstaat*) had hitherto been used by both factions as a euphemism for the forbidden word "republic," but for some reason it was abbreviated in the draft to "*Freistaat.*" Engels commented:

The "free people's state" has been turned into the "free state." A "free state," from a grammatical point of view, is a state which is free in relation to its own citizens—i.e. a state with a despotic government. All the talk about the state should be dropped, particularly since we have now had the experience of the Paris Commune

75. *Selected Works*, 2:31, 32.
76. "Foreword" (1891) to *Critique of the Gotha Program*, ibid., p. 14; cf. p. 15.

which was not really a state in the accepted sense of the word. The anarchists have thrown the term "people's state" into our faces until we are sick of it. Yet Marx's pamphlet against Proudhon and then the *Communist Manifesto* both clearly stated that a state automatically dissolves itself and vanishes when a socialist society is established.[77]

One can thus understand Marx's animus as he approached the term:

Free state—what is this?
It is by no means the aim of the workers, who have got rid of the narrow mentality of humble subjects, to set the state free. In the German Empire the "state" is almost as "free" as in Russia. Freedom consists of converting the state from an organ superimposed upon society into one completely subordinate to it, and today, too, the forms of state are more free or less free to the extent that they restrict the "freedom of the state."[78]

Marx then proceeded to dissect another ambiguous term, "present-day state," and concluded:

[Locus 8]
It is possible to speak of the "present-day state," in contrast with the future, in which its present root, bourgeois society, will have died off.
The question then arises: what transformation will the polity [*Staatswesen*] undergo in communist society? In other words, what social functions will remain in existence there that are analogous to present functions of the state? This question can only be answered scientifically, and one does not get a flea-hop nearer to the problem by a thousandfold combination of the word people with the word state.
Between capitalist and communist society lies the period of the revolutionary transformation of the one into the other. There corresponds to this also a political transition period in which the state

77. Letter to Bebel, March 18-28, 1875, *Engels: Selected Writings*, ed. W. O. Henderson (Baltimore: Penguin, 1967), p. 137.
78. *Selected Works*, 2:29.

can be nothing but the *revolutionary dictatorship of the proletariat* [Diktatur des Proletariats].[79]

Caught uncomfortably between Bakunin's charges of statism and the *real* statism of the Lassalleans, Marx was here concerned to deny that the workers strive for a "free state" or any continuing state at all. They would require a state only for the "political transition period," not forever. Marx's recent use of the slogan "dictatorship of the proletariat" in his polemic against anarchism (Locus 6) doubtless recalled it here, where he had Bakunin so much on his mind. He may incidentally have drawn a certain satisfaction from counterposing his own fiery word, *Diktatur*, to the entirely vacuous Lassallean *Freistaat*. But it is worth remarking that he did not attach enough importance to the word to urge that it be written into the program; indeed, his only lament in this connection was that legal restrictions made it unwise to call openly for a *"democratic republic."*[80] Evidently, Marx saw no logical conflict between this preferred demand for a democratic republic and his position that the transitional state "can be nothing other than" a dictatorship—which reinforces the interpretation that he conceived the dictatorship as nothing more than an extralegal provisional government by a democratically elected assembly. This was the last time Marx ever used the controversial slogan.

In the six uses of 1871–1875, Marx and Engels counterposed their idea of *temporary* class dictatorship by a *majority*, first to the Blanquist notion of educational dictatorship by a *minority*, and then to the anarchist desire for an *immediate* abolition of the state, with a sidelong swipe at the Lassallean partiality for a *continuing* "free state." It is significant that the term appeared only in minor polemical writings, for the purpose of making these distinctions, and not in any of Marx and Engels' more formal and serious publications. After having served such purposes, the slogan would again disappear for a period of fifteen years, to be revived again briefly by Engels in 1890–1893.

Marx's Notes on Bakunin

Before moving on to the 1890–1893 period, it will be appropriate to devote special attention to what is patently Marx's most significant

79. Ibid., p. 30 (except I have rendered *"Staatswesen"* as "polity" rather than simply as "state").
80. Ibid., p. 31; see Draper, "Dictatorship," p. 66.

abstinence from the phrase "dictatorship of the proletariat." This occurred when Bakunin expressly accused him of advocating an educational dictatorship and Marx responded so as to indicate he wanted nothing to do with dictatorship in that sense. This remarkable and little-known exchange came about in the following way. In 1873 Bakunin published a major polemical work, *Statism and Anarchy*, which included a long attack on Marxism as a form of "statist" socialism. Marx read the book sometime during 1874 and early 1875 and, as was his lifelong habit when reading, copied out long excerpts from the tome in one of his notebooks, interspersing his own thoughts and comments along the way. This notebook material, published for the first time in its original language in 1964, provides an invaluable new source of information on Marx's political ideas, all the more so because of its private character. The notes were intended for no other eyes than Marx's own, which ought to remove any suspicion about concealed intentions or concern for a public image. They deserve extensive quotation.[81]

Bakunin started off with an assault on the phrase *"Volksstaat"* that makes it clear why Marx and Engels were sensitive to such terminological questions in their criticism of the Gotha Program:

BAKUNIN: We already have expressed our abhorrence for the theories of Lassalle and Marx, theories which counseled the workers —if not as their ultimate ideal, at least as their next chief aim—*to form a People's State,* which, according to their interpretation, will only be "the proletariat raised to the position of a ruling class." One may ask then: if the proletariat is to be the ruling class, over

81. First published in German in *Werke,* 18:597–642. The section quoted below is from pp. 630–36. To be fair to Bakunin, I have reproduced his words from the standard English translation of this portion of *Statism and Anarchy* found in G. P. Maximoff, ed., *The Political Philosophy of Bakunin: Scientific Anarchism* (Glencoe: Free Press, 1953), pp. 286–88. Bakunin's work has never been translated in its entirety but is available in a bilingual Russian-French edition: *Gosudarstvennost' i Anarchija—Etatisme et Anarchie 1873* (Leiden: Brill, 1967). Marx's comments have recently been published in a mediocre English translation in *Anarchism and Anarcho-Syndicalism,* pp. 147–52, which I have used with several modifications of my own. An earlier even less successful translation was made by Henry Mayer, "Marx on Bakunin: A Neglected Text," *Etudes de Marxologie,* ed. Maximilien Rubel (Paris: Institut de Science Economique Appliquée, 1959), 2:91–115.

whom will it rule? The answer is that there will remain another proletariat which will be subjected to this new domination, this new State.

MARX: It means that as long as other classes, and the capitalist class in particular, still exist, and as long as the proletariat fights against them (for its enemies and the old organization of society do not vanish as a result of its coming to power) it must employ *coercive* measures, that is, governmental measures; so long it is still a class itself, and the economic conditions which give rise to the class struggle and the existence of classes have not yet disappeared and must be forcibly removed, or transformed in a process accelerated by force.

Beginning from the premise that every "rule" must have an object, every state its victims, Bakunin inquired what would be the object of proletarian rule. Marx responded predictably enough that it would be the bourgeoisie, whose restorative efforts would have to be constrained in the period immediately following the revolution. Coercive power would be required temporarily because the class enemy of the proletariat would not "vanish" overnight as the anarchists seemed to expect.

Since Bakunin never understood this elementary Marxist position, or at least pretended not to understand it, he did not address the issue of bourgeois resistance at all but went on to postulate four other distinct—and not entirely compatible—answers to his own question, beginning with the idea of proletarian rule over the peasantry.

BAKUNIN: It may be, for example, the peasant "rabble," which, as we know, does not stand in great favor with the Marxists, and who, finding themselves on a lower level of culture, probably will be ruled by the city and factory proletariat.

MARX: That is to say, wherever large numbers of peasants exist as private proprietors, and where they even constitute a more or less considerable majority, as in all countries of the West European continent, where they have not disappeared and been supplanted by agricultural day-laborers as in England, the following alternatives exist: either the peasants prevent and doom to failure every workers' revolution, as they have done in France up to now, or the proletariat (for the peasant proprietor does not belong to the proletariat; even where he does belong to it by reason of his position, he does not consider himself as belonging to it) functioning as the government must take steps that will immediately improve his position and thus win him over to the revolution; these steps moreover further the transition from private to communal ownership of land in such a way, that the peasant comes to it of his own accord on economic grounds. But one must not affront the peasant, for instance by proclaiming the abolition of the right of inheritance or the abolition of his property . . . ; still less should one strengthen small ownership by enlarging the plots, by simply transferring the larger estates to the peasants, as Bakunin advocated in his revolutionary campaign.

Comment on these most interesting assertions will be postponed until after we have heard Marx's further remarks on the same issues, as he responded to Bakunin's second postulated answer, the rule of the German workers over the backward Slavic peoples:

BAKUNIN: Or considered from the national point of view, the Slavs, for instance, will assume, for precisely the same reason, the same position of slavish subjection to the victorious German proletariat which the latter now holds with respect to its own bourgeoisie.

MARX: Schoolboy nonsense! A radical social revolution depends on particular historical conditions of economic development; they are its prerequisites. Thus a revolution is possible only where, together with capitalist production, the industrial proletariat occupies at least an important place within the population. And to have any chance of success it must *mutatis mutandis* be able immediately to do at least as much for the peasants as the French bourgeoisie during its revolution did for the French peasants of the time. A fine idea to assume that the rule of labor will include the subjugation of agricultural labor. This is where the innermost thoughts of Herr Bakunin are revealed. . . . *Will power*, not economic conditions, is the basis of his social revolution.

Here in private notes, a quarter century after the main period of our concern (but only three years after the Paris Commune), we find strong additional confirmation of the interpretations advanced in chapters 6 and 7: namely, that in countries like France and Germany Marx saw no point in an unassisted uprising by the proletariat; only with peasant support could the workers expect to be successful; only by positive help and persuasion—rather than by coercion—could they hope to win over that support. The rule of labor would not involve the subjugation of agricultural labor, for no real revolution can be made simply by the will power of a determined minority.[82]

As Bakunin worked up to his third answer, he offered some preliminary reflections on the nature of government in general, which elicited further commentary from his reader:

BAKUNIN: If there is a State, there must necessarily be domination, and therefore slavery; a State without slavery, overt or concealed, is unthinkable—and that is why we are enemies of the State.

What does it mean: "the proletariat raised into a ruling class?"

MARX: It means that the proletariat, instead of fighting individually against the economically privileged classes, has gained sufficient strength and is sufficiently well organized to employ general means of compulsion in its struggle against these classes. It can, however, use only economic means designed to abolish its own distinctive trait as a wage-earner, and hence to abolish itself as a class. With its complete victory, therefore, its rule also comes to an end, since its class character [disappears].

BAKUNIN: Will the proletariat as a whole be at the head of the government?

MARX: In a trade union, for instance, does the whole union constitute the executive committee? Will all division of labor in a factory disappear and also the various functions arising from it? And in Bakunin's construction "from the bottom up," will everybody be up at the top? Then there would be no "bottom." Will all the members of the community administer the common affairs of the area at the same time? . . .

BAKUNIN: There are about forty million Germans. Will all forty million be members of the government?

82. See above, pp. 176–98, 212–27, 235–47. On the question of winning peasant support, also see some later writings by Engels, especially *Selected Works*, 1:571–72; 2:381–99.

MARX: Certainly, for the thing begins with the self-government of the communities.

BAKUNIN: The whole people will govern and there will be no one to be governed.

MARX: When a man rules himself, then, according to this principle, he does not rule himself, for he is only himself and nobody else.

BAKUNIN: It means that there will be no government, no State, but if there is a State in existence there will be people who are governed, and there will be slaves.

MARX: That is simply to say, when class rule has disappeared a state in the now accepted political sense of the word no longer exists.

If at first the workers would rule over the "economically privileged classes," this domination would come to an end as soon as the workers abolished themselves as workers, that is, abolished wage labor. (Notice that even in these private thoughts there is no mention of abolishing the bourgeoisie in a direct physical sense.) Thereafter, however, the people would still have to rule *themselves*—just as a man rules himself—in a presumably noncoercive administrative structure resting on a foundation of self-governing local communities. Thus did Marx in his own thinking resolve Bakunin's concern about the ultimate object of the workers' "rule"—in the *reflexive* form, the verb *"herrschen"* requires no other object.

Bakunin then addressed the point he had been building up to, his third postulated answer, namely, that corrupted ex-workers would rule over the toiling people:

BAKUNIN: This dilemma is solved very simply in the Marxist theory. By a people's government they—

MARX: i.e., Bak[unin]

BAKUNIN: —mean the governing of people by means of a small number of representatives elected by the people.

MARX: This democratic drivel, political claptrap is asinine. Elections are a political form which exists in the smallest Russian commune and artel. The nature of the elections is determined not by the name, but by the economic basis, the economic interrelations of the voters, and from the moment when the functions have ceased to be political ones (1) governmental functions no longer exist; (2) the distribution of general functions becomes a routine matter and does not entail any domination; (3) elections completely lose their present political character.

Bakunin: Universal suffrage—the right of the whole people—

Marx: Such a thing as the whole people in the present sense of the word is a phantasm.

Bakunin: —to elect its so-called representatives and rulers of the State—this is the last word of the Marxists as well as of the democratic school. And this is a falsehood behind which lurks the despotism of a governing minority, a falsehood which is all the more dangerous in that it appears as the ostensible expression of a people's will. . . . Thus, from whatever angle we approach the problem, we arrive at the same sorry result: the rule of great masses of people by a small privileged minority. But this minority, say the Marxists,—

Marx: Where?

Bakunin: —will consist of workers. Yes, indeed, of *ex-workers*, who, once they become rulers or representatives of the people, cease to be workers—

Marx: No more than does a manufacturer today cease to be a capitalist on becoming a city councilman.

Bakunin: —and begin to look down upon the toiling people. From that time on they represent not the people but themselves and their own claims to govern the people. Those who doubt this know precious little about human nature.

Marx: If Herr Bakunin understood at least the position of a manager in a workers' co-operative factory, all his illusions about domination would go to the devil. He ought to have asked himself what form the functions of administration could assume in such a workers' state, if he chooses to call it thus.

Here Bakunin denied, as anarchists characteristically do, any possibility of genuine representation. If all "ex-workers" cease to represent their constituents and acquire selfish interests as rulers, then no authentic self-government is possible except at the level of a small community where continual decision-making by the whole collectivity might be possible. No doubt that is exactly what Bakunin had in mind. But it is highly significant that he unhesitatingly placed Marx alongside the "democratic school" as a believer in representative democracy. And Marx did not dispute this placement at all: he had no qualms about representation in principle, but conceived elections to have a necessary role even in noncoercive institutions. As examples he pointed to the executive committee of a trade union and the elected manager of a cooperative factory. Even in the "smallest Russian village and artel" such delegation of authority forms part of a natural and scarcely avoidable division of labor and need not involve any "domination." With respect to Bakunin's legitimate anxiety concerning the corruptibility of such elected leaders, Marx was perhaps too cavalier in dismissing the question with his comment about the capitalist city councilman, and yet the example of a part-time elective official is a revealing one. In his own mind Marx had resolved the problem of corruption by his expectation that leadership positions in the good society would be held only on a part-time or short-term basis—there would simply not be any career politicians to become corrupted.[83]

In his fourth and last answer—the most important for our purposes— Bakunin postulated a rule by "men of learning" over the ignorant masses. Note his employment here for the first time of the word "dictatorship," and Marx's crucial abstention in his response:

BAKUNIN: But these elected representatives will be convinced Socialists, and learned Socialists at that. The words "learned Socialist"—

MARX: Never used.

BAKUNIN: —and "scientific Socialism"—

MARX: Used only in contradistinction to utopian socialism which seeks to foist new fantasies upon the people instead of confining its science to the comprehension of the social movement created by the people itself; see my book against Proudhon.

BAKUNIN: —which are met with constantly in the works and speeches of the Lassalleans and Marxists, prove only that this would-be people's State will be nothing else but despotic rule over the toiling masses by a new, numerically small aristocracy of genuine or sham men of learning.[84] The people lack learning and so

83.   See above, pp. 80–84. These issues will be dealt with at length in volume 2.
84.   Here Maximoff translated the Russian *"uchenye"* as "scientists," but it is rendered as *"savants"* in the French version and is *"Gelehrten"* in the German.

they will be freed from the cares of government, will be wholly regimented into one common herd of governed people. Emancipation indeed!

The Marxists are aware of this [MARX: !] contradiction, and, realizing that government by men of learning—

MARX: Quelle reverie!

BAKUNIN: —(the most distressing, offensive, and despicable type of government in the world) will be, notwithstanding its democratic form, a veritable dictatorship, —console themselves with the thought that this dictatorship will be only temporary and of brief duration.

MARX: Non, mon cher! [We say] that the *class rule* [Klassenherrschaft] of the workers over the resisting strata of the old world can only continue until the economic basis that makes the existence of classes possible has been destroyed.

BAKUNIN: They say that the only care and aim of this government will be to educate and uplift the people—

MARX: Barroom politician!

BAKUNIN: —economically and politically—to such an extent that no government will be necessary, and that the State, having lost its political character, that is, its character of rule and domination, will turn all by itself into an altogether free organization of economic interests and communes. . . .

MARX: Leaving aside the harping on Liebknecht's *Volksstaat,* which is nonsense and contrary to the *Communist Manifesto,* etc., this means simply that since the proletariat, during the period of struggle to overthrow the old society, still acts on the basis of the old society and consequently within political forms which more or less belong to that society, it has, during this period of struggle, not yet attained its ultimate constitution [*Konstitution*], and to achieve its liberation it employs means which will be discarded after the liberation. From this Herr B. concludes that the proletariat should rather do nothing at all and wait for the *day of universal liquidation*—the Last Judgment.

Marx must have been nettled not only by Bakunin's harping on the term "*Volksstaat,*" but also by his reference to "dictatorship," a term

---

Since the word does not mean specifically natural scientists, "men of learning" would seem to be a better English translation.

Marx had himself employed in his recent polemic against anarchism (Locus 6). Bakunin obviously understood "dictatorship" in the Blanquist sense of the word, as an educational rule by the enlightened few whose mission was to "uplift" the ignorant masses. "Quelle reverie!" was Marx's instantaneous reaction to such a notion, one he deemed worthy only of a "barroom politician." For him the task of intellectuals was rather to study the "movement created by the people itself." He conceived this movement to involve the *self-education* of the masses; consequently the revolution would require no educational dictatorship but only the *"class rule"* of the workers over the resisting strata of the old world." In the context provided by Bakunin, Marx refused to use the word "dictatorship" at all, but reverted to the more familiar *"Klassenherrschaft"* and even underlined it for emphasis. Surely, in these unguarded personal notes, this constitutes Marx's most significant abstinence from the phrase "dictatorship of the proletariat."

The Echoes of the Nineties

The remaining three loci are to be found in the writings of the seventy-year-old Engels in 1890 and 1891, almost a decade after Marx died. But they all constitute echoes of Locus 8, Marx's reference to proletarian dictatorship in the *Critique of the Gotha Program*. To these last written uses, we may append as a kind of postscript a final hearsay use of the expression in 1893, reported in the memoirs of the Russian Marxist Alexei Voden.

In 1890, when the German Social Democratic Party emerged from twelve years of persecution following the lapse of Bismarck's Anti-Socialist Law, it seemed appropriate to draw up a new party program to replace the dated Gotha pronouncement of 1875. Hearing of these plans, Engels perceived a golden opportunity to influence the new program in the right direction by bringing to light Marx's never-published critique of the earlier pronouncement. Such a coup de main would strike not only at the remnants of Lassalleanism, but also at a newer brand of reformism already visible in the party's Reichstag fraction.[85]

The idea of publishing the critique evidently struck Engels immediately, and he must have reread the fifteen-year-old manuscript in anticipation. At least there is no other way to explain the sudden reappearance of the phrase "dictatorship of the proletariat," after fifteen years

85.   See *Werke*, 37:484–85.

of hibernation, in a letter Engels sent to Conrad Schmidt on October 27, 1890, scarcely a week after the decision had been taken to draft a new program. The phrase falls quite casually from Engels' pen in this long letter to the young Social Democratic economist concerning Marx's views on the relationship of political power to economic development. Political acts, he was concerned to say, are not always mere passive by-products of economic change, but can themselves affect the economy, contrary to a caricature of Marxist doctrines that had recently been published by Paul Barth:

[Locus 9]
If therefore Barth supposes that we deny any and every reaction of the political, etc., reflexes of the economic movement upon the movement itself, he is simply tilting at windmills. He has only got to look at Marx's *Eighteenth Brumaire*, which deals almost exclusively with the *particular* part played by political struggles and events; of course, within their *general* dependence upon economic conditions. Or *Capital*, the section on the working day, for instance, where legislation, which is surely a political act, has such a trenchant effect. Or the section on the history of the bourgeoisie. (Chapter XXIV.) Or why do we fight for the political dictatorship of the proletariat [*die politische Diktatur des Proletariats*] if political power is economically impotent? Force (that is state power) is also an economic power.[86]

Here, as in Locus 5b, the phrase seems nothing more than an incidental synonym for "rule of the proletariat," almost certainly reactivated in Engels' vocabulary by seeing the old slogan in Marx's critique.

Following up his scheme to publish the Gotha critique, Engels wrote his old friend, Karl Kautsky, editor of *Neue Zeit*, and received his support to print the document in the party's leading theoretical journal. In their exchanges on the practical details of publication, both men were concerned about the wounded sensibilities of old Lassalleans in the party and agreed to delete a few personal references, but they decided to leave the basic content intact. Neither man expressed any concern whatever about the old slogan.[87] Keeping the project as secret as possible, even from the other party leaders, Kautsky then suddenly

---

86. *Selected Correspondence*, p. 484.
87. *Friedrich Engels' Briefwechsel mit Karl Kautsky*, ed. Benedikt Kautsky (Vienna: Danubia, 1955), pp. 268–76.

published the document in February 1891. The bombshell did indeed cause great consternation among old Lassalleans, new reformists, and even among the top party leaders who disliked Engels' boat-rocking fait accompli. The shock waves extended even beyond party circles into the Reichstag itself. The National Liberal spokesman, Rudolf von Bennigsen, rose on February 28 to proclaim that the Social Democrats, far from appreciating their newly restored legal rights, were now publicizing Marx's call for bloody revolution and a "dictatorship of the proletariat." Stung by this accusation, one of the reformist-minded Social Democratic deputies, Karl Grillenberger, rose in response:

> Herr Dr. von Bennigsen has forgotten to add that the Social Democratic Party *rejected* this proposal Marx had made for its program. Marx was in fact annoyed that the German Social Democratic Party had worked out its program as it saw fit in view of conditions in Germany, and that therefore in our view there was never any question of a revolutionary dictatorship of the proletariat.[88]

Kautsky reported this incident to Engels, adding that "a lot of nonsense has been written about the dictatorship of the proletariat. . . . If only these people would read before they complain. Instead of dictatorship, what now figures everywhere is Liebknecht's idea of 'growing into' ['*Hineinwachsen*'] socialism."[89] Kautsky's letter arrived just as Engels was beginning an introduction for the twentieth-anniversary reedition of Marx's *Civil War in France*, and his obvious annoyance with the likes of Grillenberger found expression there in a new and provocative use of the phrase "dictatorship of the proletariat."

In the course of his introduction Engels pointed out that the Commune was led primarily by Proudhonists and Blanquists, yet "in both cases the irony of history willed—as is usual when doctrinaires come to the helm—that both did the opposite of what the doctrines of their school prescribed." Thus the Blanquists "started out from the viewpoint that a relatively small number of resolute, well-organized men would be able, at a given favorable moment, . . . to seize the helm of state. . . . This involved, above all, the strictest, dictatorial centralization of all

---

88. Incident recounted in editorial notes, ibid., pp. 286–87, with quotation from *Stenographische Berichte der Verhandlungen des Reichstags* for session of February 28, 1891.

89. Letter of January 9, 1891, *Friedrich Engels' Briefwechsel mit Karl Kautsky*, p. 285.

power in the hands of the new revolutionary government." Despite these preconceptions, the Blanquists found themselves obliged by mass pressure and force of circumstances to take part in "the shattering of the former state power and its replacement by a new and truly democratic one," a new government that renounced centralism and invited the provinces "to form a free federation of all French Communes."[90]

With glowing praise for the "correctness" of these historic steps, Engels went on to describe how the Communards had moved beyond the mere establishment of a democratic republic and actually begun the task of dismantling the state itself. It was necessary to emphasize this point, he added, "because in Germany particularly the superstitious belief in the state has been carried over from philosophy into the general consciousness of the bourgeoisie and even of many workers." He concluded:

[Locus 10a, b, and c]
And people think they have taken quite an extraordinarily bold step forward when they have rid themselves of belief in hereditary monarchy and swear by the democratic republic. In reality, however, the state is nothing but a machine for the oppression of one class by another, and indeed in the democratic republic no less than in the monarchy; and at best an evil inherited by the proletariat after its victorious struggle for class supremacy, whose worst sides the victorious proletariat, just like the Commune, cannot avoid having to lop off at once as much as possible until such time as a generation reared in new, free social conditions is able to throw the entire lumber of the state on the scrap heap.

Of late, the Social Democratic philistine [Grillenberger!] has once more been filled with wholesome terror at the words: Dictatorship of the Proletariat [Diktatur des Proletariats]. Well and good, gentlemen, do you want to know what this dictatorship looks like? Look at the Paris Commune. That was the Dictatorship of the Proletariat.[91]

Thus did the irritated patriarch of European socialism retroactively bestow dictatorial status on the Paris Commune in order to strike a "wholesome terror" into the hearts of Grillenberger and his ilk. For

90. *Selected Works*, 1:437–39.
91. Ibid., pp. 439–40.

our purposes, however, it may be more important to notice that Engels labeled the Commune a dictatorship *not* because it involved "the strictest, dictatorial centralization of all power in the hands of the new revolutionary government" (the Blanquist formula), but because it was a provisional government of the "victorious proletariat," and indeed a "truly democratic one," which had already begun to "lop off" the worst features of the state itself, to "do away with all the old repressive machinery."[92] Thus we see once more that, in Engels' conception of dictatorship, power would be exercised by a proletarian majority acting through provisionally established democratic institutions, rather than by a self-appointed vanguard committee. His specific comments on the Commune make it clear that, while power would have to be in the hands of the workers generally, it need not be in the hands of convinced Marxists or of any single party at all. Moreover, the assigned task of his dictatorship was in the first instance to destroy institutions rather than people, and particularly the repressive institutions—the standing army, the prison system, etc.—of the old regime, harking back to Marx's original 1848 assertion that every revolution required an energetic dictatorship for the purpose of "shattering and eliminating the remnants of old institutions."[93] No educational tasks of any kind were mentioned by Engels.

The final echo of Gotha followed three months later. When the party executive had worked out a first draft for the new program, they sent a copy to Engels, among other authorities, for his comments and suggestions.[94] Here was an even better opportunity to influence this important pronouncement, and Engels interrupted his vacation to write out an extended and thoughtful commentary that was later published as "Zur Kritik des sozialdemokratischen Programmentwurfs 1891," his critique of the Erfurt Program, which is every bit as essential for an understanding of the political ideas of Classical Marxism as its more famous predecessor. Engels' main object, as he confided to Kautsky, was to "let fly at the conciliatory opportunism of *Vorwärts* and at the *frischfrommfröhlichfreie 'Hineinwachsen'* of the filthy old mess 'into socialist society.' "[95]

92.   Ibid., p. 438.

93.   See n. 20 above.

94.   See *August Bebels Briefwechsel mit Friedrich Engels,* ed. Werner Blumenberg (The Hague: Mouton, 1965), pp. 420–22.

95.   Literally: "cheerful-pious-merry-free 'growth' " (letter of June 29, 1881, *Selected Correspondence,* p. 485); German words restored from *Werke,* 38:125.

Engels launched the political section of his critique with an immediate assault on the idea of *"Hineinwachsen,"* the belief that the old society might grow gradually, imperceptibly, and peacefully into the new one. Such a process, he wrote, is conceivable in democratic countries like America, France, and Britain, "where you can do whatever you want constitutionally as soon as you have a majority of the people behind you." But in Germany, "where the government is practically all-powerful and the Reichstag . . . without real power," it is sheer illusion. And the ten political demands included in the new draft program still deferentially avoided any clear call to democratize that crucial executive power. "If all these ten demands were granted we would have various new means for carrying through our principal demand but not the principal demand itself." That principal political demand was for a democratic republic:

[Locus 11]

If one thing is certain, it is that our party and the working class can only come to power under the form of a democratic republic. That is, indeed, the specific form of the dictatorship of the proletariat [*Diktatur des Proletariats*], as the great French Revolution has already shown. It is unthinkable that our best people should become ministers under an emperor, like [Johannes] Miquel. Now, it does not appear legally possible to place the demand for a republic directly in the program, . . . [which incidentally] shows how colossal the illusion is that a republic could be established there in a comfortable, peaceful manner, and not only a republic but even the communist society.

Nevertheless, one can if need be squeeze by the demand for a republic. What can and should be made, in my view, is the demand for the *concentration of all political power in the hands of the popular representative body.*[96]

Here at the end of his years, Engels reaffirmed his lifelong position as a principled democratic revolutionary: while some countries had opened a path by which a majority might peacefully and legally achieve communism, such a majority in semiabsolutist Germany would still find it necessary to employ force.[97] Even more, Engels now re-

96. *Werke*, 22:233–35.
97. These ideas will be developed more extensively in volume 2.

moved all doubt that his definition of dictatorship was unique to himself and Marx, by stating expressly that a "democratic republic" would be the "specific form of the dictatorship of the proletariat." According to twentieth-century criteria, such an assertion would be a patent self-contradiction. According to Marx and Engels' definition, however, any government during a revolutionary *Provisorium* is necessarily dictatorial by virtue of its extralegality. As his example, Engels must have been referring to the "great French Revolution" of *1871*, since neither he nor Marx ever regarded the Jacobin Republic as a proletarian government. The Paris Commune had been established through citywide elections held during the *Provisorium* that followed the violent rupture with Versailles on March 18. Functioning thus outside the framework of any established constitutional law, the Commune was both democratic and dictatorial at the same time. It was a short-lived miniature prototype of the ultimate dictatorship of the proletariat.

By tracing the history of the slogan "dictatorship of the proletaritat" through these eleven successive writings, we may understand the controversial idea in its proper historical setting. If not just a "little expression," as Kautsky would have it, neither was it "the very essence of Marx's teaching," à la Lenin. The phrase was never used in any of the masters' more substantial publications but was employed only to express factional compromises or distinctions in their dealings with other currents of the socialist movement: first as a compromise slogan with the Blanquists in 1850, and then as a counterposed idea of dictatorship to be distinguished from the Blanquist notion; next as an emphatic means of rebutting the anarchist call for an immediate dissolution of the state; and finally as a provocative way of striking a "wholesome terror" into the faint hearts of Lassalleans and reformist Social Democrats. The *rule* of the proletariat was surely "the very essence of Marx's teaching," but to label it "dictatorship" was in truth little more than factional politics.

As a kind of postscript to this chapter, we may inspect the last known reference to the dictatorship of the proletariat—a most remarkable one—in a conversation Engels had with Alexei Voden, as reported in the latter's memoirs. A young Russian student and protégé of Georgii Plekhanov, the father of Russian Marxism, Voden was just in the process of outgrowing his master's tutelage when he visited Engels in London on several occasions during the spring of 1893. They conversed about philosophy and Marx's early writings but also—inevitably—about the

Russian revolutionary movement. The increasingly bitter rivalry between Marxist Social Democrats and the Populists (*Narodniki*) was a development Engels deplored, for he found much to admire in the Populists' revolutionary zeal, and he feared Plekhanov was too doctrinaire in his dealings with them. He urged upon Voden the importance of avoiding a confrontation, and the young man felt obliged, as he remembered, "to make it clear that such an admonition might have a dour effect on Plekhanov." Voden continued:

Engels asked how Plekhanov personally stood on the question of the dictatorship of the proletariat. I had to concede that, as opposed to myself, Plekhanov had frequently asserted that when "we" would be in power "we" naturally would grant freedoms to no one but "ourselves." ... To my question, who would logically be included among these monopolists of freedom, Plekhanov had answered: the working class, under the leadership of those comrades who have correctly understood the teaching of Marx and who have drawn the correct conclusions from this teaching. To my question, is there an objective criterion for the correct understanding of Marx's teaching and for drawing the correct conclusions therefrom, Plekhanov limited himself to the suggestion that all this was set forth with "sufficient clarity" in his (Plekhanov's) works. After Engels had inquired whether I personally could put up with an objective criterion of that sort, he made the conjecture that the application of such criteria would either transform Russian Social Democracy into a sect—with unavoidable and most undesirable practical consequences—or might produce a series of splits.[98]

Engels went on to compare Plekhanov to H. M. Hyndman, the English Marxist who had a similar penchant for converting Marx's theories into a new "orthodoxy."[99] Under parallel circumstances, in reference to his French followers, Marx himself had once gibed, "All I

98. "At the Dawn of 'Legal Marxism,' " first published in *Letopisi Marksizma* (Moscow, 1927), 4:87–96 and translated in part in *Reminiscences of Marx and Engels* (Moscow: Foreign Languages, n.d.), pp. 325–34. This translation does not include the crucial passage quoted above, however, and I have translated it from the German in Marx and Engels, *Die russische Kommune: Kritik eines Mythos*, ed. Maximilien Rubel (Munich: Hanser, 1972), p. 188.
99. *Die russische Kommune*, p. 189; see also Rubel's editorial comment, p. 174; *Werke*, 22:545.

know is that I am not a Marxist."[100] Paradoxically, it was Marx and Engels' very scientism, their cavalier presumption that they were dealing in science while other socialist thinkers were dealing in dogma, that saved them from the worst excesses of the latter's characteristic intolerance. Precisely because their theories were deemed science rather than a "teaching," belief in them was conceived not as a matter of faith but as the consequence of convincing empirical evidence. Marx and Engels held their own theories, like all other scientific findings, to be provisional and subject to revision in the light of new evidence. The pursuit of new evidence, and scientific investigation generally, could take place only in an atmosphere of intellectual freedom, not in the stifling dogmatism of any orthodoxy, even a "Marxist" orthodoxy. It is justly fitting that Engels' last reference to proletarian dictatorship, in the ironic and barbed question posed above, should have repudiated the intolerant dogmatism he saw aborning among the Russian Marxists.

100. Recalled by Engels in his letter to Conrad Schmidt, August 5, 1890, *Selected Correspondence*, p. 472.

⚜[10]⚜

Conclusion:
Marxism and Totalitarian Democracy

I<small>T IS TIME TO DRAW</small> some overall conclusions about the relationship of Marx and Engels to the political tradition for which J. L. Talmon has devised the label "totalitarian democracy." With a bit of pushing and wedging, it is not too difficult to fit the two men within the broadest definition of what is supposed to distinguish totalitarian from liberal democracy. One may take their scientism and their oft-expressed intolerance of differing views as revealing an "assumption of a sole and exclusive truth in politics." In some sense, they undoubtedly regarded the classless society as a "preordained, harmonious and perfect scheme of things," although they were always reluctant to specify details. And at least down through the year 1850 they certainly treated this vision as "a matter of immediate urgency, a challenge for direct action, an imminent event."[1]

The difficulty is that such a sweeping definition, if seriously applied, would include many thinkers no one would really want to label totalitarian. Thus, for example, the belief that reason and/or the Divine will prescribe a single "correct" way to organize human society has probably been held by *most* of the great political thinkers in the Western tradition. Not very many of them have been notable, either, for their tolerance of differing, "erroneous" conceptions. Even among the tolerant minority the assumption of certainty has generally lingered until quite recent times. Such a model liberal democrat as Thomas Jefferson, for instance, gave voice to the common assumption in the very vocabulary of his classic utterance: "Error of opinion may be

---

1. See Talmon's definition cited above, chap. 1, n. 5.

tolerated where reason is left free to combat it."[2] This distinguished sentiment still presupposed one correct answer, given by reason, from which all deviations were "error," and further that it was the duty of reason to "combat" such error. Of course, to combat is not to suppress, and Jefferson remained willing to allow error to be "tolerated" in this sense. But then, would Marx and Engels have taken a different stand? Although Marx especially was not by temperament inclined toward easygoing tolerance, there is little reason to suppose that either man would have repudiated Jefferson's famous maxim, particularly if the word "science" were substituted for "reason." In 1846, it will be remembered, Marx and Engels formally censured the True Socialist Hermann Kriege for treating his ideological enemies as heretics who needed to be punished, instead of simply as opponents whom one combats (*"mit dem man* kämpft"—it is interesting that they even employed the same verb as Jefferson).[3] Had the two men been really thoroughgoing fanatics, they would have created for their followers the sort of organization that Proudhon secretly imagined, instead of the impressively open and democratic structures we have encountered. In some respects, their scientism itself encouraged tolerance rather than the opposite, as revealed in the conversation between Engels and Voden cited at the end of chapter 9. A half century after the censure of Kriege, Engels still objected to treating political and social ideas as if they were religious dogmas. Thus, an assumption of certainty may be combined with a willingness to tolerate differences, perhaps condescendingly as "error," even by personalities not temperamentally disposed toward tolerance.

In a similar vein, no one could doubt the existence of a chiliastic element in Marx and Engels' thought, although its passionate immediacy clearly declined after 1850. Even at its peak during that year, however, neither man imagined the New Jerusalem could be built in a day, and they poured water into the wine of those among their compatriots who did. They never claimed any special personal right to punish the sinful of the old world or lead the righteous into the new

2. "First Inaugural Address" (1801), in *Documents of American History*, ed. Henry Steele Commager (New York: Appleton-Century-Crofts, 1948), p. 187. Jefferson's reputation as a civil libertarian has suffered considerably in recent years after closer scrutiny of some of his presidential actions: see Leonard W. Levy, *Jefferson and Civil Liberties: The Darker Side* (Cambridge: Harvard, 1963).

3. See above, chap. 8, n. 9.

one. As has been argued before, chiliastic expectation—whether secular or religious—need not inevitably lead to totalitarian conclusions, else one would have to cast an entire pantheon of Jewish prophets and Christian saints into the hellfire of political perdition.

If the word "totalitarian" is to be more than just a synonym for fanatic, if totalitarian democracy is to be a useful concept rather than merely an abusive epithet, then the label ought to be reserved for those particular chiliasts who also endorse some or all of the characteristic features of twentieth-century totalitarianism—the elite party, the minority seizure of power, the subsequent one-party dictatorship, the systematic use of political terror, the centrally controlled reeducation of the masses. What Talmon has called "crystallized" totalitarian democracy is recognizably totalitarian according to the usual understanding of the word. It is the program created by Babeuf, and passed down to Buonarroti and Blanqui.

The central argument of the preceding chapters has been that Classical Marxism really had little connection to this specific tradition of totalitarian democracy. Contrary to widespread impressions, there is no evidence that Babeuf or Blanqui played any role whatever among the many influences on Marx and Engels' early political and intellectual development. And although our purview has not extended beyond the year 1850 (except in chapter 9), we may nonetheless draw fairly definitive conclusions respecting the four particular points that constitute the distinguishing essence of the totalitarian-democratic program.

1. Since Marx and Engels never associated themselves after 1850 with any organization that looked remotely like a vanguard party of the enlightened few, the case against them must rest entirely on the Communist League, which bore some elitist trappings, to be sure, and had its historical roots squarely in the Blanquist tradition. Before jumping to conclusions, however, one must take account of a formidable battery of confuting evidence: Marx and Engels' unvarying repudiation of conspiracies and of any responsibility for the seizure of power itself, with or without mass support; the painstakingly democratic internal structure of the league; its open-ended recruitment policies and the moderate demands made on members; and most of all, the ease with which Marx and Engels abandoned the organization in 1848, in 1850, and in 1852, showing that they did not conceive it to be indispensable at all. Rather they saw it simply as one ephemeral contribution to the many-sided efforts of the working class to organize itself into a

decisive political force. Where legal conditions permitted, the two men made it clear they preferred an open mass party such as the Chartist movement in Britain or the nationwide workers' party they tried to create in Germany in 1849.

2. The evidence that Marx and Engels supported minority revolution must also be sought almost entirely in the early period that climaxed in 1850, rather than afterwards. Of the two strategies for attaining power advanced during these early years, only the second is problematic, since Strategy I, appropriate for Great Britain, involved the overthrow of a propertied oligarchy by the proletarian majority of the nation. Strategy II may justifiably raise skeptical eyebrows when it is understood as a "permanent revolution"—initiated, to be sure, by an alliance of the majority classes in countries like France and Germany, but carried to its ultimate conclusion by the proletariat alone. The time contemplated as necessary to complete such a permanent revolution, as we have seen, then becomes the critical issue. While Willich and the exiled Blanquists projected a span of weeks or months, and frankly endorsed minority rule, the evidence makes it clear that Marx and Engels envisaged a process extending through a couple of decades at least, during which time the proletariat was expected—as a consequence of economic modernization—to develop into the majority class. The phrase "permanent revolution" itself appeared only in the compromise formulations of 1850 and disappeared thereafter, to be recalled only once, retrospectively, in Engels' final years.

3. Marx and Engels' most bloodthirsty pronouncements on the subject of revolutionary terror similarly belong to the period 1848–1850, after which they condemned terror far more often and more sharply than they ever praised it. The oft-quoted terror passages of the *Neue Rheinische Zeitung*, once set in their proper historical context, appear to be helpless cries of outrage against the physical brutality of the counterrevolution, rather than a serious program of action; in their day-to-day behavior as "practicing" revolutionaries, the two men showed distinct cautiousness and restraint. The final and renowned invocation of terror in the March *Circular* was in all likelihood the inspiration of Willich, since no similar recommendations can be found in any of Marx and Engels' other 1850 writings. While they certainly envisaged the use of force during and immediately after the revolution to "crush the resistance of the bourgeoisie," a systematic policy of terror was not integral to their vision of revolution, since they did not imagine

a minority would be imposing its will on the reluctant majority, but quite the contrary. Only a minority of dispossessed bourgeois and their hangers-on would pose any threat to the democratic revolution.

4. Among the four specific problems, only the idea of proletarian dictatorship has a significant history after the period of our concern, but by tracing the career of this slogan to 1893 we can conclude that it has little in common with the totalitarian-democratic notion of educational dictatorship by an enlightened elite. Insofar as the phrase had an exact meaning, it referred to the unavoidably extralegal character of an otherwise democratic government by the proletarian majority during the *Provisorium* that must immediately follow any revolution. The phrase figured more prominently, however, first as a tactical compromise slogan with the Blanquists, and then as a polemical device to use against anarchists and assorted reformists. While certain general repressive functions were assigned to this constituent dictatorship, the crucial educational mission of the Babouvist-Blanquist model is entirely missing from the Classical Marxist conception.

This last observation brings us back to the basic underlying assumption of any totalitarian-democratic ideology—that the masses are, alas, too ignorant or indolent to emancipate themselves. Hence the integral need for the vanguard and the other grim features of the program. Perhaps the key distinguishing feature of Marx and Engels' thinking, among the diverse currents of early socialism, was precisely their conviction, their ultimate democratic faith, that the masses could and would educate *themselves*, organize *themselves*, liberate *themselves*, and rule *themselves*. No external agent, no *deus ex machina* in the form of an enlightened elite, was required in their vision, although of course they never denied the incidental helpfulness of intellectuals like themselves. If Marx and Blanqui both proposed a constituent dictatorship, only the latter conceived it to have any educational function.

It is necessary to stress this point because so many of these totalitarian-democratic ideas have found their way *into* the Marxist tradition in the twentieth century. One need only examine one of Lenin's classic passages on proletarian dictatorship to see how strongly educational themes are sounded:

The proletariat needs state power, the centralized organization of force, the organization of violence, both for the purpose of crushing the resistance of the exploiters and for the purpose of *guiding*

the great mass of the population—the peasantry, the petty-bour-
geoisie, the semi-proletarians—in the work of organizing Socialist
economy.

By educating a workers' party, Marxism educates the vanguard
of the proletariat, capable of assuming power and of *leading the
whole people* to Socialism, of directing and organizing the new order, of being the teacher, guide and leader of all the toiling and
exploited in the task of building up their social life without the
bourgeoisie and against the bourgeoisie.[4]

Here, in a whole series of tutorial relationships, the great mass of the
population would be "guided" by Russia's small proletariat, which in
turn would be "led" by a still smaller vanguard of the proletariat, and
this vanguard in turn would be "educated" by "Marxism," that is, the
doctrines disseminated by party intellectuals like Lenin himself.

To Lenin's persistent stress on tutorial relationships, perhaps the classic response, in the spirit of Marx and Engels' original values, came
from his most sympathetic but also most devastating critic, Rosa Luxemburg:

The working class demands the right to make its mistakes and
learn in the dialectic of history.

Let us speak plainly. Historically, the errors committed by a truly
revolutionary movement are infinitely more fruitful than the infal-
libility of the cleverest Central Committee.[5]

Insofar as Marxism has become, in the twentieth century, a doctrine
exploited by the alienated intelligentsia of underdeveloped countries
to win support for, and justify, their own modernizing dictatorships,
the idea of the vanguard and of educational rule necessarily came
to play a role which had no foundation in original Marxism and which
harked back to the earlier tradition of Babeuf and Blanqui. Marx and
Engels must thus be distinguished not only from this earlier tradition
but from most of their twentieth-century "followers," as holding to the
ultimate democratic conviction that the emancipation of the masses
intrinsically must be the work of the masses themselves.

4. *State and Revolution* (New York: International, 1943), pp. 23–24.
5. "Organizational Questions of the Russian Social Democracy" (1904), in
Rosa Luxemburg Speaks, ed. Mary-Alice Waters (New York: Pathfinder, 1970),
p. 130.

BIBLIOGRAPHY
INDEX

Bibliography

Writings of Marx and Engels

A word of explanation seems appropriate regarding the various editions of Marx and Engels' writings that have been used in the foregoing book and that are listed below. Of the various collected editions, the most complete is the forty-odd-volume *Werke* published in East Germany. This set has become standard for serious scholarship in the Western world, and I have cited it throughout for those writings that are not available in English. An earlier undertaking started in the 1920s, the *Gesamtausgabe* (*MEGA*), was even more comprehensive and scholarly but was never finished. In this earlier set, each writing of the masters was published in its *original* language; thus I have used it rather than the *Werke* for Engels' essays that first appeared in the English press, as well as for a few minor items left out of the *Werke*. (A comprehensive bibliography of all Marx's writings and most of Engels' may be found in Maximilien Rubel, *Bibliographie des oeuvres de Karl Marx* [Paris: Rivière, 1956], together with its *Supplément* published in 1960.) The only significant writings for our period that remain unpublished at this date are Marx's excerpt notebooks, which I have examined at the Internationaal Instituut voor Sociale Geschiedenis in Amsterdam. They have proven useful mainly in a negative way—for example, by showing Marx's *lack* of interest in the Babouvist-Blanquist tradition, etc. For the English-speaking world, there is now in preparation a full-scale translation of the *Werke,* to be published in the United States by International Publishers under the title *Collected Works.* At the present time, however, only the more important writings of Marx and Engels are available in English, and they are scattered in numerous editions and collections. I have made an effort to use the most standard editions, except where there are more recent translations of greater merit.

GERMAN EDITIONS

Marx, Karl, and Engels, Friedrich. *Historisch-kritische Gesamtausgabe*. Edited by D. Ryazanoff. 11 vols. Frankfurt, Berlin, Moscow: Marx-Engels-Lenin Institut, 1927–35. Cited as *MEGA*.
———. *Werke*. 39 volumes with a supplemental volume in two parts. Berlin: Dietz, 1956–68. Cited as *Werke*.

ENGLISH EDITIONS

Engels, Friedrich. *The Condition of the Working Class in England*. Translated and edited by W. O. Henderson and W. H. Chaloner. Stanford: Stanford, 1968.

————. *Engels: Selected Writings.* Edited by W. O. Henderson. Baltimore: Penguin, 1967.

————. *The German Revolutions: The Peasant War in Germany and Germany: Revolution and Counter-Revolution.* Edited by Leonard Krieger. Chicago: Chicago, 1967.

Marx, Karl. *The Cologne Communist Trial.* Translated and edited by Rodney Livingstone. New York: International, 1971.

————. *Critique of Hegel's 'Philosophy of Right.'* Translated and edited by Joseph O'Malley. Cambridge: Cambridge, 1970.

————. "The Difference between the Democritean and Epicurean Philosophy of Nature." Translated by Norman D. Livergood, in his *Activity in Marx's Philosophy.* The Hague: Nijhoff, 1967.

————. *Early Writings.* Translated and edited by T. B. Bottomore. New York: McGraw-Hill, 1964.

————. *The Poverty of Philosophy.* Edited by C. P. Dutt and V. Chattopadhyaya. New York: International, n.d.

————. *Writings of the Young Marx on Philosophy and Society.* Translated and edited by Loyd D. Easton and Kurt H. Guddat. Garden City: Doubleday, 1967. Cited as *Writings.*

Marx, Karl, and Engels, Friedrich. *Basic Writings on Politics and Philosophy.* Edited by Lewis S. Feuer. Garden City: Doubleday, Anchor Books, 1959.

————. *The Communist Manifesto.* Edited by D. Ryazanoff. New York: International, 1930.

————. *The German Ideology.* Moscow: Progress, 1964.

————. *The Holy Family.* Translated by R. Dixon. Moscow: Foreign Languages, 1956.

————. *On Religion.* Moscow: Foreign Languages, 1957.

————. *The Revolution of 1848–49: Articles from the "Neue Rheinische Zeitung."* Translated by S. Ryazanskaya. New York: International, 1972.

————. *The Russian Menace to Europe.* Edited by Paul W. Blackstock and Bert F. Hoselitz. Glencoe: Free Press, 1952.

————. *Selected Correspondence: 1846–1895.* Translated by Dona Torr. New York: International, 1942.

————. *Selected Works.* 2 vols. Moscow: Foreign Languages, 1951.

————. *Writings on the Paris Commune.* Edited by Hal Draper. New York: Monthly Review, 1971.

Marx, Karl; Engels, Friedrich; and Lenin, V. I. *Anarchism and Anarcho-Syndicalism.* New York: International, 1972.

Struik, Dirk J., ed. *Birth of the Communist Manifesto.* New York: International, 1971. (Contains translation of June and October drafts and other related documents.)

Other Primary Sources

Andréas, Bert. *Gründungsdokumente des Bundes der Kommunisten (Juni bis September 1847).* Hamburg: Hauswedell, 1969.

Blumenberg, Werner. "Zur Geschichte des Bundes der Kommunisten: Die Aussagen des Peter Gerhardt Röser." *International Review of Social History* 9 (1964):81–122.

Draper, Hal. "Joseph Weydemeyer's 'Dictatorship of the Proletariat.'" *Labor History* 3 (1962):208–17.

Feuerbach, Ludwig. *The Essence of Christianity.* Translated by George Eliot. New York: Harper, 1957.

Freymond, Jacques, ed. *La Première Internationale: Recueil de documents . . . .* 2 vols. Geneva: Droz, 1962.

Gerth, Hans, ed. *The First International: Minutes of the Hague Congress . . . .* Madison: Wisconsin, 1958.

Hegel, Georg Wilhelm Friedrich. *Hegel's Philosophy of Right.* Translated and edited by T. M. Knox. Oxford: Clarendon, 1962.

Hess, Moses. *Briefwechsel.* Edited by Edmund Silberner. The Hague: Mouton, 1959.

Institute of Marxism-Leninism (Moscow). *Documents of the First International: The General Council . . . Minutes.* 5 vols. Moscow: Progress, [1964].

Institut für Marxismus-Leninismus (Berlin). *Der Bund der Kommunisten: Dokumente und Materialien.* Vol. 1: *1836–1849.* Berlin: Dietz, 1970. Cited as *Bund Dokumente.*

Maximoff, G. P., ed. *The Political Philosophy of Bakunin: Scientific Anarchism.* Glencoe: Free Press, 1953.

Nicolaievsky, Boris. "Toward a History of 'The Communist League' 1847–1852." *International Review of Social History* 1 (1956):234–52.

Schieder, Wolfgang. "Der Bund der Kommunisten im Sommer 1850: Drei Dokumente aus dem Marx-Engels Nachlass." *International Review of Social History* 13 (1968):29–57.

Wermuth, Karl, and Stieber, Wilhelm. *Die Communisten-Verschwörungen des 19. Jahrhunderts.* 2 vols. 1853–54. Reprint (2 vols. in 1). Hildesheim: Olms, 1969.

Secondary Literature

For the sake of handy reference, the following list is arranged in simple alphabetical order. Readers interested in a particular topic may consult the footnotes in the foregoing text at the point where the topic is first seriously introduced. There I have tried to comment on, or at least list, the more significant literature on each particular topic dealt with in the work.

Adams, Henry P. *Karl Marx in His Earlier Writings.* 1940. Reprint. New York: Russell and Russell, 1965.

Akademiia Obshchestvennykh Nauk (Moscow). *Aus der Geschichte des Kampfes von Marx und Engels für die proletarische Partei.* Berlin: Dietz, 1961.

Althusser, Louis. *For Marx.* Translated by Ben Brewster. New York: Pantheon, 1969.

Andréas, Bert. *Le Manifeste Communiste de Marx et Engels: Histoire et Bibliographie 1848–1918.* Milan: Feltrinelli, 1963.

Aptheker, Herbert, ed. *Marxism and Democracy: A Symposium.* New York: Humanities, 1965.

Arendt, Hannah. *The Origins of Totalitarianism.* 2nd ed. New York: Harcourt, Brace, 1958.

Ash, William F. *Marxism and Moral Concepts.* New York: Monthly Review, 1964.

Avineri, Shlomo. "Marx and Jewish Emancipation." *Journal of the History of Ideas* 25 (1964):445–50.

———. "Marx and the Intellectuals." *Journal of the History of Ideas* 28 (1967): 269–78.

———. *The Social and Political Thought of Karl Marx.* Cambridge: Cambridge, 1968.

———, ed. *Marx's Socialism.* New York: Lieber-Atherton, 1973.

Barion, Jakob. *Hegel und die marxistische Staatslehre.* Bonn: Bouvier, 1963.

Bartel, Horst, and Schmidt, Walter. "Zur Entwicklung der Auffassungen von Marx und Engels über die proletarische Partei." In *Marxismus und deutsche Arbeiterbewegung*, edited by Deutsche Akademie der Wissenschaften, pp. 7–101. Berlin: Dietz, 1970.

Becker, Gerhard. *Karl Marx und Friedrich Engels in Köln, 1848–1849: Zur Geschichte des Kölner Arbeitervereins.* Berlin: Rütten und Loening, 1963.

Berger, Martin Edgar. "War, Armies, and Revolution: Friedrich Engels' Military Thought." Ph.D. dissertation, University of Pittsburgh, 1969.

Berlin, Isaiah. *Karl Marx: His Life and Environment.* 3rd ed. New York: Oxford, 1963.

Blumenberg, Werner. *Portrait of Marx: An Illustrated Biography.* Translated by Douglas Scott. New York: Herder and Herder, 1972.

Bockmuhl, Klaus Erich. *Leiblichkeit und Gesellschaft: Studien zur Religionskritik und Anthropologie im Frühwerk von Ludwig Feuerbach und Karl Marx.* Göttingen: Vanderhoeck und Ruprecht, 1961.

Bollnow, Hermann. "Engels Auffassung von Revolution . . ." In *Marxismusstudien*, edited by Iring Fetscher, 1:77–144. Tübingen: Mohr, 1954.

Brazill, William J. *The Young Hegelians.* New Haven: Yale, 1970.

Bruhat, Jean. "La révolution française et la formation de la pensée de Marx." *La pensée socialiste devant la Révolution française*, edited by the Société des Etudes Robespierristes, pp. 125–70. Paris: Clavreuil, 1966.

Cadogan, Peter. "Harney and Engels." *International Review of Social History* 10 (1965):66–104.

Carmichael, John. *Karl Marx: The Passionate Logician.* New York: Scribners, 1967.

Chang, Sherman. *The Marxian Theory of the State.* Philadelphia: Spencer, 1931.

Cole, G. D. H. *A History of Socialist Thought.* 5 vols. in 7. New York: St Martin's, 1953–60.

Cornu, Auguste. *Karl Marx et Friedrich Engels: Leur vie et leur oeuvre.* 3 vols. Paris: Presses Universitaires, 1955–62.

———. *Karl Marx et la révolution de 1848.* Paris: Presses Universitaires, 1948.

Dommanget, Maurice. *Les idées politiques et sociales d'Auguste Blanqui.* Paris: Rivière, 1957.

Dowe, Dieter. *Aktion und Organisation: Arbeiterbewegung, sozialistische und kommunistische Bewegung in der preussischen Rheinprovinz, 1820–1852.* Hannover: Literatur und Zeitgeschichte, 1970.

Draper, Hal. "Marx and the Dictatorship of the Proletariat." *Etudes de Marxologie*, edited by Maximilien Rubel, 6:5–73. Paris: Institut de Science Economique Appliquée, 1962. Abridged version in *New Politics* 1, no. 4 (Summer 1962): 91–104.

———. "The Principle of Self-Emancipation in Marx and Engels." In *The Socialist Register 1971*, edited by Ralph Miliband and John Saville. London: Merlin, 1971.

———. *The Two Souls of Socialism*. New York: Independent Socialist Clubs, 1966.

Dunayevskaya, Raya. *Marxism and Freedom . . . from 1776 until Today*. New York: Bookman, 1958.

Dupré, Louis K. *The Philosophical Foundations of Marxism*. New York: Harcourt, Brace, 1966.

Fetscher, Iring. *Marx and Marxism*. Translated by John Hargraves. New York: Herder and Herder, 1971.

Feuer, Lewis S. *Marx and the Intellectuals: A Set of Post-Ideological Essays*. Garden City: Doubleday, Anchor Books, 1969.

Förder, Herwig, *Marx und Engels am Vorabend der Revolution: Die Ausarbeitung der politischen Richtlinien für die deutschen Kommunisten (1846–1848)*. Berlin: Akademie, 1960.

———, and Hundt, Martin. "Zur Vorgeschichte von Engels' Arbeit 'Grundsätze des Kommunismus.'" *Beiträge zur Geschichte der Arbeiterbewegung* 12 (1970):60–85.

Friedrich, Carl J. "The Unique Character of Totalitarian Society." In *Totalitarianism*, edited by Carl J. Friedrich, pp. 47–60. Cambridge: Harvard, 1954.

Fromm, Erich. *Marx's Concept of Man*. New York: Ungar, 1961.

———, ed. *Socialist Humanism*. Garden City: Doubleday, 1965.

Garaudy, Roger. *Karl Marx: The Evolution of his Thought*. New York: International, 1967.

Grünberg, Carl. "Die Londoner Kommunistische Zeitschrift und andere Urkunden aus den Jahren 1847–1848." *Archiv für die Geschichte des Sozialismus und der Arbeiterbewegung* 9 (1921):249–341.

Hamerow, Theodore S. *Restoration, Revolution, Reaction: Economics and Politics in Germany, 1815–1871*. Princeton: Princeton, 1958.

Hammen, Oscar J. "Marx and the Agrarian Question." *American Historical Review* 77 (1972):679–704.

———. *The Red '48ers: Karl Marx and Friedrich Engels*. New York: Scribners, 1969.

Harrington, Michael. *Socialism*. New York: Saturday Review, 1972.

Hertz-Eichenrode, Dieter. "Karl Marx über das Bauerntum und die Bündnisfrage." *International Review of Social History* 11 (1966):382–402.

Hillmann, Günther. *Marx und Hegel: Von der Spekulation zur Dialektik*. Frankfurt a/M: Europäische Verlagsanstalt, 1966.

Hofmann, Werner. "Die Auffassung von der sozialistischen Revolution und der Diktatur des Proletariats bei Marx und Engels und in der kommunistischen Bewegung der Gegenwart." In *Marxismus in unserer Zeit: Beiträge zum zeitgenössischen Marxismus*, pp. 137–53. Frankfurt a/M: Marxistische Blätter, 1968.

Hook, Sidney. *From Hegel to Marx.* 2nd ed. Ann Arbor: Michigan, 1962.

——. *Marx and the Marxists: The Ambiguous Legacy.* Princeton: Van Nostrand, Anvil Books, 1955.

Hyppolite, Jean. *Studies on Marx and Hegel.* Translated by John O'Neill. New York: Basic Books, 1969.

Institut für Marxismus-Leninismus (Berlin). *Ex Libris Karl Marx und Friedrich Engels: Schicksal und Verzeichnis einer Bibliothek.* Berlin: Dietz, 1967.

Jackson, J. Hampden. *Marx, Proudhon, and European Socialism.* New York: Macmillan, 1958.

Johnson, Christopher H. "Communism and the Working Class before Marx: the Icarian Experience." *American Historical Review* 76 (1971):642–89.

Johnstone, Monty. "Marx and Engels and the Concept of the Party." In *The Socialist Register 1967,* edited by Ralph Miliband and John Saville, pp. 121–58. New York: Monthly Review, 1967.

Kamenka, Eugene. *The Ethical Foundations of Marxism.* New York: Praeger, 1962.

——. *Marxism and Ethics.* New York: St. Martin's, 1969.

Kandel, E. P., ed. *Marx und Engels und die ersten proletarischen Revolutionäre.* Translated from Russian by Richard Sperl. Berlin: Dietz, 1965.

Karl Marx: Chronik seines Lebens in Einzeldaten. Edited by Marx-Engels-Lenin Institute. Moscow: Marx-Engels, 1934.

Kautsky, Karl. *The Dictatorship of the Proletariat.* Translated by H. J. Stenning. 1919. Reprint. Ann Arbor: Michigan, 1964.

Kowalsky, Werner. *Vorgeschichte und Entstehung des Bundes der Gerechten.* Berlin: Rütten und Loening, 1962.

Künzli, Arnold. *Karl Marx: Eine Psychographie.* Vienna: Europa, 1966.

Kupisch, Karl. *Vom Pietismus zum Kommunismus.* Berlin: Lettner, 1953.

Landauer, Carl. *European Socialism.* 2 vols. Berkeley: California, 1959.

Laski, Harold. *Harold Laski on the Communist Manifesto.* New York: Random House, 1967.

Lichtheim, George. *From Marx to Hegel.* New York: Herder and Herder, 1971.

——. *Marxism: An Historical and Critical Study.* New York: Praeger, 1961.

——. *The Origins of Socialism.* New York: Praeger, 1969.

——. *A Short History of Socialism.* New York: Praeger, 1970.

Lobkowicz, Nicholas, ed. *Marx and the Western World.* Notre Dame: Notre Dame, 1967.

Löwith, Karl. *From Hegel to Nietzsche: The Revolution in Nineteenth-Century Thought.* Translated by David E. Green. New York: Holt, 1967.

Lowy, Michael. *La théorie de la révolution chez le jeune Marx.* Paris: Maspero, 1970.

McLellan, David. *Karl Marx: His Life and Thought.* New York: Harper, 1973.

——. *Marx Before Marxism.* New York: Harper, 1970.

——. *The Young Hegelians and Karl Marx.* New York: Praeger, 1969.

Maihofer, Werner. "Recht und Staat im Denken des jungen Marx." In *Karl Marx 1818–1968: Neue Studien zu Person und Lehre.* Mainz: Hase und Koehler, 1968.

Mandel, Ernest. *The Formation of the Economic Thought of Karl Marx.* Translated by Brian Pearce. New York: Monthly Review, 1971.

BIBLIOGRAPHY [351]

Mautner, Wilhelm. "Zur Geschichte des Begriffs 'Diktatur des Proletariats.'" *Archiv für die Geschichte des Sozialismus und der Arbeiterbewegung* 12 (1926):280–83.

Mayer, Gustav. *Friedrich Engels: Eine Biographie.* 2 vols. The Hague: Nijhoff, 1934. Abridged edition in English translation: *Friedrich Engels: A Biography.* New York: Knopf, 1936.

Mayer, Henry. "Marx, Engels and the Politics of the Peasantry." *Etudes de Marxologie*, edited by Maximilien Rubel, 3:91–151. Paris: Institut de Science Economique Appliquée, 1960.

Mayo, Henry B. *Democracy and Marxism.* New York: Oxford, 1955.

Mehring, Franz. *Karl Marx: The Story of His Life.* Translated by Edward Fitgerald. 1935. Reprint. Ann Arbor: Michigan, 1962.

Mende, Georg. *Karl Marx' Entwicklung vom revolutionären Demokraten zum Kommunisten.* 3rd ed. Berlin: Dietz, 1960.

Meyer, Alfred G. *Marxism: The Unity of Theory and Practice.* 2nd ed. Cambridge: Harvard, 1970.

Meyer, Hermann. "Karl Marx und die deutsche Revolution von 1848." *Historische Zeitschrift* 172 (1951):517–34.

Miliband, Ralph. "Marx and the State." In *The Socialist Register 1965*, edited by Ralph Miliband and John Saville, pp. 278–96. New York: Monthly Review, 1965.

Miller, Susanne. *Das Problem der Freiheit im Sozialismus.* Frankfurt a/M: Europäische Verlagsanstalt, 1964.

Molnár, Erik. *La politique d'alliances du marxisme (1848–1889).* Budapest: Akadémiai Kiadó, 1967.

Monz, Heinz. *Karl Marx und Trier.* Trier: Neu, 1964.

———. "Die rechtsethischen und rechtspolitischen Anschauungen von Heinrich Marx." *Archiv für Sozialgeschichte* 8 (1968):261–83.

Moore, Stanley. *The Critique of Capitalist Democracy: An Introduction to the Theory of the State in Marx, Engels, and Lenin.* New York: Paine-Whitman, 1957.

———. *Three Tactics: The Background in Marx.* New York: Monthly Review, 1963.

Mühlestein, Hans. "Marx and the Utopian Wilhelm Weitling." *Science and Society* 12 (1948):113–29.

Na'aman, Shlomo. "Zur Geschichte des Bundes der Kommunisten in Deutschland in der zweiten Phase seines Bestehens." *Archiv für Sozialgeschichte* 5 (1965): 5–82.

Nicolaievsky, Boris. "Who Is Distorting History?" *Proceedings of the American Philosophical Society* 105 (1961):209–36.

——— and Maenchen-Helfen, Otto. *Karl Marx: Man and Fighter.* Translated by Gwenda David and Eric Mosbacher. Philadelphia: Lippincott, 1936.

Nova, Fritz. *Frederick Engels: His Contributions to Political Theory.* New York: Philosophical Library, 1967.

Noyes, P. H. *Organization and Revolution: Working-Class Associations in the German Revolution of 1848–1849.* Princeton: Princeton, 1966.

Obermann, Karl. *Zur Geschichte des Bundes der Kommunisten 1849–52.* Berlin: Dietz, 1955.

——. "Zur Geschichte des Kommunistischen Korrespondenzkomitees im Jahre 1846, insbesondere im Rheinland und in Westfalen." *Beiträge zur Geschichte der deutschen Arbeiterbewegung* 4 (1962):116–43.

Papaioannou, Kostas. "Le parti totalitaire." *Le Contrat social* 10 (1966):161–70, 236–45.

Payne, Robert. *Marx.* New York: Simon and Schuster, 1968.

Plamenatz, John. *German Marxism and Russian Communism.* London: Longmans, Green, 1954.

——. *Man and Society.* 2 vols. New York: McGraw-Hill, 1963.

Popper, Karl R. *The Open Society and its Enemies.* Princeton: Princeton, 1950.

Pranger, Robert J. "Marx and Political Theory." *Review of Politics* 30 (1968):191–208.

Rosenberg, Arthur. *Democracy and Socialism: A Contribution to the Political History of the Past 150 Years.* Translated by George Rosen. London: Bell, 1939.

Rossiter, Clinton. *Constitutional Dictatorship: Crisis Government in the Modern Democracies.* New York: Harcourt, Brace, 1963.

Rubel, Maximilien. "Les Cahiers de lecture de Karl Marx." *International Review of Social History* 2 (1957):392–420; 5 (1960):39–76.

——. "Le concept de démocratie chez Marx." *Le Contrat social* 6 (1962):214–20. Modified version in English in *New Politics* 1, no. 2 (Winter 1962):78–90.

——. *Karl Marx: Essai de biographie intellectuelle.* Paris: Rivière, 1957.

——. *Marx–Chronik: Daten zu Leben und Werk.* Munich: Hanser, 1968.

——. "Remarques sur le concept du parti prolétarien chez Marx." *Revue Française de Sociologie* 2 (1961):165–76.

Sanderson, John. *An Interpretation of the Political Ideas of Marx and Engels.* New York: Ferhill, 1969.

——. "Marx and Engels on the State." *Western Political Quarterly* 16 (1963):946–55.

Schefold, Christoph. *Die Rechtsphilosophie des jungen Marx von 1842.* Munich: Beck, 1970.

Schieder, Wolfgang. *Anfänge der deutschen Arbeiterbewegung: Die Auslandsvereine im Jahrzehnt nach der Julirevolution von 1830.* Stuttgart: Klett, 1963.

Schmidt, Walter. "Der Bund der Kommunisten und die Versuche einer Zentralisierung der deutschen Arbeitervereine im April und Mai 1848." *Zeitschrift für Geschichtswissenschaft* 9 (1961):577–614.

Schraepler, Ernst. "Der Bund der Gerechten: Seine Tätigkeit in London 1840–1847." *Archiv für Sozialgeschichte* 2 (1962):5–29.

——. *Handwerkerbünde und Arbeitervereine, 1830–53.* Berlin: deGruyter, 1972.

Schuffenhauer, Werner. *Feuerbach und der junge Marx.* Berlin: Wissenschaften, 1965.

Schwartzschild, Leopold. *Karl Marx: The Red Prussian.* Translated by Margaret Wing. New York: Scribners, 1947.

Silberner, Edmund. "Was Marx an Anti-Semite?" *Historia Judaica* 11 (1949):3–52.

Skrzypczak, Henryk. *Marx Engels Revolution.* Berlin: Colloquium, 1968.

Sowell, Thomas. "Marx's 'Increasing Misery' Doctrine." *American Economic Review* 50 (1960):110–20.

Spitzer, Alan. *The Revolutionary Theories of Louis Auguste Blanqui.* New York: Columbia, 1957.

Talmon, J. L. *The Origins of Totalitarian Democracy.* New York: Praeger, 1960.

———. *Political Messianism: The Romantic Phase.* New York: Praeger, 1960.

Tucker, Robert C. *The Marxian Revolutionary Idea.* New York: Norton, 1969.

———. *Philosophy and Myth in Karl Marx.* Cambridge: Cambridge, 1961.

Turetzki, W. A. *Die Entwicklung der Anschauungen von Marx und Engels über den Staat.* Berlin: VEB, 1956.

Ulam, Adam B. *The Unfinished Revolution: An Essay on the Sources of Influence of Marxism and Communism.* New York: Random House, 1960.

Ullrich, Horst. *Der junge Engels.* 2 vols. Berlin: VEB, 1961–66.

Varain, Heinz Josef. "Die Entwicklung der Revolutionstheorie bei Karl Marx bis zum Jahre 1844." *Geschichte in Wissenschaft und Unterricht* 14 (1963):342–59.

Wolfe, Bertram D. *Marxism: One Hundred Years in the Life of a Doctrine.* New York: Dial, 1965.

Index

—constituent: concept of, 288–90;
Marx and Engels on, 291–97
—educational: Babeuf on, 8–9, 289–90;
Weitling on, 11, 153, 155–56,
197–98; Marx and Engels on,
197–98, 290, 296, 326–28, 341–42;
Lenin on, 341–42. *See also*
Intellectuals, role of
—of the allied majority classes, 232,
233, 300
—of the bourgeoisie, 231, 234, 300–01.
See also Revolution, bourgeois
—of the proletariat: Locus 1a, 301;
Locus 1b, 302 (also 231); Locus 2,
298 (also 249); Locus 3, 303; Locus
4, 304–05; Locus 5a, 312–13; Locus
5b, 313–14; Locus 6, 314–15; Locus
7, 310 (also 299); Locus 8, 318–19;
Locus 9, 329; Locus 10, 331; Locus
11, 333; hearsay use of, 1871,
308–09; hearsay use of, 1893, 335;
functions of, 290, 295–97, 315–16,
321, 331–32; lack of educational
functions, 290, 296, 316, 326–28,
332; and "rule" of the proletariat,
290, 297, 304, 313–14; as compromise
slogan with the Blanquists, 297–302,
305–06, 308–09; as distinguished
from Blanquist conception, 299,
310–12, 319; temporary character
stressed, 302, 303, 305, 308, 313, 315,
318–19, 331; equated with demands
of *Manifesto*, 303–04, 313; as
contrasted to anarchist program,
308–09, 318–19, 320–21; equated
with democratic institutions, 314,
319, 331–32, 333–34; used to shock
reformists, 318–19, 331, 333;
abstinence from use of, 326–28;
factional nature of phrase, 334, 341
Diets, provincial, of Prussia: Marx on,
39, 40–41, 64; Hegel on, 55
Division of labor, transcendence of. *See*
Deprofessionalization
Doctors' Club. *See* Young Hegelians
Draper, Hal, 285, 297, 302, 306

Eccarius, Georg, 239, 242, 268, 269, 270
Economic ideas: of the young Marx,
73–74, 75–77, 87–88; of the young
Engels, 109–10, 114–15, 124; as
developed in the *Manifesto*, 138–42;

of Marx and Engels thereafter,
182–83, 219, 228, 233, 253, 329
Education. *See* Intellectuals, role of;
Self-education of the masses
Engels, Friedrich: *for Engels' relation
to other persons, see name of person
concerned; for his relation to
organizations, see name of organization; and for his ideas, see individual
topics.* Birth, 94; schooling, 94–95;
apprenticeship in Barmen, 95–100;
in Berlin, 100–04; first meetings with
Marx, 105, 113; in Manchester,
105–13; return to Barmen, 113–16;
in Brussels and Paris, 124, 148–49,
154, 170–71, 191; during 1848
revolution, 172–73, 192–93, 203–05,
223–27; in London, 227, 240, 249,
257, 272–73, 279–80. *See also* Marx
and Engels contrasted
Engels, Friedrich, Sr., 94, 105, 114, 124
Enlightenment: as origin of totalitarian
democratic ideas, 4, 12*n*; H. Marx
and, 18, 20; Marx and, 20–21, 24, 45;
Young Hegelians and, 29–30
Equality before the law: young Marx
on, 37; young Engels on, 98, 99. *See
also* Law
Erfurt Program of 1891: Engels tries to
influence, 328, 329–30; Engels'
critique of, 332–34
Ethics of revolution: Marx and Engels
on, 111, 133–35, 142, 143–47,
209–10; Mazzini on, 142–43. *See also*
Peaceful transition to communism;
Rioting; Terror
Ewerbeck, Hermann, 90–91, 149, 154,
175*n*
Executive branch of government: Marx
and Engels on, 41–44, 80–81,
194–95, 317, 333. *See also* Armed
forces; Bureaucracy; Dictatorship;
Separation of powers

Fanaticism. *See* Intolerance, political;
Totalitarian democracy
Feuerbach, Ludwig: ideas of, 28, 35,
56–58, 70; Marx and, 46, 58, 59,
68–71, 89; Engels and, 100–01
Flocon, Ferdinand, 170, 263
Fourier, Charles, 9, 52, 119
France, Marx and Engels' views on: